RON BROWN'S BODY

HOW ONE MAN'S DEATH
SAVED THE CLINTON PRESIDENCY
AND HILLARY'S FUTURE

JACK CASHILL

WND Books
A Division of Thomas Nelson Publishers
Since 1798

www.thomasnelson.com

Published in Nashville, Tennessee, by WND Books.

Library of Congress Cataloging-in-Publication Data

Cashill, Jack.
  Ron Brown's body : how one man's death saved the Clinton presidency and
Hillary's future / Jack Cashill.
    p. cm.
  Includes bibliographical references.
  ISBN 0-7852-6237-7
  1. Brown, Ronald Harmon, 1941–1996. 2. Brown, Ronald Harmon, 1941–1996—Death and burial. 3. Cabinet officers—United States—Biography. 4. United States. Dept. of Commerce—Officials and employees—Biography. 5. United States—Politics and government—1993–2001. 6. Political corruption—United States—History—20th century. 7. Clinton, Bill, 1946– —Friends and associates. 8. Clinton, Hillary Rodham—Friends and associates. I. Title.
  E840.8.B77C37 2004
  973.929'092—dc22   2004000522

Printed in the United States of America
04 05 06 07 BVG 5 4 3 2 1

Dedicated to the memory of Captains Ashley Davis and Tim Shafer, Staff Sergeants Gerald Von Aldrich II and Robert Farrington Jr., and Tech Sergeants Cheryl Turnage and Shelly Kelly, all of whom died in honorable service to their country through no fault of their own.

CONTENTS

INTRODUCTION

"ENRON CORP. CONFIRMS *NO* ENRON EXECUTIVES ON BOARD COMMERCE SECRETARY RON BROWN'S MISSING PLANE."[1]

Throughout the day on April 3, 1996, even as America's power brokers scrambled to spin their respects, the man whom they presumed to honor lay face up amidst the mud and debris of a barren Croatian hillside.

Death, as it often does, humbled its victim, this man of impeccable style, and left his body in ironic disarray, his arms thrown helplessly over his head, the shirt ripped clean off his back, his pants severed at the knees like a careless frat boy's, the mocking vestige of a tie draped around his neck.

His name was Ron Brown, the United States secretary of Commerce and an all too appropriate icon of this time and place. No man's life more clearly embodied the cynical ethos of official Washington, and yet, given that cynicism, no man's death was more fully welcome therein.

For the two most desperate years of the Clinton presidency, 1994-1996, Ron Brown found himself at the nexus of White House machinations, the central exchange, the point where presidential power alchemized into hard cash more crudely and less discreetly than at any time in a hundred years. Here, Brown was both exploiter and exploited, victimizer and ultimately victim, the classic "man who knew too much."

"Why Ron Brown Won't Go Down." So declared the grimly ironic title of a just-released article in the *American Spectator*.[2] But the article's author miscalculated the physics of Washington power. Ron Brown did go down. Just before 3:00 PM Croatia time, the Air Force CT-43A that bore him drifted "inexplicably" off-course, sideswiped a hill nearly two miles from the Dubrovnik airport where it was headed, and skidded to a wrenching stop.

Hours before the first American arrived at the crash site to confirm

Brown's death, while at least one American passenger still lived, President Bill Clinton descended on the Commerce Department and, in the artless words of CNN, "eulogized his friend nonetheless."[3]

"Nonetheless"?

With the president were his wife, Hillary Rodham Clinton, and Vice-President Al Gore. The reason Clinton cited for his unseemly haste was an odd, almost unbelievable one: "I wanted to come here today, as it is almost Passover for American Jews and I know a lot of you will want to be leaving soon."

"Leaving soon"? As though—what?—the department's few Jewish employees would not trouble themselves to wait for news or to find time over the next eight days to mourn Brown and their other deceased colleagues?

Speaking of those colleagues, there were eleven other Commerce Department employees on that doomed plane. The president dedicated but one paragraph to the lot of them, "some of them very young," and mentioned none by name, not even Assistant Secretary of Commerce Charles Meissner.

Those assembled likely felt the death of their colleagues much more deeply than they did Brown's. No matter. After that one desultory paragraph, the president got back on message: "I also want to say just one last thing about Ron Brown."

No, the president was not speaking to Commerce Department employees about their loss. He was speaking to his base in black America, searching, as he often did in such circumstances, for an advantage—and doing so in time for the evening news.

Helping Clinton with that base was Alexis Herman, then a White House liaison and soon to be secretary of labor. The president described Herman as a long-time friend of Brown, which was true enough. What the president did not say was that Brown had ceased to trust Herman, his one time protégée on the Democratic National Committee. Although she represented Brown's best access to the president, Brown felt that access narrowing, choking. Herman had turned her back on him, he was sure, and cast her lot with the president.

Throughout his presidency, Clinton enjoyed an immunity from the paranoia regarding church-state separation that infected the capital and the Caucasian base of his own party. For strategic reasons, he exercised his immunity that day. He attributed this bit of spiritual insight to Herman.[4]

"His favorite scripture verse was that wonderful verse from Isaiah," said Clinton of Brown. "They who wait upon the Lord shall have their strength renewed. They shall mount up with wings as eagles. They will run and not grow weary. They will walk and faint not."

This verse would provide the essential metaphor for Brown in the days to come. He was the man "who walked and ran and flew through life." Clinton would repeat this line in the introduction he wrote for a biography written by Tracey Brown about her father.[5]

This was all fabrication. Brown did not know the Bible. He could not cite a single verse. His quest for spirituality had begun only in the last weeks of life and only then out of desperation. Still, on the dishonesty scale, this bit of presidential dissembling barely registers.

To be sure, eulogies almost invariably aggrandize the virtues of the deceased, but Clinton was not so much eulogizing Brown as he was constructing his own defense:

> [W]hen we met earlier this week, right before he left for the Balkans, he was so excited because he thought that, along with these business leaders and the other very able people from the Commerce Department on this mission, that they would be able to use the power of the American economy to help the peace take hold in the Balkans, to help people in that troubled place have the kind of decent, honorable and wonderfully ordinary lives that we Americans too often take for granted.

In truth, Brown was not excited at all. When they met earlier in the week, Brown begged not to go. At this, the most anxious moment of his life, he dreaded the prospect of the trip. There was nothing decent or honorable about it. There no longer was on such junkets.[6] He was sick of being, in his words, "a motherf—ing tour guide for Hillary Clinton."[7]

What troubled Brown more, however, was this trip had no point, not even the dark one of Hoovering up campaign cash. Worse, the trip was all too spontaneous and improvised. It bordered on chaotic.

For the first time on any of his trade missions, Brown had to twist arms to fill the plane and even then not successfully. Nor did he attract the caliber of business executives his pride demanded. Still, the White House insisted. And as much as Brown loathed the extortionate nature of the trips, he sensed that if he ceased to oblige the Clintons, "to carry the bag," they would cut him loose.

And this leads to the essential deceit of Clinton's hasty eulogy. The president and his wife did not love Brown as Clinton avowed. Nor did they enjoy much, if any, of "his friendship and his warmth." No, the relationship, always cool, had turned cold. Brown feared the Clintons, feared to even call them, and they deeply distrusted him.

This, the opinion-shapers in the major media chose not to know. They had already chosen their story line. Rather than recount Brown's fate as a cautionary tale on the perils of power, as they might have, as they did upon the untimely passing of White House counsel Vince Foster, the media routinely meshed the death of "this great American hero" on April 3 with Martin Luther King's death on April 4, twenty-eight years earlier. President Clinton, in fact, unblushingly claimed Brown, like King, died "answering a very important challenge of his time," and no one dared to call the comparison profane.

And so the story would have ended: Ron Brown buried at Arlington National Cemetery with more pomp than any government official since RFK, a nation in mourning for its fallen hero, and a president bereft. But Ron Brown's body had one more story to tell.

At the U.S. Army base at Dover, Delaware, three days after his death, Armed Forces Institute of Pathology photographer, U.S. Navy CPO Kathleen Janoski, noted a nearly perfectly circular hole in the top of Brown's head. It would measure just about .45 inches in diameter.

"Wow. That looks like a bullet hole," said Janoski.[8]

The pathologists who heard her cry and heeded it would soon enough wish they hadn't. They opened the door on a mystery that simply refuses to stay shut. And, like many others who questioned the official story line during the Clintons' most desperate years, they have suffered for it.

"We do not know for sure what happened there," said Clinton of the crash in Croatia. This much was likely true. It is also true he did not want to know. His administration's lack of curiosity would stoke the already over-heated fires of conspiracy and forge an astonishing range of theories.

The theorists, credible or not, were starting with the wrong question. The right question—the first question—was not why did the plane come down.

The right question was why did it ever go up.

1 | THE HANDSHAKE

Fixed in the national imagination is the one youthful image of Bill Clinton, oversized and conspicuously eager, jumping out of line, separating himself from his Boys' Nation colleagues, to shake the hand of his presumed idol, President John F. Kennedy.

There is an equally telling, but much more composed, image of the young Ron Brown. The year is 1955.[1] The thirteen-year-old Brown in a crisp polo shirt stands amidst a crowd of onlookers outside Harlem's legendary Theresa Hotel, a hotel his father manages. There, he smartly shakes the hand of Vice-President Richard Nixon. The adults in the crowd, all properly dressed, eye not Nixon but Brown.

One can all but read Brown's future in this picture. Though he gives away thirty years and half a foot to Nixon, young Brown seems unabashed. He looks Nixon directly in the eye and smiles broadly but not deferentially. It is hard to imagine any thirteen-year-old anywhere, white or black, with Brown's cool and poise.

If Republicans were not yet unwelcome in America's inner cities—Eisenhower and Nixon would pull 40 percent of the black vote a year later—they were not quite at home, especially Nixon. Yet here he smiles back warmly, looking pleased and more human than one remembers him. Even then, Brown had that power. It was his great gift.

"I was always amazed at the way he was continually reaching out trying to bridge the differences between people," said Clinton of Brown in his Commerce Department eulogy. It was the eulogy's one honest moment.

Ron Brown was born to build bridges. The date was August 1, 1941. The place was Washington. His parents, Bill and Gloria—or "Nan" as she was later called by the family—had settled there to launch their ascent into the middle class. Bill and Gloria were both college graduates, and they had greater ambitions for their son. This was not unusual among the emerging black middle class, or presumptuous, even in 1941.[2]

If there was any young black American destined for what social theorist W.E.B. DuBois famously referred to as the "talented tenth," it was Ron Brown. Writing in 1903, DuBois imagined an upper tier of black society, proud and college-educated, groomed to serve as "the group leader, the man who sets the ideals of the community where he lives, directs its thoughts and heads its social movements."[3] DuBois would later lose faith in this concept, in America for that matter, but Bill and Gloria Brown never really would, certainly not when it came to their son.

When Ron was five, the Browns moved to New York after a stop in Boston and soon settled in Harlem, a softer place then than now, a name no more off-putting to the white ear than, say, Chinatown. An only child, Ron lived amidst the luxurious trappings of America's premier black hotel but commuted from the first grade on to smart, largely white schools across town. Brown spent summers at YMCA camps in upstate New York or on family vacations at Martha's Vineyard or Sag Harbor, where he waited tables even through college. From his earliest days, he would ride the crest of racial progress and do so with deceptive ease.

Progress was in the air the summer of the handshake, 1955. Young Emmett Till was deceived by it. A Chicago boy, one week older than Brown, Till ventured naïvely into the murky racial swamp of Mississippi and was brutally murdered for his naïveté. His crime? Saying "Bye, baby" to the white wife of a storeowner. Most of America had at least the good sense to be horrified. If Brown was at all scarred by the event, or even aware, he left no account of it. Of more immediate interest to Brown, in this summer of mixed signals, was the imminent triumph of the Brooklyn Dodgers, led by Jackie Robinson to their first World Series win. Indeed, Richard Nixon was not the only Republican Brown looked up to that summer.

That same year, in Alabama, an unsung twenty-six-year-old minister had stepped up to lead the now legendary Montgomery bus boycott. His name was Martin Luther King. His emergence fulfilled the prophecy of DuBois that the black church would produce a "Negro Gandhi."[4]

Not every black man could be a Ghandi. Speaking in 1948, a more realistic DuBois had publicly re-examined the ideal of the talented tenth and found it overly ambitious. With segregation in decline and freedom beckoning, too many among DuBois' imagined elite "wanted to be Americans, and they did not care so much what kind of folks Americans were, as for the right to be one of them."[5] Here, alas, DuBois foretold the fate of Ron Brown as presciently as he had foretold King's. That they would both be labeled "civil rights leaders" and casually compared at Brown's death says less about their likeness than it does about the corruption of the phrase "civil rights."

The community that nurtured both King and Brown and shaped their dreams was slowly coming undone. For Brown, the unraveling started at home. Brown's parents separated when he was in high school and soon divorced. It is hard to calculate the effects of divorce on a personality, but they are almost always soul-shaking in a quiet, simmering way, especially then, when most children, white and black, proudly lived with both parents. Brown seemed to lose his bearings because of it, and his performance in school began to decline.

The unsettled nature of his life at home may well have influenced his choice of college—Middlebury in rural Vermont. His daughter Tracey attributes this decision to his desire for the "romanticized, all-American image"[6] of an ivy-coated campus life. It is also true that because of his lackluster grades Brown could not get into the Ivy League colleges towards which his father had pushed him.[7] In any case, given its very name and location, its tidy lawns and venerable buildings, one must strain to imagine a life more stable and serene than that of Middlebury in the 1950s.

When Brown enrolled, he was but one of three black students at Middlebury, a school so unreflectively white it evokes the derisive label "white-bread." But whiteness was not alien to Brown. It was in his blood. His maternal great-grandfather had posed as a Confederate soldier to escape the South. His maternal grandmother had blond hair. His mother passed for white at the exclusive Steuben Glass store on Fifth Avenue where she worked. In size and coloring, Brown took more after his father but inherited enough of his mother's shading and absorbed enough of her airs to make whites feel comfortable around him.

At Middlebury, Brown seemed to revel in his uniqueness, his status as an "F&O," a first and only. He kept his distance from the few other blacks on campus, partly perhaps to preserve his distinctiveness and partly because, for him, the idea of class solidarity rivaled that of race. He felt no particular kinship with inner-city blacks. He never really would.

It would be wrong to read too much of the "race traitor" into the young Brown. Before fashion dictated otherwise, and even after, students from all ethnicities would seek out colleges like Middlebury to re-create themselves in a kind of standard American mold, one gleaned from movies and TV. This was, after all, a time when shows like *Leave It To Beaver* and *Father Knows Best* aired without irony.

In 1958, when Brown started college, there was no such concept as multiculturalism and almost no intellectual desire anywhere to preserve the customs and grudges of one's ancestors. That was something parents pushed on children, and children almost inevitably pushed back.

In the late 1950s, despite the vestigial horrors of the South and the everyday indignities in the North, "Negroes" were optimistic about the future and idealistic about the American promise. Integration was the operating paradigm in progressive America, and almost no one, black or white, had cause to doubt its eventual success. Like his parents' marriage, this worldview would also collapse, and Brown would be left to find his way among its ruins.

As with so many of the roads to hell, this one, too, was paved with good intentions. At Middlebury, Brown began to learn the arts of navigation. In the second semester of his freshman year, Middlebury put him "on warning" because of his poor academic performance. He was placed on warning again in the beginning of his sophomore year, and after the first semester of that year the administration declared Brown an "academic failure" and flunked him out.

Three days later, the college readmitted him. This was decidedly unusual. As one might expect, college officials have denied that Brown's hasty return was "simply" a matter of race—they always do. Tracey Brown attributes Brown's rapid readmission to her father's powers of persuasion. Still, it is hard to imagine race did not play a part in the way Brown made his case or in the way the administration received it. The fact that legendary Harlem congressman Adam Clayton Powell Jr. intervened on Brown's behalf could not have hurt either.[8]

As it happened, exactly one week before Brown flunked out of Middlebury, four black college students from North Carolina A&T sat down at a Woolworth's lunch counter in Greensboro and asked to be served. Despite threats of violence, they remained there all day waiting and returned the next day, as did reporters and a TV news cameraman. Within a week, black and white students throughout the South were staging comparable protests in solidarity, and the national media were paying attention.

Having had to confront its own racial guilt, now tangible and inescapable thanks to television, white America began to seek atonement. On a campus like Middlebury—where awareness was high but the means of expiation few—the faculty would feel the burden most heavily.

Enter Ron Brown stage right. At this keen historic moment, he would help pioneer a corrosive new phenomenon, one that black social theorist Shelby Steele aptly labels "redemptive liberalism." As Steele describes it, an institution like Middlebury displays its "conspicuous and social virtuousness" not by rewarding the strength of a given minority but by tolerating its weakness.[9] The institution gets its "virtue-credit" for this act of seeming tolerance, even if the recipient inevitably suffers for it.

With his easy readmission, Brown learned all the wrong lessons. He had to have seen just how vulnerable white society was to the right kind of appeal, and he had the rhetorical skills to pull one off. Brown would not have to work hard after all. And he did not. Despite his natural gifts, Brown graduated with a C- average, deeply mired in the bottom third of his class.

"Race absolutely corrupts those who use it for redemption," says Steele, "and absolutely weakens those who use it for advancement."[10] So saying, Steele describes the tragic synergy that would undo Ron Brown and the political culture that embraced him.

As to historical context, in the fall semester after Brown graduated from Middlebury, James Meredith enrolled at the University of Mississippi, the first black student to do so. Two students were killed in the riots that erupted in protest over his courageous enrollment. But Mississippi was a world away.

Closer to home, Brown would find one more opportunity for genuine redemption, and he would make the best of it. For male students at Middlebury in the 1950s, ROTC was mandatory for two years. Brown signed up for the optional, additional two final years, less because of a career interest in the army than for the spare cash ROTC offered. Like most everything else Brown did at Middlebury, he did his ROTC service indifferently or worse.

In the summer of 1962, Brown completed his basic training and received his commission as a second lieutenant in the U.S. Army Reserve. A week later, he married Alma Arrington, a fine-featured beauty whose relative darkness must have unsettled the color-conscious Gloria Brown. Alma more than compensated in the Browns' eyes, however, with status. The wedding took place at the proper Episcopal Church in Brooklyn favored by her upper middle-class family, one whose expectations, as filtered through Alma, would always intimidate Brown.

The combination of marriage and the military, as it often does, solidified the man. "For the first time in his life," writes Brown biographer Steven Holmes, "Ron Brown had to face the immediate consequences of his actions."[11] By all accounts, Brown performed exceedingly well in his work as a transportation officer in Germany and then, after being promoted to captain, in Korea. Indeed, Brown was chosen to command the motorcade when President Lyndon Johnson toured Korea in 1966, the first of many presidential tours on which Brown would work and, ironically, the most honorable.

In this latter posting, Brown also ran a school for the training and orientation of Korean soldiers. In an army that could ill afford the luxury of redemptive liberalism, Brown honored his own potential and was rewarded for it. "He built the school into one of the most unique and outstanding schools of the United States Army," wrote his immediate supervisor, Lieutenant Colonel Milford Downey. "Beyond doubt, he is one of the most competent officers I have ever known in service."[12] Col. Downey's evaluation was not the exception. Brown consistently received enthusiastic reviews.

Col. Downey strongly encouraged Brown to remain in the Army after his four-year posting expired. Had Brown done so, and had he survived the inevitable rigors of Vietnam, his path in a racially sensitized army might well have mirrored that of another product of ROTC and Harlem, Colin Powell. But, for a variety of reasons, Brown chose not to.

This was unfortunate. Washington DC would prove more dangerous to both body and soul than Vietnam ever could have.

2 | RON BEIGE

W hen scholar and theologian Cornel West writes of the "the tremendous pull of the white world and the tragic need for white recognition and affirmation among so many black people,"[1] he may or may not have had Ron Brown in mind.

But other blacks imagined Brown just so, perhaps none more bitingly than Chicago congressman, Gus Savage. It was Savage who, after Brown backed a white candidate in a Chicago mayoral race, gave him the enduring label, "Ron Beige."[2]

If Brown seemed "beige" to some or if his needs seemed "tragic" to others, it is only from the perspective of a later date and only among people who have lost faith in the uplifting effects of the American experience. When Brown left for Germany in 1963, he left an America in which ambitions like his were normative. Through college and the army, he aspired not so much to be "white"—there is no real record of that—as to be "American."

"You can't grow up in Harlem, surrounded by legendary figures in black sports and entertainment, and come away without a strong ethnic identity," he would later protest, perhaps a bit too much.[3] "I went to school with white kids. That doesn't mean I turned color to be accepted."

Although the barriers he faced were at first a bit higher, Brown dreamed the same dreams as the ethnic Italians and Irish and Hispanics with whom he served in the army. The problem was that by the time he returned in 1967, those dreams already seemed, to a certain class of people, suspect.

The world would change a great deal in his absence, perhaps more than any four years in American history save those of the Civil War. Brown left an America in which John Kennedy presided, hope flourished, and idealism reigned, nowhere more so than in the black community. The young Hillary Rodham would wistfully describe these as the "years dominated by men with dreams,"[4] and few would have disagreed.

In fact, it was in August of 1963, just two months after Ron and Alma Brown left for Germany, that Martin Luther King led 250,000 people at the historic March on Washington. The march's principle organizer, Bayard Rustin, captured its integrationist spirit: "The March was not a Negro action. It was an action of Negroes and whites together. Not just the leaders of the Negro organization, but leading Catholic, Protestant, and Jewish spokesmen called the people into the street."[5]

The fire behind this march would never again burn so brightly or so purely. Just eighteen days later, a bomb racked the Sixteenth Street Baptist Church in Birmingham, Alabama, killing four black girls and scarring the psyche of every African American. Two months later an assassin's bullet felled President John F. Kennedy in Dallas.

The nation's mood was growing dark and cynical. No one anticipated that change more concisely than the then little-known Malcolm X. Said he famously of Kennedy's death, it was a case of the "chickens coming home to roost."[6] His take on the March on Washington was no more charitable:

> The whites didn't integrate it; they infiltrated it. Whites joined it; they engulfed it; they became so much a part of it, it lost its original flavor. It ceased to be a black march; it ceased to be militant; it ceased to be angry; it ceased to be impatient. In fact, it ceased to be a march. It became a picnic, an outing with a festive, circus-like atmosphere . . . CLOWNS AND ALL.[7]

In the summer of 1964, the summer after Kennedy's death, the first major "race riot" in a generation erupted in the epicenter of black America, Brown's beloved Harlem. Fittingly perhaps, the two black reporters assigned by the *New York Times*, Junius Griffin and Ted Jones, set up a temporary bureau in the Theresa Hotel. The riot soon spread to Brooklyn's Bedford-Stuyvesant, and the spirit behind it spread across America.

In 1965, just as Malcolm X was growing more universal in his sympathies, his fellow black Muslims gunned him down in Harlem. Malcolm X proved more popular in death than in life. His un-evolved, hard-line, black nationalism, so alien in 1963, had become part of the American fabric by decade's end.

Ron Brown returned to America from Korea in the summer of 1967 just in time to watch the suppressed passions of America's inner cities swell to a firestorm and all but raze Newark, Detroit, and scores of other cities. It was to Brown's advantage that he came to prominence when he did, years later. In 1967, America had little tolerance for bridge-building or the color beige. The nation was experimenting with a new word and a new concept—"polarization."

The inner cities had no monopoly on the concept or its consequences. For the first time in history, a nation's youth—at least those with access to the microphones—rejected the very foundations on which the nation was built. True, fashion drove the campus rebellions of the late 60s as much as any ideology. And fashions, to be sure, pass. But the sentiments forged in the cauldron of that ill-focused movement would leave a vestigial mark on a whole generation of future American leaders, none more significant than Bill and Hillary Clinton.

Hillary Rodham was one of those with her hands on the mike. At decade's end, May 1969, she was chosen to deliver a commencement address at Wellesley College. The speech proved to be so wonderfully presumptuous, so true a testament to her time and place, that *Life* magazine reprinted it in full.[8]

Rodham began by upbraiding the man who had spoken before her, Senator Edward Brooke of Massachusetts, the first African American senator in a century. She had found his cautious take on social progress wanting. "How can we talk about percentages and trends?" she scolded him. "We're not interested in social reconstruction; it's human reconstruction."

Rodham's message was, if nothing else, ambitious. She took on the whole of the American psyche—"our prevailing, acquisitive, and competitive corporate life, including tragically the universities"—and bared its unredeemed soul. This "is not the way of life for us," she told her peers and their bemused parents. "We're searching for more immediate, ecstatic, and penetrating modes of living."

On Hillary's speech one can all but see the fingerprints of the so-called critical theorists, then *au courant* in America's elite universities. Sometimes called "cultural Marxists," these ideologues extended Marxist structural critique beyond the economy to the larger culture and urged, as Hillary did, "human reconstruction." They and their professorial acolytes imbued many of the nation's brighter youth with a sense of societal self-hatred so deep they lost all sense of American exceptionalism. This loss would affect foreign policy for decades to come.

Two months later and an ocean away, a young man Hillary Rodham had yet to meet would reveal, if anything, an even greater contempt for the culture that produced him. In Bill Clinton's infamous letter from Oxford to Colonel Eugene Holmes—among the most chillingly prophetic in the history of American letters—contempt quickly morphs into cynicism:

> I decided to accept the draft in spite of my beliefs for one reason; to maintain my political viability within the system. For years I have worked to prepare myself for a political life characterized by both practical political ability and concern for rapid social progress. It is a life I still feel compelled to try to lead. I do not think our system of government is by definition corrupt, however dangerous and inadequate it has been in recent years. (The society may be corrupt, but that is not the same thing, and if that is true we are all finished anyway.)[9]

Clinton thanked Holmes for "saving me from the draft" and then went on to explain why he had to be saved. Among other reasons, young Clinton wanted nothing to do with "a war I opposed and despised with a depth of feeling I had reserved solely for racism in America before Vietnam." Even as a young man, Clinton was savvy enough to equate militarism with racism and brandish anti-racism as his moral shield. He would never stop doing so, even in his eulogies for Ron Brown.

What the Clintons and Brown abandoned in the late 1960s was faith in their country. Although all would make patriotic gestures throughout their careers—Brown most sincerely—none of them would ever again express confidence in America's moral imperative or the uniqueness of its destiny. This disinterest would cost America dearly.

By decade's end, those who actually struggled for genuine progress seemed relevant only to those who hated atavistically enough to kill them. In April 1968, one such killer murdered Martin Luther King. Two months later, an assassin gunned down another would-be bridge-builder, presidential aspirant, Robert F. Kennedy.

In five years, most of which Ron Brown missed, Martin, John, Malcolm, and Bobby were all murdered. Not one of them made it past forty-six years of age. And none of the killings seemed sufficiently comprehendible to satisfy anyone. The most commonly asked question in those years was the amorphous "Why?"

As insightful as he could be, Ron Brown had no more answers than anyone else. In 1967, at loose ends upon his return to America, Brown used his family's connections to secure an interview with the National Urban League, historically the most moderate of civil rights groups. Once hired, he was posted to a Bronx employment recruitment center as a trainee advisor. He also enrolled in the evening program at St. John's Law School to escape a life of social work. By this time he had one child at home, Michael, and one on the way, daughter Tracey.

Tracey writes that her father saw his work at the Urban League as "a perfect fit for him."[10] No one else would spin it thus. By all other accounts, Brown lacked any particular gift or interest in urban uplift. Nor did he have much enthusiasm for law school. Biographer Holmes writes that he "struggled to stay current in his school work and was not always the best prepared in class."[11]

One professor told him, "If you ever do learn to study you're going to be a world beater."[12] But the professor did not understand that the rules for a person like Brown were changing. Indeed, the professor would soon help accelerate that change. His name? Mario Cuomo. Student Brown never did learn how to study. He wouldn't have to.

Fresh out of the military, Brown cut an impressive figure. He also made friends with people who believed in him. And even then, his "people skills" were exceptional, particularly his ability to negotiate with the more radical elements of the civil rights movement. The Urban League put Brown on its fast track. He was quickly brought downtown and made a special assistant to legendary Urban League executive director, Whitney Young.

If Brown was prospering, Young and the Urban League were not. In 1970, The Ford Foundation slashed the League's funding by nearly two million dollars a year. Hat in hand, Young appealed to the Nixon White House. Never popular in the black community, Nixon saw an opportunity to curry favor at relatively little cost and urged his cabinet to shore up the League. In accepting the president's largesse, Young made the Urban League a veritable ward of the federal government. From then on, it would have to maintain a strong lobbying presence in Washington to assure its survival.[13]

In 1971, Brown passed the New York bar, and in 1972, the Urban League's new executive director, Vernon Jordan, appointed him general counsel. As general counsel, Brown showed the same indifference to routine work as he had at Middlebury and in law school. This work, he fobbed off on others. But Jordan, a veteran schmoozer himself, recognized Brown's true gifts and soon enough sent him back to the one city in the world where those gifts could be best exploited and rewarded, the city of Brown's birth and the city of his undoing, Washington DC.

3 COMING HOME

If there has ever been a more disturbing year in American history than 1973, it escapes easy recall.

In January, The U.S. Supreme Court invalidated the abortion laws of every American state in *Roe v. Wade*. In that same month, America signed a sham cease-fire with North Vietnam and began its slow, dishonorable abandonment of the South. In April, President Nixon fired his loose-lipped counsel, John Dean, too late to stop his ship from sinking. In October, Israel and the Arab states fought an unwanted war to an inconclusive end, and OPEC launched an oil embargo that left everyone feeling embattled. In between these two October events, Vice President Spiro Agnew gave the nabobs of negativism something about which to natter as he resigned under a cloud of miscellaneous corruption charges.

In the midst of this unsettling year, Ron Brown descended on Washington. In the long run, his timing proved unfortunate. Brown's great gift was his adaptability. Like Zelig in the Woody Allen movie of the same name, he became a master of appearances. He could absorb the mores of a time and place and make them his own.

Growing up in a hotel had to play a part in this inchoate formation. He had never really known a "home." Living as an only child in a strange city, without the traditional black cultural supports of church and extended family, Brown learned etiquette but not virtue, manners but not morality. His choices in clothes and cars and, almost inevitably, women were sure-handed. His moral choices, however, were uncertain and unguided. Had

13

Brown arrived in some more inspired age, a more structured one, even the early idealistic days of the New Frontier, he might have matured and flourished. But such was not his destiny.

In the short run, however, Brown's timing proved exquisite. He returned to the city of his birth, a city where the Brown family was known and well connected, a city that in virtually all its quarters valued style over substance.

When Brown arrived, the city was more open to a young black man on the make than it ever was before or ever would be again. There were at least two reasons why. As it happened, the increased crime and riots of the 60s had driven away a good slice of the white population and left the city of Washington more than 70 percent black. The population shift put an unprecedented amount of city power in black hands, a power made tangible by the advent of home rule at the end of that fateful year, 1973.

Then, too, the spirit of redemptive liberalism Brown first encountered at Middlebury had overwhelmed official Washington. Lyndon Johnson introduced the spirit on a large scale through the Great Society, and the Nixon White House institutionalized it by administrative fiat throughout the various bureaucracies.

This redemption, as Shelby Steele argues, was less about helping blacks than it was about redeeming whites from a legacy of guilt, a guilt suburban flight had only intensified. The results would have surely appalled Malcolm X. Writes Steele convincingly:

> Suddenly, a people strong enough to win freedom in a society in which they were outnumbered ten to one had to make a case for their own weakness, had to offer up their own helplessness as a vehicle for the redemption of others, had to reimagine themselves and advertise themselves primarily as victims.[1]

Worse, by 1973, this spirit had loss much of its sincerity. It had already begun to formalize and calcify. The superficial benefits it would generate would go not to those who had suffered most but, ironically, to those who had suffered least, those who were building resumes while other blacks were building a movement.

Ron Brown would tell one story time and again that spoke, he believed, to his own sense of victimization but that, in reality, spoke to his exemption from the same. The year was 1963. Brown, then a second lieutenant, and his wife, Alma, loaded their gear into his "snappy-new '62 navy-blue Mercury Comet convertible with light blue leather interior"[2] and headed south to Fort Eustis, Virginia. In Hampton, Virginia, they pulled into a drive-in restaurant.

When the white waitress apologetically told them she would have to bring their food in a box away from the other customers, the Browns drove off indignantly and would not stop until they reached Fort Eustis.

To be fair, Brown tended to tell this story knowingly, for effect, especially to white reporters. He had to sense that among an emerging black leadership, many of whom had earned their stripes riding freedom buses, not snappy convertibles, this slight would seem trivial, almost laughable.

Among a white audience, the story had its desired effect. However charming and accommodating Ron Brown might seem, he had suffered in ways whites would never understand. Unlike, say, a Jesse Jackson, who opened with the proverbial race card, Brown kept this card up his sleeve, but, as will become evident, he would not shy away from playing it when he had to.

In his first three years in Washington, Brown learned to maneuver through the halls of Congress where he testified often on behalf of the Urban League and found himself in the unlikely role of "civil rights leader." He also quickly ingratiated himself with the leadership in the city of Washington, as his 1976 appointment to the board of the University of the District of Columbia would testify.

In 1977, with Democrat Jimmy Carter in the White House, Brown made a play to chair the troubled Equal Employment Opportunity Commission. Launched twelve years earlier in a sea of optimism, the EEOC had long since foundered on the inexorable shoals of bureaucracy and bad management. Predictably, the struggle to control the chair had less to do with righting the ship than with seizing the helm for its own sake. Even misdirected, the commission offered a substantial base of power and patronage.

Organized labor backed Brown. The liberal feminist wing of the party backed Eleanor Holmes Norton. Brown counted on the support of his boss, Vernon Jordan, arguably the preeminent civil rights leader of the moment, to sway the Carter camp in his direction. When Jordan backed Norton—a rational decision given her superior credentials—Brown felt betrayed and always would. This, after all, was a world in which connections almost always trumped credentials. Brown had no other prism through which to view Jordan's decision.

From this moment on, Brown knew he would have to leave the Urban League. Although Jordan would forever downplay the rift, those who knew Brown best knew "Vernon and [Brown] could not be in the same room together."[3] Even the usually sanguine Tracey Brown acknowledges, "Dad felt disillusioned by his friend and mentor."[4]

Casting about for some meaningful role for himself, Brown flirted with a run for mayor of Washington DC. With the advent of home rule, the city's power potential was great, and its hierarchies were still unsettled. Brown had the right look and the right pedigree. What he lacked at the time was the proverbial fire in the belly, not to mention popular support. There could be no ground swell for a man who had no particular interest in the people he would represent. In February 1978, when he called reporters to tell them he would not be a candidate, there is little evidence anyone much cared.[5]

Indirectly, it was Jimmy Carter who rescued Brown from the Urban League. His floundering presidency had inspired Senator Ted Kennedy to make a run at the Democratic nomination, a run that in the beginning had a high likelihood of success. Kennedy needed at least one credible African American to represent his campaign to the black community, and Ron Brown got the call. This was the breakout Brown had been looking for, the chance to find his way in the wider world.

In December 1979, right after Christmas, Brown found himself sitting out on the grounds of Kennedy's West Palm Beach estate, talking to and being taken seriously by men who had the power to shake the universe. This son of Harlem was not yet forty. Like Jay Gatsby, he had not quite arrived and never quite would. But he wanted it, and on that soft, sweet evening, he could all but taste it, never quite knowing what that "it" really was.

4 | CASHING IN

As history has duly recorded, the Kennedy campaign sputtered and died in 1980, and Jimmy Carter was re-nominated. For all the bridges Ron Brown built to the black community and beyond, the only bridge that finally mattered was the one Ted Kennedy failed to cross at Chappaquiddick.

No one faulted Brown for the defeat. He had performed well. Grateful for his help, Kennedy hired Brown to be chief counsel of the Senate Judiciary Committee. Neither Brown nor Kennedy, however, counted on the Republicans' riding Reagan's coattails to control of the Senate. This reversal cost Kennedy his committee chair and Brown his job. At loose ends, Brown accepted a position as a Kennedy aide, but the gig had the whiff of purgatory about it from the moment he took it.

As to what heaven might hold, Brown did not have to look much further than his one time mentor, Vernon Jordan. Tall and imposing, self-important to a fault, Jordan was proudly pioneering a new field—civil rights entrepreneur. He had seen the light early on. While still at the Urban League, Jordan was making a serious income by sitting on a variety of corporate boards and speaking at high-dollar events. Brown had no objection to Jordan making money, even on Urban League time. What he objected to was Jordan's refusal to let him do the same.[1] This forced disparity in their respective incomes and lifestyles stung.

So lucrative was Jordan's calling and so ambiguous were his sources of income that Jordan chose not to accept a cabinet position when president-elect

17

Clinton offered. To fill out a financial disclosure form was to tell the world more than the world needed to know. Except in the case of women—and Jordan had the scars to prove the exception[2]—Jordan would manage his affairs more prudently than Brown did or would. He would make his sacrifices for Clinton, but only to a point. It is hard to imagine Jordan on that fatal plane trip to Croatia.

When the spotlight fixed on Jordan during the Monica Lewinsky scandal—a scandal not of his making—they revealed just how profitable a career in civil rights could be. Although Jordan neither lobbied nor practiced law, his power law firm paid him more than $1 million a year. The eleven blue chip corporations on whose boards he sat paid him an additional $947,000, and that did not include the income from his wife's six corporate boards.[3] Not bad for a guy who, in the words of one insider, "partied all night and slept all day."[4]

What was not known was how much more income Jordan was earning from side deals in the flourishing shadow world of "minority capitalism," a world that would also shape Ron Brown's life but not, alas, for the purer. This was not his father's kind of capitalism. It was a new and different breed of cat. The man who let the cat out of the bag—as President Clinton would often remind America—was none other than Richard Nixon. Clinton had no better way to defend the phenomenon.

In March 1970, Nixon issued Executive Order 11518, directing the Small Business Administration to "particularly consider the needs and interests of minority-owned small business concerns." The result of this and similar orders was astonishing. Authorities would begin to use the words "disadvantaged" and "black" interchangeably. They gave themselves authority to ignore the newly minted civil rights acts. Indeed, they would "set aside" contracts for preferred minorities solely on the basis of race.

Without benefit of a public airing or even Congressional debate, America had quietly exempted blacks from its historic opportunity-based model and schemed instead to arrange appropriate outcomes. This "proportional" model of justice was so far removed from the notion of individual rights that at the time it disturbed even the liberal U.S. Commission on Civil Rights.[5]

Historically, capitalism had served as an end-run around discrimination. "With his fate in his own hands," writes Shelby Steele of the ambitious African American before the 1960s, "his energies must go toward the development of excellence, even if there is racism in the world where he functions."[6] The Theresa Hotel was a case in point. So was Hollywood: America's Jews had responded to the exclusion they faced in established industries by pioneering altogether new ones. The Japanese and Chinese in America had done much the same.

Minority capitalism, on the other hand, developed excellence—or even basic entrepreneurial skills—only by chance. What it did more routinely, in every large city and state capital in America, was create a wholly gratuitous class of well-connected middlemen.

These newly minted entrepreneurs exchanged their race preferences and connections for the rights to distribute other peoples' products and services. Brown himself came to manage a pointlessly random portfolio of *stuff*—bonds, burlap bags, insurance, oil contracts, natural gas, pay phones, pension services, radio shows, sludge treatment—without knowing much about any of it. Like so many others of this spurious class, he added cost but not value and produced nothing.

Worse, the whole phenomenon had no real justification, not even the redressing of historic wrongs. In a dispassionate, academic text on the minority rights revolution, John Skrentny argues pointedly that minority capitalist programs "were developed for blacks as a way to mitigate the urban riots of the 1960s and to win their votes." There never was any evidence "government was responding to complaints of discrimination."[7]

Skrentny's comments track with Malcom X's from earlier in the decade. "Politically the American Negro is nothing but a football," said Malcolm, "and the white liberals control this mentally dead ball through tricks of tokenism: false promises of integration and civil rights."[8]

Malcolm X framed the debate as one between conservatives and liberals and found them both deficient. Malcolm, however, does idealists in either camp an injustice. The real dialectic exists between those hopeful souls who imagined these new programs and the opportunists who executed them. The resulting synthesis almost inevitably favors the opportunists. Their motives are sharper and more enduring. The results that matter to them are better calculated. It was Vice President Hubert Humphrey, for instance, who initiated the first minority capitalist programs within the Small Business Administration, but it was Nixon who institutionalized them and took the credit.

In an historic eye-blink, opportunists turned the inner core of the civil rights movement into an enterprise zone, especially in the city where it mattered most, Washington DC. There, a small handful of insiders created a veritable civil rights cartel that controlled a disproportionate amount of the available money.

Twenty years of "reform" after Brown launched his entrepreneurial career, Senator Kit Bond of Missouri, ranking Republican on the Senate Small Business Committee, would still be lamenting that the continued dominance of such insiders "really undermines" the SBA's set-aside program.[9]

It is not hard to understand why "minority capitalism" proved so seductive. For one, it was all entirely legal. For another, those distributing the rewards made it seem like a natural continuation of the undeniably moral civil rights movement. Better still, they could—and would—applaud themselves for their largesse, even if with other people's money.

"The urgency is made to seem so intense," writes Shelby Steele, "that it becomes *virtuous* to set principle aside."[10] And then, as Steele adds, there were always "the prerequisites of interventionism—the preferential patronage of jobs, careers, grant money, set-asides, diversity consulting businesses, black political districts, and so on."[11]

In time, these perks would claim no other reputation quite as publicly or completely as they would Ron Brown's. This was a shame. There was much to like about the young Ron Brown. He was bright, ambitious, and altogether charming. He had the rare ability to cross racial lines without guile. He had been a good and honest soldier. He was a dedicated father, one who loved his children more than life itself, and that says a lot about a man. Had fate placed him in an environment where virtue was rewarded, he might have become the person others hoped he could be. He might even still be alive.

Brown's undoing began when Ted Kennedy contacted a certain Washington law firm on Brown's behalf. The left-leaning *New Republic* would charitably describe the firm as "one of Washington's most powerful and unprincipled"—the legendary Patton, Boggs & Blow.[12]

The defining partner during Brown's tenure was the irrepressible Tommy Boggs. "Ted [Kennedy] and Tommy partied together," says a woman who knew them both. "That was during the days of a lot of partying."[13] One rightly reads between the lines here. Tommy Boggs could make things happen, even parties. The son of famed congressional leader, Hale Boggs, and his successor in Congress, Lindy Boggs, and the brother of

ABC TV's Cokie Roberts, Boggs was entirely well wired from the moment he joined the firm in 1966.

Boggs had any number of reasons for hiring Brown—his connections, his affiliation with Ted Kennedy, and, above all, his race. Admitted Brown, "Every firm wanted a black lateral partner who had status."[14] This was not, however, mere tokenism. Brown gave Patton Boggs entree to that set-aside slice of the revenue pie the firm could not access on its own.

Brown had one reason above all for signing on with Patton Boggs. In fact, there was no other reason. Money. Brown had been developing a taste for luxury, and Patton Boggs could satisfy it. Brown tripled his salary right out of the gate from roughly $65,000 on the Hill to $200,000.[15] Now, he could at least begin to indulge his affection for fine clothes and cars. He could send his children—Michael and Tracey—to the finest prep schools and colleges. He could move to the kind of pricey enclave his self-image demanded. All he would have to offer in return was his soul. And Boggs did not hesitate to ask for it.

The partners at Patton Boggs took sufficient pride in its unofficial motto—"You eat what you kill"—that they might as well have put it on the letterhead. "For a bunch of liberal Democrats," said one partner, "we sure do believe in the free enterprise system. Socialism is not an ethic at Patton Boggs."[16]

The Patton Boggs ethic, such as it was, worked well for Brown: what mattered here was not what one practiced but what one professed. As filtered through the sensibility of daughter Tracey, Brown would find a liberal justification for every unsavory client he represented, every sleazy move he made. Such rationalizations were not unique to Brown. They defined late–twentieth century Washington.

To get him started, Boggs threw Brown some bones. His first lobbying job was to help derail pending legislation on behalf of Burlington Industries. That the legislation was being debated before his former committee made Brown all the more valuable.

On his first major project, Brown represented a consortium of Japanese electronic firms fighting a tax on the sale of VCRs and blank videocassettes. The purpose of the tax was to compensate American producers for the likely unwarranted duplication of their product. Boggs had selected Brown for the project because the Senate Judiciary Committee handles copyright issues, and Brown knew his way around the committee well.

The Japanese, however, were not thrilled by Boggs' choice. Brown would attribute their resistance to his race, but his inexperience might have concerned them even more. In any case, he proved a skillful negotiator, helping to hold the consortium together and defeat the proposed tax. Ron Brown had found his profession.[17] That he would often represent foreign countries at the expense of his own troubled him little. After all, as Tracey Brown reminds us, the Japanese "had corporate offices as well as manufacturing plants within the United States, thus providing jobs for U.S. workers."[18]

By 1985, Brown was making nearly $350,000 a year from Patton Boggs and looking around for ways to make more. To do that he would have to bring in his own business and perhaps even start a business or two on his own. In time, he would do both, and it would cost him dearly.

Texas 1969:
Nolanda Hill, right, then 24, and her sister, former Miss Texas Mary Lou Butler Blaylock, help promote
"The Stock Market Observer," a program on KDTV-Channel 39 in Dallas-Fort Worth.

5   NOLANDA

Nolanda Hill remembers the moment vividly. It was in the early 1980s. She and her then husband, Billy Hill, had stopped by Patton Boggs to talk to an old law school friend of Billy's named Joe Reeder about some potential business.[1]

When the conversation strayed to old school talk, Nolanda ventured into the corridor to check out the firm's pricey art collection. It was then she noticed Ron Brown—tall, mustached, exquisitely tailored as always—walking coolly down the stairs. And he noticed Nolanda, a tallish, blue-eyed brunette in her late thirties, three years younger than Brown, not bad-looking at all, but a Texan of the old school and a serious entrepreneur; she was never a "babe," nothing close, no matter what the newspapers would one day say or imply.

Brown approached her. It was not unlike him to do so. "He brought new meaning to the word womanizer," says Hill wryly. Hill was charmed. How could she not be? All who met Ron Brown were charmed. Hill had no way of knowing, of course, this chance meeting would in time transform her life and very nearly destroy it.

At that point of near destruction, when the media presented Hill to the world, they did so selectively, grudgingly. To the degree she plays any role at all in Brown's reported life, it is almost inevitably as vixen, villainess, the Eve to his Adam—"a controversial, flamboyant Texas wheeler-dealer fond of showing up at business meetings on a motorcycle."[2] So contrived was the reporting on Hill that a careful reader of the major media would not learn as essential a fact as her race.

In her retelling of Brown's life, Tracey Brown scarcely mentions Hill, relegating her relationship with Brown to one sentence late in the book and her identity to one word: "businesswoman."[3] Hill does not even get a mention in the index.

One can forgive Tracey Brown a daughter's discretion, but Brown's biographer, Steven Holmes, has no such excuse. He pays only a little more attention to Hill than does Tracey, virtually all of it cruel. In his lowest blow, he cites unnamed sources who label her as "untrustworthy, a gold digger, neurotic, a habitual liar."[4] And although Hill talked to Holmes at length and shared with him her deep affection for Brown—"He was my best friend. He was my everything"—Holmes reduces their relationship to the crudest common denominator. "In their own way," says Holmes with more authority than he has any right to, "each saw the other as a meal ticket."[5]

By denying Hill her due, Holmes and other journalists missed the real story of Ron Brown. There is no understanding his life, and especially his death, without Hill. For not only was she his business partner and lover, but she was also his most trusted confidante, the keeper of his secrets. Brown would call Hill at least twice a day from all over the world, often five, six, seven times a day in times of crisis. Hill's sister and attorney can attest to the same. When Hill was with them, they would grow weary of Brown's calls. The calls drove her assistant, Jane Solt, almost crazy. "It was kind of like I was his diary," says Hill almost matter-of-factly.

Why the media denial? No doubt, Hill made some enemies in Washington, a city that for all its feminist sympathies prefers its women in stereotypes. Hill fit none of them. She was an Edna Ferber character in a Nora Ephron kind of town. In Washington not many women ride Harleys. Not many use "rodeo" as a verb as in "I loved to rodeo." Not many worked against the ERA, the Equal Rights Amendment, especially among Democrats. (Hill figures she got all the rights there were to get with the Civil Rights Act of 1964, a law she took at its word.) Not many have faith in the Lord or in free enterprise, and there is a general distrust of those who do, especially those like Hill who have faith in both.

"My first belief," says Hill, "is that outside of spiritual the only other real opportunities are economic." In Texas, in most of America, that kind of sentiment doesn't even turn a head. In the District, it causes heartburn.

For a variety of reasons, none of them good, the Washington media allowed Hill's enemies to define her. The *New York Times*, for instance, turns to an imprisoned former partner of Hill's for a character reference. "She had a real inferiority complex," Thomas Gaubert told the *Times*, "because, one, she was a woman; two, she had no education; and three, she came from the wrong side of the tracks."[6]

It is hard to understand how Gaubert—and by extension the *Times* and the rest of the media—got everything wrong but her gender. Hill has a college degree as do her two sisters, as do, for that matter, her mother, Francile, and her father, Nolan—a rare pattern for a family presumably from "the wrong side of the tracks" in pre-air-conditioned Texas.

In reality, Nolanda Sue Butler grew up comfortably if modestly in Irving, Texas, then a "little bitty town" halfway between Forth Worth and Dallas. Nolan Butler owned a service station and then a lumberyard before settling on a career as a commercial real estate broker. Francile Butler was an educator and school administrator.

Something of a tomboy, Hill was torn between her love of the rodeo—she favored barrel racing—and her affection for classical music. In fact, she was one of America's rare music majors to minor in physical education. Her sisters—one, two years older, one, two years younger—also had a gift for music, and so they did what musical singers once routinely did—formed a singing group named, of course, "The Butler Sisters."

Hill helped pay her way through college in the mid-1960s by touring a four-state area with her sisters. They sang in a wide range of styles. Hill preferred the blues and suffered the show tunes in the spirit of sisterly compromise. At the height of their game, the Butler Sisters hooked up with the late Bob Hope, a man who happily lived up to his image. "He was very nice, very kind, very wise," says Hill. With Vietnam now coming home to America, the sisters performed at many a military hospital—inspiring work, yes, but never easy.

As Hill rounded into her early twenties, she and her sisters saw where their road was inevitably heading, and none of them much wanted to go there: Las Vegas. Instead, unwittingly, Hill chose a career path that would lead to her to the one city in America that could surpass Vegas in both sin and intrigue, Washington DC.

The inspiration came to Hill early and lit a fire underneath her. In working with Hope, she observed that the people who dominated his business were people who looked, well, like Bob Hope. "There was nothing but wealthy white men," says Hill of the early television industry. She was undaunted. From early on, Nolan Butler had encouraged his little rodeo star to seize the proverbial bull by the horns. "He told me," says Hill proudly, "I could be anything I wanted to be."

Hill also attributes her father with a keen sense of justice long before it was fashionable, back, in fact, when it was borderline dangerous. So encouraged, Hill began her one-woman assault on the closed shop of Texas TV. "I didn't have anything but the commitment and desire," says Hill. "I was dedicated to the proposition that women and minorities would have a voice."

Had Hill infused her energy into almost any other field—say music or ranching or real estate—she would likely have emerged successful and fulfilled without ever having been threatened and slandered and, finally, incarcerated. But television management differed from these other fields in one critical respect: it was highly regulated. And virtually all that regulatory power resided in Washington.

Television knew no halcyon period before regulation. In 1927 Congress took the power to license newly emerging commercial radio stations away from the Commerce Department—of all places—and gave it to a new five-member Federal Radio Commission. Seven years later Congress expanded the re-christened Federal Communications Commission (FCC) to seven members and extended its responsibilities to include telephone and telegraph regulation.[7] The pattern was set. The FCC casually absorbed television into its expanding dominion as soon as it came on board.

In drafting the Communications Act of 1934, Congress allowed that "the public" owns the airwaves. The FCC only grants a station the use of a broadcast frequency for a certain period of time. One problem. Public ownership never works in America quite as intended. Never really has.

Settlers of the Plymouth Plantation learned this lesson the hard way. In year one, they tested their belief that "the taking away of property and bringing in community into a commonwealth would make them happy and flourishing as if they were wiser than God," and even these good souls were brought up short. "For this community was found to breed much confusion and discontent," wrote the chastened Governor, William Bradford, "and retard much employment that would have been to their benefit and comfort."

The FCC has bred its own share of confusion and discontent. Instructive in the same is the rise of the Johnson media empire—as in Lyndon Baines

Johnson. Not surprisingly, Johnson launched his media career only after he had been elected to Congress. In 1943, using wife Ladybird as a cut out, he bought a failing Austin, Texas radio station for $17,500.[8] As biographer Robert Caro observes of Johnson, "In truth, he oversaw, in detail, every aspect of KTBC's operation."[9]

Various FCC restrictions had helped keep the price low, but the Commission proceeded to lift those restrictions uniquely for the Johnsons. The ambitious young congressman and his wife were allowed to obtain a better frequency, increase transmitting power fourfold, and broadcast at all hours. It didn't hurt that LBJ had a very good friend in FCC board member Clifford Durr. LBJ also made new friends at CBS. Its president, Bill Paley, decided a station owned by the congressman's wife would make an excellent addition to the CBS family. Needless to say, these considerations dramatically inflated the station's value.

In 1948, after some ballot box stuffing that was impressive even by Texas standards, "Landslide Lyndon" was elected to the U.S. Senate where he took a seat on the Commerce Committee. This just happened to be the very same committee that watched over the FCC and managed communications bills that came before the Senate. The fox was officially in the henhouse.

In June of 1952, after a four-year freeze on television license grants, that same FCC just happened to bestow one of its first unfrozen grants on none other than the good wife of the new Senate minority leader. In fact, Ladybird applied for and received the sole VHF television license in Austin, Texas, for KTBC-TV. Over the next two decades the FCC would continue to exercise its power to protect the Johnson TV monopoly in Austin and to extend it to Waco. By the time Johnson became president in 1963, Ladybird's company was registering a $500,000 annual profit. And it was all more or less legal.

A few years later Hill and then husband, Sheldon Turner, looked into the possibility of launching a rival UHF station in Austin. Says Hill, "We got laughed at." Hill, still recovering from an impetuous early marriage, had met Turner at a Dallas TV station where he was the general manager. She had taken a job there in the late '60s after the Butler Sisters had gone their separate ways. Ambitious and eager, Hill absorbed everything she could about the industry. She remembers writing words down on the palm of her hand at meetings and going back and looking them up, "So I looked like I knew what I was doing."

She and Turner set their sights on acquiring their own TV station. VHF stations—very high frequency, channels 2 through 13—were prohibitively expensive. By arbitrarily restricting licenses, Austin being a case in point, the FCC had driven the price up. "Politics," says Hill with ironic understatement, "played a role in keeping the spectrum closed."

The coming revolution was in UHF, ultra high frequency, the then second tier channels 14 through 83. As one might expect, VHF stations and their friends in government resisted UHF mightily, and the FCC helped by restricting their commercial viability. In the early '70s at least, this kept UHF stations available enough to allow Hill and Turner to apply and win the license for KNBN in Dallas, previously owned by preacher Pat Robertson.

To make UHF stations competitive, new television sets needed a simple device called, colloquially, a "click tuner." As Hill explains it, laws had to be changed to allow their installation. The place where laws got changed was Washington. And so Hill and a handful of others—Ted Turner among them—went to work to change the laws. "That's how I learned about politics," says Hill, "and how you get things done in Washington."

Along the way, Hill and husband Sheldon Turner, twenty years her senior, suffered the kind of setbacks that in a novel critics would dismiss as melodrama. But real they were, and none more frighteningly so than Turner's brain tumor, which left him blind. "To keep the TV dream alive," Hill launched a publishing company and found herself selling books out of the back of her car.

The melodrama only intensified when she met Billy Hill, a young attorney who was assigned to work on a copyright issue for her publishing company. She soon made him a 15 percent partner in the television business, and, in time, they became romantically involved. Turner, still incapacitated, released her to marry Hill, and the three remained more or less amiable partners.

Even in the age of Bob & Carol & Ted & Alice, even in Dallas, this arrangement tilted towards the unorthodox. Hill's critics, as one might expect, hold it against her. Holmes coldly describes it as "part of what was an emerging pattern of mixing profit and pleasure,"[10] a pattern he would extend to her relationship with Brown. Hill contends otherwise. Says she with genuine conviction about her late husband, "Sheldon was the best friend I ever had."

In any case, Metromedia bought the UHF station for $15 million in 1983, and the three partners were, if not rich, at least pretty dang close. It was then that Hill, her star ascendant, went to Washington to chair a symposium on women in telecommunications conducted by the FCC.

"I have a lot of money now," she told her audience, "but I didn't marry any. I didn't inherit any, and I never slept with any as far as I know. But the men in every one of those categories are now in pretty good shape."

It was when she was in Washington for this event that she accompanied Billy Hill to discuss a business deal at Patton Boggs. It was at Patton Boggs, of course, that she met Ron Brown.

In 1985, Hill launched Corridor Communications, through which she operated a Boston area TV station she had bought in 1983 and another station in Washington. So involved was the litigation surrounding the establishment of Corridor that Hill retained Joe Reeder and got her own desk at Patton Boggs. She spent many a week in Washington and would commute home to Billy Hill and their young son, Andrew, on weekends.

From the beginning she was attracted to Brown, and he to her. What she saw in Brown was what everyone saw. Potential. He had "a tiny little office" then and a job that asked little of him. "He lived," says Hill, "in a very me, me, me world." Brown wanted more, and both knew that Hill could help him.

"When I met Ron," says Hill. "I knew instinctively that his ability to cross between cultures and ethnicities was God-given." Then and now a passionate believer in the transforming power of television, Hill saw TV as a way to give minorities and women more of a voice and inevitably more of a stake.

What Brown saw in Hill was likely a source of calm and order, a mother as much as a lover. Brown wanted advice, and Hill was not at all hesitant to give it. "He was not managed," says Hill. "He was undisciplined. He didn't work hard. He played hard. He was nowhere near coming to the place where he was using his talent and his intellect and his ability for the good of others."

Hill felt strongly Brown would find real happiness and a sense of peace only when he started using that talent. She even disciplined him about his "zipper problem," which at the time was largely an academic discussion. Brown and Hill had developed an intense relationship without sex. That would change.

As her marriage to Billy Hill crumbled towards decade's end, she saw more and more of Brown, and their relationship deepened. "I didn't like the adultress part of the relationship," says Hill. "It was just wrong." As she would learn in time, others did not like it either.

6 | HAITI

With the reader's kind permission, the narrative jumps ahead here ten years. Nolanda Hill and Ron Brown sit in the dining room of her apartment at the semi-glitzy 2401 Pennsylvania Avenue, a long stone's throw from the White House, the kind of building where life and work mesh more seamlessly than they do anywhere else in America.

Amidst the trappings of power and faux luxury, Hill and Brown are doing what thousands of people across the country are doing at the same moment—watching the evening news and eating Chinese take-out. It's just that they are watching with more interest. Much more. The stunned Brown, in fact, watches with something near horror. Finally, unable to reconcile himself to what he is seeing, he picks up his chopsticks, throws them violently at the television, and explodes in a paroxysm of hurt and fury, "cussing," Hill would remember, "like a sailor."[1]

To the ordinary, news-watching, eggroll-eating middle American, the images on TV would not have seemed unduly provocative. They simply showed President Clinton meeting with a group of advisors to control the simmering mess the nation of Haiti had become.

In truth, this benighted country had been a geo-political disaster since the French first set foot on its ill-fated soil. In the most recent dust-up of note, the Haitian military had overthrown its elected president, Jean-Bertrand Aristide, the latest in a long line of coups to plague Haiti since it emerged as the world's first black republic in 1804. Although President Bush had pledged to restore Aristide to power, he and his people must have realized how unfixable the whole situation was and left the mess for his successor.

As irrelevant as Haiti might have seemed to Bush or to the rest of the world, it mattered deeply to Clinton. There was a specific reason why: black America cared about Haiti, at least its leadership, and Bill Clinton cared about black America. Eighty-two percent of African-Americans would vote for him in 1992's tight three-way race. He could not have been elected—or be re-elected—without their support.

And so in the 1992 campaign, Clinton chided Bush for his lack of resolution, attacked the president's policy of sending refugees back, and promised to return Aristide to power. At their 1992 convention, Democrats embedded Clinton's stand on repatriation into their platform with unusual boldness: "Forcible return of anyone fleeing political repression is a betrayal of American values."[2]

As Clinton knew it would, his position played well with Kweisi Mfume and his colleagues on the Congressional Black Caucus. Mfume admits he was "very concerned about that situation."[3] The caucus chairman had reacted viscerally to the scenes of Haitian refugees risking death in the Caribbean and expected Clinton to offer them asylum as promised until the situation in Haiti improved.

To Mfume's astonishment, however, Clinton quickly reneged on his pledge. He was not long in office before he announced plans to send the refugees picked up at sea right back to Haiti, the exact policy for which he had scolded Bush. This decision angered the Black Caucus and threatened Clinton's hold on the black voter.

"We're not going up there and pose for any pictures with him," Mfume would tell his colleagues, "until he keeps his promise."[4]

Despite Mfume's concerns, Clinton only sank deeper into the Haitian morass. The Defense Department and the CIA seemed to be flouting Clinton's plan to return Aristide to power. This "public display of indiscipline," as Haiti expert Robert White describes it, climaxed with the unseemly spectacle of an American military ship, the USS *Harlan County*, reversing course when confronted by a gang of wild-eyed Haitian thugs along a Port-au-Prince dock.[5] The ignominious retreat of the ship on October 11, 1993, just four days before Aristide's scheduled return, forced Clinton to get serious about Haiti in a way he had yet to be.

At some point in this sequence, the matter became serious enough—or visual enough—to attract TV news people and force Brown to recognize he had been cut out of the loop. Had the White House meeting been about Bosnia or Somalia or some such place, Brown would not have been troubled. But Haiti? No one in the Clinton administration knew half as much about Haiti as Brown did. Thus, the throwing of the aforementioned chopsticks.

Brown had a long and uneasy history with Haiti. He had met its front men early on in his tenure at Patton Boggs, back when the infamous "Baby Doc" Duvalier was still in power. Nolanda Hill believes it was Brown's friend, the inimitable Lauri Fitz-Pegado, who made the introduction.

Fitz-Pegado deserves a sidebar of her own as she so nicely embodies the ethos of late twentieth century Washington. An African American with an Angolan husband, Fitz-Pegado looked good, had decent foreign-service credentials, and did not shy from playing the diversity card. With this combination, she smoothed her way into some of the most influential lobbies of Washington in her role as public affairs specialist with Hill & Knowlton, an international PR firm.

Brown returned the favor on the Haitian referral by later nominating Fitz-Pegado to be assistant secretary of Commerce and director general of the United States and Foreign Commercial Service. This position was to put Fitz-Pegado in charge of a global network of two hundred trade offices in seventy countries.

Fitz-Pegado's nomination received the strongest endorsement from Brown and the president and passed through two committees unscathed. Along the way, however, someone tipped off the minority Republicans on the Senate Banking, Housing, and Urban Affairs committee about Fitz-Pegado's involvement in an extraordinary bit of PR legerdemain. Indeed, so over-the-top was this incident that it came to be known, even on the Senate floor, by its own legendary name: "the baby incubator fraud."

Senator Lauch Faircloth discussed the incident in detail in his opening remarks to this committee on May 25, 1994.[6] As Faircloth related, just before the Gulf War, Fitz-Pegado had coached a fifteen-year-old Kuwaiti girl on how to testify before Congress.

The girl proved to be a quick learner. Hidden behind a screen, allegedly for safety's sake, and identified only as "Naira," she told a story so chilling that at least six Senators would cite it as a reason to liberate Kuwait. Iraqi soldiers, claimed Naira, had snatched Kuwaiti babies from hospital respirators and left them "on the cold floor to die."

Under Fitz-Pegado's tutelage, other witnesses came forward to add horrifying detail. The most critical was a surgeon who called himself Dr. Ebrahim. The good doctor told the United Nations Security Council he had personally buried forty of those very babies the Iraqis pulled from incubators.

One problem. Troublesome as they might be, the Iraqis never threw babies out of incubators. The girl testifying proved to be the daughter of the Kuwaiti ambassador to the United States. The surgeon in question proved to be a dentist who had never buried any of the babies because, well, he had never actually seen any.

The Republican opposition's summary statement on "professional scam-artist" Fitz-Pegado was withering. Much of the criticism could have applied to Brown as well:

> Lauri Fitz-Pegado has coached perjured testimony before Congress. She has served as a lobbyist for the Communist Government in Angola. She has worked for the murderous Duvalier regime in Haiti, a regime which has left us with the tragic legacy we are attempting to deal with today. She has been a hired gun for disreputable foreign interests. She has deliberately attempted to mislead Senators about her past. In short, Lauri Fitz-Pegado has disqualified herself from service in the position to which she has been nominated.

No matter. Brown did some serious arm-twisting, and only three Democrats in the full Senate voted to send her nomination back to the Banking Committee for further review. Fitz-Pegado was duly confirmed. Said Faircloth, "There are few people in America who have less business being in charge of our nation's trade secrets than Lauri Fitz-Pegado." This warning would prove entirely prophetic, but more on that later.

Back to Ron Brown and the Haitians. In October 1983 the Duvalier regime decided it needed help in Washington and reached out to Ron Brown for representation. To be fair, Baby Doc was not quite as ruthless as his father, Francois "Papa Doc" Duvalier, but he was not much of an improvement. Case in point: the normally gracious Pope John Paul II had blistered the regime for "divisions, injustices, excessive inequality, misery, hunger" and "the fear of many people."[7] And he had made these charges publicly—in Haiti itself—while on a goodwill mission earlier in that year.

Daughter Tracey Brown refers to Haiti as a "major client" and puts the best possible face on her father's decision to represent it. "Although Haiti was ruled by a dictator," she writes, "Dad didn't think the Haitian people should be punished because of their leadership." But as Tracey also notes, "Dad earned quite a bit for this work and that increased his ambivalence."[8]

To put a further gloss on her father's motives, Tracey Brown also claims that at the time of her father's hiring, the "Duvalier government received no foreign aid from the United States because of its human rights violations."[9] This was one problem Brown allegedly hoped to address.

As sympathetic as he may be, biographer Steven Holmes does not begin to buy Tracey Brown's rationales. "The claim that Brown was simply trying to get U.S. aid restored to Haiti in order to alleviate the suffering," writes Holmes, "is simply wrong."[10]

At the time of Brown's hiring, the Haitian government was indeed receiving foreign aid. During Brown's tenure as a lobbyist, he helped raise the annual allowance from $38 million to $55 million. More to the point, Brown worked to get that aid passed through the Duvalier regime and not through private aid programs.

For obvious reasons, Duvalier wanted the money coming to him and his people. So did Brown. To help spread that money around, Brown organized a prototype of what would become his signature foreign policy initiative, the "trade mission." According to Tracey, he reserved the mission for "black-owned American businesses" as a way of introducing them to the Haitian marketplace.[11] In effect, however, Duvalier and his cronies *were* that marketplace.

Brown himself had launched one of the black-owned businesses in question. He called it "Harmon International"—Harmon being his middle name—and through it hoped to get the concession on all the grain bags into and out of Haiti.

"Ron's goal was to make money," says Nolanda Hill. "He saw a considerable amount of money changing hands at the top in Haiti, and he wanted a piece of that pie."

And yet for all of the venality of his deal with Haiti, Brown took on Duvalier as a client less out of greed than fear, specifically fear of failure. Brown had good cause to worry. He was always uneasy at Patton Boggs, and especially so in those early days. Its culture, as defined by Boggs, was Southern good-old-boy, and Brown was neither.

What is more, Patton Boggs had hired Brown less for his talent than for his race and his connections to Ted Kennedy. Beyond Kennedy, Brown had few meaningful affiliations in Congress and no access at all to the heads of any powerful committees. If he were to survive at the firm, he needed to bring in clients of his own and nurture them. At the time he was already living beyond his means. All moral judgments aside, Duvalier was a godsend.

Happily for Brown, at least in the short haul, all moral judgments were set aside at his new firm. Boggs gloried in his role as "fixer." "You fix things by virtue of what you know and who you know," says Hill. "Sometimes money, more often not." This was a dirty business. As hard as Brown tried to fit in, he could not. He would never be a "fixer" in the Boggs tradition. He would always feel sullied by the work he did at Patton Boggs.

Brown had good reason to feel sullied. Much of the work he did was demeaning, especially his work with Haiti. Lobbying was only a small part of the job. His primary task, according to Hill, "was helping them move money around." He would assist various well-connected Haitians as they attempted to get into the country, often illegally, and establish themselves. This might mean finding them jobs, getting them credentialed, even turning on their utilities—in his own name if need be.[12]

Brown also made some new associations at the Haitian embassy, none more troublesome than the beguiling Lillian Madsen. Biographer Holmes, although normally reticent about describing women, loses it over Lillian. The daughter of a white Spanish father and a black Haitian mother, Madsen dazzled Holmes with her "clear golden skin, long flowing blond hair, light brown eyes, a petite though well proportioned figure, a full sensuous mouth, and a gleaming smile."[13]

A "full sensuous mouth"?

One wonders what Holmes' colleagues at the *New York Times* thought of that turn of phrase. Adds Holmes, as if the reader needed to be told, "Madsen was stunning to behold." Curiously, Holmes does not share with the reader a single physical detail about Nolanda Hill—no slouch in the looks department herself—not even her race. What is more, the friends of Brown that Holmes consults routinely denigrate Hill and dismiss her claims of intimacy while they elevate the status of Madsen.

"There was far more to their relationship than that this was just his squeeze," says one friend proudly of Brown. "He had almost a family sense about Lillian."[14] Lillian, by the by, had a family of her own—including a husband and children.

Aware of Madsen and Hill and presumably others, these same anonymous "friends" insist Brown "remained a loving husband to Alma."[15] Tracey Brown maintains the same fiction. "For all their thirty-four years together," writes Tracey, "my parents had a smooth, loving relationship."[16] Hill believes Alma Brown had reconciled herself to Brown's philandering with other black women. "She knew all about them," says Hill. "It was pretty common knowledge."

Hill's problem was she was white. No need to be coy. There is something going on here that will affect the course of Hill's life and lead ultimately to her undoing. In the course of her relationship with Brown, Hill would encounter a good deal of resistance to that relationship, almost exclusively from African Americans. Indeed, Holmes, who is black, and Brown's quoted friends can barely hide their contempt.

Brown, in fact, would go to some lengths to hide his relationship with Hill from his black colleagues. Said Willie Brown, later the mayor of San Francisco, Hill "was not a blip, not a blip . . . Ron Brown made sure that [Hill] simply did not register perception-wise. He was very careful about that."[17]

Yet for all his seeming discretion, the black insider community in the District was well aware of Hill. To get Brown's goat, Vernon Jordan, among others, would report Hill's whereabouts to Brown if he saw her out and about without him, and Brown in turn would call Hill "mad as a hornet."

The Clinton Justice Department surely understood that Hill could expect little sympathy or support from the black community in Washington DC. In time, this understanding would shape its legal strategy. As to Madsen, she would never have to face charges. She would shamelessly exploit the all too willing Brown and cause him what Holmes describes as "extreme legal difficulties."[18]

Meanwhile, Baby Doc was facing difficulties of his own. In 1985, unrest swept his country, and he and his police responded as the instigators hoped they might—with his customary brutality. The ensuing repression inspired the Reagan State Department to suspend all direct aid. While Brown lobbied them to restore the aid, the Reagan administration was quietly negotiating through a back channel to arrange Duvalier's departure. His government was in full collapse.

The State Department dealt with the unwitting Brown only to provide cover for its real plans. These plans became obvious even to Brown in February 1986 when Baby Doc and his wife hightailed it out of the country on board a U.S. military transport. Although Baby Doc Duvalier had paid Brown more than $500,000 for less than three years of service, no amount could make amends for the damage this service would do to Brown's reputation.

Even after Duvalier fled the country, Brown would keep abreast of Haiti's affairs. As Brown grew in stature, Haitians in Washington paid more and more attention to him. Hill reports being in the room once when Aristide called, a man Brown thought of as harsh and corrupt. Says Hill, "The looting of Haiti didn't stop just because Duvalier left."

By late 1993, however, Haiti was just one of the albatrosses hanging from Brown's weary neck. Vietnam was another, a heavier one at that, and more on this later. After he had thrown the chopsticks and regained his composure, Brown rationalized to Hill that it was "the Vietnam thing" that must have precluded the president from consulting with him about Haiti.

Hill would not let Brown delude himself. She may have been the one person other than his wife who, when asked, gave advice without deference. "Ron, that makes no sense," Hill told him in her tough-love style. "If they thought you had any value, they would quietly consult you."

Clinton did, for instance, quietly consult Kweisi Mfume about Haiti. Despite his reservations about Clinton, Mfume was enormously flattered. "Can you imagine that," Mfume would relate, "the president of the United States calling me?"[19]

For no obvious strategic reason, Clinton also called William Gray III, the president of the United Negro College Fund. He, too, was highly flattered. "The president asked me for my views on the [Haitian] situation and how I would solve it," Gray would later report. "Imagine the significance of that."[20] The significance, of course, was political. Clinton was trying to shore up his bridge to black America. Who knows how many black leaders he called to seek their opinion on a subject about which most of them knew little?

Clinton refused, however, to call the one black leader who might have actually helped him. As Brown was becoming painfully aware, the Clintons no longer valued him even as a bridge-builder to black America. He was beginning to see he had only one role of value left, a dangerous one at that.

"Bagman."

7 JESSE

From early on, Ron Brown saw himself as a potential president of the United States. It was a heady vision, but not an unrealistic one. He was smooth, well spoken, and looked good on television. He had the right credentials, great connections, plenty of ambition, and all the charm in the world. Plus, he was one of very few Democrats to have served in the military, an asset in that party at least one year out of every four. What slowed his journey to the White House and ultimately derailed it was not his race. No, it was that damnable baggage.

For all his heft, Baby Doc Duvalier would weigh Brown down less than would Jesse Jackson, the well-known activist and perennial presidential candidate. As it happened, Brown did not come looking for Jackson. Jackson came looking for Brown.

It only made sense. When Jackson went trawling for support prior to his 1988 run for the presidency, black leaders were slow to sign on. The feedback Jackson got went something like this: If you are going to run, do it right. Don't repeat the chaotic effort of 1984. Several major players pointed Jackson towards Brown. Brown had hands-on experience from the Kennedy campaign and his occasional work with the Democratic National Committee. More importantly, Brown translated well into the white world, certainly much better than Jackson did or could, and this was widely understood.

In Tracey Brown's account, which seems entirely credible, Jackson approached Brown at a fund-raiser. With him were Percy Sutton, a New York politico and the chair of Jackson's campaign, and Alexis Herman.

Herman was still another of the well-born, light-skinned African Americans who would come to dominate the highly profitable Washington civil rights enterprise.[1]

At this time, Herman served as president of A.M. Herman & Associates, a consulting firm that, among other things, "guided corporations on human resources issues," occasionally in the lucrative wake of a Jesse Jackson scolding. Herman's path to the top—she would eventually become secretary of labor and earn her own independent counsel—would intersect Brown's at many a critical juncture, including his final one.

Although flattered by Jackson's offer, Brown turned it down. "I wasn't ready to stop what I was doing to run a campaign that clearly wasn't going to win," Brown would later say. "My commitment wasn't deep enough."[2]

Even without Brown's help, Jackson ran a sufficiently energetic campaign to come into the convention with twelve hundred delegates. If he lacked the strength to stop Massachusetts Governor Michael Dukakis, he had more than enough to scare him. The Dukakis camp lived with the fear Jackson would demand the vice-presidential nod. Such a demand, whether satisfied or not, would doom Dukakis' then-promising bid for the presidency. This, everyone knew.

Once again, it was Jesse Jackson who made the preemptive move. Wanting to signal party regulars that he was willing to play ball, he approached Brown during a reception at a Georgetown club, put his hand on Brown's shoulder, and told him "it was time to bring the first team in."[3] The game now was the convention. Jackson wanted Brown to manage his efforts.

Always calculating, Brown asked for time and made a series of phone calls to party leaders, including those in Massachusetts, the home base of both Dukakis and Brown's old mentor, Ted Kennedy. After a week of vacillation, Brown finally agreed.[4]

"The party people were relieved because they figured it would hold the party together," Brown would acknowledge, "but I was not serving multiple masters. The person I was advocating was Jesse Jackson."[5]

Jackson's people were not so sure. When he heard of Brown's appointment, longtime Jackson aide Frank Watkins recalls thinking, "That's Baby Doc's lawyer!"[6] Others on Jackson's staff shared Watkins' dismay. They saw Brown as too centrist, too self-interested, too white.

"Within the Democratic Party there was them and there was us," said Howard University political scientist Ron Walters, who worked for Jackson.

"Ron Brown had a different profile. He was part of the establishment. It's logical that people should suspect him. He's not part of 'the movement.'"[7]

Those who presumed Brown had an agenda beyond helping Jackson were correct. On one level, the obvious one, Brown knew a successful performance at the convention would polish his resume and smooth his access to Congress, a major plus for his Patton Boggs business. Less obviously, Brown had set his sights on the chairmanship of the Democratic National Committee.

As busloads of potentially volatile Jackson delegates descended on the Atlanta convention, Brown did what Brown did best: he negotiated. He arranged a role for Jackson at the convention that was high enough in profile to satisfy the reverend but not so high that it obscured Dukakis and his message. Dukakis left the convention with a solid lead in the polls, and Brown left with an enhanced reputation.

"The individual who put Ron Brown on the map was Jesse Jackson," said Democratic activist Tony Coehlo. "No question about it."[8] Following the convention, Brown served as an advisor to the Dukakis campaign and watched it unravel from up close, the third straight presidential flameout for the party that controlled both houses of Congress. If he were Democratic chair, Brown knew he could only do better.

And here came the rub. No sooner did Brown begin lobbying for the job than he realized he had a new liability to deal with; no, not "Baby Doc," but "Jesse." George Bush had beaten Dukakis by branding him with the "L" word, "liberal." Jackson had the "L" word written all over him and, in some reactionary quarters, even within his own party, the "N" word. The very people that had encouraged Brown to involve himself in the Jackson campaign were now discouraging him from pursuing the DNC chair because of the taint from that very involvement.

A good deal of resistance came from Jewish members of the party and with good cause. In January 1984 while joshing with a black *Washington Post* reporter, Milton Coleman, Jackson famously referred to Jews as "Hymies" and to New York City as "Hymietown."[9]

These words from the mouth of any other candidate would have ended not just his campaign but his career. Not Jackson. As America's most prominent African American, he enjoyed unparalleled immunity from media criticism. The *Post* only reported his remarks several weeks after the fact and then deep in an article by another *Post* reporter on Jackson's uneasy relationship with American Jews. Still, all hell broke loose.

After first denying he ever said such things, Jackson accused the party's Jews of conspiring to defeat him. Trying to be helpful in his distinctive way, the Nation of Islam's Louis Farrakhan threatened Coleman and warned Jews in Jackson's presence: "If you harm this brother [Jackson], it will be the last one you harm."[10]

Despite a public atonement some weeks later, not the last in his career, Jackson refused to denounce Farrakhan. Understandably, not all Jews were quick to forgive Jackson, and many extended their suspicions to Brown. Brown would have to work hard to overcome them.

White Southern Democrats were even less enthusiastic about Brown than their Jewish colleagues. "The public perception about his election is probably that Jesse Jackson is in charge of the party," Bobby Kahn, executive director of the Georgia Democratic party, said at the time. Alabama party chairman John Baker was even more blunt in his public assessment of Brown's candidacy: "I think this is a giant step backward."[11] As to Arkansas Governor Bill Clinton, he and his colleagues on the centrist Democratic Leadership Council consciously and conspicuously supported no one.

When approached personally, Clinton himself refused to endorse Brown. "I was basically disgusted," said Brown supporter Steve Cobble. "I felt, what a wimp!"[12] Cobble's disgust with Clinton was widely shared in the Brown camp. Despite Clinton's self-definition as a civil rights pioneer and despite the civil rights aura attached to this race, Clinton washed his hands of it, a pattern that would be repeated when he was elected president.

Opposition to Brown came from some surprising quarters. Until strong-armed by Jesse Jackson, Ted Kennedy refused to commit. Brown's former law professor, Mario Cuomo, hesitated to endorse him. Catching the drift within the party establishment, even Alexis Herman declined Brown's request to work on his campaign for chair. Although sympathetic, she did not think Brown had a chance to realize his "dream chase" and told him so.[13]

"The problem for the Democrats isn't that Ron Brown is black, it's that he's a liberal," said Republican consultant, Roger Stone, an opinion that captured the prevailing sentiment at the time.[14] But Brown himself wasn't buying. He dismissed the distinction between his color and his presumed political beliefs as "slightly disingenuous," adding, accurately enough: "If I was white and I had been the convention manager for Jesse Jackson, these issues would not be raised, certainly not with the same vehemence."[15]

To prevail in this environment, Brown was not above playing the race card himself. "Suddenly anyone who remained opposed to Ron Brown was a racist," said one DNC member who, like others among the opposition, has bitter memories of the contest.[16] Tracey Brown, less diplomatic than her father, affirms these critics in their suspicions, writing off in-party resistance to Brown as "blatant racism."[17]

It was during this campaign that Brown demonstrated another talent that would come back to haunt him—raising money. In no time at all, he had mustered nearly $350,000, an unprecedented amount for this kind of insider campaign. Much of the money came from his colleagues at Patton Boggs who could easily calculate the value of a partner as DNC chair. Brown used some of the money to lease a plane and unleash a whirlwind campaign.[18] His combination of energy, organization, and charm left his two opponents breathless.

As Brown proved himself an effective campaigner and a likely winner, certain key figures began to understand the consequences for themselves. One was Bill Clinton. Late in the campaign, Clinton claims to have endorsed Brown. He would tell Tracey Brown that after much deliberation and consultation, "I thought it would be a good thing for the party to have its first African American chairman, especially since he was the ablest person interested in the job."[19] Clinton's admission that Brown was the "ablest" of the candidates, as he obviously was, leaves no other conclusion but that Clinton hesitated earlier only because of Brown's race.

As Bill Clinton warmed to the Brown candidacy, Jesse Jackson began to cool. When Brown made a point of his "independence," Jackson understood just who it was Brown was being independent from, namely Jesse Jackson. With Brown's triumph, the separation was complete, and the hierarchy was reversed. Brown was now "the man," and Jackson was not pleased.

Nolanda Hill was none too pleased either. Brown chose not to invite her to his three-hundred-person-strong victory party at the Ritz-Carlton in Washington on February 10, 1989. "I had worked damned hard and put a lot of myself into his getting elected," says Hill. "And he'd hidden me for so long."[20] Although not yet intimate, they were much too close for Brown to risk his standing in the black community by surfacing Hill in the presence of his wife, Alma.

Brown knew he had done Hill wrong. He sent roses to her apartment and to her unofficial office at Patton Boggs, but Hill refused to acknowledge them. Finally, he tracked her down at Patton Boggs and asked what he had to do to make amends. Said Hill, "You have to take me to the most high-visibility restaurant in Washington DC, and I'll choose it."

The soiree at the power restaurant Tiberio proved eventful beyond expectations. The first night they both had free just happened to fall on Valentine's Day. Amidst a sea of single-race couples, black and white, they were the only couple both black and white.

No sooner had they sat down than Brown learned he had an urgent message from Jesse Jackson at the DNC headquarters. Brown dispatched his driver to pick it up, and he and Hill read the angry, three-page, single-spaced letter over dinner. The letter called Brown a "traitor" and accused him of abandoning both Jackson and black America in his quest for power. "It blessed [Brown] out," says Hill.

Growing more uncomfortable by the minute, the couple left the restaurant early only to find that Brown's driver, a Jackson loyalist, had quit his job and abandoned the car. Brown drove Hill to her apartment, and this time, he stayed.

Jackson has acknowledged sending the letter. As he tells the story, he just wanted to remind Brown that "oppression forces" have long tried to play moderate blacks off against their more radical brethren.[21]

The letter targeted what Steven Holmes calls "a vulnerable spot in [Brown's] psyche—his racial identity."[22] Still, it did not deter him. Two weeks later, Brown chose to endorse Richard M. Daley, who was running for mayor of Chicago as a Democrat, against an African American running as an independent. At issue was how Brown would make the endorsement. A personal appearance by Brown would have much more impact than, say, a press release.

Here, things got ugly. Jackson and his supporters urged Brown to stay out of Chicago. "When Brown brings his Oreo you-know-what into Chicago," said Congressman Gus Savage, "I'll guarantee I'm going to organize a reception party for him at the airport and to follow him all the way to some white hotel to denounce his coming in."[23] But despite enormous pressure—and in the face of dancing Oreo cookies—Brown did go to Chicago, not once but twice. In so doing, he crossed a racial Rubicon and left Jackson on the distant bank.

At this moment in his career, had Brown fixed his star on the presidency, he might well have succeeded. He had cleared himself of his Jackson baggage. Baby Doc was fading into the background like a youthful indiscretion. And the press was warming up to him as a racial pioneer and potential crossover candidate.

"Until 1989," says Nolanda Hill knowingly, "Ron did not feel proud of himself." But the DNC race, for the first time since the Army, showed Brown who he was and what kind of potential he really had. He was in the position to do genuine good, and he had the ability to do it.

If only there had not been so many temptations.

8 ENTITLED

M iserable creature!"
This is how retired innkeeper Bunny Engler of Harlingen, Texas describes Ron Brown, and she has, alas, good reason to describe him thus.[1]

In retrospect, the pattern seems self-evident: Ron Brown was quietly destroying himself. Every major step he took only seemed to ease him closer if not to death itself than at least to moral self-destruction, the kind that would transform one of God's more gifted children into a "miserable creature." This he could not see, of course. But had he been more aware of self and surroundings, he would have understood, at least, the nature of the seduction.

Even as Brown pursued the DNC chair, he would yield to the siren song of "minority capitalism." The black Jag, the gold Rolex, the monogrammed shirts, the Hermès ties, the French cuffs, the Haitian mistress—they did not come cheap. But the bounty available to a well-connected black man in late-century DC came easily, so easily, in fact, and so easily rationalized, one can understand why Brown had come to feel it his due.

In December 1988, with the DNC race heating up, Brown involved himself in an all too classic bit of preferential enterprise. He and some colleagues bought a Washington radio station. This purchase cost Brown not much more than his signature and a little time. Yes, it was that easy and that legal. The laws that made this possible were a testament to the powers of redemptive white liberalism.

Here is how these laws came to be. As late as the 1960s, the FCC rejected racial preferences in the awarding of TV and radio licenses, and the courts supported the FCC. At the time, claimed the Commission, "The Communications Act, like the Constitution, is color-blind."[2]

Feeling the need to atone for the nation's sins, progressive activists continued to press their case. The Constitution, of course, was not about to change. They knew that. Nor was the opinion of the general public, which has always rejected racial preferences. They knew this too. And so progressives took their case to the courts in the hope of finding judges equally indifferent to the public will and constitutional niceties.

They were not disappointed. In 1974, a DC court of appeals breached the constitutional walls on the communications front. The case in question involved two African Americans who had each hoped to become 7 percent partners in an Orlando TV station. In this case, the court ruled, "Merit should be awarded for minority ownership where it is likely to increase the diversity of program." This case was one of the first anywhere to make "diversity" an end it itself. It did not involve compensation for past wrongs.

Once given the court's blessing, and fully in the spirit of the times, administrative law judges at the FCC prided themselves on how much unearned preference they could dispense. In 1978, impatient with its own progress in reducing the "extreme disparity" between minority percentages at large and in the industry, the FCC took what it calls, "further Commission action."

Did it ever. The FCC started by formalizing the use of minority preferences in the awarding of licenses. Bolder still, it chose to award generous tax credits to companies that sold to "minorities," a term the FCC never really defined in the first place.

Whether one agrees with the FCC decisions or not, the absence of legislative or executive oversight stuns the student of democracy. An appointed board reversed the "color-blind" principles of constitutional law and all but drafted a major tax law, and citizens effectively had no voice in the process. In 1995 Congress finally got involved and repealed the tax credits, not because of any abuse to the Constitution but because of "perceived abuses" to the program.

The purchase of WKYS by Ron Brown and his associates would not have been seen as an abuse. This deal went more or less by the book. The minority purchasers may not have been "purchasers" in the traditional sense, but they were at least minorities, if not exactly "disadvantaged" ones.

The playing field had indeed been leveled. In the past only powerful insiders like Lyndon Johnson could benefit from FCC-rigged sweetheart deals. Now, the FCC was prepared to corrupt just about any minority with juice.

The ownership corporation was known as Albimar Communications, and Brown had a 10 percent share. Heading up the deal were Brown's friend Bertram Lee, a Boston broadcasting executive, and Jim Kelly, a New York entrepreneur who would soon marry Sharon Pratt Dixon. Dixon had kicked off her successful campaign for the mayor's job in Washington a few months back with a lavish party at the Democratic national convention.

NBC, a General Electric subsidiary, sold WKYS to Albimar for $42.5 million. Under the FCC's tax credit program, NBC saved about $15 million in federal income taxes by selling to a minority-owned enterprise. Feeling generous with the money saved, and perhaps hoping to generate goodwill in the minority community, NBC went so far as to finance $10 million of the purchase price.[3]

Albimar's investors put up less than $1 million. To secure his own $4.2 million ownership share, Brown invested only $87,000. This he borrowed from the loosely run and soon-to-fail National Bank of Washington, on whose board sat Tommy Boggs.[4] Shortly after the purchase, WKYS hired Brown's wife, Alma Brown, as public affairs director. This was minority capitalism at its purest: if one excludes the taxpayer from the equation, win-win-win.

Brown and his Albimar partners Lee and Kelly also launched a company called Kellee Communications Inc. Kellee provided a perfectly gratuitous layer of involvement in the pay telephone service at several major airports, including Dulles and National. The Kellee partners knew nothing about pay telephones. They did not have to. MCI Communications Inc. and AT&T Corp. provided the technical wherewithal, and Kellee provided the connections, a well-wired job from end to end.

There is sometimes a fine line between old-fashioned cronyism and minority capitalism, and Brown walked that line as well. In 1991, he interceded with the city of Washington, now headed by his business partner's wife, to get Patton Boggs a $200,000 contract to represent the city on a bond issue. Although he had no real experience with bonds—nor for that matter did Patton Boggs—no one much cared. Brown secured the account by arguing that he would handle it.[5]

It is a shame Brown was so seduced. By all accounts, he was doing a first-class job reviving the fortunes of the DNC. Knowing his own strengths, he focused on rebuilding relationships and hired skilled operational people to manage the organization. In the process, he became the most visible DNC chair in the organization's history.

"Brown has hit the media stratosphere," reported the *Washingtonian* magazine in a pre-election puff piece in 1992, "where he's mentioned as secretary of state one day, baseball commissioner the next, and a Senate candidate from New York the day after that."[6]

Brown would achieve none of the above. As he never seemed to grasp, his rising political profile made insider deals progressively more risky. Like mushrooms, his enterprises grew best in the dark. There, no one could discern the various shadings of ethics and law, and no one could judge.

The deal that finally shed light on Brown's shadow world came by way of Tommy Boggs. Always the opportunist, Boggs saw a chance "to get minority credit and preference"[7] by making Brown a stockholder and director of a Louisiana company called Chemfix Technologies, Inc.[8] Chemfix, however, had better contacts than credentials. This came out only after New York City had awarded it half of a $210 million sludge-removal contract, a contract Patton Boggs had negotiated.

Newsday of New York led the charge. Beginning in March 1991, the paper launched a series of articles detailing serious operational problems in at least five cities that had contracted with Chemfix. In two of the five, operations had to be shut down.

Sludge stories have little intrinsic appeal, even in New York. What attracted *Newsday's* interest were the deal's all too conspicuous players. Los Angeles mayor Tom Bradley helped stir this unseemly pot by writing city officials to praise Brown's venture. Los Angeles, unfortunately, was one of Chemfix's five problem cities. To help negotiate with the city, the venture also hired Harold Ickes. Ickes would later become Brown's uneasy liaison to an increasingly distant Oval Office as well as the booking agent for his fatal trip. At the time, however, he was New York City mayor David Dinkins' campaign counsel, and that was controversy enough.

Most troublesome of all was the involvement of Brown himself and Dinkins, his old family friend. What gave the stories jazz was the revelation that the DNC chose New York City as the site of its 1992 convention just two months after New York City settled on Chemfix. Brown, reported *Newsday*, was the "major force" in that decision.[9]

Brown and Dinkins, of course, denied any deal, and the media reported the same. It's just that no one believed them. The irony here is this was one of those rare instances where there was no deal, at least no convention deal. Nolanda Hill, who was involved in communications planning for the convention, insists such charges were "totally wrong."

"Ron wanted New York because he was a New Yorker at heart, and this was the most powerful city in the world."

Still, there was more than enough for an admirably vigilant press to chew on. ABC's *20/20* picked up on the story, and through continued exposure, the media forced Brown and Chemfix to give up the contract. "It's a victory for the people," declaimed Staten Island Borough president Guy Molinari. "The stench from this contract was more than just sewage sludge."[10]

One additional deal merits discussion, not only because it captures the dubious gist of minority capitalism but also because it would serve as a catalyzing agent in the chain that led to Brown's death.

In 1992, at the peak of his game, the *Washingtonian* reported Brown "had personally negotiated a deal that brought a $700,000 contract to his firm, Capital/PEBSCO, to help manage and promote all of the District of Columbia's retirement funds."[11] One should make note here of the dollar figure and move on. To Brown's good fortune, at least in the short-term, the media would lose track of it.

Brown first made contact with the Ohio-based Public Employees Benefit Services Corporation, or PEBSCO, in 1984—an appropriate year, given the Orwellian spin used to justify the relationship. Historically, the company administered retirement programs for municipal workers, a subject about which Brown knew nothing. But as Steven Holmes acknowledges, Brown had two things going for him: "his political contacts and his race."[12]

Several of the cities in which PEBSCO wanted to do business now required that vendors form partnerships with minority firms. Washington was one of those cities. Although by all accounts Brown had little business acumen and less pension experience, he formed a company called Capital/PEBSCO, which promptly secured half the city's retirement fund business. After his partner's wife, Sharon Pratt Dixon, was elected mayor, Capital/PEBSCO snared the whole contract, despite the fact another company had reportedly made a lower bid for the work.[13]

"I think he saw a growing niche market that he was able to capitalize on," said PEBSCO attorney Mark Koogler of Brown, casually debasing the language of business to justify a pure insider scam. But Koogler was just warming up. In a bit of sophistry so breathtakingly cynical it deserves to be read in full, he fixes the scam as a kind of natural stage in the evolution of the civil rights movement:

> There was a kind of moral symmetry in Brown's being able to help enrich himself as a black front man for a white company. Arguably, being able to capitalize on his race in getting municipal contracts was no more than compensation for the racism that kept him from getting private clients. If affirmative action simply made one already well-to-do black man that much richer, then so be it. He was probably comfortable with the thought that he, after all, had done his part for civil rights and was still supporting the cause. Others would now have to put themselves on the line to lift the downtrodden out of poverty.[14]

What PEBSCO and other high-minded companies could not assure— and barely even addressed—was successful management. For Brown, this failing became most apparent in his radio venture. Says Nolanda Hill, who knows more than a little about broadcasting, "They were in way over their heads."

Fortunately for Brown and his colleagues, NBC came to the rescue. In 1995, when Brown was secretary of Commerce, the always-generous NBC quietly forgave Albimar virtually its entire $10 million loan. NBC executives would tell their media colleagues its attorneys "were not aware Ron Brown was a partner in Albimar" when they negotiated the write-off.

When the *Washington Post* learned of the deal, Brown was in Brussels discussing international communications policy with the Group of Seven major industrialized nations. True to form, his office assured the *Post*, "There is not and never has been any conflict of interest for Secretary Brown on matters pertaining to telecommunications."[15]

As to the loan of $87,000 for Albimar, when the National Bank of Washington went under, Hill persuaded a friend of hers, Val Boerkskevy, to buy the note lest it fall into the wrong hands. Brown had promised to pay it off when he got his money from Patton Boggs, but he never did. Hill finally paid it off herself.[16]

Someone always seemed to be coming to Ron Brown's rescue. In 1992, as the Center for Public Integrity was about to release a report raising serious conflict-of-interest questions about Brown, the center's director, Charles Lewis, a former *60 Minutes* producer, got a call from a union leader on the center's board. The leader had been asked by Brown to hold the highly critical report—"Private Parties: Political party leadership in Washington's mercenary culture"—until after the election.

When Lewis refused to honor Brown's request, the labor leader withdrew from the center's board and canceled his financial commitment to the center. Within a month, Lewis told the *New York Times*, "Half the labor money dried up." Said Lewis of Brown, "He knows where the edges are. And he is willing to walk right up to the edge. To the absolute edge."[17]

It was at the edges where Brown was of the most value and where most of the money was to be made. In Brown's financial disclosure report, signed by him on January 1, 1993, he reported an income for 1992 in excess of three-quarters of a million dollars, only $89,000 of which came from his job at the DNC.[18] It's just too bad his riches cost him his soul.

Shelby Steele tells of how as a young black man he and his friends enjoyed "the sense of innocence that is always entailed in feeling victimized" and how that sense "filled us with a corresponding feeling of entitlement, or even license."[19] Steele was able to wean himself from its false nurturance. Brown never could. Throughout the twelve years of his tenure at Patton Boggs, there was always someone like attorney Koogler whispering in his ear and telling him about the "racism" that confronted him at every step and the "compensation" that was his due for enduring it.

Bunny Engler never dreamed she would be expected to contribute to Brown's compensation package. In the fall of 1992 she and her husband Franklyn owned a restaurant called the Oriskany Inn near Davis, West Virginia. Brown often visited their restaurant because he owned two homes in Canaan Valley's Timberline Ski area. Sometimes he came with his wife, the Englers report. Sometimes he came with another woman.

Stephen Dresch, a high-level forensic economist who has requested his clients not be named, had been contracted to learn what he could about Brown. In the course of his investigation he came across a $3,000 watercolor by Austin Deuel that had been in Brown's possession. With the help of one of Brown's female friends, whom Dresch chooses to identify only as "not Nolanda Hill," he was able to trace the painting to the Oriskany Inn and return it to the shocked Englers.

The story of how Brown came to possess this painting speaks so powerfully to the unraveling of the civil rights ethic that it hurts. Apparently Brown and the woman had visited the inn one night in the late fall of 1992 at the very peak of Brown's acclaim. They were the last ones to leave. As they were walking past the unmanned reception area, Brown reached over to the wall and grabbed one of two watercolors hanging there. When they reached the parking lot and the woman realized what he had done, she was shocked and asked him why he took it.

Said Brown matter-of-factly, "I'm entitled to it."

9 | GUANXI

If there was one luncheon Ron Brown should not have attended it was the one that took place at Matteo's Restaurant in Waikiki in December 1991. At the lunch were arguably the three people most directly responsible for his demise: Gene and Nora Lum and Michael Brown, Ron's then twenty-six-year-old son.

Hawaii was just one stop, but a fateful one, on a ten-day Asia junket. Later on this same trip, Ron Brown would meet the one other person of Asian origin who would most complicate his life, the altogether enigmatic John Huang. At the time, Huang worked for the now-notorious Lippo Group, an Indonesia-based conglomerate owned by the ethnic Chinese Mochtar Riady and his sons, James and Stephen.

It may be impolitic to admit, but Asian names are not easy for occidentals to follow. The unfamiliarity of these names and the size of the cast have had the ironic effect of protecting those involved in Clinton's misadventures on the Pacific rim. For the sake of simplicity, this story will focus mainly on five recurring characters of Asian origin:

- John Huang, born in Mainland China, raised in Taiwan, an American citizen since 1977, the chief American representative for the Lippo Group.
- Mochtar Riady and his second son, James, the owners of the Lippo Group, the latter a permanent American resident.
- Gene and Nora Lum, Hawaiian wheeler-dealers and American citizens.

54

The five have little in common save for the collective, "Asians," the rubric to which they would be assigned by westerners like Brown, with whom they worked. As shall be seen, the interests of the five merge only rarely, though all play central roles in Brown's demise. If the Riadys and Huang would do more long-term damage to American interests, the Lums would cause more immediate problems for Brown.

The Lums, in particular, were a piece of work. Nora, a Japanese American, began her career selling clothes in a tourist shop on Waikiki before moving into real estate. Gene, Chinese by origin and an attorney, took a run at politics without success and eventually settled into a job with the Honolulu city council as an advisor on land-use policy. When the Japanese flooded Hawaii in the 1980s with a veritable tsunami of investment money, no couple was better situated to part the waters than the Lums.

What interested the Japanese in particular was real estate. If they had had their way, they would have turned the whole of the state into a golf course. Hawaii resisted. Given its natural wonders, the state had been keen on protecting the environment long before it was fashionable. To do so, the state government had erected a veritable barrier reef of regulation. This would have been all well and good in a world of saints, but in the real world, regulation inevitably breeds opportunism.

This is where the Lums came into play. They emerged from the swampy Hawaiian symbiosis of business and government as full-blown fixers. And fix they did. By the end of the 1980s, the Japanese had no fewer than seventy golf courses in various stages of development, and the Lums had helped ease a good share of them into existence. Working as a team, Gene and Nora were able to match developers with politicians willing to finesse projects through the regulatory maze. The currency of this realm was the "campaign donation."[1]

The Lums were not alone in their calling. "The political influence over the governor's office, major political entities, was monumental," public interest attorney Anthony Locricchio told the producers of a PBS *Frontline* presentation. "The remarkable thing for the Japanese was how cheaply they could buy Hawaiian politicians."[2]

So blatant had the pay-offs become that the Federal Elections Commission (FEC) was forced to intervene. Its investigators found a staggering number of violations, particularly of those campaign laws designed to protect against foreign influence. These violations included the payment of tens of thousands of illegal dollars to the governor, the Honolulu mayor, and more than one hundred other politicians, all of which had to be given back. That this pattern of abuse would soon repeat itself on a national scale was more than mere coincidence.

The FEC was not the only organization interested in the Lums. The FBI had its eye on them as well. The bureau enlisted a golf course developer by the name of Charles Chidiac as a cooperating witness. He shared with *Frontline* how he had come to employ this ambitious couple:

> I was told that this woman and her husband can fix anything in Hawaii, so I hired her to advise me how to work in this corrupt system and help me out with my zoning. . . . She is a convincing woman. She can convince people that she can do things. So I gave her $50,000 in cash and she said, "I'll get you the approval in two months."[3]

The FBI secretly tape-recorded the Lums and caught Nora Lum bragging about her ability to launder campaign funds. The case against the Lums, however, would eventually be dropped for lack of what the Justice Department called "admissible evidence." Nora Lum would boast that Webster Hubbell shut down the Hawaii investigation during his tenure as associate attorney general, and she was likely telling the truth.[4] In the meantime, the Lums had decided to take their fund-raising skills to a larger stage.

"I'm going to move into the hierarchy of the Democratic Party," Nora Lum told Chidiac.[5] And as the Brown luncheon would prove, she was as good as her word. When Ron and Michael Brown met with the Lums, they had to have been aware of the Lums' reputation. Why else would they have met?

In 1991 Ron Brown had no higher goal than to get a Democrat elected president. Prospects, however, were none too bright. After the Gulf War early in the year, incumbent President George Bush's approval rating crested at an astonishing 91 percent, the highest ever recorded. It had even reached more than 55 percent among African Americans. To have any chance of victory, Brown had to find a new source of votes and, even more importantly, a new source of revenue. He knew one good place to look, the self-designated APA (as in Asian Pacific American) community.

Brown had turned to this community before—back in 1988 when he had launched his own improbable bid for DNC chair. In seeking APA support, Brown had vowed to include Asian Americans in the DNC and to pay attention to their needs. This is one vow he chose to honor.[6]

In seeking to woo Asian money, foreign or domestic, Brown had two primary sources of competition. One was obvious. One was not. The obvious one was the Republican party. Before the 1992 election, Democrats worried out loud about the inroads Republicans had been making into their APA base. If Japanese Americans tended to vote Democratic, new immigrants like the Koreans and Vietnamese skewed to the Right and were finding a home in a welcoming Republican party. "Entrepreneurship, strong defense, strong foreign policy, anti-communism," said Tony Chen, the Republicans' chief APA strategist, "That is what basically captures the hearts of most Asian Americans."[7]

By contrast, Democrats lacked much of a message. Rep. Bob Matsui, (D-CA) argued, "We're much better when it comes to civil rights or the issue of hate crimes." Matsui had to admit, however, those issues did not play well to an APA citizenry that had little, if any, experience with "hate."[8]

The truth is that by the time of the 1992 election anti-Asian sentiment in America had dwindled to almost nothing. The weary politics of victimization just were not working in communities that routinely outperformed American norms economically and educationally.

And then—if one can jump ahead a little—Democrats caught a perverse break. In exploiting the Asian community for its money, they stirred a new wave of anxiety about Asian influence. When Republicans in Congress dared to investigate, Democratic operatives accused Republicans of singling out Asians for attack and stoking the anxiety. The politics of victimization had life once more.

If Republicans were the obvious source of competition for the hearts and pocketbooks of the APA community, the less obvious one was Bill Clinton. Nolanda Hill traces Brown's recognition of the potential challenge as far back as 1989. It was then Brown first expressed his concern about the mother lode of Asian largesse, "the Riady money."

The Riadys derived their considerable income from their corporate flagship, the Lippo Group, "lippo" being a Chinese word for "energy." Lippo began as a banking enterprise in Indonesia and then diversified into securities, land development, coal mining, insurance, and a variety of other interests. As the business grew, its reach expanded throughout Southeast Asia, including China, and into America.

In 1977, the year of Jimmy Carter's inauguration, Mochtar Riady tried to buy the National Bank of Georgia. Given future events, one does not have to speculate too wildly to sense a pattern here. As it happened, the deal fell through, but one of its brokers, Jackson Stephens, persuaded Riady to join his family's investment bank.

Forget about its Little Rock location. Stephens Inc. was reportedly the largest American investment bank outside of New York. It was through Stephens that James Riady met and began to cultivate an aspiring young politician, Bill Clinton, then Arkansas's attorney general. The Riadys grounded their Arkansas connection in 1984 when James Riady and Jackson Stephens purchased the Worthen Bank, Arkansas's largest.[9]

To be fair to the Riadys, and Asians in general, their notion of "friendship" differs significantly from that of the West. Generally speaking, friendship in the East is not based on an established pattern of loyalty and trust. Rather, friendship precedes that trust and possibly results in it. In much the same way an arranged marriage is not based on love but, ideally, results in it.

Willingness to enter into a friendship is often marked by the exchange of gifts or favors. When done respectfully, such an exchange is seen as a sign of genuine courtesy. Once the gifts are accepted, a friendship is formed and with that friendship comes a series of rights and expectations. In this context, friendship becomes a kind of formalized and serious game that often goes under the name of *Guanxi*.[10]

In 1984, the Riadys made their first investment in their new friendship with Clinton. That year the Worthen Bank under Riady/Stephens management lost tens of millions of dollars of Arkansas state pension funds in a disastrous investment scheme. Instead of passing the loss along to the state as they were legally entitled to, they ate the loss and saved Clinton's reputation and career.[11]

Without question, *Guanxi* informs the business culture of the Far East. The Clintons would prove willing to sacrifice their own cultural norms and the strategic interests of their own country to exploit *Guanxi*. The Riadys, however, only had to finesse their norms to exploit the Clintons.

In 1991, Clinton was just one presidential aspirant of many and not the most likely. Brown did not want Clinton to have exclusive access to what he saw as an undeveloped gold mine of Asian money, especially the Riady money. With access to this money, Clinton had the potential to usurp Brown's power as DNC Chair.

To keep the Asian money in general play, Brown had to find an opening to that community. On the 1991 Asian trip, Brown's assistant Melinda Yee offered up one contact who had perhaps more potential to open doors than any other, the ineffable John Huang, a man who would haunt the futures of both Ron Brown and Bill Clinton. Yee described his role in the memo that follows:

> John Huang is our key to Hong Kong. He is also interested in renewing his trusteeship to us on this trip through his Asian banking connections. He has agreed to host a high dollar event for us in Hong Kong with wealthy Asian bankers who are either U.S. permanent residents or with U.S. corporate ties. He will make sure that all of the hotel accommodations, meals, and transportation are paid for by his bank. He should be invited to be part of our delegation.[12]

Given the prickly nature of modern sensitivities, one hesitates to uses the word "enigmatic" to describe Huang. But the word fits. The man is, in fact, elusive. Slight and unassuming, he has eased his way through life almost unnoticed. The many investigations into his career have yet to fix even his date or place of birth.

At the Thompson Committee hearings in 1997, one Lippo colleague after another would tell the gathered senators that they had "no idea how Huang passed his day." All they knew was Huang was James Riady's "man in America." At the end of the day, even the committee had to admit Huang was "something of a mystery."[13]

A mystery Huang might have been, but he had a very real function, and the Thompson Committee worked hard to discern it. According to its best evidence—a Lippo insider's memo—the committee pegged Huang as "the political power that advises the Riady Family on issues and where to make contributions."[14]

At this stage of the game, Bill Clinton was still a long shot. By working with Brown, Huang could better survey the field and spread his bets. On Brown's 1991 junket, Huang scheduled numerous meetings for Brown's DNC delegation. Among them, as noted on the DNC schedule, was a "DINNER ($$) HOSTED BY LIPPOGROUP [*sic*] (JOHN HUANG)."

The Burton Committee would later report a bit too dryly, "The dollar signs appear to refer to the fact that the dinner was held for the purposes of fund-raising." As to how much money was raised and where it went, the committee made the following, mildly astonishing observation: "The DNC is unable to account for any contributions which may have been raised in conjunction with the Hong Kong trip."[15]

When the *Los Angeles Times* later tried to track this money, its reporters descended into an informational black hole. The DNC's attorney, Peter Kadzik, argued the meetings were designed to "raise Ron Brown's stature as someone who was familiar with foreign policy, economic affairs, and other international issues." When asked about fund-raising, Kadzik admitted, "There certainly could have been some sort of attempt to see whether some kind of fund-raising was possible." He then added lamely, "We don't have a firm indication that this did occur." The 1991 Hong Kong affair would not be the last time Asian money would go unreported.[16]

Brown knew the rules. Only U.S. citizens or legal residents could donate to the party. Foreign nationals could not. But if the money raised were not being reported, such distinctions were irrelevant. Much to the embarrassment of the Democrat party, Huang and others would get caught blurring these same distinctions in the 1996 election cycle.

In any case, it appears the trip met whatever goals Brown had set for it. When he returned from Asia, he thanked Mochtar Riady and the Lippo Group for hosting the DNC delegation during their stay in Hong Kong.

Wrote Brown, "I especially wanted to recognize my friendship with John Huang and the tremendous asset that he is to the Lippo Group."[17] The money from Hawaii, by contrast, was duly reported. A few days after the meeting, the Lums donated $26,000 to the DNC. By the following summer, the extended Lum family had kicked in another $80,000 and found themselves a couple of choice seats at the Democratic National Convention.[18]

Although the Lums would never set their sights much higher than a quick buck, the Riadys entertained greater ambitions, not only for themselves but also for their business partners in the People's Republic of China. Publicly at least, perhaps because he did not know the Riadys well, Brown approached the China question with caution.

Brown had impressed the business leaders he met in Hong Kong by telling them he was "not there to speak, but to listen and learn."[19] He then asked each of them to express his own thoughts about doing business with the U.S. One businessman, the largest exporter of jade in Hong Kong, advised Brown to be cautious in any future dealings with China.

"China," said the businessman, "would rather give up the country than lose face before the world."

The message Brown pulled from this cryptic comment was the intended one: American "commercial engagement" with China should not hinge on any guaranteed improvement in human rights or military restraint. Such improvements would presumably follow engagement. This message might not have appealed to the average Asian American citizen, but it did have a nice ring for those affluent Asians, American or otherwise, who were involved in foreign trade.

Brown, however, had spent too much time on the Korean DMZ to get sentimental about the People's Republic. If he refrained from comment during the campaign, it was only to coax more money from the new friends he made.

Candidate Clinton showed no such restraint. On the election trail, he could not have been more emphatic in his contempt for the People's Republic. In his campaign book, *Putting People First*, he explicitly denounced Bush for rewarding China with improved trade status "when it has continued to trade goods made by prison labor and has failed to make significant progress on human rights since the Tiananmen Square massacre."[20] On the campaign trail, he was even more blunt, hectoring Bush repeatedly for "coddling tyrants" in Beijing and conducting "business as usual with those who murdered freedom at Tiananmen Square."[21]

In retrospect, one has to wonder whether the Riadys understood Clinton's campaign rhetoric to be something of an inside joke. As shall be seen soon enough, they favored something of an open door policy with the misunderstood gentlemen of the People's Republic—a wide open door. And they were buying their way into a position of indispensable influence with the Clinton campaign.

In the spring of 1992, for instance, when Clinton was facing the critical New York primary without any money to speak of, James Riady used his influence with the Worthen Bank to arrange a $3.5 million line of credit. Just a little more *Guanxi*. At the time, the Riadys had no official ties to the bank. A series of major irregularities had forced them out of the banking business in Arkansas.[22]

Soon after the Worthen intervention, James Riady hosted and John Huang organized a dinner at Riady's Brentwood, California, home for the Democratic Senatorial Campaign Committee. The *Los Angeles Times* would call the $110,000 worth of fund-raising "a flirtation with deft book-keeping."[23] There was a pattern afoot here.

Still, for all their power, it was more important that Clinton please the voter, Asian American or otherwise, than the Riadys—at least on the campaign trail. In 1992, few in the APA community identified their fates with that of the People's Republic. Republicans understood this and geared their efforts accordingly. Not only was their message more coherent, but so also was their organization. Bush had already appointed more Asian Americans to positions in his administration than all previous presidents combined, a claim the White House was not shy in broadcasting. In addition, the Republican party had formally established its Asian Victory 92 fund, 75 percent of which was to be designated to boost Republican causes or candidates within the Asian community.[24]

Democrats had no such apparatus, not at least until the Lums came to the mainland to gear one up. With Ron Brown's blessing, they set up shop in a shabby Southern California warehouse in Torrance and grandly christened themselves the Asia Pacific Advisory Council-Vote Group, or APAC-Vote.

Helping the Lums was John Huang. By all accounts, APAC was an unusual political organization. The Lums did little precinct walking or voter targeting, if any. They supported no Asian American candidates anyone knew of and developed no relations with Asian American officials. And although they claimed APAC to be a part of the DNC, the DNC had no record of APAC.

What the Lums were doing—and doing well—was raising money. What they were not doing was accounting for any of it to anyone. Hawaiian developer Charles Chidiac, still on good terms with the Lums, reported seeing piles of $100 bills stashed in shopping bags in Nora Lum's back office. Nora also introduced Chidiac to John Huang, a daily visitor whom she credited with having raised half of APAC's $700,000 total.

"The money disappeared though," claimed Chidiac. "Nobody knows what happened to the money."[25] As long-time Democratic volunteer Trudy Owens breezily observed, "Of course, it was illegal money from Korea and Taiwan, anyway." Ron Brown had asked Owens to help set up the Torrance, California operation. This is an experience she came to regret.

"All the Democrats I've known have been wonderful people," said Owens. "I've only met two bad ones."[26] The two bad ones in Owens' calculation were the Lums. They managed to blend the potentially honorable concept of *Guanxi* with good old-fashioned Western graft to create a toxic and potentially lethal mix.

The Lums' operation climaxed with a gala awards dinner shortly before the 1992 election that bordered on the burlesque. One award was given to a representative of each of the APA ethnic subsets. Nora Lum received one award. So did John Huang. Chidiac even received an award as a representative of the apocryphal Lebanese American Advisory Council. As something of a highlight, candidate Bill Clinton contributed a letter under his own signature, claiming the event would honor the APAC volunteers for their hard work on behalf of the campaign. As one might expect, the money raised at this event also quickly disappeared.[27]

The only thing that removes the event from the realm of the comic is that future dealings of the Lums would lead to the death of Ron Brown. The future machinations of Huang and the Riadys meanwhile would lead to the imperilment of American security.

Otherwise, it was all quite amusing.

10 | MIRROR IMAGE

In the run-up to the 1992 election, Ron Brown stayed relentlessly on message. The Reagan-Bush years were not "a glory period for America." No, he argued with self-deluding passion, they were "a time of cynicism and greed and self-centeredness."[1]

Brown's message tracked well with the one being spun by Bill and Hillary Clinton. As early as September 1991, when Clinton was just one candidate out of many in a seemingly weak field, he was posturing much as Brown was: "The 1980s were not just a decade of greed and self-seeking," railed Clinton, "they were a decade of denial and blame."[2]

In almost comically ironic fashion, Clinton and Brown reveal just how deep was the "denial" of that decade. One marvels at the ability of both men to absolve themselves of their own overt self-absorption and to project it onto the unredeemed masses.

This denial, however, did not necessarily make them hypocrites. "Hypocrisy" implies conscious deception. The careers of both Brown and Clinton suggest that the first person each deceived was himself. In his own mind, Ron Brown was a pioneer in the emerging new field of entrepreneurial civil rights. Everyone told him so.

In Clinton's mind, he too deserved all the many perks he could squeeze out of his office. These were just compensation for the sacrifices the Clintons endured in their bold attempt to engineer what Hillary so eloquently called "human reconstruction."

The two men had more in common than a gift for self-deception. There were the obvious points of comparison: each was tall, good-looking, gregarious, charismatic, ambitious, at home in the world, and recklessly promiscuous. As seen, each had the ability to project his private failings on the rest of humanity. And each had a comparable range of failings to project. "There were more similarities than differences between them," says Nolanda Hill, "especially in regards to pathologies."[3]

Hill's analysis of Brown—an analysis largely substantiated by Brown's daughter Tracey—works for Clinton in many particulars. Each came of age as their parents' marriage collapsed. Brown's Theresa Hotel was not unlike Clinton's Hot Springs, an artificial universe where life revolved around their respective needs and in which each shone like the sun.

Says Hill of Brown, "He was accustomed to not hearing things." Brown was an only child. Clinton had an irrelevant and all but unnoticed half-brother, the regrettable Roger Clinton. As happens in such situations, neither ever learned how to lose. Ted Kennedy tells Tracey Brown that her father "was not a gracious loser" and would throw tantrums when he lost at tennis.[4] Clinton would do much the same at golf where he was, by all accounts, an inveterate cheater.

Both men had facile minds and a gift for processing information. For all that, according to Hill, "[Brown] had a tendency to run away from problems. But when you focused him, when you insisted he focus himself, he had a good analytic mind." Much the same has been said about Clinton.

They were both also astute readers of people and skilled manipulators. They could make a person feel like he or she was the only one in the room and extract from that person whatever was worth extracting. But they could turn on a person just as easily. "He was a screamer," says Hill of Brown, "real hot-tempered, not laid back."

Tracey Brown tells one story of how her father "kept on berating" an aide, Morris Reid, who "horrified, apologized repeatedly" for a minor error of judgment but to no apparent avail.[5] Tracey tells a second story about how her father verbally and even physically assaulted the same pathetic aide on a commercial airline for mistakenly booking him in first class.

"We were on that plane," recalled Reid painfully, "with the secretary sitting in the aisle and me at the window. Everybody walked by and he was humiliating me."[6] To his good fortune, Reid missed Brown's final flight. Brown compelled him to stay behind in Zagreb to take care of a problem that had emerged between the Croatian government and an up-and-coming Texan energy company called Enron. So Reid has told Tracey Brown.

Clinton literature is redundant with comparable scenes of browbeating and borderline violence, the victims, like Browns,' almost always physically small—Dick Morris, George Stephanopoulos, Harold Ickes—and powerless. Although both Brown and Clinton had volatile tempers, their flare-ups were quick and their good humor easily restored. Despite the more than occasional rant, they genuinely liked people and tended to avoid confrontation.

The confrontations, the hard and decisive choices, they left to the women in their lives. At the end of the day, it was Hill who had to push Brown to what would prove to be a literally fatal showdown with the president. The president's response to that showdown is undocumented. History suggests, however, if any firm decisions were made about Brown's future, it was likely Hillary Clinton who made them.

There were differences between the men, most attributable to Brown's being black in a largely white world. Brown had, as Hill notes, "the ability to mask how he really felt," a useful survival skill in that world and one Clinton lacked in the extreme.

Brown was also more than a little insecure, especially around whites. Unlike himself, he saw Clinton as something of a wonk, a guy who preferred to surround himself with ideologues rather than to mix it up in the community. Importantly, Brown had less interest than the Clintons in remaking society in his own image and more in making the most out of the society at hand. Brown may have been spoiled, even corrupt, but he was no megalomaniac.

And yet for all their differences, when Brown looked at Clinton—and he was one of the few in the cabinet tall enough to see eye to eye—he saw much of himself. And he did not necessarily admire what he saw.

Says Hill pointedly, "Ron and Clinton did not like each other." They never really did. In time, Brown's dislike would turn to fear. He would intuit, if not fully understand, that the pathologies of Bill Clinton, and of Hillary as well, ran deeper than his own, and when the two combined, much deeper.

Even in the glory days of 1992, when all was going so swimmingly for Brown and eventually for Clinton, the two distrusted each other. Brown never forgot Clinton's belated and half-hearted endorsement of his run for the DNC chair. Partly out of payback and partly out of good judgment, Brown was equally slow in endorsing Clinton.

It was not until April 1992, after the New York primary, that Brown revealed his willingness to fuse their respective campaigns. Technically, Brown broke a DNC tradition by making a public overture this early, but the now front-loaded primaries had revealed Clinton's strength. There was no point in waiting for an anti-climactic convention. In a way, however, it was already too late. Hillary Clinton, in particular, demanded loyalty, indeed fealty, and Brown did not signal his obeisance early enough.

"Hillary was always against him," says Hill of Brown. "He was not a supporter of Clinton early." Hillary Clinton intimidated Brown from the moment he became dependent on the Clinton White House. The fact that he vigorously defended Clinton against what Tracey Brown calls "the manufactured scandals"[7] cut no ice with the frosty Mrs. Clinton. In time, his anxiety about her support would inspire him to do things he knew he never should have.

There was one other source of conflict between the two men, an inevitable one. Biographer Steven Holmes writes accurately of his tenure at the DNC, "Brown was a star from opening day."[8] As Clinton's campaign gained momentum, Brown's star shone even brighter. But then again so did Clinton's. And so did vice-presidential candidate, Al Gore's. "Political egos are interesting," says Hill insightfully. "They're more like film stars, not team players."

On the two occasions Brown rode the post-convention campaign bus with Clinton and Gore, he rather wished he hadn't. On the most obvious level, the Clintons' lack of organization dismayed the former Army captain. "I cannot f—ing believe it," Brown told a former aide. "The only way I can get anything done on this god-damned campaign is to go sit on a bus for four days, talk to his wife, talk to him, talk to both of them, make sure nobody else talks to them, get a final decision, and then stay on the bus until it's implemented."[9]

On a deeper level, it was Brown's own popularity that caused him discomfort. On one occasion, he boarded the bus in Arkansas and rode it down through Texas. All along the route African Americans showed up holding signs not for Clinton and Gore but for Ron Brown. The warmer the reception for Brown, the chillier grew the environment on the bus. Brown could feel it. Finally, he called Hill from the tour and said, "I don't think I can do this." Al Gore, in particular, came to resent Brown. The reason was basic. Whatever air was left around candidate Clinton, Brown was breathing. "He did not have a good relationship with Al Gore," says Hill emphatically, "*at all*."

If Brown were less than thrilled with the bus tour, the media were enchanted. "Something was happening out there on Highway 61," wrote *Newsweek's* Joe Klein, "an emotional connection that mocked and then demolished the industrial-strength cynicism of the 150 journalists tagging along."[10]

The *Washington Post's* Joel Achenbach headlined Clinton and Gore as the "New Heart-throbs of the Heartland."[11] The *Post's* Edward Walsh summarized the image of the two as "Youth, vigor, energy. And change." On the McLaughlin Group, *Newsweek's* Eleanor Clift accurately summed up the collective media swoon: "They got more positive coverage on this bus tour than the Beatles got on their first tour of America. More reporters were oohing and aahing. It was almost embarrassing."[12]

The media had spent their enthusiasm for political campaigns by the time of the Republican convention that same August. "The whole week was double-ply, wall to wall ugly," wrote *Newsweek's* Joe Klein fresh off the Clinton campaign bus. "The Republican Party reached an unimaginably slouchy, and brazen, and constant level of mendacity."[13]

Given the consistency of the coverage, one could understand why analyst Stephen Hess of the liberal Brookings Institution would be inclined to tell the *Washington Post*, "You read the papers and you'd think it was going to be a runaway election for Bill Clinton."[14] Reality would soon enough intrude on the love fest, but the major media remained the bedrock on which Clinton would root his presidency. Nolanda Hill would be just one of many women to learn that to threaten this presidency was to antagonize the media that sustained it.

It was in the weeks just before the election that Brown hit the media stratosphere. "In my view Ron is the number-one black leader, nationwide," Tony Coehlo, the former House majority whip, told the *Washingtonian*. "Ahead of Jesse. Ahead of Vernon Jordan," added *Washington Post* columnist David Broder with a casualness that had to sting Brown's two eclipsed rivals.[15]

The author of the lengthy *Washingtonian* article, national editor Harry Jaffe, argued that Brown stood to win no matter how the election turned out. A Clinton victory, Jaffe argued, meant "a top job in the new administration." That much was true. But there was a point Jaffe missed. The moment Clinton won, the position of DNC chair became almost irrelevant.

Ron Brown would have to depend on the whims of Bill and Hillary Clinton if he wished to remain in politics. True, Brown could choose to "stay on the outside and make millions as one of the best-connected lawyers in town." But if Jaffe had stripped away Brown's patina of cool, he would have seen that for the highly ambitious Brown lobbying was no longer an option, not for a man who seriously aspired to be the "first black president."[16]

"I remember Ron sitting at the counter," says Hill, "and saying, 'If I am not at that table when first picture is taken I will die.'" The "table" in question was the one around which the cabinet sat. And for all his good work, Brown had absolutely no guarantee of a seat.

11 | NEW WORLD ORDER

Shortly after the 1992 convention, candidate Bill Clinton found himself short of crucial cash once again. If he hoped to win six tightly contested states, he needed a quick infusion of funding. Anxious, he turned to the one person he knew he could count on.

In mid-August 1992, he and the man took a memorable limousine ride. Although the conversation between the two has not been preserved, James Riady's subsequent actions suggest its general outlines. The Riady family poured $600,000 into the DNC and a number of the state parties in question. Clinton and Gore won five of the six including Georgia and Ohio, both squeakers.[1]

As to the money raised by the Lums in their Southern California warehouse, that has proved more difficult to track. Some of it, perhaps most, went no further than the Lums' pockets. The rest likely made its way into that great sloshing pool of "walking around money" that Democratic operatives sprinkled around inner-city neighborhoods to stimulate the vote.

As history has duly recorded, these investments paid off. Bill Clinton rode the crest of his freshly minted post-convention popularity to the presidency, winning 43 percent of the vote in a provocative three-way race that produced the highest voter turn out in twenty years.

In one of the sadder, more self-deluding periods of his life, Ron Brown spent the days after the election pining to become secretary of state. Unaware of the pathos of the scene she describes, Tracey Brown relates how her father had Lauri Fitz-Pegado assist him in composing a letter "that would list his qualifications for this top level job."[2]

And what might those qualifications have been? That Brown had gained his most noteworthy foreign policy experience by servicing the now-exiled tyrant, "Baby Doc" Duvalier? That he had worked as an agent on behalf of any number of other disreputable nation states like Fitz-Pegado's own client, Angola? That he had lately toured the Far East in search of illicit campaign cash? In the run-up to the election, Clinton had famously promised "the most ethical administration in history," and at this early date, when at least some part of the electorate took him at his word, he could not even begin to entertain the idea of Brown at the State Department.

Of course, Clinton could not tell him this. On November 19, two weeks after the election, when Brown met Clinton at the Hays-Adams Hotel across Lafayette Park from the White House, Clinton stressed the need to balance his own perceived youth and inexperience by putting someone older and more seasoned at State, someone like Warren Christopher. Brown took little comfort when Clinton told him the words he would paraphrase at his memorial service, "I wouldn't have gotten it without you."[3]

The only position Clinton even mentioned at the Hays-Adams was the ambassadorship to the United Nations; this held no charm for Brown at all. "Andy Young has already done that," he had told Nolanda Hill earlier.

A civil rights leader and Atlanta mayor, Young had uneasily served under Jimmy Carter as ambassador to the U.N., a position rich in perks but low in power. As Tommy Boggs had unceremoniously reminded Brown, "That's a nigger job."[4] When Brown did manage to tell Clinton he had no interest in the United Nations, Clinton unconvincingly responded, "I'm going to find the best place for you."

In their respective retellings of the Hays-Adams meeting, Tracey Brown and Steven Holmes make it sound like a casual chat between equals. Tracey has Clinton offering Brown the secretary of Commerce position.[5] Holmes has Brown boldly refusing the U.N. offer as testament to the fact that "Brown, no less than Clinton, defined the new establishment."[6] Tracey Brown's account is flat-out wrong. Holmes errs in his inference of equality. Equals they no longer were. The power had shifted almost entirely into Clinton's hands, and Brown knew it.

Brown and Hill had role-played beforehand to help Brown through the quiet terror of the meeting. "He was scared to death," says Hill. "He knew he was finished if he didn't get anything." After leaving the hotel, a dismayed Brown called Hill from the car and asked her to call ahead for Chinese food. He wanted to stop by to "debrief" her and get her read on things. Hill remembers that his stomach was upset and his nerves were on edge. The only Chinese he could handle was the tea.

A late-night phone caller, as the nation would one day learn, President Clinton contacted Brown's home at 2:00 AM three fretful weeks later. He had an offer to make, not the U.N. but Commerce. Unaware another person had already turned down the job, Brown was receptive.

Immediately after talking to the president, Brown called Hill from his basement TV room. He asked her to find out what it was Commerce actually did, as he had to leave the next morning for Little Rock. Hill went to the Commerce Department first thing and took notes from the materials she gathered. Brown called her as planned when he changed planes in Memphis, and Hill briefed him. She was not encouraging.

Hill flew to Dallas later that same day. The next day, as she and her mother drove to Hill's farm, Brown called once more, and he and Hill argued vehemently. Hill was dead set against his taking the job. Not only would it undo their business partnership, but it would also allow the Clintons "to use his weaknesses for their own purposes." Too upset to drive, Hill pulled over to the side of the road, her mom listening to every word. "The Clintons are bad actors," she prophetically told Brown. "You are digging your own grave and mine."

But the glory was too much for Brown to resist. A day later, his family flew to Little Rock for the public announcement. In Little Rock, Clinton told those gathered that he wanted Commerce to become the "powerhouse of government" and Ron Brown was the one person who could accomplish that. Brown knew he had his work cut out for him. As he himself admitted, Commerce had historically been something of a "dumping ground"[7] for political hacks and fund-raisers of dubious talent.

The Department of Commerce and Labor, as it was originally called, owed its creation to the progressive surge that swept America in the latter years of the nineteenth century, a period of great industrial growth but minimal corporate oversight. A Republican progressive, President Theodore Roosevelt, signed the department into law in 1903. In the beginning, one of the department's primary roles was to investigate corporate behavior, which it did through its "bureau of corporations."[8]

In the boosterish climate of the 1920s, the new and dynamic Commerce secretary Herbert Hoover redefined the department's mission.[9] Appointed by Warren G. Harding in 1921, Hoover transformed Commerce from a corporate watchdog into a veritable service organization, a highly effective one at that.

A successful and relentless engineer, Hoover helped standardize a dazzlingly wide range of industrial products as well as many of the government's more amorphous services like safety, statistics, the census, the air waves, and even fisheries. Hoover did try to develop foreign markets for American products, but as the Hoover Museum makes a point of noting, "He kept in mind the delicate line between government power and private enterprise."

Save for the loss of its original energy and enthusiasm, the Commerce Department Brown inherited had not changed much from Hoover's day. The department oversaw a sundry lot of semi-useful functions that had no other more likely place to call home. These included the U.S. Census Bureau, the National Institute of Standards and Technology, and the National Oceanic & Atmospheric Administration. Beyond these services, the department had a generalized mission of promoting American trade, sort of like an international chamber of commerce. So irrelevant had the department seemingly become, in fact, that when the Republicans targeted it for extinction in the "Republican Revolution" of 1994, few objected. The department had no popular constituency.

By 1994, however, at least a few Republicans knew what the Clintons knew. Commerce had a very real role indeed. It had become the conduit through which the Clintons were exporting their vision of the world and importing the means to pay for it. That vision was an odd, improvised one—less traditional Western democratic capitalism than a corrupted, Westernized version of *Guanxi*.

That the Democratic party allowed this to happen is one of the great, untold stories of our time. The party's deep, almost desperate need to win a presidential election opened the gates. Coming into 1992, Democrats had lost the last three, and five of the last six elections, the only win being the unrepeatable post-Watergate fluke of 1976, the one that put Jimmy Carter in office. To win again, Democrats had to do a better job of courting the American business classes—both for their votes and for their money.

For victory's sake, Democrats felt the need to sacrifice a good deal of tradition. That tradition harkened back to Presidents Thomas Jefferson and Andrew Jackson, whose shared distaste for "government-assistance seeking Whig elites" is the kind of rock solid principle on which parties are founded.[10]

In the twentieth century, Democrat presidents carried on the tradition. Woodrow Wilson chastised "the money power" and called the fight against monopolies "a second struggle for emancipation."[11] Despite his own family fortune, Franklin Roosevelt aroused the party's populist base with his spirited attacks on the "money changers" and the "economic royalists." As he told Congress, "I should like to have it said of my first administration that in it the forces of selfishness and lust for power met their match."[12]

In 1948, Harry Truman scored a surprise win by keeping the heat on these same forces, specifically, as he was fond of repeating, "big business and special privilege."[13]

After their third straight presidential drubbing in 1988, party leaders faced a dilemma: how to woo "big business" without cooling the ardor of their traditional anti-business forces. They caught the break they needed with the recession of 1991. Essentially, they would cloak their move to the middle with rhetoric of economic recovery. "It's the economy, stupid." This tacit understanding among party regulars helped produce a presumed centrist like Bill Clinton as candidate and a party platform that was openly business-friendly.

"We reject both the do-nothing government of the last twelve years," read the *Opportunity* section of that 1992 platform, "and the big government theory that says we can hamstring business and tax and spend our way to prosperity."[14] This one eye-popping paragraph had to sting traditional Democrats. Their leaders had turned the Republicans' "tax and spend" language against their own base.

Only desperation—and compromise—kept the traditionalists in line. What the leadership proposed as middle ground is the now-celebrated, if still entirely ambiguous, "third way." Under its banner, Democrats vowed "to create a far better climate for firms and independent contractors of all sizes" because business, after all, was a "noble endeavor."[15]

To help articulate this "third way," Clinton descended to what the party's hard core had to see as the ninth circle of capitalist hell, the archetypal Wall Street investment firm, Goldman Sachs. There he found its co-chairman, Robert Rubin, and recruited him to be chairman of his National Economic Council and later his secretary of the treasury.

In his much praised opus, *Wealth and Democracy*, Kevin Phillips summarizes the brave new Rubin/Clinton vision thusly: "The U.S. economy, like a major Wall Street investment firm, would be run to make money and attract it from around the world."[16] Phillips' critique is hardly partisan. His 1990 book, *The Rich and the Poor*, served the Clinton campaign as a semi-official reference guide to the Reagan-Bush 1980s, in Phillips' words, "a decade of greed and wealth concentration."[17]

This new Democratic worldview focused on the radically non-traditional issue of deficit reduction as a way to "cheer the bond market, bring down interest rates, and stimulate economic expansion."[18] It culminated in an era of leverage and speculation and cleared the way for labor-rattling corporate perks like the North American Free Trade Agreement (NAFTA) and the World Trade Organization (WTO). Argues Phillips, "Market economics might be the claim, but globalized U.S. economic management was the game."[19] Hoover's "delicate line" between government power and private enterprise was about to be rubbed out.

For two centuries the Democratic party had provided the philosophical restraint on corporate ambition. Those restraints had been all but removed. The party's intellectual Left would continue to protest "globalism," more specifically global capitalism, but almost no one in power was listening.

Under Clinton, global capitalism would rule as it never had before. The Left would chafe but not rebel, its protests devolving to the level of harmless street theater. More problematic still, given its inherent self-definition, the Left was not inclined to challenge the ambitions of government. That was the province of the Right, and with the Right fully out of power in Clinton's first two years, the corporate world and the federal government were free to merge.

Still another restraint was about to collapse as well, the one traditionally provided by the mainstream media. A now-famous Roper poll of 139 bureau chiefs and Washington correspondents revealed a stunning 89 percent preference for Clinton over the incumbent Bush and the upstart H. Ross Perot in the 1992 election.[20] Eager to see Clinton succeed, reporters and pundits of the mainstream expressed almost no objection to his administration's embrace of the corporation.

Holmes, himself a *New York Times* reporter, nicely captures the prevailing media *zeitgeist*. He chides the Reagan and Bush administrations for being "in the thrall of the conservative Republican ideology that shunned government intervention in the marketplace."[21] For America's future, Holmes looks hopefully to the "nexus of America's political and commercial strength" of which Brown is the avatar, "an uncanny fit in the New World Order."[22]

Holmes was hardly unique. Writing in those hazy, lazy days before the Enron scandals broke, few in the mainstream media expressed concern when the government *did* intervene in the marketplace. With little guidance from the media, America was venturing into uncharted territory, one in which the mutual exploitation of the government and its corporations would reach a level heretofore unimagined, and few would even notice.

One other major variable fueled the transformation of the Commerce Department: Ron Brown's scruple-free ambition. From a philosophical perspective at least, Brown would feel more at home in the Clinton administration than he would have with any of his Democratic predecessors. And unlike the Republicans who had recently held the job, Brown felt no internal restraint—nor faced any external one—on extending the reach of government. In fact, he immediately sought a 12 percent increase in his department's budget.[23]

From a purely practical perspective, Commerce was, as Clinton promised, "the best place" for Brown. He was in sync with the administration's aspirations and was eager to make headlines. Says Holmes, "Brown soon realized that there was only one function of the Commerce Department that could provide [acclaim]—international trade."[24]

Brown may have had no experience in international trade, but he had spent the last ten years practicing a version of capitalism in which connections mattered far more than competence and in which the law mattered little at all. He would feel right at home in the age of bastardized *Guanxi*.

Or so he thought. In time, this "New World Order" would prove disastrous in ways even Brown could not have anticipated. He was moving beyond the safe confines of petty minority capitalism and into a no-man's-land where the stakes were higher, the rules of engagement more ambiguous, and the potential casualties much more severe.

In the meantime, however, Brown had some self-inflicted wounds to attend to.

12 | OKLAHOMA

Although it was not obvious to anyone who knew their lifestyle, Hawaiians Gene and Nora Lum were, in the language of the bureaucracy, "disadvantaged."

Their Asian origins made them such, more or less automatically. As disadvantaged business people, they were able to compete for certain contracts with a high probability of success. No one understood the potential fruits of such success better than Ron Brown. His knowledge of how the game was played would lead him, the Lums, and his son Michael to, of all places, Oklahoma. Here, finally Brown would outsmart himself in a scam that would ultimately leave two people dead, one of them himself.

Those who are so inclined can pin minority capitalism on Richard Nixon. Bill Clinton often did. At its inception, the Nixon administration reserved the minority set-aside contract for African Americans. There was some logic for this. African Americans, as a group, had suffered legal discrimination, and their ancestors had been enslaved. One could make the argument, and some did, that this legacy shaped black economic performance.

No such argument could be made for Asian Americans. By 1989, when Brown first hooked up with their political people, native-born Chinese Americans were earning 50 percent more per family than the American norm and nearly as twice as much as African American families—and Japanese Americans were out-earning Chinese Americans.

"You know, we know how to make money," an Asian American Democratic consultant would unabashedly tell producers of PBS's *Frontline*.

"A lot of us are businessmen, right, and a lot of them are very successful entrepreneurs."[1]

Twenty years after the fact, Nixon's Commerce Secretary Maurice Stans recounted how Asian Americans came to be "minorities." As remembered, he approached Nixon with an idea to advance the cause of any number of ethnic groups. "I'd like to wrap them all together into one program," he remembers, "and call it 'Minority Business.'"

Nixon did not need much prompting. He saw the idea as a way to attract a range of minority voters, particularly Hispanics. Said he in response, "All right, let's do it that way." And that was that. Without vote of the people or of Congress or even discussion in the cabinet, an arguably unconstitutional race-based spoils system sprang into full flower. In time, without the benefit of any additional legislation or public discussion, this system came to include Asian Americans and the even more elusive Pacific Islanders as well.[2]

To understand how it is an Hawaiian couple came to seek the fruits of minority capitalism in the gas fields of Oklahoma, one needs to understand a little about the state of those fields circa 1980. At that time, for a variety of reasons, the demand for natural gas was unusually high. A small gas "gathering system" firm, called Creek Systems, a subsidiary of Golden Arrow Gas Energy, was in a position to supply it.[3]

Oklahoma Natural Gas (ONG) needed its product. A well-established firm in a non-competitive, highly protected utility market, ONG enjoyed a captive customer base that had little choice but to absorb the rising prices, certainly if approved by the Corporation Commission of the State of Oklahoma, which regulated such things.

"It was like watching *Dallas*, the television show," remembered Creek Systems co-owner Ron Miller of those heady times, "except taking place in Oklahoma. Limousines were around a lot. Corporate jets were in vogue. The real affluents used to fly Bell Jeff [*sic*] Ranger helicopters to go out for dinner."[4]

Given the reality of a seller's market, ONG signed a fifteen-year contract with Creek, in which the latter would provide ONG a fixed supply of gas at a fixed high price for the length of that contract, regardless of whether ONG needed the gas. It was a good deal for Creek, but there was nothing untoward about it.

In the mid-80s, however, the bottom fell out of the natural gas market, and Oklahoma Natural Gas found itself stuck with a contract for an expensive supply source it no longer needed or wanted. Worse, an honest administrative judge at the Corporation Commission had ruled the deal "imprudent" and prevented ONG from continuing to pass the costs along to its customers.

Clearly, ONG needed a creative solution. In August of 1989, its attorneys found one or at least claimed they did. They informed Creek of a loophole in the "Priority Rules" of the Corporation Commission. As the ONG attorneys interpreted those rules, ONG did not have to "take" Creek gas if they no longer needed it.

"Out of the blue they just called us up," claimed Creek's Miller, "and said, 'Shut your pipeline down.' It was a gut shot because it potentially was a death blow."[5]

Shocked at the loss of a $15 million per year contract, Creek attorneys were set to file suit in state court, when ONG attorney William "Tater" Anderson persuaded them to settle the dispute before the Corporation Commission. Human nature being something of a constant since the fall of Adam, the good commissioners in Oklahoma proved no more immune to seduction than those in Hawaii or Washington.

"Every time we would make an appearance, to me it was sort of obvious that the rulings that we were getting were . . . were bizarre," recalled Miller.[6] Bizarre indeed. After hearing both sides, commissioners overruled one of their own senior administrative judges and voted two to one in favor of ONG. The contract was void. ONG did not have to buy any more Creek gas.

At this point, late 1990, the only recourse open to Creek was to appeal the commission's ruling to the state supreme court, which is just what Miller and his partner, Jim Kitchens, did. The case languished for a couple of fee-eating years and might have slipped quietly into history.

But on October 2, 1992, a month before Bill Clinton's election to the presidency, one of the Oklahoma commissioners came forward with a bit of news that turned not just Oklahoma—but the Clinton campaign— inside out: Commissioner Bob Anthony announced publicly he had been working with the FBI for the past four years to uncover corruption at the Oklahoma State Corporation Commission.

"I had no idea," Commissioner Anthony would later tell the producers of a PBS *Frontline* production, "The Fixers," "that within the first few weeks of my taking office in this agency, that utility lawyers, utility lobbyists, utility executives would come into my office, close the door, and count out thousands of dollars in hundred dollar bills."[7]

Among the cases Anthony cited, two deserve special attention. One, of course, was the dispute between ONG and Creek. In the one instance, with the FBI tape recorder capturing every word, ONG attorney "Tater" Anderson laid $5,000 in $100 bills on Anthony's desk to help him see right reason.

Wanting to establish the willful nature of Anderson's violation, Anthony said to him, "The Oklahoma Statue Title XVII is sort of interfering with this."

"The law makes hypocrites out of all of us," replied Anderson with old-school oil country flair. "That damn statute does."[8]

Tater Anderson had one other important client, Arkla, the Arkansas-Louisiana Gas Company. In the very sentence after the above bribe was secured, Anthony remembered Tater Anderson saying, "An Arkla representative would be in on Friday to make arrangements for some more."[9] Although the Clinton camp had no stake in the ONG-Creek dispute, Arkla was another matter.

Serving as chairman and CEO of Arkla at the time was one Mr. Thomas F. ("Mack") McLarty III. An Arkansas state representative at twenty-three, McLarty had parlayed his political contacts into a seat on the Arkla board and eventually its chairmanship. He had been walking the edge where politics meets business all of his adult life without ever losing balance. Now, here he was, the treasurer of the 1992 Clinton campaign as well as Clinton's intended chief of staff, and he risked embarrassing everyone, most notably his boyhood pal, Bill Clinton.

McLarty had to be one anxious man that fall. Anthony had recorded a 1989 meeting with Arkla's president and other senior executives, including Arkla's general counsel. On tape, the executives can be heard promising Anthony major money to retire his campaign debt. Anthony then recorded a follow-up meeting at which two Arkla executives actually delivered the cash.

Says Anthony, "At the time that five or six Arkla officers or attorneys illegally gave me cash and checks and we discussed the illegal nature of the transaction, Mack McLarty was chairman of the board and chief executive officer of Arkla." As such, McLarty was either complicit in these deals or incompetent, and neither quality bode well for the president's new chief of staff.[10]

For all of the anxious parties, the news would only get worse. A few weeks after Commissioner Anthony's shocking disclosure, Creek co-owner

Ron Miller filed suit against Tater Anderson, the attorney who lobbied both for ONG and Arkla. Miller's lawsuit threatened to expose bribery and other crimes committed not only by ONG but also by Arkla and its executives and the commission and its employees. In the process, Ron Miller made himself one very unpopular man in the state of Oklahoma.

"We're talking about a thirty-year history of bribery and corruption and wrongdoing in the state of Oklahoma," Commissioner Anthony observed. "There's a lot of people that just couldn't afford to have any of that story told."[11] In fact, by challenging the establishment, as Miller was about to do, he may well have signed his own death warrant, but more on this later.

Creative damage control was definitely in order. Given the outcome of the 1992 election, the FBI investigation could be contained. A friendly Justice Department could see to that. This may have been just one case out of many that inspired the newly inaugurated president to fire all U.S. Attorneys in one early stroke—something no other president had ever done before.

Even if the FBI were taken off the case, the continuing, even escalating, dispute between Creek and ONG was proving problematic. As a private matter, it was beyond reach of the White House. If, however, Creek could somehow be convinced to drop its lawsuit, none of this need ever be made public, and everyone could go home happy.

In the middle of October 1992, some two weeks after Commissioner Anthony had disclosed his involvement with the FBI, Ron Miller's partner, Creek's Jim Kitchens, approached Miller with a new angle.

"He said that he had a phone call from a friend that had overheard a conversation in California at a DNC fund-raiser," recalled Miller, "and that he had heard Creek mentioned and it was this friend's understanding that Jim was going to get a phone call."[12]

Miller recalled that the friend, who was from "Torrance," hinted Creek would get a call from "some people" who wanted to put this thing to bed. At the time, Creek was hard-pressed to pay its bills and keep its doors open, largely due to the ONG cutback in gas purchases and mounting legal expenses. Miller and especially Kitchens were taking all calls.

This is where Ron Brown enters the picture. Brown may have learned of McLarty's "Oklahoma problem" from Oklahoma governor David Walters. Brown had helped Walters win the governorship in 1990, and Walters was not above a little chicanery himself. In 1993, he would plead guilty to charges that he had accepted illegal campaign contributions and narrowly escape an impeachment inquiry. The guilty plea did not prevent Walters from finagling a seat on Brown's final flight through which Walters hoped to advance the interests of his newly formed Walters Power International. Only a relative's funeral kept Walters off that plane.[13]

No record exists of the conversations between McLarty and Ron Brown, but Brown clearly had a solution. Brown envisioned Creek under different ownership—*minority* ownership. Who could object to that? Certainly not McLarty. Under his leadership, according to his official bio, "Arkla was praised for its efforts to promote minority business growth and to enhance the company's efforts to employ minorities." For his good work, in fact, McLarty had received a Fair Share Award from the NAACP just a year earlier.[14]

Brown saw the fuel supply contracts at the new Denver airport as one highly tempting target for such an enterprise. And this was a job he would have had wired from beginning to end. He had close ties to Colorado governor Roy Roemer and Denver mayor Frederico Peña, soon to become secretary of transportation. And he himself had lobbied for the airport's federal funding. Oklahoma's military bases also looked promising.[15]

Brown had a couple in mind, an Asian American couple that was perfect for the job. Gene and Nora Lum had one virtue that endeared them to Brown. They were not afraid to get their hands dirty. During the campaign, they had proved their ability to divide cash in their Torrance warehouse and keep their mouths shut. One imagines Brown had to have gotten a slice of that pie as well. True, the pair knew no more about gas and oil than they had learned at the self-service pump. But that mattered little. The real work they could and would hire others to do. Brown had always done just that on his own minority ventures.

In any case, someone gave Brown the "nod" to proceed. As Commissioner Anthony observed, "I think somebody at an awfully high level had the connections to get something done that they needed to get done."[16]

This was a beneficial maneuver for Brown in many ways. It gave him a chance to demonstrate his usefulness and loyalty to the White House. And so, late in the fall of 1992, at the same time he was contemplating a cabinet position, he was dispatching the Lums to Oklahoma, hoping they too could find their fortunes, like many before them, in its gas and oil fields.

This deal would prove to be a cluster backscratch like no other. It would only make sense for the Lums to "buy" Creek if they could be assured of a sweetheart deal with Oklahoma Natural Gas. The Lums needed such a deal as they did not have money of their own.

It would only make sense for ONG to make a deal with the Lums if they could be assured Creek would drop the lawsuit. The beauty of it all was ONG could chalk up a new contract with the Lum-owned Creek to a newly discovered interest in helping minority business and maybe win a few awards in the process, much as Mack McLarty already had. ONG would also make some new and useful friends in Washington.

At about the same time McLarty was assuming his new responsibilities as chief of staff, the "mystery buyers"[17] entered negotiations with Jim Kitchens to purchase Creek. When Ron Miller would ask his partner Kitchens with whom he was meeting, Kitchens would say at first only that it was "the lady" or "the woman." In time, he would add the detail that there was a lawyer husband involved and that "they were very close friends and very involved with Ron Brown."[18]

It was not until early 1993—after President Clinton's inauguration—and after many further conversations between Kitchens and his California friends that Kitchens revealed to Miller the identities of the potential buyers. As fate would have it, Kitchens had once been a "dirt contractor" in Hawaii. There he, like many other contractors, had made the acquaintance of the ubiquitous Lums.

"When [the Lums] started coming over to the office," observed Miller, "practically the first thing that would come out of their mouth is, 'We're from Washington and we're here to help.' I mean it was . . . it was a bizarre thing."[19]

Under considerable pressure, ONG offered the Lums a seriously sweet, no-cut, ten-year gas contract. In turn, the Lums divided the contract into two and arranged to pre-sell the halves for a combined $18.75 million. They then agreed to pay Miller and Kitchens $6.3 million upfront for Creek, almost all of which went to pay down debt, with a promised $3.1 million to be paid over the next three years.[20]

The Lums' new company, almost comically named Dynamic Energy Resources, would no longer have any gas contracts, but it would have a $12 million pile of cash. Like many wildcatters before them, the Lums were about to strike it rich. This was minority capitalism at its purest. Everyone would win—except of course the ratepayers who would have to pick up the "excess charges" imposed over the life of the contract.

In later testimony before the Oklahoma Corporation Commission,

$250-an-hour economist Stephen Dresch was asked why he qualified the Lum's deal as only an "apparent" windfall. Dresch replied dryly that Dynamic had "provided at least one very valuable service to ONG," namely the dismissal of all pending litigation. This, he added, was "absolutely" a condition of the deal.[21]

Immediate payback for Brown came in early spring 1993 in the form of a surprise invitation. Hillary Clinton had invited him to a private luncheon for the two of them on the balcony of the White House.

"Ron felt very uncomfortable with Hillary," Nolanda Hill recalls. "He did not think she liked him."

Understandably, this was no small event in Brown's life. But the lunch went well. Hill remembers Brown's good mood because afterwards he picked her up in his chauffeur-driven limousine and joked that Hill and Hillary were wearing the same outfit. As Brown told Hill, Clinton expressed her appreciation for Brown's work in getting her husband elected. More to the point, she thanked him for his help with "Mack McLarty's problem in Oklahoma."[22]

To close the deal, the Lums contracted with John Tisdale, who had handled Clinton's legal work in Arkansas and partnered with Clinton confidant Bruce Lindsey. People in Oklahoma paid attention to that, especially when Tisdale received faxes from the White House and phone calls from the likes of Clinton aide George Stephanopoulos.[23]

Miller, however, was not easily impressed. He refused to settle on promises. He and Kitchens wanted their money up front. Nolanda Hill has testified before the Oklahoma Corporation Commission that in November 1993 Brown made a call directly to Mack McLarty from her apartment to make him aware of the need for financing. Testified Hill, "Secretary Brown talked of a glitch in the timing of the [Creek] deal and the need for bridge financing to keep the deal from falling apart."[24]

On November 9, 1993, the day before Creek's case against ONG was scheduled to go to trial, a $4.5 million bridge loan showed up in Dynamic's account in State Bank of Tulsa and was immediately wired to Creek's account at Republic Bank in Norman. Reportedly, the financing came from Llama Capital Corporation, headquartered in Fayetteville, Arkansas, a commercial banking firm formed by Alice Walton, daughter of Wal-Mart founder Sam Walton and a "big buddy" of Hillary Clinton. At the time, Hillary served on the Wal-Mart board of directors.[25] This clinched the deal.

Within days of the closing, the Lums chartered a plane and flew to the Asian Pacific Economic Cooperation (APEC) summit in Seattle. Ron Brown attended along with his new staffer, Trisha Lum, the Lums' daughter. At the invitation of the DNC, the Lums attended a breakfast for McLarty and were White House invitees at an APEC trade ministers reception. Nora Lum then joined John Huang and James Riady at the APEC presidential dinner.[26]

Soon afterwards Nora Lum made gifts of Dynamic stock to several individuals, most notably to Michael Brown. Accustomed to operating with impunity and now emboldened by his relationship with the White House, Ron Brown offered up his only son as conduit to the Oklahoma money. "Hubris," the Greeks called this brashness, and it would prove Brown's fatal flaw.

For the moment, however, Brown felt he had penetrated the Arkansas wall around the Clintons and had found a safe spot within. Better still, he was set to get a nice cut of the Oklahoma action. He had no way of knowing, however, that this cut would one day prove the unkindest cut of all.

13 VIETNAM

If there was a literary theme to Ron Brown's life, it would be that of pure naturalism: Brown, the unwary soul in an uncaring universe, compelled by internal forces he scarcely understands to do things he knows he ought not do.

Brown calls to mind Clyde Griffith in Theodore Dreiser's *American Tragedy* or the eponymous hero of Frank Norris's *McTeague*. Indeed, when Hollywood transformed the latter of the two into celluloid, it gave the film a one word title that works all too well for the epic sweep of Ron Brown's life—*Greed*.

At this point, to shed light on that life, it might be helpful to introduce a gentleman named Ly Thanh Binh. The story that follows comes largely from his recollection. To his credit, every detail Binh provided that can be verified has been verified. What is more, he has made only specific and limited claims about his own involvement, and these have held up as well.[1]

In 1973, the year Ron Brown came to Washington, Ly Thanh Binh came to America. He left his native South Vietnam to finish his schooling. When his government fell in 1975, he found himself stranded and alone. He made the best of it, getting a degree in economics from Tulane in 1978 and becoming an American citizen soon after. He tried a number of careers, none with great success, and was looking for a new opportunity when, in 1992, he met an older Vietnamese gentleman adrift in America, Nguyen Van Hao.

Hao had quite a history himself. In 1975, as a deputy prime minister of South Vietnam, he proved his cunning, perhaps his treachery, by securing a position in the incoming communist administration. He was the only high-ranking South Vietnamese official to have made the switch. Apparently, he had curried favor by harboring some of the South's gold reserves and handing it over to the new government.

From 1980 to 1984, improbably enough, Hao found himself in Haiti advising the Duvalier regime on industrial development projects for the World Bank.[2] It was in Haiti he made the acquaintance of Marc Ashton, a former financial adviser to "Baby Doc" and, by 1992, president of a gourmet food company in south Florida. It was through Haiti that Ashton met Ron Brown. Ashton also just happened to have one very well-connected sister-in-law. Her name was Lillian Madsen—she of the golden locks, sensuous mouth, and prominent American boyfriend.

At the time Binh and Hao met, Hao was running a convenience store in south Florida. Hao showed Binh a set of jumbled plans, the logic of which made more sense than the details. The plans represented Hao's strategy for stimulating investment in Vietnam once the trade embargo was lifted.

Binh liked what he heard. Hao had the connections, and Binh, with his Tulane education, had the language and business skills to put the plans in order. It seemed a good fit. Binh offered his help without salary. The two agreed to be partners in an endeavor called the Vietnam Development Corporation.

The pair ran the fledgling enterprise out of Hao's home in Coral Springs, Florida. In the beginning, the two men did little more than send their plan to likely investors. One can only imagine their delight, indeed their astonishment, when Marc Ashton managed to set up a meeting with the celebrated chairman of the Democratic National Committee.

In November 1992, Brown flew to Florida on a private jet. At a local restaurant he met with Lillian Madsen and her brother-in-law, Ashton, and their old friend, Nguyen Van Hao. Not yet nominated to anything but fully expecting to be, Brown listened to Hao's plans and told him he wanted to be "the exclusive lobbyist" for Vietnam.[3]

Hao had one specific goal—lifting the trade embargo against Vietnam. Brown had one specific goal too. He wanted money. After the meeting, he headed off to a DNC executive session in the Bahamas. Somewhere along the way, he hatched an idea and called Nolanda Hill to get her take on it: How about if he intervened on behalf of the Vietnamese for cash?[4]

Hill was horrified. "I can't believe you're really talking about this," she scolded him, "especially on a cell phone." She suspected Brown was being set up and told him so. And that was the last she heard of it, at least for a while.

Although Binh had not been at the meeting with Brown, he had excellent reason to believe Hao's enthusiastic account. So confident was Hao of Brown's interest that he flew back to Vietnam and took his new partner with him.

Once in Vietnam, the American Binh could see his Vietnamese partner had not oversold his pull. The two were treated like dignitaries and even met with Prime Minister Vo Van Kiet. This meeting concluded with a private discussion between Kiet and Hao in which Hao received the prime minister's official blessing to hire Brown.

Hao and Binh returned to America with a letter from the prime minister to Brown, urging Brown to continue discussions with the pair.[5] The Vietnamese government denied any such meeting ever took place or that a letter was ever written, but on all verifiable points Binh would prove reliable, including his description of Hao's past history in Vietnam.

By the time Hao and Binh arrived home in December, Brown had already been nominated to Commerce. Upon accepting the cabinet nod, Brown had to do two things, both unpleasant: one was opening his finances to inspection in order to win Senate approval; the other was learning to live on a $145,000 income once the approval was secured. The latter adjustment would catch up with him first.

For starters, Brown found himself in a nasty row with his partners at Patton Boggs. To smooth his passage through the Senate, Brown had to completely divest himself of Patton Boggs' obligations. This meant his partners were forced not only to buy him out but also to pay Brown's anticipated earnings in advance. Brown estimated the worth of his partnership to be in the $1 million range. The accountants advising Patton Boggs had figured it to be more like $700,000. An indignant Brown eventually acquiesced, but it was beginning to dawn on him that his pursuit of glory would take a toll.

Nolanda Hill could see this clearly. When she helped Brown structure his Capital/PEBSCO buyout, she noted how it pained him to let that settlement money, also coincidentally $700,000, slip through his fingers. It didn't even matter that the money was heading, for tax purposes, directly into a protected account. To keep up his lifestyle Brown needed not just net worth; he needed cash.

Hao must have sensed this need. He returned to Washington without Binh and sought a second meeting with Brown. Despite the discouragement from Hill and despite his recent nomination, Brown proved willing. His need for money was no longer merely speculative. He was about to lose his Patton Boggs income, and he was also about to acquire some new expenses.

Brown's relationship with Madsen came at a price. As Hill observes, Brown had been paying the rent at Madsen's apartment "forever" and writing it off as his "insurance office." No sooner had Brown been nominated to the cabinet than he upped his investment. He bought the lovely Haitian a new townhouse on Westover Place, not far from his own residence. This deal struck close to home in more ways than the obvious. Brown had enlisted his son Michael to co-sign on the mortgage from PaineWebber.[6]

Despite his genuine affection for his son, Brown had chosen to expose him to the dark side of his life. In fact, Brown was no longer quite able to tell the dark from the light. On the "edge" where Brown operated, questions of morality and legality had so blurred that he had ceased to ask them.

It was at the Madsen townhouse in December 1992 that he met again with Hao and Marc Ashton and, of course, Madsen. It was at this second meeting, according to Binh, that Brown made a specific and telling request—$700,000 in cash.[7] The money was to be placed in a Singapore bank account controlled by Marc Ashton. Brown demanded other economic concessions as well.

If Hao was unfazed, Binh was getting queasy. Said the American Binh, "My guts turned upside down." He told Hao that with Brown now in government he had serious doubts about their course of action. Hao tried to persuade him to see the deal through.[8]

In a sworn affidavit, prepared in the spring of 1993, Binh was altogether specific in his account of what transpired. "Mr. Hao, after his trip to visit Mr. Brown, told me that the price was demanded by Mr. Brown for his lobby effort to be carried out by Patton, Boggs and Blow but with close supervision and office coordination with Mr. Brown's contacts." In addition, Brown provided further detail about the "$700,000 in cash to be deposited in an off-shore bank account." Binh elaborated:

> This price was personally delivered to Hanoi by Mr. Hao on his second trip to Vietnam and upon his return he told me that everything was "in order." He told me that money was underway to be transferred to a Singapore bank account at Banque Indosuez. This account was

opened by Mr. Le Quang Uyen, a partner of our group and a current vice president of Banque Indosuez Bangladesh branch.[9]

By the time of the third meeting in February, the Senate had already confirmed Brown with surprising ease as secretary—in the full Senate only Republican Paul Coverdell of Georgia voted against him.[10] This time Brown met Hao and Ashton at a Washington restaurant. Madsen was not present. Brown later took Hao alone to the Commerce Department for a brief tour, a fact later verified by Brown's own staff.

According to Binh, Brown reached a tentative agreement with Hao to include oil royalties or concessions and interests of at least 30 percent in other business ventures in Vietnam as well as the cash. In exchange, Brown would work to adopt an eight-point agenda for U.S. assistance to Vietnam. This would start with the lifting of the trade embargo and the establishment of most favored nation trading status for Vietnam, and it would include proposals for financial aid and industrial development.[11]

The problem was that Brown was no longer a lobbyist or a DNC official and what he sought could no longer be dressed up as a contract or even a campaign donation. Brown was asking for a bribe. "He had been carrying the bag for so long," laments Hill, "that he had not made the transition from politician to a statesman."

It was about this time, in the reflexively amoral words of Brown's biographer Steven Holmes, "the unthinkable happened." The "unthinkable" was not that Brown solicited a bribe from a Stalinist regime that was likely still holding American POWs. The unthinkable was the two Vietnamese partners, Hao and Binh, had "a falling-out."[12] Holmes neglects to mention the falling-out occurred because of Binh's apparent and understandable revulsion at the turn of events.

Binh was sufficiently upset that he began telling his story to the media and federal officials. In the beginning, the media blew him off, but the FBI took him seriously. In late February 1993, with Brown confirmed less than a month as secretary of commerce, the Miami office of the FBI launched a probe.[13]

For six months, no news of the investigation made its way into the media. It was not because of a lack of effort on Binh's part. The *New York Times* described his endeavors with characteristic lack of sympathy: "For seven months, the small-time businessman has been spinning a wild tale of international intrigue."[14] It should be noted that the *Times* offered up this bit of condescension *after* major parts of the "wild tale" had already been confirmed.

On air, CNN confirmed Binh had come to its offices early on and acknowledged he had passed an FBI lie detector test, but "several holes remained in his story." What is more, he had an "ax to grind" because of a financial dispute with Hao.[15]

In fact, the "financial dispute" angle surfaced as part of White House spin control and only after the story broke. Instead of trying to fill the "holes" in Binh's story, CNN and the other media held back until *U.S. News and World Report*, in the artless but apt words of CNN, "broke the media silence."

Hill remembers well the August 1993 day the story surfaced. She was returning to her Washington apartment at night when she was "blind-sided" by a stringer from the *Washington Post*. He had "all these facts and figures" and wanted to know about Brown's involvement with the Vietnamese. After eluding the man, Hill called Brown's cell phone unsuccessfully and finally located his advance man. Brown was apparently in the air on his way to California.

"You tell Ron," said Hill, "that when he gets off that plane to get back on it." When Brown called, Hill was still fuming. Brown at first assumed it was the Lillian Madsen angle that troubled her, and it likely did, but the real problem went deeper. Hill had already received letters from Republican congressman Bill Clinger about her own business deals with Brown; the last thing she needed was for Brown to stir up more dubious publicity. "You better be here before daylight comes," she warned him.

What scared Hill most was the amount solicited—$700,000. She knew this was the exact amount in the Capital/PEBSCO buyout she had structured for Brown, and she remembered how it vexed him to see that money pass through his fingers.

"The coincidence was too much," she says. Hill, quick to exonerate Brown when the charges are baseless, as she does with the alleged Chemfix quid pro quo, cannot do so here. For her, the figure of $700,000 had the ring of truth about it.

The media caught up with Brown in California. "I don't know anything about it. I have no comment," Brown told CNN's Wolf Blitzer on August 13. "No credible news media has ever picked it up. It's totally without foundation."[16]

Brown stopped to elaborate: "It's an absolutely ridiculous report, has no validity to it. I have never been involved with any such thing. I have never had any kind of business relationship, any kind of financial relationship, any kind of relationship of any kind on this matter."[17]

Upon his hasty return to Washington, Hill proved less accepting than the media. "You better find yourself a lawyer," she told Brown. "You are about to get in major trouble."

Now it was Brown's turn to be furious. He repeated to Hill what he had told the media: he never had anything to do with any Vietnamese. This made Hill angrier still. "That's funny," she told him. "You called me right after that [first] meeting." Brown had forgotten.

After the initial brushfire, the heat subsided. Both the solicitor of the bribe and the would-be recipient denied they had even met, and this sucked the air out of the reporting, at least for a while. Through his spokesman, Jim Desler, Brown was emphatic in his denials. Desler had told the *Washington Times* as early as May that Brown "never had any contact with any of the people named, not Mr. Hao or Mr. Birth [*sic*], and never had any business dealings with the company."[18]

On at least one other occasion Desler repeated the denial, telling the *New York Times* Brown "didn't recall meeting with this man."[19] Until he absolutely had to, Brown made no effort to counter the impression Desler was giving.

Brown's biographer, Steven Holmes, traces the roots of the whole controversy to a "grievous error" made by Desler. After receiving calls as early as March 1993 about Binh's charges, Desler asked Brown if they were true. "It's absolutely preposterous," Brown told him, "all of it." Rather than fixing the truth or falsity of each specific charge, Desler assumed all of Binh's charges were false, including the three meetings.

"With a little bit more experience," Desler tells Holmes, "I probably would have handled it better." Holmes does allow, however, with an "allegation as serious as bribery," Brown should have made sure that statements issued under his name were accurate.[20] One should think so.

On September 26, the brushfire flared up into a firestorm when the *Miami Herald* reported that despite all the denials, Brown and Hao had met three times, just as Binh had been alleging. Brown's attorney, Reid Weingarten, finally acknowledged the meetings. One of these meetings, in fact, had occurred after Brown's installation as secretary. Weingarten tried to justify the meetings, saying Hao had merely "sought advice on trade issues involving Vietnam."[21]

Left unsaid was why the secretary of commerce would host a convenience store manager he barely knew. This question no one seems to have asked. Binh had the answers, and his credibility was further strengthened when the *New York Times* reported that authorities "had found evidence that suggested the Vietnamese were preparing to establish a bank account in Singapore."[22]

It was also credibly reported that the FBI had copies of two faxes Hao had sent to Vietnam officials in December saying Brown's reaction to his offer had been "positive."[23]

In October, while a Miami grand jury reviewed the evidence in Brown's Vietnam case, House Republican leaders, then in the minority, called on Attorney General Janet Reno to name a special prosecutor. Their disingenuous claim that Brown was "entitled to something better than prolonged trial by press account" offered Brown little solace.[24]

"You have some serious problems, buddy," Hill had told him, and neither of them knew the half of it.

14 | THE BLACK PRESIDENT

Ron Brown had dreamed of becoming America's first black president from the time he was a little boy. By 1992, the dream had entered the realm of the realistic.

Bus rides through the South during the campaign of that year raised Brown's hopes and turned his head. The blacks along the route were cheering for him. Those cheers, however, only irritated the man who would prove to be his greatest rival for the position of first black president, the entirely unlikely Bill Clinton.

For starters, Bill Clinton was white, something of a handicap right there. Plus, he was a wonk. He had no feel for the streets. Clinton also had to play white enough to attract the white southern and northern ethnic vote.

To secure critical black support, Clinton made a conscious effort to develop an appropriate style. According to Nolanda Hill, it was Vernon Jordan who taught Clinton the "patois" he needed to communicate to African Americans. As he mastered that patois, Clinton began to create an image for himself that appealed even to sophisticated African Americans.

The hard work paid off in 1998. At the climax of the Monica Lewinsky scandal, with Ron Brown long since dead, famed author Toni Morrison anointed Clinton as "our first black president." "After all," Morrison continued in this much-discussed *New Yorker* article, "Clinton displays almost every trope of blackness: single-parent household, born poor, working class, saxophone-playing, McDonald's-and-junk-food-loving boy from Arkansas."[1]

The Morrison nomination was not entirely fanciful. It was grounded in hard numbers. Democratic party strategist Donna Brazile observed that in the last three years of his presidency, in every poll she ran, "Bill Clinton was the number one African American leader."[2]

Black support would prove particularly useful to Clinton during his impeachment ordeal. It stiffened the resolve of his fellow Democrats and helped persuade them not to jettison their beleaguered president. In August 1998, the same month as his ill-tempered and ill-received public apology, Clinton's approval rating among African Americans registered at 93 percent, higher even than Jesse Jackson's.[3] Even after the ugly final weeks of his presidency, Clinton scored an 87 percent approval rating among blacks, nearly twice as high as was it among whites. Indeed, black support for Clinton had been critical at every step of his presidency.

For his valuable book, *Bill Clinton and Black America*, columnist Dewayne Wickham invited some forty prominent African Americans to lend their impressions of Bill Clinton and explain why he was "wildly popular with the vast majority of African Americans."[4] Their observations are worth noting. To Clinton's credit, he apparently does have a great gift for putting people at ease. If his white allies took this for granted, blacks did not. Says attorney Johnny Cochran, "Bill Clinton is probably the most comfortable Caucasian around black people that most of us have ever seen."[5]

This level of comfort was possible, however, only because African Americans bought into a carefully crafted myth about Clinton's life. The Clintons had spun this fiction out of whole cloth and, amazingly enough, got away with it.

"He had a poor upbringing," observes TV reporter April Woodard of Clinton.[6] "He came from the other side of the tracks," elaborates business executive Gwynne McKinney. "In some circles he was probably called poor white trash."[7] "What separates him from every other president—and basically from most white politicians—is that he grew up with a lot of black kids," adds Michael Frisby.[8] Indeed, the chapter in Wickham's book from which several of these observations come is titled, "A Kindred Soul."

Congressman Jesse Jackson Jr. comments that Clinton's "experience as a poor white Southerner growing up is comparable to the experiences that poor African Americans in the South have grown up with." Jackson adds, "He ran on that personal story and that personal experience."[9] Although Jackson's last observation is accurate, all those that preceded it are not.

For black audiences, Clinton added detail that showed his sensitivity to black causes. On the occasion of the fortieth anniversary of the integration of Little Rock schools in 1997, Clinton reminisced about the lessons learned in his grandparent's small grocery store in Hope. Despite a sixth-grade education, his grandfather taught young Bill "America's most profound lessons." These included the understanding that "we really are all equal" and "we really do have the right to live in dignity."[10] Clinton elaborated it was the events at Little Rock "that made racial equality a driving obsession in my life."

In his semi-famous "Mend It, Don't End It" July 1995 speech on affirmative action, Clinton added more specifics about his path to racial awareness. On this occasion he told his audience how he had "wept" in the privacy of his own home as he watched Martin Luther King and the landmark March on Washington.[11] A year later, on a national radio address at the height of the church-burning hysteria then sweeping America, Clinton would tell his audience, "In our country during the '50s and '60s, black churches were burned to intimidate civil rights workers. I have vivid and painful memories of black churches being burned in my own state when I was a child."[12]

If any of the above is true, there is simply no evidence to back it up. There is, however, much evidence to the contrary. In her 1994 autobiography, *Leading With My Heart*, Clinton's mother, Virginia Kelley, refers to only one moment of racial instruction from her parents. This came as a three-year-old when her otherwise "vindictive, manipulative" mother spanked her for saying "Hi, nigger" to an old black woman.[13]

Kelley's mother was more likely striking a blow for Southern etiquette than for civil rights, but Kelley, buffing the Clinton myth, has another take: "Bill and Roger's enlightened views on race started long before they were born, with that furious spanking in Hope in 1926."[14] Roger Clinton, at least, did not quite learn the lesson. Bill's younger half-brother would later be caught on a 1984 police surveillance tape in a less than enlightened moment:

> Some junior high nigger kicked Steve's ass while he was trying to help
> his brothers out; junior high or sophomore in high school. Whatever
> it was, Steve had the nigger down. However it was, it was Steve's fault.
> He had the nigger down, he let him up. The nigger blindsided him.[15]

If Arkansas state trooper Larry Patterson is to be believed, brother Bill was no more sensitive. In his audio book, *More than Sex: The Secrets of Bill and Hillary Clinton Revealed,* Patterson claims Bill Clinton would occasionally use the word "nigger" when angry with black opponents. He cites its particular use in reference to Arkansas activist, Say McIntosh, a Clinton critic. Patterson contends Clinton referred to Jesse Jackson as a "nigger" as late as 1992 and routinely tolerated racial slurs by others. The last of these claims can be verified.[16] During the 1992 campaign, Gennifer Flowers taped the following conversation:

> *Clinton*: Mario Cuomo is a mean son of a bitch.
> *Flowers*: I wouldn't be surprised if he does not have Mafiosi major connections. (Clinton laughs.)[17]

In an all too indicative moment, candidate Clinton denied the voice on the tape was his and then apologized to Cuomo for the remark.[18]

In many salient details the mythic life Clinton evoked did not match the one he lived. Although his presumed father, Bill Blythe, died before he was born, Clinton did not exactly grow up in the archetypal poor single-family household.

After Clinton spent much of the first few years living with his doting grandparents, his mother returned from her training as a nurse anesthetist and took him back. In 1950, Kelley married Roger Clinton, the youngest son of an affluent Hot Springs family. Whatever lessons young Clinton was learning about racial equality from his grandfather more or less ceased when Clinton went to live with his mom and new stepfather. He was three years old at the time.

As Virginia Kelley reminisces about her husband, "Nobody ever loved Bill Clinton more than Roger did."[19] In his first act as stepfather, Roger Clinton bought Bill a new set of model trains. Soon enough the new family decamped to Hot Springs where Roger found work in his family's car dealership and Kelley found the flashy lifestyle that suited her tastes.

Says Kelley, "Hot Springs seemed to afford me a wonderful life."[20] The "seemed to" part refers not to any lack of material goods but to Roger Clinton's chronic alcoholism. This part of the myth is true. The fact that Clinton strategically exposed his stepfather's problems on the campaign trail provoked, as Kelley admits, a good deal of understandable anger in the extended Clinton family.[21]

For all of their very real problems, Clinton was the apple of his parents' eyes. In *First In His Class*, the *Washington Post*'s David Maraniss reports on a life that was almost uniquely luxurious given the time and place. The Clintons had turned the living room of the family's comfortable middle class home into a veritable "shrine" to young Bill's many accomplishments.

"The refrigerator was stocked to his taste." His bedroom, and he never had to share one, was the largest in the house. He had his own bathroom, perhaps the only teen in the state so blessed. Meanwhile in the carport sat the black four-door finned Buick that young Bill drove to Hot Springs High School. For special occasions, like a trip to the whites-only country club, there was also the family's cream yellow Henry J coupe. By nineteen, Clinton was driving a white Buick convertible with red interior.[22] The notion he was "poor" or came from "the wrong side of the tracks" is laughable.

Of note, neither Kelley nor Marannis show Clinton interacting with any African Americans at any time in his Arkansas youth. Nor do we sense any particular racial sensitivity about a life lived in the already archaic world of the Old South. Kelley, in fact, sent young Bill to the best of Hot Springs' still segregated schools all the way through high school. If the desegregation of Little Rock High in 1957 troubled Kelley or her eleven-year-old son, it did not affect their real-world decisions.

At his high school graduation, Clinton had the chance to share with his audience just how "racial equality" had become a "driving obsession" in his life. He chose not to. Other than a wistful hope that his generation would "remove complacency, poverty, and prejudice from the hearts of free men," and this buried deep in the benediction he offered, one sees no sign at all of this passion.[23]

As to the church burnings that caused such "vivid and painful memories" for the young Clinton, there were none. Jim Johnson, a retired Arkansas state supreme court justice, demanded Clinton name "one black church which has been burned in the state of Arkansas or else apologize for the shame which you continue to bring to your native state!" He was not alone in his protest. The state historian and the leaders of several black organizations joined him.[24] A Clinton spokesman later clarified he meant "black community buildings," but there is no record of these either.[25]

The same month Clinton graduated from high school, just a few hundred miles away, Mississippi Klansmen brutally murdered three young civil rights workers, two of them white, all of them scarcely older than he was. There is no evidence their murders distracted Clinton from a summer of saxophone playing and skirt chasing. When Clinton ran for freshman class president at Georgetown in the fall, he ran a non-ideological campaign, says Maraniss, on "a platform of dry moderation."[26]

At Georgetown, especially on racial issues, Clinton proved to be the soul of restraint. When the student council debated whether to fund a group heading to Alabama to participate in a civil rights march, Clinton waffled before finally supporting the funding request. Despite his "driving obsession," he showed no inclination to march himself.[27]

In the summer of 1966, Frank Holt appeared to be the favorite to succeed vintage school-door-blocker Orville Faubus as governor of Arkansas. Although slightly more progressive than Faubus—who wasn't—Holt had inherited the Faubus political apparatus and used it. Among those running against Holt was Brooks Hays, a Democrat and former congressman who made the courageous decision to support the integration of Little Rock schools.[28]

Clinton backed Holt. He used his family connections—Uncle Raymond Clinton was a force in Arkansas politics—to land a spot on Holt's campaign. Although Republican Winthrop Rockefeller beat them both, Clinton parlayed his Holt connections into a job on the Washington staff of Senator William J. Fulbright, an unrepentant segregationist.[29]

And thus a political career was launched, not on a driving obsession for racial equality but on pure political calculation. Indeed, had Roger Clinton taken his young family to Wichita instead of Hot Springs, Bill Clinton today would be a Republican. When the prevailing winds in the Democratic party shifted, as they soon would, Clinton would tack to port.

By June 1992, Clinton had a lock on the Democratic nomination but was still a long shot for victory in November. Even Perot was leading him in the polls. To win, Clinton knew he would have to play all the angles in the race game. The first obstacle was the same one Dukakis faced in 1988: Jesse Jackson. His advisors, Paul Begala and George Stephanopoulos, sold Clinton on a deft but risky maneuver.

At the end of an address to Jackson's Rainbow Coalition, Clinton "dissed" Jackson for providing a forum the previous night to Sister Souljah, an arguably racist black rapper. Although Clinton worried he had miscalculated, the media applauded his courage. And as to Jackson, although he felt "violated," he still presented Clinton with a memo outlining his credentials for the vice-presidency. After all, who else could he offer it to?[30]

Clinton did not make the Sister Souljah gambit in a vacuum. Ten days earlier he had appeared on the *Arsenio Hall Show*, playing the saxophone and talking to Hall for half an hour. According to Wickham, Clinton banked enormous good will with millions of African Americans that night. This appearance, adds Wickham, "helped cushion him" against any criticism for his comments before the Rainbow Coalition.[31]

"The fact that he just blew a saxophone," notes civil rights leader Joseph Lowery, "made white folks hate him."[32] It obviously did not matter that Clinton learned to play this instrument of Belgian origin in the altogether vanilla band of an all-white high school. The Clinton myth trumped all logic.

As Lowery's improbable comment suggests, both Bill and Hillary Clinton employed another cushioning strategy, a deeper, more destructive one. With Manichean flair, the Clintons divided the world into good and evil and positioned themselves among the good, in what Shelby Steele calls "the zone of decency." Once so established, they gained the power to "decertify" others. Says Steele, "No politician in modern times has mined this vein more effectively than President Clinton."[33]

The decertified "other" was almost inevitably, in Hillary Clinton's immortal phrase, "the vast right-wing conspiracy." If that phrase jarred the average viewer of the *Today Show*, it rang true among the base, particularly among African Americans who had been long-conditioned to think of political conservatives, black or white, in terms bordering on the demonic.

The Clintons played this game relentlessly. While President Bill Clinton reassured the nation at large that "It is simply wrong to play politics with the issue of affirmative action,"[34] the black president quietly stoked the fears of African Americans by warning them in private conversations of "right-wing attacks" on affirmative action.[35]

The enemy had been identified. The message had sunk in. And the strategy worked its magic. "I think anything that would upset those right-wing conservatives is a good idea," retiree Norma Johnson tells Wickham. "They hate his guts—and that's exactly why black folks love Bill Clinton."[36]

Upon his election, Clinton made one move that resonated well with the black community. He appointed the highly visible Vernon Jordan to co-chair his transition team with Warren Christopher. "It was the first time in history that a president of the United States publicly stated that his best friend was an African American," says civil rights activist Mary Frances Berry.[37]

In fact, this was a new and expedient friendship. Marannis' biography, which takes Clinton through 1991, has not a single mention of Jordan. Roger Morris' exhaustive biography of the Clintons, *Partners in Power*, likewise makes no reference to a friendship with Jordan, and this book covers 1992. [38] Still, it was a highly public friendship that would prove useful to Clinton and to Jordan as well—at least until the Monica misadventure.

Jordan helped Clinton choose a cabinet conspicuously designed to "look like America." This cabinet included four African Americans: Ron Brown at Commerce, Hazel O'Leary at Energy, Mike Espy at Agriculture, and Jesse Brown at Veteran's Affairs. It also included two Hispanics, Henry Cisneros at HUD and Frederico Pena at Transportation, and three women in addition to O'Leary: Janet Reno, the attorney general, Donna Shalala at Health and Human Services, and Madeline Albright, ambassador to the United Nations.

"He put black people in real power positions," observes former Atlanta mayor Bill Campbell. "That alone goes a long way in explaining why this guy was so popular with black folks."[39]

This willful sharing of power with minorities quickly became part of the Clinton myth. Ron Brown learned the hard way, however, just how illusory the myth was. He sensed the depth of that deception with the publication in 1994 of Robert Woodward's *The Agenda*.[40]

The "agenda" in question was the domestic one embodied in the contentious budget bill of 1993. Woodward tells the story with his typical insider detail about the fierce, if chaotic, struggle between the "investment hawks" and the "deficit hawks" within Clinton's cabinet to shape the bill and with it the Clinton presidency. For the record, the deficit hawks won.

What mattered to Brown about the story, what stung and humiliated him, as he told Nolanda Hill, was that he seemed to have played almost no part in the contest.[41] Woodward's book made this clear. There is, in fact, only one reference to Brown, and it is an insignificant one. Brown's power was chimerical.

In the beginning of the book, Woodward lists Clinton's nine-member "economic team." Brown is not on it. Nor is Brown among the thirty-one Democrats who comprise Woodward's "cast of characters." What intrigues the observer about this cast is it looks less "like America" than it does like, say, Idaho.

Of the thirty-one Democrats listed, twenty-two of whom are part of Clinton's official team, not one is a racial minority of any kind. Of the seventy identifiable faces (including repetitions) in the photo section of the book, all are white. Indeed of the twenty-two members of the Clinton team, only four are female, and that includes Hillary Clinton.[42] And this is the "domestic" team. On the national security front, minorities did not even enjoy the illusion of power.

Curious, too, is the absence of any meaningful role for Vernon Jordan. Although Woodward acknowledges Jordan is the co-chair of the transition team with Christopher, that acknowledgement is the last one sees of Jordan. Christopher, soon to be nominated secretary of state, appears to be the one managing the appointment process, even on the domestic front.

The only identifiable "ethnics" with any real power in the Clinton administration were Jewish. In *The Agenda,* Jews play a prominent role. Three of them—Robert Reich, Robert Rubin, and Alan Greenspan—are essential. In Clinton's second term, people of Jewish origin would head the Departments of State, Defense, Treasury, Commerce (briefly), and serve as national security advisor and director of central intelligence. It was in part to allay the inherent tension between Jews and blacks within his own administration—remember "Hymietown"—that Clinton made the otherwise pointless "Passover" reference at Brown's eulogy.

Although the Clintons respected the competence of the Jews in their party, they could be as vile towards them as Jesse Jackson was. In his dispassionate book on the Clinton marriage, *State of a Union*, veteran reporter Jerry Oppenheimer observed that early in the Clinton career Hillary Clinton had called campaign aide Paul Fray "a f—ing Jew bastard" in front of at least two witnesses. The witnesses verified the accusation.[43]

When this charge surfaced during Hillary's 2000 Senate run, she promptly denied it and predictably set the Clinton attack machine on Fray and the witnesses. In 1999, however, Trooper Larry Patterson observed it was "fairly common" for both Clintons to slur Jews with much the same language Oppenheimer would expose a year later.[44]

Advisor Dick Morris, himself Jewish, added evidence of his own. As he observed on FOX News' *Hannity & Colmes*, he had once been arguing with the Clintons about his fee when Hillary exploded, "That's all you people care about is money!" Morris revealed he had also shared this newsworthy anecdote with high profile reporter Gail Sheehy for her then-yet-to-be-published biography, *Hillary's Choice.* Not surprisingly, Sheehy chose to protect the Clintons' "zone of decency" by not reporting this story.[45]

Unlike Jews, Blacks and Hispanics in the Clinton administration enjoyed little more than the trappings of power. As Brown learned, the appointment of minorities served largely to appease key voting blocs. He and the other minorities in the cabinet were not even allowed to pick their own seconds in command. That person was inevitably a Clinton plant in place to do the administration's real work.[46]

Time after time, the Clintons exploited the trust of their minority appointees and used them less for information than insulation. This pattern became apparent at the time of the Monica Lewinsky affair. As the president told the story, it was Betty Currie that Monica came to see. It was Bill Richardson who offered her a job at the United Nations. It was Vernon Jordan who chose to intercede for her at Revlon. These interventions cost the three a huge amount of anxiety and some staggering legal bills.

Hillary Clinton was not above a little exploitation herself. In unrelated incidents, it was not Hillary but her loyal aide Maggie Williams who cleared out Vince Foster's office after his death and accepted Johnny Chung's $50,000 donation in the White House. These acts led to huge legal bills for Williams as well.

Hillary Clinton had her own plans for Ron Brown. Although she could not bother herself to talk to him on the campaign bus in April 1993, as mentioned earlier, she invited him to a one-on-one lunch on the balcony of the White House. The given reason was to talk politics and thank him for his help with the "McLarty problem." But, in fact, she wanted more. She was about to test Brown, to see whether he would be a "good soldier."

According to Hill, who "debriefed" Brown after the patio lunch, the Clintons had a mission for Brown. They were about to give him the unofficial title "California Czar," ostensibly to show their commitment to the rebuilding of the California economy after the Los Angeles riots two years earlier. In reality, as Brown would soon enough realize, the "czar" claptrap was cover for a deeper California assignment.

Incredible as it may sound, the Clintons were prepared to approve the sale of the former Long Beach Naval Station to a company wholly owned by the People's Republic of China. The company was called COSCO, the China Ocean Shipping Company, and it was part of the Chinese navy. Says Hill of Brown's participation in the proposed sale, "This was his first big water to carry."

In time, U.S. intelligence sources would learn of Chinese plans to use the station as a base for espionage—no surprise there—and Congress would kill the deal. But Congress intervened only after Brown had died.[47] While alive, Brown knew more about the Chinese than he wanted to. And Long Beach was just one thing out of many that he knew he shouldn't have known.

Like the other minorities in the cabinet, Brown was not just exploitable. He was expendable.

15 | BETRAYAL

For Ron Brown, the most critical appointment in 1993 was one Bill Clinton decided not to make.

The nominee's name was Lani Guinier. When Clinton scuttled her nomination for the position of the deputy attorney general for civil rights, he boxed himself in on the question of Ron Brown, and he knew it.

The Guinier story sheds light not only on how Brown escaped from the Vietnam morass, but also on why, ultimately, black leadership abruptly ceased to challenge the cause of his death. As such, it deserves to be told.

Lani Guinier had good reason to feel excited in early 1993. Her Yale Law School classmates, Bill and Hillary Clinton, had reached the pinnacle of world power, and they were still her friends. Just three days after the inauguration, in fact, she and two other classmates had hosted a small dinner party and were "giddy with disbelief"[1] that the Clintons were actually going to attend. There was no political posturing here, no photo ops, just dinner "at the modest home of an honest-to-goodness" black friend.[2]

In February 1993, the same month Brown was meeting with Hao at the Commerce Department, Guinier began to receive job overtures from the White House. Although Guinier's credentials were solid—she had just received tenure at the University of Pennsylvania Law School—her legal writings were provocative. Guinier had championed, among other things, "proportional" voting, a phenomenon common enough in Europe but somewhat alien in the United States. Dissent began to build.

If the Clintons had problems with Guinier's scholarship, they showed no early signs of it. Guinier's would-be boss, Janet Reno, openly welcomed her. Other than Reno, however, Guinier worried "no one else in the administration was taking the nomination process seriously."[3] And Reno herself had her hands full. The Justice Department was focusing its attention on a small religious community on the dusty plains outside of Waco, Texas.

As the world knows, the Waco assault ended in tragedy. Following an FBI tank attack on April 19, eighty people burned to death, twenty of them children. The assault did not, however, end in political disaster. That would have occurred only if the Justice Department had shared with America what it knew and concealed about the Branch Davidians' ethnicity. More than half the dead were, in fact, racial minorities. Twenty-eight of them, aged six to sixty, were black.[4] It is unlikely Lani Guinier herself knew this. In her book, *Lift Every Voice*, she never mentions Waco.

Ten days after the Waco conflagration, at the end of a chaotic vetting process, Bill Clinton formally nominated Lani Guinier to head the Civil Rights Division. In introducing her to the assembled crowd at the Justice Department, he reaffirmed his commitment to civil rights and even praised Guinier for having sued his state for voting rights irregularities when he was governor and Guinier was a staff attorney for the Legal Defense Fund (LDF).

An incident during that ordeal should have alerted Guinier to Clinton's character. Her LDF colleague, Dayna Cunningham, had been in Arkansas to witness it. As Cunningham recounted, Clinton "irresponsibly pandered" to a hostile white crowd during a meeting in the Mississippi Delta region of southeastern Arkansas, a crowd more than a little intimidating to a young black woman. After the meeting, Clinton approached Cunningham in the rear of the room, grabbed the flesh of her upper arm, and seductively declared, "I love Lani Guinier. I love the Legal Defense Fund."

Cunningham was outraged. "Where is your core?" she thought. "What do you stand for?" Cunningham warned Guinier that Clinton would not defend principle unless his own political neck was on the line. At the time of her nomination, Guinier was in no mood to listen.[5]

In the days ahead, Guinier would begin to see the wisdom in Cunningham's warning. As the criticism against Guinier's nomination picked up on the Right, some of it rough, support from the White House began to ebb away. This troubled Guinier because she believed, perhaps rightly, that her views would seem less controversial if she were able to defend them. Her courtesy calls with U.S. Senators had been going well, including those with Republicans like Arlen Specter of Pennsylvania. He had told reporters, "If you turn down Guinier on the state of this record, no potential nominee with any intellect or courage or guts is going to come forward."[6] The White House was not nearly as encouraging.

In the middle of May, about a month after the nomination, a friend was giving the increasingly anxious Guinier a tour of the Oval Office to cheer her up. The two were walking down the hallway when Hillary Clinton and a staffer approached them. As Hillary breezed past, she said, "Hey, kiddo," and just kept walking. Guinier was astonished at the slight. About ten steps later, Hillary looked back over her shoulder and explained she was late for lunch. Those were the last words Hillary ever would utter to her embattled law school buddy.[7] In Hillary Clinton's book, *Living History*, there is no mention at all of Lani Guinier.[8]

On May 23 of that year, the *New York Times* joined the fray, questioning whether Guinier had the appropriate "philosophy and political sense" for the job, but allowing that the upcoming Senate hearings would be the appropriate place to answer the question.[9] Guinier was confident she would prevail in a hearing before a Senate with a Democratic majority, but she was beginning to doubt whether she would ever get the chance. She no longer trusted Bill Clinton.

"So far, I could look under every rock," Guinier writes, "but could not find him." The nominating process offered a "window on the presidential soul," and Guinier did not like what she was seeing.[10]

On June 3 the president finally called Guinier in for a private meeting. He was not encouraging. He warned her that the three weeks before the hearings would be brutal. Although of course he would "go to the mat" for *her*, it was her "writing" that was causing him political problems.[11]

Guinier reminded Clinton of an interview he had given during the campaign. When PBS's Bill Moyers asked him if there were any one issue on which he would not equivocate, Clinton answered, "The one thing I would not back down on is racial equality."[12] Taken aback by Guinier's observation, Clinton did not ask her to withdraw at that meeting. She took some consolation in that.

Within an hour of leaving the meeting, however, Guinier got a call from the president. "Lani," he said, "I have decided to withdraw your nomination." He then promised he would spend the rest of his life making it up to her. Despite his promises, that was the last Guinier would ever hear from either of the Clintons.[13]

Guinier watched the ensuing press conference in horror as the president dismissed her views as "undemocratic" and thus indefensible. She felt almost physically assaulted. "My friend, the president, was humiliating me on national television."[14]

On June 6, the forty-ninth anniversary of D-Day, Clinton sent letters to the Senate explaining his retreat. "I concluded," he wrote them, "that I could not ask for confirmation of a nominee with whom I disagreed."[15] In their meeting in the Oval Office, he had not been able to specify with which position of hers he disagreed. No matter. It was all over, at least for Lani Guinier.

But not for Ron Brown. Almost immediately, Clinton began to see what a furor his abandonment of Guinier had stirred within the black community. The Black Caucus denounced the president's move as a "capitulation" and froze him out of their deliberations. Entertainer Bill Cosby abruptly cancelled his master-of-ceremonies commitment for the White House Jazz Festival later in June. In July when Guinier spoke at the NAACP's national convention, thousands stood on their feet and chanted, "Lani, Lani, Lani." NAACP chairman William Gibson told the crowd the president had "kicked us in the teeth."[16] Clinton's approval rating among blacks, which had been 87 percent a few months earlier, fell precipitously to 53 percent.[17]

So in August, when Ron Brown's Vietnam problem flared up in the press, Bill Clinton was in no position to abandon him, no matter how egregious Brown's actions might have been. Jesse Jackson adviser Ron Walters defined Clinton's dilemma: "You've got a very popular figure in the black community and the black business establishment. If he doesn't stick by Ron Brown, it will be politically untenable for Bill Clinton."[18]

It should come as no surprise then that Janet Reno would turn down the request made by Republican House leadership to appoint a special prosecutor in the Vietnam affair. Nor that President Clinton would prove resolute in his support of Brown.

In late September 1993, right after it became known that Brown had in fact deceived the public about his three meetings with Nguyen Van Hao, Brown met with Clinton at the White House. Here, once again, Clinton declared his support. Said Clinton, "He's told me that he hadn't done anything wrong, and he's done just about everything right as Commerce secretary. I think he's done a great job, and I have no reason not to believe him."[19]

And so the investigation was thrown back to the cloistered confines of a federal grand jury in Janet Reno's Dade County, now under the watchful eyes of the Justice Department's Public Integrity Section. Stephen Dresch believes that then-Deputy Attorney General Webster Hubbell undermined this investigation just as he had the Hawaii investigation into the Lums. The prosecutor never even called Ron Brown to testify.

The media showed remarkably little curiosity when in February 1994 the Justice Department announced it was preparing to clear Brown of these unpleasant allegations. The grand jury, as the *Washington Post* reported matter-of-factly, "found no evidence to support claims by Florida businessman Binh Ly that the two businessmen recruited Brown to help develop business ventures in Vietnam as soon as the trade ban could be lifted."[20]

Of course they had found evidence. At the least, they had the consistent and specific testimony from Binh and the acknowledgement that Hao, a convenience store manager, had met with Brown three times, the last time in his Commerce Department office. They also had copies of faxes from Hao to the Vietnamese assuring them Brown was on board as well as evidence the Vietnamese had opened an offshore bank account for Brown in Singapore.

Brown had been predicting for several months he would be exonerated. He had reason to be confident. For one, as he would tell Nolanda Hill shortly before his death, he had gotten an inside tip about the investigation from the Justice Department almost as soon as Binh went to the FBI.[21] FBI agents on the case would tell ABC News that they always suspected just that.[22] As a result of the tip, Brown never did actually accept the money. The Lani Guinier brouhaha just sealed the deal.

At the end of the day, in an entirely unusual move, the Justice Department agreed to demands by Brown's attorney, Reid Weingarten, that Brown was "entitled to a public exoneration" because of his prominence and the publicity given the investigation.[23] A remarkably complacent media duly trumpeted his "innocence." One can find no trace of an independent media inquiry into Binh's charges or any interest in the fate of this intrepid whistleblower. The fact that the secretary of commerce had almost undeniably negotiated a large bribe with a communist country was quickly forgotten.

By April, Brown would once again be the subject of flattering profiles like the one in the *New York Times* headlined, "Ron Brown Re-emerges in Halls of Power, and Thrives." As to the grand jury investigation, that was a mere "detour." After all, had not the Clinton Justice Department declared, "Mr. Brown had not misused his position"?[24]

"Rather than holding blacks to higher collective standards," writes William McGowan in his much praised *Coloring The News*, "newspaper, magazine, and television journalism has set the bar much lower, implicitly endorsing a kind of cultural separatism that minimizes the value—sometimes even the possibility—of common cultural standards for all Americans."[25] Just as at Middlebury, Brown would gain a seeming advantage in the lowering of standards. But in the long run, these deviations were destroying him.

In the short term at least, fate was not as kind to Lani Guinier as it had been to Brown. She was about to learn that an idealist like herself could expect little lasting support in a town as opportunistic as Washington DC. Although the ubiquitous Vernon Jordan promised his and the president's lasting support, that quickly evaporated. The Black Caucus refused to meet with the president for over a month, but then its members also began to back away from Guinier.[26]

Guinier had her own "moment of epiphany" at the occasion of the congressional Black Caucus Dinner in September 1993. Although the group had invited both Guinier and the president, the White House had negotiated all the terms. The president would leave before Guinier received her award and had a chance to say anything. She was to be seated as far from the president as possible in "a virtual island of untouchable space."

There with her husband, Guinier felt very much isolated and alone. "My friends in the DC-based civil rights community still acknowledged my presence," Guinier remembers, "but they seemed determined to maintain some distance to protect their ability to play in this field."[27]

Guinier was seeing for herself how the civil rights community had "withered because of this instinct to insider politics." Indeed, this once proud movement had devolved into something of a court at whose center sat the almost blindly revered "black president" and his wife, Hillary Clinton. Here, says Guiner, "access is the coin of the realm."[28]

Guinier's unsparingly observant friend, Dayna Cunningham, explained to Guinier that these would-be courtiers had traded their "sepia-bronzed movement résumés" in for cash and expected Guinier to do the same. "Blacks with their plaques," is how Guinier and Cunningham came to see the movement's insiders. For Guinier, this was all very disillusioning.[29]

As to Brown, he would never experience the kind of betrayal at the hands of this community that Guinier did. That betrayal would not occur until nearly two years after his death.

16 MOST FAVORED NATION

"Now Mr. Brown is back," trumpeted the *New York Times* in April 1994, two months after the Justice Department cleared him of wrongdoing in the Vietnam affair. "While other Administration officials duck over the Whitewater matter, the Commerce Secretary has been winning extravagant praise."[1]

That's how easy it was for Ron Brown—at least publicly. Given this kind of coverage, after an incident that should have killed his career, one can at least understand how he had come to feel "entitled." But while the *Times* gloried in Brown's "ability to play in the symphonies of power," Brown himself knew he himself had been played, been had.

The White House had intervened to save him from being indicted—or so Brown suspected. He knew such intervention always came at a price. And he knew too that, when called upon, he would pay it. "Ron was so worried that the White House would withdraw support," says Nolanda Hill, "that he was willing to do anything."

If Ron Brown were prepared to sacrifice his freedom, so too, ironically, were the Clintons. As the *Times'* article suggests, early 1994 was a time of high anxiety at the White House. That irksome "Whitewater matter" was beginning to take a toll.

On February 24, Deputy Treasury Secretary Roger Altman admitted to the Senate Banking Committee he had given the White House a "heads-up" on likely criminal referrals. He would have to step down before the summer was out. On March 5, White House Counsel Bernard Nussbaum resigned under fire, a victim of Whitewater fallout. Ten days later, Associate Attorney General Webster Hubbell resigned in disgrace amidst accusations he had stolen from his clients back in Little Rock. A week after that, former Arkansas judge David Hale accused the president of pressuring him to make an illegal $300,000 loan in 1986.

In the Clinton White House, small scandals had a way of spawning larger ones. In this case, Arkansas would soon bleed into China. Despite his seeming horror on the campaign trail about doing business "with those who murdered freedom at Tiananmen Square," President Clinton would prove to have no qualms about doing just that—and much more.[2]

Attorneys at the public interest law firm, Judicial Watch, would come to think of China as "the most serious scandal in United States history,"[3] and few who have studied it disagree. It dwarfed all the others of the Clinton years and pulled into its orbit those without the freedom to pull away. Compromised by his own recklessness with the Vietnamese, Ron Brown ranked high among those snared.

To understand how Brown and the Clintons came to the point where they were prepared to betray not just their principles but their country, it is useful to reintroduce the elusive John Huang. The reader will recall Huang proved very helpful to Brown on his 1991 trip to the Far East. Huang, an American citizen since 1977, was technically the chief executive of the Riady family business in the United States. All evidence suggests, however, his real job was overseeing the Riady investments in the Democratic party in general and Bill Clinton in particular.[4] As early as 1989, Brown was convinced "the Clintons were owned by the Riady interests."[5]

Huang first met Bill Clinton, already a Riady family friend, in Hong Kong in 1985 and gave him a tour of the city. A little *Guanxi*. In 1988, he met the governor once again at the Democratic National Convention in Atlanta where Clinton, a rising star within the party, made his infamously prolix keynote address. When deposed in 1996 by Judicial Watch, Huang would claim these were the only two times he had ever met Bill Clinton before he went to work for the Commerce Department in 1994.[6]

Understandably, Huang would never consent to being questioned under oath again. He had perjured himself. Starting on March 15, 1993, Huang had, in fact, made forty-seven visits to the White House *before* he joined the Commerce Department. At least nine of those visits were with the president, most of these in the family quarters.[7] One of these meetings proved particularly memorable.

On April 19, 1993, Huang and James Riady met Clinton in the Oval Office. Riady recalls the day vividly because a television in the corner was showing the Mount Carmel community at Waco in full flame. Ever gracious, Clinton escorted his guests to the White House situation room to observe key staff then in the throes of mismanaging the crisis. Huang and Riady also dropped in on Robert Rubin, head of the president's Economic Council. White House entry logs confirm Riady's memory and Huang's multiple visits.[8] Three days later, Hillary Clinton held a press conference to address the press's concerns, not about Waco but about Whitewater.

Whatever conversations Huang had with the Clintons have been lost to history. Hillary Clinton certainly did not think them worth recording in *Living History,* and it is likely her husband will extend the respectful silence in his forthcoming book. One does not have to be a cynic to suspect Clinton's discussions with Huang and Riady focused on a decision the president soon would make—renewing most favored nation (MFN) status for the People's Republic of China (PRC).

In the way of background, China had been granted MFN status in 1980 after a thirty-year abeyance. Once restored, this status had to be renewed annually. After Tiananmen Square in 1989, liberals in Congress had pressured President George Bush to place conditions on MFN because of China's disregard for human rights.

A believer in "constructive engagement," Bush consistently vetoed legislation to do just that, and Clinton attacked him for it on the campaign trail. "We believe that the Bush administration erred by extending most favored nation trade status to China," argued Clinton and Gore in *Putting People First,* "before it achieved documented progress on human rights."[9]

Understandably, Congressional liberals had high hopes for Clinton. But unknown to them, the Riadys had come to take a special interest not only in Bill Clinton but also in Communist China. The 1997 Senate hearings headed by Tennessee senator Fred Thompson made this clear. "Over the past five years," reads the report, "the Lippo Group has shifted its strategic center from Indonesia to the People's Republic of China." Those five years, by the way, backdate to 1992, the year of Clinton's election.[10]

The Thompson Committee cited any number of large-scale Riady joint ventures in China, including the construction and development of apartment complexes, office buildings, highways, ports, and other infrastructure. Lippo's principal partner in the People's Republic was an enterprise called China Resources, "a company wholly-owned and operated by the PRC government."[11]

One of the Clintons' most useful tools for advancing China's interests was to be Ron Brown. This role would prove a bit awkward for Brown. Like most liberal Democrats he had positioned himself as a champion of human rights. Says Hill, "Ron had been very vocal about his belief that China should not be granted most favored nation status."

But like too many of those in public office, this sentiment was not deeply felt. Brown had taken this position while at the DNC largely to differentiate himself from the more moderate Democratic Leadership Council and target the core of his party more effectively.

When the campaign was over and Clinton began to shift direction, self-preservation dictated Brown follow. "Human rights, schmuman rights," adds Hill. "He was not hardcore anything." His public change of heart mattered. As an African American and certifiable "civil rights leader," Brown had a certain moral weight about him others did not. The Clintons compelled him to use that weight in a bit of strategic jujitsu to advance their plans for Asia.

One cabinet member who resisted the president's seeming change of direction on China was Madeline Albright, then ambassador to the United Nations. The president charged Brown with winning her over.

Says Hill, "He was going to pull the race card on poor old Madeline Albright." Before a critical cabinet meeting, Brown offered to take Albright on a limousine tour of the largely poor and black southeast section of Washington. As he told her what they would see, Brown made his pitch, culminating with an appeal to the ambivalence about American justice rife within his party: "Who are we to talk about human rights?"

Brown zeroed in on the epicenter of that ambivalence, the liberal unease about all things racial. Albright teared up. Brown had done his job well, too well. Immediately after the cabinet meeting, he repaired to Hill's apartment. From there, he called Albright and apologized. Clinton, says Hill, had turned Brown "into a full-blown hypocrite, a public one," and it sickened him.

In late May 1993, a week before he would betray Lani Guinier and a month after his meeting with Huang and Riady, President Clinton betrayed the billion or so people in Mainland China—at least in the eyes of Chinese dissidents and their supporters—by renewing China's most favored nation status.

To buffer the shock from this renewal and to show his continued concern, the president issued Executive Order 12850. This half-hearted decree spelled out the conditions necessary for China to retain its MFN status next year and in the years to come.

"President Clinton will examine China's actions in several areas," promised the White House with great solemnity.[12] These included a range of human rights issues, among them free speech, the treatment of prisoners, broadcast rights, respect for Tibet, freedom of emigration, and prison labor. Only the latter two conditions did Clinton make "binding and absolute."[13] And even these conditions would prove considerably less than binding or absolute.

Although he promised to deal with weapons issues separately, Clinton seemed willing at least to confront China's role in their proliferation. He claimed the United States was examining reports that China had shipped M-11 ballistic missiles to Pakistan in violation of the Missile Technology Control Regime.[14]

On this score Clinton was talking tough. He vowed if he could prove China had transferred M-11 missiles or related equipment, he would "not hesitate to act." Satisfied with the president's tough talk, liberal Democrats in Congress dropped their demands for additional human rights legislation.[15] As to the Chinese, they made a show of outrage at the president's conditions and continued to do business as usual.

It does a disservice to the honorable souls within the Clinton administration to imply they all abandoned their principles and fell into lockstep behind Clinton. That did not happen. The year following EO 12850 saw the rough dialectic within the administration play itself out in the public square with much of the pressure to hang tough coming from Warren Christopher and the State Department. Pressure also came from an unlikely congressional alliance of liberal Democrats and conservative Republicans. The moderates in either party were more willing to play ball.

As it turned out, China did sell M-11 ballistic missile technology to Pakistan, and the administration was forced to respond. It did so in August 1993 by banning the export of satellites and related equipment. Relations took another hit when the U.S. Navy stopped and inspected a Chinese merchant ship wrongly thought to be carrying chemical weapons to Iran.[16]

In that same summer, both Congress and the European Parliament passed separate resolutions urging the International Olympic Committee not to hold the 2000 summer Olympics in Beijing. In September, China released dissident Wei Jingsheng, but this last-minute gesture was not enough to save the games.

One has to admire, if nothing else, Chinese bravado in the face of such nearly universal scorn. In February 1994, when Assistant Secretary of State John Shattuck met secretly with Wei Jingsheng, the highest-ranking party member to have become a dissident and one of the founders of the "Democracy Wall" movement, the Chinese went public with *their* fury. They dared to break off what the Human Rights Watch called "an almost non-existent 'human rights dialogue.'"[17]

Why such bravado? After being released from prison, Wei Jinsheng would tell British journalist Christopher Hitchens it was "hard to lobby against the Beijing dictatorship in Washington, because Washington's China policy was determined in Beijing."[18] To the degree this was true, 1994 was the year America moved its China policy offshore.

Just ten days after Shattuck's provocative meeting with Wei Jingsheng, Warren Christopher was dispatched eastward, if for no other reason, than to smooth the waters. The Chinese never gave him a chance. To set the tone for Christopher's trip, authorities arrested Wei Jingsheng a week before his arrival. They were just warming up.

Soon after Christopher deplaned on this, his first visit as secretary of state, Tiananmen hard-liner Li Peng verbally assaulted him. His insults were shrewd and studied. In a biting turn of phrase, he accused Christopher and Clinton of "losing China," a charge that in a slightly different context had haunted the Democratic party since the days of Harry Truman.

Li Peng then used a comparable trope on Christopher that Brown had used on Albright. How, he argued, could America be so sanctimonious about human rights in light of the riots that had flared up in Los Angeles in the wake of the Rodney King affair? Given the moral self-doubt that infected the Democratic party, this charge had to sting as well.[19]

So violent was his tirade that the American contingent actually contemplated getting back on the plane and going home. They might as well have. The trip did not get much better after this rude welcoming. Although the Chinese made a few concessions, Christopher's return to Washington was "funereal."[20]

Problems were brewing at home as well. In fact, when Clinton's next emissary, Michael Armacost, visited the Oval Office in early May 1994 to discuss some major face-saving concessions before his China trip, he found the president and his advisors distracted beyond discussion. He would not learn until the next day that Paula Jones had just filed her sexual harassment lawsuit against the president.[21] Such were the seeds of the new China policy.

As word began to spread that Clinton was preparing to kowtow unconditionally to China, the liberal base of his own party grew alarmed. "China has not made overall significant progress and therefore hasn't complied with the President's executive order," said California representative Nancy Pelosi. "Let's get real about this. It is important for us to have sanctions that are real and that pressure the Chinese."[22]

Clinton wasn't listening. On May 26, 1994, he shocked those who had ever taken his China position seriously by "de-linking" human rights from renewal of China's most favored nation status. Although he admitted China had not made much progress on the issues outlined in his 1993 executive order, he suggested that, by following a new voluntary set of principles, American businesses could somehow turn things around.[23] Now, almost no one was taking Clinton seriously. As the BBC News would report in its own nicely understated way, "The Clinton administration's China policy has generally lacked coherence and seen a number of sharp turns."[24]

There is any number of reasons why these turns might have been taken, some of them legitimate. Members of both parties of presumably good conscience have long believed open trade would do more to advance human rights than would sanctions.

In his authoritative book on the subject, *A Great Wall*, veteran *New York Times* China correspondent Patrick Tyler paints an entirely credible picture of two "competing constituencies" locked in a battle for dominance within the Clinton administration. Tyler himself favored the position that America had to maintain a stable and constructive relationship with China despite its "thuggery and brutality." This had been George Bush's position, the one Clinton had attacked so mercilessly on the campaign trail in a burst of what Tyler calls "tactical moralism in the matrix of deconstructing Bush."[25]

Given his biases, Tyler turns a blind eye to one undeniable force in the ongoing China dialectic. Something more than logic was necessary to turn Clinton 180 degrees away from a position that was still popular in his party.

That something revealed itself during a crucial week in June 1994, the fifth anniversary of Tiananmen Square.

This time the decision-making likely involved Hillary Clinton. A week earlier, on June 12, Independent Counsel Robert Fiske had questioned both her and her husband under oath about Whitewater-related issues. They both had to know just what was their most vulnerable point.

Or more precisely, who.

At the time, Hillary's former law partner, Webster Hubbell, was broke, disgraced, and jobless. He was staring at a mountain of debt and serious time in prison. After the past eighteen chaotic months, the last thing the Clintons needed was an Arkansas insider making a deal with the Office of the Independent Counsel or the Senate Banking Committee. This was not about to happen. What follows is an outline of the week that headed it off:

- On Monday, June 20, Hillary Clinton meets with Hubbell.
- On Tuesday, James Riady and John Huang meet with trusted Clinton staffer Mark Middleton in the White House. That evening they attend a reception with the president on the South Lawn.
- On Wednesday, Riady and Huang meet again with Middleton at the White House.
- On Thursday Riady has breakfast with Hubbell. On that same day, Riady has lunch with Hubbell. That afternoon Riady and Huang meet with a commissioner of the Export-Import Bank.
- On Friday, Riady and Huang visit the White House twice, once to meet with Middleton and once to meet with Robert Rubin.
- On Saturday, Riady and Huang attend the president's weekly radio address in the Oval Office. A video, recorded both before and after the broadcast, shows Riady to have changed clothes, suggesting he was an overnight guest. After the other guests have left, Riady and Huang remain behind. The tape concludes with Clinton saying, "Just set everybody down wherever you want 'em, James," and then goes blank.
- On Monday, June 27, Webb Hubbell receives $100,000 from a Riady company account, Hong Kong China, Ltd. On the same day, Huang receives a memo from the Lippo Group in Jakarta congratulating him on his new position in the Commerce Department and informing him of a nearly half-million dollar severance package from Lippo.[26]

"Clinton was owned by Riady," claims Nolanda Hill, cutting to the chase. "It was in their best interests to open China." In his book, written two years after the Thompson hearings, Tyler never mentions the name "Riady." Tyler positions Robert Rubin at the head of the pro-engagement forces, but he fails to mention that Riady had a veritable open door to Rubin's office.

Nor does Tyler mention John Huang. And at every turn, there he was, international man of mystery, frontman for an Indonesian outfit deeply involved in the People's Republic of China, and candidate for a top spot in the Clinton administration. That he should choose to sacrifice his considerable Lippo income to serve this nation should have raised alarms throughout the White House and beyond.

According to the Thompson Committee, Huang had expressed interest in working for the government as soon as the president was elected in 1992. He was not particularly fussy. A bit immodestly perhaps, he was prepared to accept an assistant or undersecretary position at State, Treasury, or even Commerce if need be. Aware of his many talents, the Democratic National Committee put him on its "must consider" list. Senator Tom Daschle, among others, sent a letter of recommendation on his behalf.

And what were Huang's talents? A letter sent by an Asian outreach advocate on the stationery of David Roberti, the president pro tem of the California state Senate, was frank to a fault: "John is the Riady family's top priority for placement because he is like one of their own." The Riady family, in case anyone needed reminding, "invested heavily in the Clinton campaign."[27] To some, those were credentials enough.

In 1993 Huang's future in American government had been as unsettled as Clinton's China policy. His application bounced around the bureaucracy for nearly a year until January 1994 when the White House personnel office found Huang a potential spot as deputy assistant secretary at the Department of Commerce. It was not until that fateful week in June 1994 that Huang would actually be hired.

There is a good deal of dispute as to how and why he was hired, a problem compounded by the deaths, both on a Croatian hillside, of his immediate boss, Charles Meissner, and Meissner's boss, Ron Brown. According to his subordinates, Meissner felt pressured by Brown to achieve "ethnic diversity."[28] Nolanda Hill, however, would tell Brian Ross on ABC's *Prime Time Live* that Brown believed "the White House put [Huang] there," and in this instance, added Hill, "The White House meant Hillary Clinton."[29] Whoever was responsible, Huang went to Commerce not to advance America's interests but the Riadys' and, by extension, China's.

Huang himself has taken the Fifth Amendment on this and other questions. So has Mark Middleton, the only White House aide to do so. So indeed has Webb Hubbell. As to James Riady, he has fled the country.

The sequence of events beginning with the meeting between Hillary Clinton and Hubbell on June 20 adds credibility to Hill's claim. A week after that meeting, Hubbell received a $100,000 payoff from the Riadys for no other ostensible purpose than to keep his mouth shut. Ever since the transaction, Hubbell has done just that. On that same day, in a likely quid pro quo, Huang received notice of his imminent hiring. He went to work at Commerce a few weeks later. Adds Hill with conviction, "Ron did not know that Huang had been hired until after the fact."

Huang's actual work was icing on the cake. The Thompson Committee makes this striking admission: "Although Huang's first day at Commerce was July 18, 1994, he was granted his first security clearance in January 1994."[30] In the case of both the appointment and the hiring, however, Brown was in no position to protest.

Just as Huang was receiving "three security clearances in succession, each at the top secret level," Brown was receiving his own "clearance" in the Vietnam affair. To secure that clearance, Brown ceded his ability to say *no* to the White House. To secure its own clearance on Whitewater, the White House ceded its ability to say *no* to the Riadys.

They had all given up so much for so little. Nineteen ninety-four may have been an anxious year, but no worse. Desperation was yet to come.

17 | FLYING HIGH

As things turned out, the Justice Department cleared Brown of his Vietnam charges rather in the nick of time. Just a week later, on February 10, 1994, without the taint of scandal, he was able to head up a delegation to Russia on the first of many large-scale trade missions.

As it also happened, on the very same day Brown left for Russia, an obscure Republican congressman from Pennsylvania, William Clinger, sent a letter of inquiry, the first of many he would send to Brown.[1]

The timing of these two events was coincidental. But there is a haunting fatefulness about it nonetheless. The pressure Clinger generated would eventually spur Brown to lead his last, fatal trade mission to the Balkans. But on that day in February 1994, neither Brown nor Clinger could have conceived of such an end.

At the time, Clinger was the ranking Republican member of the House Committee on Government Operations. In 1994 this meant little. Republicans had not controlled the House in forty years, and no one expected them to do so for another forty. In truth, Clinger had more title than power and far less of either than Brown.

The congressman had sent the letter at the urging of one of his staffers. When the staff member had learned of the Vietnam bribe allegations, he decided to pull Brown's financial disclosure forms and have a look. Although he found nothing about Vietnam in the file, he did discover Brown had once had holdings in telecommunications, an industry that comes under the purview of Commerce. Among the holdings that troubled

Clinger was one called First International, a company that had, in fact, been conceived to explore communications opportunities in Eastern Europe and Russia. Remember the name.[2]

Clinger began by sending letters to Nolanda Hill. Brown begged her not to respond, and she obliged him. Concerned, Clinger sent Brown a polite letter warning that the "mere appearance of a conflict of interest could severely erode public confidence." Brown blew him off. Three weeks later the Commerce ethics officer wrote back to Clinger telling him "we do not think it is appropriate" to answer many of the questions he had asked.[3]

"It was sort of arrogant," said Clinger. "He felt he didn't have to respond. We were in the minority, and at that point, we couldn't compel him to do anything."[4] Brown would come to regret his arrogance. Vexed and more than a little vengeful, Clinger would become Brown's Javert. Unknown to Clinger, however, the rock he turned over was but a small one in a field of boulders. Starting that fateful day, February 10, Ron Brown was about to redefine the meaning of "conflict of interest."

Even in a party of saints, the international trade mission had the potential to corrupt. And few who traveled with Brown to Russia ran any immediate risk of beatification, certainly not Roger Tamraz.

Tamraz would get his Warholian "fifteen minutes" by serving up the one moment of comic relief in the otherwise plodding 1997 Thompson hearings. The Lebanese oil financier had donated $300,000 to the DNC and gotten in return an invite to several White House functions, including a dinner at which he had asked the president for help on a Central-Asian pipeline deal. When questioned by Senator Joseph Lieberman whether he got his money's worth in access, Tamraz, brash and self-aware, joked, "I think next time I'll give $600,000."[5]

At the time of the Russian trip, however, about the only place one could see an image of Tamraz was on an Interpol bulletin board. As Senator Thompson pointed out, a Lebanese court had charged Tamraz with embezzling $200 million from a bank. A Jordanian court had convicted him *in absentia* for the same fraud and sentenced him to two years in prison. A French court had ordered him to pay $56 million in connection with a financial dispute. And there was an outstanding Interpol warrant for his arrest. Said Thompson in dismay, "That was information that presumably [the Clinton administration] had access to."[6]

No matter. In February 1994 President Clinton authorized Tamraz to travel with Brown on the "presidential business development mission" to Russia. Once there, administration officials arranged a series of meetings between Tamraz and Russian energy officials from the GAZPROM bureau. A month later, according to a now declassified telegram, Commerce Department representatives in Russia were ordered to arrange meetings between Tamraz and the Russian first deputy minister of fuels and energy.[7] "Commerce" to be sure, but one cannot envision Herbert Hoover authorizing anything of the sort.

Of course, not all those traveling with Brown were as shady as Tamraz. On board, too, were executives from more reputable energy companies like Enron. In fact, Enron execs would become frequent flyers on Brown trade missions. On the last one, with impressive clairvoyance, they chose to take their own plane.

In retrospect, there was a relative innocence about the Russian trip. No doubt, by picking and choosing among industries, the Clinton administration was creating a sense of indebtedness among those chosen. But at this stage, even if there were expectations of future donations, there was no known quid pro quo.

Besides, the idea of selecting specific companies for promotion was not at all alien to Democratic party principles. In his ambitious 1983 book, *The Next American Frontier*, Labor Secretary Robert Reich made the case for doing just that.

"Business enterprises," he argued, "will largely replace geographic jurisdictions as conduits of government support for economic and human development."[8] Not all business enterprises either. In Reich's America, government support would focus on those businesses that had willingly restructured themselves along government-specified lines.[9] This practice, known informally as "picking winners," would be much bruited about in Democratic circles before Japan's fall from economic grace cast doubt on the wisdom of a formal "industrial policy."

Despite his Harvard professorship, Reich's sway extended well beyond the ivy tower. Over the past decade, he had emerged as the most influential economic philosopher of his party. The 1984 Democratic nominee for president, Walter Mondale, called *The Next American Frontier*, "One of the most important works of the decade."[10]

Clinton was also a fan. Every one of Reich's books, some of them dog-eared, sat on the shelf next to his desk in the Arkansas governor's mansion.

Reich's most recent book, *The Work of Nations*, had served as the blueprint for the Clinton campaign book, *Putting People First*.[11]

Reich, however, had written his books for people like himself—idealists, old-fashioned liberals who really did believe in "putting people first." There were, however, too few such people in the Clinton administration to achieve anything like critical mass. In the first-year budget battle, cabinet liberals had been steamrollered by the likes of Texan treasury secretary "Loophole Lloyd" Bentsen and Wall Street wizard Robert Rubin and reduced to near silence ever since.

Once at a cabinet meeting, as Reich listened to the president "drone on," he made a list of the *"real* cabinet." His quick synopses are instructive. Two relevant samples:

> Secretary of the Treasury—Secretary of Wall Street (bond traders, investment bankers, institutional investors, money managers, the very rich)
>
> Secretary of Commerce—Secretary of Corporate America (Fortune 500 companies, global conglomerates, top exporters and importers, local chambers of commerce)[12]

In the hands of political opportunists, Reich's ideas were potentially dangerous. They could be used to justify the creation of a favored class of oligarchs who would be "picked" not for their value to the nation but for their value to the White House. With the active backing of the United States government, they would then go forth to exploit the world and share their riches with the administration that made it possible. In this light, Roger Tamraz differed from his fellow petitioners largely in his self-awareness.

The one industrialist who perhaps best embodied this phenomenon was Loral Aerospace's chairman, Bernard Schwartz. An accountant by background, Schwartz took over the small, struggling Loral Corporation in 1972 when its stock was valued at thirty-six cents a share. He then produced ninety-six consecutive quarters of improved earnings before selling it to Lockheed Martin in 1996 for fifty-one dollars a share.[13] The two things Schwartz had lots of were moxie and money.

In 1994, nearing seventy, the ever-ambitious Schwartz was about to shift his area of interest from the defense industry to telecommunications, specifically a cellular satellite network. Not coincidentally, he was about to get interested in politics. In the 1992 election cycle, Schwartz had donated only $12,500 to help elect Clinton, chump change for a man of his wealth. In the 1996 cycle, he would donate $632,000 and emerge as the single largest donor to the Democratic party.[14] In return for his largesse, he was allowed to sell out this country and walk away a free man. Ron Brown would help—but only to a point.

In 1994, Schwartz had almost as much baggage as Brown. Five years earlier Loral had pled guilty to charges of conspiring to defraud the U.S. government on an Air Force radar contract. As a consequence, the company had to pay a $1.5 million fine and was put on a "watch list" for national security officials. Schwartz understood, however, that for him to launch his planned satellite network he would need to clean the slate.

Schwartz had a specific goal. In 1986, in the wake of the *Challenger* disaster, the U.S. government had decided to allow U.S. satellite makers to launch civilian telecommunications satellites in, among other countries, China. It was understood such a technology transfer might well help China, but America's real focus at the time was the Soviet Union. Strengthening China's hand in that rivalry had its advantages.

Understandably, after the massacre of pro-democracy students in Tiananmen Square in 1989, the U.S. ceased all military and space cooperation with China. Congress promptly passed a law suspending the licensing of exports of certain items to China, including U.S.-origin commercial satellites for launch on Chinese vehicles. To waive these suspensions, the president was obliged to report to Congress on a case-by-case basis that it was in the national interest to do so. President Bush signed nine such waivers before leaving office in 1993, and Clinton quietly reissued the waivers on those missiles yet to be launched.[15]

By 1994, when Schwartz was seeking his own waivers, the geo-political balance had shifted significantly. The Soviet Union no longer existed, and Russia was not an active threat. As the Pentagon fully understood—if the White House refused to—America faced only one potentially hostile, nuclear-capable superpower in the foreseeable future, and that was the People's Republic of China.[16]

Schwartz had a good idea how to ease potential White House resistance. In the early summer of 1994, just about the same time the Riadys were bailing out Webster Hubbell, Schwartz made a "soft-money" contribution to the DNC in the amount of $100,000. In two months, Ron Brown would be leading a major "presidential business development mission" to Hong Kong and three cities in the People's Republic, and Schwartz wanted to make damn sure he was on board.

One searches in vain here for a coherent, overarching conspiracy. The hallmark of the Clinton White House was its utter disorganization. In his memoirs, aide George Stephanopoulos calls its atmosphere "dysfunctional."[17] In his book, *The Choice*, Robert Woodward describes a White House that "teetered on the edge of management chaos."[18] Robert Reich talks about a "chronically undisciplined president"[19] and a "wildly disorganized White House."[20] The strategy to extort campaign donations on trade missions seems equally improvised and chaotic, but no less real for its contrivance.

As to the orchestration of that China trip, according to Nolanda Hill, "Ron didn't have anything to do with it." She contends the Clintons used Undersecretary Charles Meissner as facilitator because they did not trust Brown with the Riady connection. "It was Ron's [belief]," says Hill, "that it was a lucrative and closely held association, and they didn't want to share the pie." She believes the real decisions were being made in "Hillary's office."

China was a lucrative pie indeed; many executives wanted a slice. One was Sanford Robertson, a partner in Robertson, Stephens & Company, a San Francisco investment banking firm. Given the modest size of his business, Robertson, too, knew he would have to hustle to get a seat. On April 11, he sent a fawning letter to Brown, a classic of its type.

"I have read with great interest of your efforts in providing an economic balance to the current China MFN debate," Robertson begins with a bit of flattery. "The *Wall Street Journal* indicated that you have a trip of businessmen planned for August of this year. I would like to be considered a candidate for the trip."

In the body of the letter, Robertson lays out his company's plans in China and boasts of its clever hiring of the son of a prominent Tiananmen henchman, all of which is fairly straightforward. It is in the seemingly casual "P.S." that Robertson makes his strongest case:

> It has been fund-raising season out here for the Senate, and we've had events at our home for Feinstein, Lieberman, and Cooper. I wish you were still head of the DNC for the December [*sic*] elections, but you are obviously doing a great job at Commerce.[21]

Much to his good fortune, Robertson had been an early Clinton supporter and fund-raiser. In the 1991-92 election cycle, Robertson and his wife each gave the Democratic party $35,000. In the 1993-94 election cycle, Robertson gave the Democratic party $50,000. He got to go.

Ed Lupenberger, chairman and chief executive officer of the Entergy Corporation, likewise worked all the angles to get on board. A later investigation turned up an Entergy inter-office memo written by "JCB"—since identified as J. "Chip" Brown, the head of Entergy's Hong Kong office—that illuminates the company's efforts.

Chip Brown had traveled to Washington and there met with Jude Kearney, a deputy assistant secretary at Commerce and a former staffer to Clinton when governor. According to the memo, Kearney "indicated competitive nature of being selected to ride on the plane with the secretary. Also [Kearney] indicated that politics of the situation were important and he as a political appointee would push those that were 'politically connected' to the Clinton administration and to the Democrats."[22]

As the parent company of Arkansas Power & Light (AP&L), Entergy was nicely connected. Clinton had enjoyed a mutually beneficial relationship with AP&L for years. Entergy had also given generously to the DNC and to the Democratic Leadership Council at the time Clinton served as its chairman. Lupenberger also got to go.

In the final count, twenty-five executives flew to China with Brown on a modified 707 that once served as Air Force One. Research done by PBS's *Frontline* showed that more than 70 percent of the business delegates on the China trip were donors to Clinton and the Democrats.[23] From her conversations with Brown, Hill took the impression the solicitation was "explicit." It was, she says, "a thinly veiled shakedown situation."

Those who were not donors had other ways of repaying favors. Brown also invited along a woman by the name of Yla Eason, CEO of Olmec Toys. This was heady company for Eason. With Brown and her fellow executives, she stopped first in Hong Kong and then traveled on a midnight cruise aboard the so-called "love boat," the Pacific Princess. Not surprisingly, Eason was reported to be "close" to the late commerce secretary. After the trip, Brown sent her a short standard thank-you note, personally writing in, "You are wonderful!" One cannot imagine his writing the same to Sanford Robertson.

Eason had taken credit for pioneering the term "ethnically correct" in the toy industry. Her toys were to have the appropriate skin tones and features of blacks and Hispanics. This Harvard MBA, however, had no intention of enabling blacks and Hispanics to make these toys at her facilities in a Richmond, Virginia tax-free enterprise zone.

According to recently declassified materials, Brown arranged for Eason to meet in Beijing with the president of the China National Toy Association, which was under the direct control of the communist State Council and the Chinese Army. Eason contracted with her Chinese partners to transform a line of modified GI Joe dolls into so-called "Bronze Bombers" and unleash them on American minority families in 1995. As a result of her efforts, President Clinton personally gave her the 1997 Business Enterprise Award.

The story, alas, has an unhappy denouement. When the relentless reporter and researcher Charles Smith attempted to question Eason about her relationship to Brown and whether, as he suspected, Brown had been taking a cut of her profits for his efforts on her behalf, Eason promptly left Virginia and disappeared.

Probably just as well. Creditors filed in court against Eason and seized the remaining Olmec inventory, including her final unwittingly ironic inspiration—sixteen hundred Malcolm X dolls made by slave labor. As of last report, she was still in hiding after leaving $1.2 million in unpaid debts, and Olmec was history.[24]

The other participants fared better. Entergy signed two major contracts while on the trip, with Brown in attendance at the first signing ceremony. According to the contract, Entergy would receive a $465 million share of a $1 billion deal with the Lippo Group to manage and expand Lippo's power plant in northern China. Entergy's second contract for an estimated $400 million was signed in Guangzhou to help build two 660-megawatt generating stations.[25]

As to Loral, Brown publicly praised its Globalstar cellular telephone system before an audience of Chinese telecommunications officials. Soon afterwards, Loral nabbed a $250 million cellular phone deal with the Ministry of Telecommunications. The *Boston Globe* would report that during the same trade mission Schwartz cut a deal with China's Commission on Science Technology and Industry for National Defense, the notorious COSTIND, which involved the use of highly sensitive encryption technology. By all accounts, COSTIND was an intelligence agency whose primary function was to acquire advanced technology with military applications. More on encryption later. [26]

The ever fulsome Sanford Robertson did not do too badly either. "Although my projects were less visible than the billion dollar contracts you were helping consummate," he wrote Brown afterwards, "the trip was extremely worthwhile for our firm. By basking in the reflected glow of your trip we were able to underwrite projects in China, and Hong Kong (as well as Japan)."

Robertson followed this up with a letter to the president, thanking him for allowing Robertson to participate in such an "economic and diplomatic triumph." The next paragraphs make one suspect Brown put him up to it:

> One of the highlights was observing Ron Brown in the way he represented the United States. His diplomatic skills were superb, particularly in the meeting with Li Peng. He deftly navigated the human rights issues by obtaining an agreement on further talks, and then moved directly into the economic issues at hand, i.e. helping Chrysler, Sprint, and others with their joint ventures.
>
> The twenty-five CEOs were all very impressed with his diplomatic and commercial skills. We all hoped that you and your administration could find increasing ways to utilize these abilities. [27]

"Human rights, schmuman rights" indeed! Brown was loving it. How could he not? Says Nolanda Hill, "He thought [the trip] was the greatest thing since blue cheese." He would call Hill, then in Uganda on business, to describe the sights, the food, and even the elegant jewelry of the women. The Chinese were so respectful and so deferential. They treated him like he was more popular than Clinton.

It would never get any better. The world of the Clintons would fall to hell in two months, and as to Brown, his repressed anxiety about the Chinese would soon enough surface as a very real and irrepressible fear.

18 | CALAMITY

In the early morning of November 8, 1994, Nolanda Hill was one agitated woman. She had just voted in Dallas, and the vibes were all wrong. After voting, she flew immediately back to Washington. Soon after she arrived, Ron Brown called and asked to come over to watch the returns.

Brown was feeling uneasy as well, less about the outcome of the election than his own role in it. The White House had been consulting him for nothing other than the distribution of "preacher money." His last official act, in fact, had been to deliver a large pile of it to Jesse Jackson.[1]

If this money followed its historic flow, it would pass through some select middlemen and into the hands of those black ministers who had long since sold out their respective flocks for the perks of political power. After deductions for "campaign jackets" and "buttons" and other such untraceable transactions, the ministers would pass out what was left to those would-be voters who needed a little incentive to get to the polls for a midterm election about which they could otherwise care less.[2]

Brown hated this assignment. He was the man who had engineered the Democratic comeback in 1992—"I couldn't have done it without you," Clinton would eulogize him—and here he was two years later, reduced to the role of a bagman.

By saving the dirty work for Brown, the White House freed the less sullied among its key people to stump for candidates. As the most popular of the White House aides, with his own quasi-rock star aura, George Stephanopoulos got to play some of the better venues. For him, the most memorable appearance as well as "the most foreboding" was one he made in his native Queens on behalf of Democratic party icon, Mario Cuomo, then running for reelection as governor of New York. "Within a few minutes," remembers Stephanopoulos, "I knew something was wrong."[3]

Cuomo was no longer his eloquent, inspirational self. "His voice was tired, and his words were hard—his new favorite seemed to be 'vindication.'" As Stephanopoulos flew back to Washington that night, he allowed that perhaps the governor had just had a bad night, "But it sure feels down out there."[4]

The White House sent Robert Reich out on the stump as well. Lacking Stephanopoulos's star power, the diminutive Reich was dispatched to outposts like Steubenville, Ohio, to champion obscure candidates he had never before met. And yet, for what it was worth, when Reich delivered the traditional liberal Democratic message in that particular Steubenville union hall, he managed to rouse the geriatric audience to a standing ovation.[5]

Reich found his fellow cabinet members much harder to rouse. The day after the Steubenville speech, November 3, he sat among them and marveled how far they had drifted off base and how deeply they had sunk into denial.

"Disaster looms," recalls Reich, "but you wouldn't know it sitting here." Leon Panetta dryly introduced the subjects of the day: the president's upcoming trip to Indonesia, free trade with Chile, passage of GATT, deficit reduction. The cold bureaucracy of it all disheartened Reich.

"What about good schools," he dared to venture, "tax credits for college, job training, a higher minimum wage, stronger unions?"

Treasury Secretary Lloyd Bentsen cut him off. "I don't think we need to worry about union support in 1996." Panetta then finessed the meeting back on course, and that was all for Reich. For a moment he contemplated making a scene, but that might have resulted in the one consequence all minor cabinet members feared—"banishment from the loop." In this regards at least, Ron Brown was not unique.[6]

Only one man in America seemed willing to tell Bill Clinton the truth, and that was his on-again, off-again consultant Dick Morris. Feeling alone and isolated in the days before the election, Clinton called Morris for advice. Morris laid it out unsparingly: the 1994 congressional elections were going to be "a calamity."[7] Morris predicted the Democrats would suffer huge losses.

Clinton didn't want to hear it. Sure, the Democrats would lose a few seats. If historical patterns prevailed, they would give up maybe one seat in the Senate and a dozen in the House, but they had seats to spare. The Democrats, after all, had controlled the House for forty years. That, they could not lose.

On Election Day, November 8, Clinton went about business as usual. He did a few radio shows in the morning to jump-start some critical races, met with the president of Iceland, of all places, and inevitably checked with Morris on the exit polls. The early results were horrifying. Clinton could not believe what was taking place all across America, and he was powerless to stop it.[8]

Hill and Brown ate barbecue that evening and sweated through the results. One state after another was evicting its Democratic office holders from positions of power. "You better fasten your seat belt," Hill told Brown. "We have had it." For the two of them, the threat was imminent and personal. Republicans in Congress, those Brown had been ignoring for the last two years, were no longer going to be a nuisance. They were going to be a danger. Adds Hill, "I knew that Ron's goose was cooked."

After dinner, Brown stopped by the war room in the White House. He called Hill on the way home and told her the scene was like a funeral, only much worse.

"Pompeii after Vesuvius," recalls Reich. "Rome after the sacking. Richmond after Grant. Washington after yesterday's vote."

The results rocked DC. "People are dazed," notes Reich. "No one had expected quite this."[9] In a time of peace and economic growth, Democrats had lost an incredible fifty-two seats in the House and eight in the Senate. Mario Cuomo lost. House speaker Tom Foley lost. Popular Texas governor Ann Richards lost to George Bush's almost unheard of oldest son, George W. Bush. Of the twenty candidates Reich stumped for, seventeen lost, including Greg Didinato of Steubenville fame, who lost badly. Incredibly, not a single Republican incumbent running for the House, the Senate, or governor had lost anywhere in America.

"The 1994 defeat devastated Clinton," remembers Dick Morris.[10] But this was more than a defeat for his party. This was personal. "The election itself is being described as a total repudiation of Bill Clinton and the Democrats," Reich observed at the time, a "fundamental realignment."[11] "His presidency," writes Evan Thomas in his sympathetic account, "was in tatters."[12]

After days of anger and self-pity, Bill Clinton began to focus again on the one organizing principle that had directed his life to date. "All that mattered was his survival," Clinton aide George Stephanopoulos writes of his former boss. "Everyone else had to fall in line: his staff, his cabinet, the country, even his wife."[13] Stephanopoulos speaks here of another circumstance, but the principle was eternal. It had guided Clinton's entire political career. Forget the party. Forget the promises. Clinton had to be reelected.

Serendipitously, just a week after the election, Ron Brown and the Clintons headed to the one place in the world most capable of nurturing a Clinton comeback, the Riady home base of Indonesia.

The Riadys had bailed Clinton out as governor when he mismanaged Arkansas's Teacher's Retirement Fund. They had rescued him twice on the 1992 campaign trail. They had seemingly bought off Webster Hubbell before he had to seek a deal with Whitewater prosecutors. In the spirit of *Guanxi,* they had shown their friendship.

Soon enough, in Utah of all unlikely places, Clinton would appear to reciprocate in what may have been the most shocking single transaction of his presidency.

Indonesia set the terms for the visit. Only a few days before Clinton's departure, an Indonesian court sentenced labor leader Muchtar Pakpahan to three years in prison, the sixth union official to be convicted in connection with recent worker riots. Sixteen of his colleagues were still on trial in what looked to the world like the busting of a "dangerously independent" union. U.S. officials "deplored" the sentence and then headed east to do business.[14]

Says Nolanda Hill, "It was major-league Riady payback time."

The mood on this trip was sour from the beginning. On the seemingly endless flight over, Stephanopoulos reports, "The president and Hillary rarely left their cabin."[15] Given the nature of that relationship, this could not have been Bill's idea. Again, what transpired in those long painful hours has been lost to history—in *Living History,* there is no trip to Indonesia—but from this moment on, the presidency would assume a much sharper edge.

Ron Brown too was feeling the pressure. As chief international fundraiser, how could he not? The Clintons had "heavily stressed" the trip's importance.[16] They not only had to impress the Riadys on their own home turf, but they also had to start squeezing the CEOs accompanying them in a more systematic way. Hill believes it was about this time that the $100,000 donation morphed from a discreet expectation into the price of admission. As she told Brown, "They are going to use you and use you and use you until you are such damaged goods they can't use you anymore."

The Indonesian trip boasted an impressive cast of characters. Traveling with the president and first lady were Bruce Lindsey, the president's tight-lipped confidant, and the soon-to-be-indicted Webster Hubbell. This group met twice with Indonesian plutocrats James and Mochtar Riady.

Joining them all at the Asian Pacific Economic Conference in Jakarta were the notorious Hawaiian fund raisers Gene and Nora Lum as well as any number of shadowy figures like Little Rock restaurateur Charlie Trie and Thai citizen Pauline Kanchanalak, both later charged by the Justice Department's campaign finance task force with funneling hundreds of thousands of dollars in foreign contributions to the DNC.

Ron Brown, of course, was there as well. He could sense the chill in the air. The charmed trip to China, just two months behind him, seemed a lifetime ago. As he often did when he was fretful or depressed, he called Hill frequently. In this particular case he was anxious about the way Clinton was treating him. Hill describes it as a kind of a black version of *Guanxi*—Clinton was letting it be known that Brown "carried his water."

It was Brown who introduced Clinton to an International Business Community meeting in Jakarta on November 16. "I thought if I keep coming back here," joked the president, "I might become as well-known in Asia as Secretary Brown is." Dispensing quickly with the odd, ironic humor, Clinton plunged into a speech that had to have dismayed any traditional Democrat or human rights activist who chanced to hear or read it.

"Keeping America on the front lines of economic opportunity has been my first priority since I took office," Clinton claimed, adding later, "The second thing we are doing is working hard to expand trade and investment."

Clinton then chided traditional Democrats for their historic "adversarial" relationship with business and Republicans for their "inactive" one. In a "departure" from the philosophy of both parties, boasted Clinton, "We have unashamedly been an active partner in helping our business enterprises to win contracts abroad."

Unashamedly?

As to human rights, Clinton's ambivalence about his own nation left him seemingly powerless to recommend much of anything. "We do not seek to impose our vision of the world on others," he groveled. "Indeed, we continue to struggle with our own inequities and our own shortcomings."[17]

If Clinton's comments dismayed Indonesian union leaders and the oppressed residents of East Timor, they surely warmed the heart of host Mohamed Suharto, the president of Indonesia. Human rights activists would credit the murderous, long-reigning autocrat with as many as two million notches on his very crowded belt.

The observer has to marvel at the implosion of this party's moral base, certainly this administration's. Just a few years earlier, Democrats in power routinely championed the so-called Sullivan Principles, which absolutely "imposed our vision of the world" on South Africa.

This time, although human rights groups pressed the White House for a comparable set of business guidelines, the White House would not respond. When Brown did circulate the draft of a voluntary human rights code to several major CEOs before the Indonesia trip, they and their allies successfully lobbied the White House to scotch it. [18]

The CEOs, like John Bryson of Mission Energy, had more important things on their minds than human rights. On August 26, Bryson had written a "Dear Ron" letter to Brown. In it, he asked Brown to "indicate your support for ADB funding" for a massive new coal-fired electric plant for Indonesia called the Paiton project. [19]

Also in August, John Huang met with the CIA on the same subject. On September 30, seven weeks before the trip, a team from Mission had met with the Commerce Department and the State Department to review Mission's plans. [20]

For the record, the "ADB" referenced above is the Asian Development Bank, a multinational institution created to fight poverty in Asia and the Pacific. The bank has no larger shareholder than the United States. Mission CEO Bryson asked Brown for his support because the ADB was reluctant to approve the loan. There was one good reason for its reluctance. According to handwritten Commerce Department notes, retrieved by researcher Charles Smith through the Freedom of Information Act, "ADB is still considering this, [because] of very minimal involvement of Indo ruling family in the Mission project."

Although Paiton was hailed as the first "private" electric plant in Indonesia, "private" had a different meaning in Indonesia than it did elsewhere. In this case it meant owned and operated, at least in part, by the "Indo ruling family," the Suhartos.

According to Commerce Department notes from John Huang's file, a certain percentage of this project was set aside for a management company owned by Suharto's daughter, Titek Prabowo, and her brother-in-law Hashim Djojohadikusumo. The cut for her and the other relatives was to be a $50 million upfront loan to be paid back through presumed profits generated by the plant.

This arrangement could not have shocked Ron Brown. No doubt it reminded him of everyday business in the city of Washington. According to Commerce notes, however, it did trouble the Asian Development Bank. The ABD was reportedly "skiddish" [sic] about offering what amounted to a $50 million bribe to the family of a corrupt oligarch paid, at least in part, by the U.S. taxpayer.

It was on the issue of "first family" involvement with the Paiton power project that Huang had met with the CIA. What the CIA did not know is that after the meeting Huang left the Commerce Department and walked across the street where, according to the Thompson Committee, he had "a secret office." This office was located within the larger offices of Stephens Inc. Stephens, one recalls, is the Little Rock-based investment-banking firm with which the Riadys had a long relationship. There, in private, Huang proceeded to place a three-hour call to his former employer, the Riadys' Lippo Group. [21]

Lippo had a lot at stake. Mission Energy, as it turns out, was part of a larger consortium known as Edison International, and Edison was a Lippo partner. There is more. Suharto in-law Hashim had secured an exclusive, no bid, no-cut contract to supply clean coal to the Paiton power plant. Hashim's financial backer in his Indonesian coal mining business was none other than Mochtar Riady. The Lippo Group controlled one of the only two commercially viable low-sulfur coal mines in the world, this one conveniently located near the Paiton plant in Indonesia.

It gets worse. Mission CEO John Bryson donated money to the Clinton-Gore campaign and also to President Clinton's new and voracious legal defense fund. And so the Mission Energy people did get to go to Indonesia with Brown and the Clintons.

Although the Asian Development Bank had the good sense not to make the loan, Mission plowed right on, securing the loan through commercial sources. When the deal went through, Bryson thanked Brown profusely for his help in making it happen. [22]

What happens next on the American end of this saga raises a host of seriously troubling questions. The CNN.com report on the day it happened, September 18, 1996, well captures the general tenure of the reporting. "Clinton Declares Utah Canyons A National Monument," reads the headline.[23]

CNN's usually observant Wolf Blitzer reported that using the Grand Canyon as "his picture perfect backdrop," Clinton "unilaterally" declared a new 1.7 million-acre national monument seventy miles away in southern Utah.

"We're saying, very simply, our parents and grandparents saved the Grand Canyon for us," Clinton told the cheering crowd. "Today, we will save the Grand Escalante Canyons and the Kaiparowitz Plateaus of Utah for our children."

To his credit, Blitzer did not shy from the implicit controversy. He reported the people of Utah were "furious." They claimed it was "a land grab" by the federal government "at the economic expense of the state." The fact that Clinton made the announcement in Arizona, a potentially winnable state in the upcoming election, only angered them more.

The question looms, of course, as to why Clinton would make so bold a move just two months before the election. True, it would play well to environmentalists, but Clinton had their votes already, and there were many safer gestures he could have made. Blitzer raised the issue of coal, perhaps $1 trillion worth of clean, low-sulfur coal that would never be mined.

Blitzer, however, did not know the deeper significance of the coal. Clinton surely must have. Said the president of this grand environmental gesture, "We can't have mines everywhere and we shouldn't have mines that threaten our national treasures."

No, not everywhere, just in Indonesia. In a stroke of the pen, Clinton had handed the Riadys a monopoly on the world's supply of low-sulfur coal.

One does not need to be a conspiracy theorist to connect the dots between Utah and Indonesia. The FBI had made the connection as well. Consider the following field notes from an FBI interview with Huang:

> HUANG laughed in response to questions concerning J. RIADY's interest in Utah coal restrictions. J. RIADY's coal interests were minimal. Indonesia had significant infrastructure problems which prohibited the development of its coal resources.[24]

Huang was lying. The Riadys had a powerful interest, and they would exploit it for all it was worth. In fact, at the Paiton plant, the price of the coal exceeded the price of the electricity it produced. Each kilowatt generated drove the plant deeper into debt. Of course, this meant there were no profits, which meant Suharto's daughter and her brother-in-law did not have to pay back their up-front $50 million loan. (If this plot sounds familiar, it is because it is nearly identical to that of Mel Brooks' play and movie, *The Producers*.)

PLN, the state Indonesian power company, caught the drift of the plot. In 1999, the company sued the Clinton administration. Its attorneys charged U.S. officials knew the Paiton power plant contract to be awash in "corruption, collusion, and nepotism" from the beginning. In December of that year, an Indonesian court ruled in its favor. The PLN estimated it had lost over $18 billion in total from Suharto corruption inside U.S. government sponsored power plant contracts.[25]

By the way, Enron contributed its own share to that $18 billion loss. But in the crush for cash after the 1994 election, how was anyone to notice?

19 DARK BUDDHA

January 6, 1995, was not a cheery day at the White House. The poll published in the *Washington Post* that morning surely rattled the Clintons and sent the more ambitious among their staff scurrying for the want ads.

The president's approval rating had dipped to an unnervingly low 45 percent. The rating of his most likely Republican opponent, Senate majority leader Bob Dole, was cresting at 62 percent. The only place where Clinton bested Dole was in the "disapprove" column, and here by a chilling 51-25 percent. Bill Clinton was staring down the barrel of a one-term presidency.[1]

"I can tell you," DNC finance chair Terry McAuliffe would later testify, "the political mood at the time clearly was that he had no chance of winning again."[2]

Ron Brown was one of those thinking about his career options. Republicans surely weren't going to hold him over. Indeed, the Republican "Contract with America" that had swept the party to power called for the elimination of his own bailiwick, the Commerce Department. The libertarian Cato Institute, then at the peak of its influence on Congress, trashed Commerce, calling it "perhaps the worst example of political pork"[3] and "a cog in the racial spoils system."[4]

Like the Russians at Stalingrad, the Clintons had few options but to fight on. In early December 1994, in the White House treaty room, Bill and Hillary Clinton held a secret meeting with the one man who could possibly turn the tide of battle, political consultant Dick Morris.

As is well enough known, Morris had worked both sides of the aisle throughout his career, a flexibility that merely sowed distrust on either side. More than a decade earlier, he had helped Clinton regain the governor's office after an embarrassing post-first-term defeat. In 1990, however, Morris and the Clintons went their separate ways. The story behind his departure from the Clinton camp is worth telling as it reveals both Bill Clinton's capacity for violence and Hillary's for covering it up.

To date, Hillary Clinton has shown no inclination to share unpleasant truths. *Living History*, her autobiography, is almost as free of conflict as her book on Socks the Cat. There is no tension with Ron Brown, no bitter trip to Indonesia, no fight with Dick Morris, no Lani Guinier at all. She casually attributes Morris's refusal to work on the 1994 congressional campaign to his problems with their staff. "People were so mean to me," says the Dick Morris of Hillary's memory.[5]

In an open letter to Hillary Clinton in *National Review Online*, Morris offered a more vivid accounting of events. At the time, as Morris relates, Clinton was facing a serious challenge in the gubernatorial primary. Worried he was falling behind his opponent, Clinton "verbally assaulted" Morris for not giving his campaign more time. When the offended Morris turned and stalked out of the room, Clinton followed.

> Bill ran after me, tackled me, threw me to the floor of the kitchen in the mansion and cocked his fist back to punch me. You [Hillary] grabbed his arm and, yelling at him to stop and get control of himself, pulled him off me.

Morris also volunteers that when the story threatened to surface again during the 1992 presidential campaign, Hillary told him to "say it never happened."[6]

Desperate times, however, called for desperate measures, and so Morris was summoned once again, this time by Hillary herself.[7] At their first get-together, Morris insisted on weekly meetings thereafter, and the president agreed.[8] For the first month, Hillary attended the meetings and then strategically withdrew.

As Morris relates, Clinton would share Morris's advice and the polling data with Hillary, and "she read every word." When he encountered Hillary, Morris adds, "She showed familiarity with every bit of it." It would be April before anyone else in the White House even knew these meetings were taking place.[9]

In late January 1995, David Maraniss's book on Clinton, *First in His Class*, hit the bookstores. The book recounts a less than flattering story Morris had told about Hillary Clinton, and upon its publication, she promptly froze him out.

"There is no colder feeling on the planet," says Morris.[10] By the summer, however, the relationship had thawed, and Morris and Hillary Clinton began to hold private biweekly meetings.

The rules of the game, which had been only loosely followed to this point, were about to be scrapped altogether. With more discipline than they had done in regards to anything else since coming to town, the Clintons were preparing to launch what Senator Fred Thompson would call "the most corrupt political campaign in modern history."[11]

From the beginning, Morris insisted on one strategy above all others: filling the airwaves with TV ads early and relentlessly. "Week after week, month after month," says Morris, "from early July 1995 more or less continually until election day in '96, sixteen months later, we bombarded the public with ads."[12]

In the 1992 campaign, the unknown Clinton spent roughly $40 million on advertising. In the 1996 campaign, the incumbent Clinton would spend $85 million.[13] Morris also insisted on a "virtually unlimited budget" for polling, and he got that too.[14]

With the DNC broke and demoralized after the 1994 rout, raising this much money was not easy. "For the Democrats," McAuliffe noted, "it was not a very optimistic time."[15] The lack of enthusiasm for Clinton even within his own party put the onus for raising money on the White House itself.

"You don't know, you don't have any remote idea," Clinton would tell Morris, "how hard I have to work, how hard Hillary has to work, how hard Al [Gore] has to work to raise this much money."[16] They were not the only ones who had to work hard. The White House started to lean on Ron Brown to gin up some revenue as well.

"There was nothing that was done after 1994," says Nolanda Hill, cutting to the quick, "that did not have payback."

The bulk of the money went to TV. An adept strategist, Morris understood the sympathies of the media and devised a strategy to accommodate their willful innocence. It was painfully simple, and it worked. To achieve "relative secrecy," he chose not to advertise at all in New York City or Washington DC and only occasionally in Los Angeles. "If these cities remained dark," recalls Morris, "the national press would not make an issue out of our ads—of this we felt sure."[17]

"No one in the media really caught on," confirms Robert Woodward in his book on the election.[18] The reason they did not catch on, as Morris well knew, is because they did not want to. The story the media chose not to watch unfold was an extraordinary one. The Thompson Committee does a concise job of summarizing what that story was:

> The president and his top advisors decided to raise money early for his re-election campaign. To accomplish their goal, the president and his top advisors took control of the DNC and designed a plan to engage in a historically aggressive fund-raising effort, utilizing the DNC as a vehicle for getting around federal election laws. The DNC ran television advertisements, created under the direct supervision of the president, which were specifically designed to promote the president's re-election.[19]

In the afterword to the paperback edition of *The Choice*, Robert Woodward has the grace to admit he "vastly underestimated the significance of money" in the campaign.[20] He notes too that the ads themselves—the most memorable of which showed Newt Gingrich and Bob Dole conspiring to let Medicare "wither on the vine"—"were deceptive enough to be appalling."[21] Evan Thomas, primary author of *Back from the Dead*, also admits that "one of the great underreported stories" of the campaign was how the Democrats, not the Republicans, engaged in "the really effective negative campaigning."[22]

Neither Thomas nor Woodward explains why, during the campaign itself, no one in the major media chose to tell the true story. An unprecedented series of untruthful, arguably illegal ads, which reached about 125 million Americans three times a week, should have been obvious to the media and scandalous from the outset. The scandal would have exploded if the media had asked where the money was coming from to pay for the ads and how it was being raised. Again, the Thompson Committee report proves instructive:

> The president and his aides demeaned the offices of the president and vice president, took advantage of minority groups, pulled down all the

barriers that would normally be in place to keep out illegal contributions, pressured policy makers, and left themselves open to strong suspicion that they were selling not only access to high-ranking officials, but policy as well. Millions of dollars were raised in illegal contributions, much of it from foreign sources.[23]

To get some sense of the media's self-deception, one need only contrast the Thompson version of the campaign with the one captured by the staff of *Newsweek*. As Joe Klein tells the story in the foreword of Thomas's book, "Bill Clinton, by shrewdness, luck and love of the game, came back from a near-death experience to win a second term."[24]

In his biography of Brown published two years after the Thompson Committee hearings, Steven Holmes makes no mention of the Thompson Committee per se and dismisses the work of the various congressional committees and news organizations in a paragraph. "With the lack of solid proof of the charge [selling seats]," writes Holmes approvingly, "it was constantly mocked by Brown's allies."[25]

Another unsung victim of the president's will to survive was the traditional Democratic agenda. In terms of policy, Morris' first priority was to insist Clinton "compete for the center."[26] The urgency of this competition maddened liberals in the White House. Stephanopoulos, among others, despised Dick Morris, the "dark Buddha" of his fevered imagination, and all he stood for.[27]

"I hated him," he says bluntly. "I wanted him gone." To Stephanopoulos, "triangulation" was little more than a "fancy word for betrayal."[28]

Labor Secretary Robert Reich felt the betrayal more deeply than anyone in the White House. In many ways, Reich represented what Brown might have been but never was: a sincerely committed liberal who used his office for advancing at least his own idea of the common good.

As might be expected, Reich had no use for Morris and his agenda. He conceived of Morris as "Mephistopheles, the corrupter of all means to an end that is never fully realized; the ultimate betrayer."[29] Reich watched with despair as Morris worked his dark magic on Bill Clinton, a man who he had once thought shared his ideals.

In fact, there may be no more damning account of Clinton's presidency than Reich's. He documents in painful detail Clinton's ongoing slouch to compromise. "To the extent B [Bill Clinton] relies on [Morris]," observes

Reich, "B will utter no word that challenges America, no thought that pricks the nation's conscience, no idea that causes us to reexamine old assumptions or grapple with issues we'd rather ignore."[30]

To Ron Brown, Robert Reich was simply "the midget."[31] In the beginning at least, Reich's conspicuous idealism bored Brown almost as much as did his pontificating on economics, a subject that held little interest for the more worldly Brown. As Brown got to know Reich better, he came to see his convictions were genuine. After a fashion, he even warmed up to him. Reich, in fact, would be the last cabinet member Brown would ever see. Still, rather than emulate Reich, Brown merely pitied him. This White House, he understood, had little use for sincerity.

Although Brown had few illusions about what this White House expected of him, he could still be surprised. Nolanda Hill shared one such surprise with Brown in early 1995, namely an impersonal fund-raising letter from Terry McAuliffe and the Democratic National Committee. The letter suggested that if Hill donated $100,000 to the DNC she too could go on a trade mission.

"I could speculate that in the Business Leadership brochure there might be the opportunity for donors to go on overseas trips with fellow donors and DNC personnel," McAuliffe would one day grudgingly admit under oath. "That I would concede."[32]

Hill was in Ecuador on business when the appeal reached her. "I got this letter," she remembers, "and just went ballistic." She immediately called Brown from the ambassador's house. "He was livid. He was furious," says Hill. "It made him so mad." Brown recoiled less at the ethics of McAuliffe's request than at the casual way the White House prostituted his services. He had begun to believe his own press clippings and see himself as a statesman, not a fundraiser. Says Hill, "He felt that [fund-raising] cheapened his missions."

For altogether different reasons, McAuliffe's appeal disturbed Larry Klayman as much as it did Hill or Brown. A little known trial lawyer for twenty years, Klayman had just launched a public interest firm called Judicial Watch. From his experience in trade law, he knew Commerce was one department that deserved watching.

When Klayman saw seat-hawking appeals coming from the DNC, Judicial Watch proceeded to submit a series of Freedom of Information Act (FOIA) requests to the Commerce Department for more information.

Brown sloughed these off, but as he would soon learn, one did not slough Klayman off easily.[33]

Nor William Clinger. As it happened, the same day Hill received the fund-raising letter from McAuliffe, she also got a letter from Clinger. The Republican sweep in November had elevated the Pennsylvania congressman from an easily ignored member of the minority to chairman of the House Committee on Government Operations. To say the least, he had not forgotten the slights of the past year. Brown's financial disclosure forms still intrigued him, and he was particularly keen on knowing more about a company called First International in which Hill and Brown were partners.

Despite Hill's entreaties, and with watchdogs now gnawing away on either leg, Brown still could not slow down. The pressure to raise money was too intense. Clinton shared with Dick Morris just how smothering that pressure was:

> I can't think. I can't act. I can't do anything but go to fund-raisers and shake hands. You want me to issue executive orders; I can't focus on a thing but the next fund-raiser. Hillary can't. Al can't—we're all getting sick and crazy because of it.[34]

And no one was getting sicker or crazier because of it than Ron Brown.

20 CO-TARGETED

It was tornado season in Dallas, mid-May 1995. An angry bruise of a cloud hung low over the corporate office park where Nolanda Hill had gone to meet her attorney on a routine matter. The wind whipped the trees outside the wall-to-wall windows, and the rain lashed the windows. For Hill, the weather seemed altogether appropriate for what would happen next.

Her secretary announced a call, an important one. It was the secretary of Commerce. Hill had grown used to these calls. Ron Brown called her often, sometimes too often. She took it nonetheless.

"I have some news for you that you are not going to like," said Brown, unsettling Hill right out of the chute. "That f—ing bitch did it. She did it. We have both been named as co-targets." Hill's head spun, and her stomach fell to her feet.

The woman in question, the subject of Brown's wrath, was Attorney General Janet Reno. What she "did" was call for an independent counsel, primarily to assess whether Brown had "accepted things of value" from Hill in exchange for his influence. Reno's going after Brown did not shock either of them. He had been the subject of an inquiry for months. Targeting Hill, however, had no precedent, and it unnerved them both.

When first conceived as part of the omnibus Ethics in Government Act of 1978, the Independent Counsel Act was written for the kind of people that had made "Watergate" a household word just a few years earlier. Although amended over time, the act continued to target much the same people as it did in 1978—government officials who betrayed their trust.

Specifically, the law—28 USCS § 591(b)—applied to the president and vice president, any number of executive officers above a certain salary, the director of the CIA and the commissioner of Internal Revenue, even the chairman and treasurer of the principal national campaign committees. Although Brown clearly fit the profile, one reads the law in vain trying to find any references to business partners or confidántes outside of government.[1]

"It was unlawful," says Hill of her own targeting. "I was the only such person in history."

Such details did not deter Janet Reno. She sought an independent counsel for Hill to investigate "possible violations of criminal law by Hill or her companies" as well as by Brown. Reno claimed Hill's business dealings and Brown's were "inextricably intertwined."[2] And who was there to protest the law's abuse? Not the party in opposition. The Republicans in Congress had set the machinery in motion.

The process had begun in 1993 when then-minority congressman William Clinger launched a search through Brown's financial disclosure forms and found many a shady deal in the penumbra thereof. In January 1995, with the White House still reeling from the electoral debacle of November 1994, the newly empowered Clinger went public with his accusations against Brown and, by extension, Hill. And this time, he had something to show: three checks made out to Ron Brown, each worth $45,000, from a company called First International.

In the way of background, Nolanda Hill formed First International with Brown in the wake of communism's collapse. Her goal was to explore broadcasting opportunities in the newly liberated Eastern Europe. She chose to set up a separate company because her primary business, Corridor Broadcasting, was a tightly regulated FCC licensee. There was nothing improper about the First International venture or the way Hill had set it up.

At the time, Brown was still chairman of the DNC. Neither he nor Hill expected Bush to lose in 1992. When his tenure at the DNC ended, Brown figured he could use his high profile and enhanced clout to help Hill secure business. The fact he was a minority wouldn't hurt either.

To Hill, Brown's stature made him a valuable partner even without any investment of cash. Brown saw it the same way. Heck, he had made a career out of getting something for nothing. It did not trouble him that Hill was doing all the work and running all the risk. For Brown, that was business as usual.

First International had several projects in the works when Clinton was elected. "It was not yet profitable," says Hill, "but it was about to be." Indeed, on his initial financial disclosure form for 1992, Brown had properly identified First International as his largest asset, worth $500,000 to $1 million—such forms allow for broad ranges—and his estimate was not unreasonable.[3]

Ironically, it was Clinton's victory and Brown's subsequent appointment to the cabinet that bollixed Hill's plans. "I am in a regulated business," claims Hill. "The last thing I wanted was someone in government." Her claim makes sense. As was true in the Vietnam issue, any action by Brown as commerce secretary to influence the outcome of an international deal would be conspicuous and illegal, especially in that First International was involved in privatizing once-public entities.

Brown understood this. Just before entering government, he pressured Hill, much as he pressured his partners at Patton Boggs, to pay him his share of potential future earnings. As a full partner in the business, he was legally entitled to make such a claim.

Ethically, however, Brown had lost his bearings. He had developed a cash jones as ravenous as any drug habit. His demand for money demoralized Hill even more than it had Tommy Boggs. Given her relationship to Brown, how could it have done otherwise?

Not having the cash at hand, Hill offered Brown a buyout agreement—a fixed note worth $500,000 that would not fall due until 1996. The ethics officer at Commerce granted Brown a waiver to accept the offer and maintain a passive interest in the company. And since Brown had listed the asset in his disclosure forms, all seemed more or less in order.

But not for long. As Brown's income contracted, his yearning for cash grew. Needing to pay his Vietnam-related legal bills, Brown turned to Hill or, more precisely, *on* Hill. Always careless with details, he had neglected to sign the promissory note for the $500,000. This self-inflicted loophole allowed him to demand Hill pay at least some of the First International money up front.

"I felt more than betrayed," says Hill of Brown's demand. "It was the most unfair thing I had seen in my life. I could not believe it."

Hill, who saw herself as a shrewd businesswoman, likely deceives herself on one point: the degree to which her affection for Brown impaired her business judgment. She seems to have offered him more of First International than he was worth and yielded to his demands more readily than he deserved. On April 15, 1993, First International Limited Partnership cut a check to Brown for $45,000. The company cut additional checks for $45,000 on July 21, 1993, and on October 15, 1993.[4]

For understandable reasons, Brown chose not to report these transactions on his next annual financial disclosure. Someone unknown, however, had gotten hold of actual copies of the checks and sent them to Clinger's office. On January 26, 1995—the day after President Clinton's rambling, self-pitying State of the Union speech, by all accounts the worst of his career—Clinger drove still another nail into Clinton's presumed coffin. He went public with the checks. He had to suspect Brown had done much worse, but the checks were tangible. These, the media could see.

The charges from Clinger and other Republicans prompted the humbled Clinton administration to respond. In mid-February 1995, Janet Reno announced the launch of a formal ninety-day inquiry to determine whether Brown deserved his own independent counsel.

Hill still thinks Reno acted "unilaterally," but she also believes Reno went forward only because "no great hue and cry" came from the Clintons to stop. Some reporters, especially on the Right, believe the Clintons let Reno proceed for strategic reasons. An independent counsel, after all, would keep the scandalous details of the affair in confidence and out of the news.[5] In truth, the Clintons weren't all that clever. And at this stage of the game, they weren't all that powerful. In early 1995, they had little political capital to invest in anyone, let alone a man they did not trust and had bailed out once already.

Besides, the Clintons could not know for sure how deep was the well of Brown's corruption. The financial disclosure forms suggested no discernible bottom. Brown had made the kind of "mistakes" in filing out these forms that would have sent a less adroit cabinet member packing.

On one form, for instance, Brown identified a housing development that he co-owned, the Belle Haven Apartments, as being in "Potomac, Maryland." In truth, as Brown had to know, the project was actually in Landover, Maryland.

Brown likely chose Potomac because it was among the most exclusive of Washington suburbs. Upon hearing "Potomac," few would associate the project with the "dismal, drug-infested" Belle Haven of Landover, Maryland. Yes, *that* Belle Haven, the notorious one whose units had been periodically declared "unfit for human habitation."

Brown had invested $71,000 in the project ten years earlier, an investment that would net him an estimated $175,000 in tax write-offs alone over the next ten years. A California multi-millionaire by the name of A. Bruce Rozet had arranged the deal.

"He got filthy rich off this program," said HUD secretary Henry Cisneros of Rozet in 1994, unaware of Brown's involvement, "and he left filthy places behind him for people to live in." Rozet, in fact, had enhanced his riches by defaulting on a $6.1 million loan from the Maryland Housing Fund that was allegedly used to renovate the buildings more than a decade earlier.

Ron Brown, however, could see the good in a man like Rozet. After all, the California slumlord helped end the famed "decade of greed" by donating nearly $75,000 to the DNC between 1987 and 1994. Rozet had also obliged Brown by using the services of Patton Boggs to extricate himself from a separate scrape with HUD in 1989.[6] Had all this been known at the time of his nomination to Commerce, Brown would likely not have been confirmed.

Reno's ninety-day period of inquiry would prove to be a ticklish one for the White House and the media. The two other cabinet members facing independent counsels were both minorities: Mike Espy, the African American secretary of agriculture, and Henry Cisneros, the Hispanic secretary of HUD. The White House had even felt compelled to force Espy out soon after his counsel had been appointed in October 1994. Cisneros's case was still in the pipeline.

Brown's performance at Commerce cried out for exposure, but neither the White House nor the media had any interest in portraying Brown as the antagonist. That role would fall to Hill. To read contemporary accounts of the case one would think it was she who had betrayed the trust of a public office, not Brown.

In a major profile written in February 1995, the *Los Angeles Times* identifies Hill as "the main character" in the Brown saga. The thrust of the *Times'* story, and much of the reporting on Hill, is that her payments to Brown represented an attempt to buy his influence. The *Times'* story traces their first meeting to 1990, at least seven years after their actual first encounter. This later date allows the reporter to spin a picture of Hill as gold digger, a woman who hoped to satisfy her "expensive tastes" and "opulent lifestyle" by hitching a ride on Brown's clearly ascending star.[7]

Like most reporting on Hill, the *Los Angeles Times'* piece is disturbingly inaccurate. From the outset of the article, the reporter deliberately creates the picture of Hill as a con artist. The article has Hill telling acquaintances she was either a professional singer or a classical pianist, "but none claim to have seen her perform." The college she claims to have attended has "no record of her." The reporter goes on and on insinuating fraud where none exists. Hill, in fact, has worked as a classical pianist and a singer. She did graduate from Stephen F. Austin University. These facts are easily verified.

In its February 1995 profile of the "flamboyant" Hill, the *New York Times* creates an entirely fictitious scandal. According to the *Times*, Columbia Productions, a company allegedly owned by Hill, had created the introductory video for the 1992 Democratic National Convention and charged the DNC the princely sum of $75,000 to do so.

The real story is fascinating, and all too typical, but it has nothing to do with the story the *Times* reports. According to Hill, Ron Brown had given the concession business at the convention to his business partner, Jim Kelly, the husband of the Washington DC mayor. Kelly had no experience in this line of work, and there had been no competitive bidding. When Hill realized what was going on, she persuaded Brown to undo this conspicuously shifty deal before Kelly's competitors found out. She even flew to New York to back-out the paperwork, not easily done at this point.

Kelly did not take the news well. He allegedly turned on Brown and threatened to cancel the pension business Brown did with the city of Washington. To pacify Kelly, Brown offered to have the DNC pay him $75,000. The only questions were how and for what. Since Hill had written, produced, and edited the video in question as an in-kind contribution, Brown figured the cleanest way would be to write off the $75,000 as the cost of video production and pass the check through Columbia Productions to Kelly. Hill did not own Columbia Productions and did not get a dime out of the deal.

The *New York Times* reporter also questions why Hill used Columbia Productions to make the video and not her primary company, Corridor Broadcasting. This is the nub of his argument, and it is clear that Congressman Clinger has steered him to it.[8] In fact, Corridor had defaulted on a loan from a defunct savings and loan that is reported to have cost "the taxpayers" $23 million. Each of the profiles on Hill implies she drained money out of Corridor not only to support her own presumably lavish lifestyle but also to purchase Ron Brown's influence. "Everything that we look at has sort of questionable elements to it," Clinger would cagily tell the *New York Times*.[9]

Not surprisingly, Hill has a different take on events. She and her partners took out the loans to buy Corridor in 1985 long before Brown had any influence to sell. These loans were backed by real equity—namely two TV stations, one in Washington, one in the Boston area—that appreciated annually. For her, the failure of this partnership and the eventual default on the loans is a tale of anguish and heartbreak, not casual exploitation as imputed by the media. By 1993, in fact, Hill had lost all ownership in the stations, although she continued to manage them.

"Get yourself a high profile," Hill had told a convention of would-be entrepreneurs in 1986. "Let people know who you are."[10] For years Hill had worked to create that profile, partly by just being who she was, an archetypal hard-charging west Texan, more feminine than most of the women in Washington and more masculine than most of the men. When her lawyers refused to allow her to cooperate with the media—a mistake, Hill now realizes—the media simply defined her by the dark Hollywood spin on that very persona.

The *Washington Post*, for instance, in a lengthy March 1995 profile on Hill, details how Hill *dresses* and then, through the use of an unnamed source, casually depicts her as "the stereotype of a soap-opera Texas businesswoman who might have appeared on the TV show *Dallas*."[11]

Any number of people had an interest in reinforcing this stereotype, including Ron Brown. His attorney, Reid Weingarten, did not shy from painting Brown as the innocent victim of Hill's wiles. For a Republican like Clinger, always squeamish about race, an attack on a woman held fewer risks than an attack on an African American. The White House was at least as sensitive to racial nuances as Clinger. The major media were even more so.

In mid-May 1995, having used the full ninety days at her disposal, Janet Reno called for an independent counsel to probe Brown's business dealings. When revealed, the details of this probe had to have raised the collective blood pressure at the Brown household. In addition to the charges concerning his financial disclosure forms and his relationship with Hill, Brown faced a third unwelcome charge—the improper purchase of a townhouse for his Haitian mistress, Lillian Madsen.

Brown had arranged for an associate, a wealthy Brazilian by the name of Jose Amaro Pintos Ramos, to put up the $108,000 down payment. Brown had lied about this on his mortgage application and his financial disclosure forms. Given that he had accepted Ramos's largesse *after* being nominated Commerce secretary, Brown had good reason to keep his involvement quiet.[12]

The media, however, showed little interest in Madsen or in Brown's other disclosure issues. They zeroed in, like Reno, on Brown's dealings with Nolanda Hill. Not only had Hill paid Brown $135,000 through First International, but she had forgiven him a $300,000 personal loan as well as the $72,000 in debts Brown owed First International.[13]

The media asked the legitimate question: what had Brown done to merit roughly $500,000? They also raised the less substantial but more sensational question of whether Hill had siphoned the money from publicly held loans to buy Brown's influence.

Publicly at least, the White House seemed to take Reno's call for an independent counsel in stride. For the Clintons, independent counsels had become something of an occupational hazard. Once appointed, Brown's would be the fourth such counsel investigating either them or their cabinet.

As to Ron Brown, he managed to improvise a cool he certainly did not feel. When this story broke, reporters asked him whether he had thought of resigning as Espy had. "I certainly have not," Brown replied. "You'll have to raise those questions with others."[14] The most significant of those others, the ones in the White House, had their own reasons for keeping Brown on the job and in tow.

"I am confident at the conclusion of the process, the independent counsel will find no wrongdoing by Secretary Brown," Clinton told the media. "In the interim, I value his continued service on behalf of this country."[15]

When pressed on the difference in treatment between Espy and Brown, White House spokesman Mike McCurry replied lamely, "There are different facts, there are different issues involved."[16] Two issues, in particular, concerned the White House. One was Brown's status, in the words of biographer Holmes, as "a politically well-connected, wildly popular black man."[17] Espy was none of those things other than black and male.

Even more sensitive, however, was Brown's role in the reelection of the president. Janet Reno had been assessing Brown's guilt at the very same time the Clintons and Dick Morris were conceiving their radical strategy to retain the White House. The Clintons had a job for Brown, but it had nothing to do with managing the 1996 campaign. On this latter point, anonymous White House "aides" could not have been more clear. The "best" Brown could now hope for, they uniformly told the media, was "to avoid indictment and a forced resignation."[18]

Brown was damaged goods, and the White House was letting him know it. As Hill saw it, the worse the damage, the better a bagman Brown would be. If his fund-raising missions were ever exposed, the White House could lay it all off on a corrupt black man kept on the job only because of the White House's otherwise admirable sensitivity to racial issues. "He felt extremely abused," says Hill of Brown. But by this time, he had few options and no good ones.

Still, on the surface at least, Brown was handling the pressure better than Hill. Unlike Hill, he had a Washington support network that would interpret the charges against him much the way his daughter Tracey did, namely as "the measures that the white Establishment will take whenever an African American becomes too powerful."[19] In times like this, Brown, like others before and after, would find psychological refuge in his blackness. He would not have to face his own culpability.

Hill had no such support. "I didn't have anywhere to turn," she says, still barely comprehending what happened to her. In addition to the media, at least five separate agencies of government were hounding her. Helicopters tracked her on one day. The FBI staked out her mother's house on another. The enemies she had made in the media business continued to feed Clinger and the media any suggestive evidence they could find. "As we began to develop the Hill connections," Clinger would admit, "we had stuff coming over the transom from her employees."[20]

An ordinary citizen cannot begin to sense what it feels like to endure the crushing resentment of a hostile nation despite one's innocence. During the Clinton years, such sufferers were all vulnerable and disproportionately female: Paula Jones, Linda Tripp, Billy Dale, Gennifer Flowers, Richard Jewell, Nolanda Hill.

For Hill, the burden was unshared. "It was horrible," says Hill. "My son didn't want anything to do with me. I was watching my mother age in front of me. Nobody believed me." At the time, no interest group, ethnic group, or political faction supported her.

The weight of the investigation all but suffocated Hill. So profound was her despair at one point that she could scarcely drive or discern where she was. Shocked by her condition, ex-husband Billy Hill and an attorney friend executed what Hill calls "an intervention." They took her car keys and drove her to her sister's house, telling the sister, "You have to watch her."

Billy Hill then identified a doctor and convinced Nolanda to see him. The doctor promptly checked Hill into an intern's overnight room so no one—especially no one in the media—could find her. And there she stayed for two weeks. For the first week, she took no calls from outside her family, not even from Brown.

"I read the Bible a lot," says Hill, "all the time." Just prior to Reno's decision to name an independent counsel, Hill had spent several months in Central America, much of that time assessing her faith and "getting it in order." Her priorities, Hill admits, had been "so wrong." Although the ordeal to follow would test her faith, Hill is sure she could not have endured without it.

On July 6, 1995, Daniel Pearson was appointed independent counsel. On that same day, a still shaky Hill came to Washington at Brown's request. To duck the media, she paid cash for her airline tickets and checked into the Mayflower Hotel under the name of Sue Butler. When Brown came to see her there, Hill demanded to know what beyond the obvious Brown had done to cause all of this.

"We had a huge, huge fight," says Hill, "the worst ever." Brown left in a huff and headed for his place in West Virginia. Thinking more clearly, he turned around, came back and called Hill at 3:00 AM.

"We have to stay in the same boat," Brown implored her. He wanted to talk. Concerned about listening devices at the Mayflower, he picked Hill up in his Cadillac—the British-made Jag had to go once he entered the cabinet—and drove her to a Maryland IHOP. They never left the parking lot. Hill was crying, unable to fathom what had happened to her.

"If you know you have done nothing illegal," says Hill, "you know it."

For a mix of reasons, the political Right was leading the attack against her. Hill now believes a select few among them desired her media properties, and others hoped to neutralize Brown's fund-raising abilities. Most, however, as well as some on the deep Left, saw the Brown phenomenon as a cancer in the body politic and wanted it cut out. Believing what they read and heard in the media, they saw Hill as an intrinsic part of that phenomenon.

Then, too, there was the Reno factor. The fact that Daniel Pearson, like Reno, came from Miami raised Hill's suspicions. It is Hill's belief that

Reno was still brooding over the seemingly unnatural death of the Miami grand jury in Brown's Vietnam case.

"She did not believe Ron to be an honest person," says Hill of Reno. And in 1995, Reno still had enough independent power to be dangerous. Her desire to hang on to her job had not yet grown so desperate that she could be easily manipulated. That would happen later.

One of the frequent complaints about the independent counsel law was it gave the counsel a veritable "hunting license." In this case, however, the further the hunt roamed from the inconsequential boudoir of Lillian Madsen's townhouse and the equally irrelevant halls of First International, the more productive it became. In time, the trail would lead Pearson and his team of investigators through Hawaii and Southern California to the one place neither Brown nor the White House wanted it to go.

Oklahoma.

21 DEAR RON

O n July 5, 1995, the day before Janet Reno named Daniel Pearson the independent counsel for Ron Brown, Gary Tooker, the vice chairman of Motorola, sent Brown a letter. One suspects it cheered Brown less than Tooker might have hoped.

Tooker begins the letter with the cloying gambit of crossing out the typed "Secretary Brown" and writing in "Dear Ron." "I am writing to thank you and some key members of the Commerce Department," continues Tooker, "for your assistance in obtaining the presidential waiver for encryption sales to China."

The letter goes on in fulsome detail about how Brown and his staff manned "the front line" in the battle against those irksome "national security controls" that hamper American business. "The outcome of this waiver is good both for U.S. economic security as well as our broader natural security interests," concludes Tooker in the kind of winking self-deception that had become the *newspeak* of the international business community. Brown, in fact, had helped write the lexicon.[1]

A year or two earlier, Brown might have been flattered by a letter of this sort. But by this stage of the game, he had received too many unduly intimate "Dear Ron" letters to be charmed. Indeed, they had begun to oppress. Motorola. Loral. Hughes. MCI. RSA Security. They all wanted the same thing—an open door to China, national security be damned.

With reelection at stake, the White House was willing to throw that door open just about as wide as the corporations and their Chinese consumers could afford. Johnny Chung, who has admitted funneling $100,000 from the Chinese Military to the DNC,[2] would tell the Thompson Committee, "The White House is like a subway: You have to put in coins to open the gates."[3] When he wiped the stardust from his eyes, Brown was beginning to see himself as little more than a glorified gatekeeper.

That very first paragraph of Tooker's letter had keyed in on the two words that made Brown's gatekeeping assignment so touchy, *China* and *encryption*. *China*, Brown knew. The promise and peril of that country he understood about as well as anyone. *Encryption* came harder.

It was Nolanda Hill who first introduced him to the concept back when she and Brown were trying to launch First International. At the time, Brown was still chairman of the DNC, and Hill was doing the heavy lifting. This, she soon wearied of and let Brown know it. He got the message and at least tried to pitch in.

The first opportunity Brown spotted was in Egypt. The minister of finance had asked Brown if he knew anyone with experience in over-the-air television, better known in the U.S. as Pay TV. Hill was just the person. Brown called her from the minister's office.

What the Egyptians told Brown was they were having problems with the country's non-Muslim citizens. These would-be viewers were apparently chafing at the restrictive fare on regular TV. Pay TV would solve that problem. It would scramble and code shows offensive to the Muslims, and decoder boxes would deliver the signal only to those homes that wanted it. This made sense to Hill, and so she put a deal together.

The Egyptians had asked for five encryption systems. This request puzzled Hill given that five such systems could handle all of the United States. A fax that arrived at her office just hours before the deal was to be closed clarified the picture considerably. The Egyptians were demanding the schematics of the encryption systems. As Hill knew, only the manufacturer had these. If the Egyptians needed encryption schematics, it was not for their TV programming.

Hill immediately went to a pay phone and called Brown. "You can't deal with these people," she warned him. "They just want the technology. An encryption system doesn't care what it decodes."

Hill killed the deal. Humbled, Brown sent no more business First International's way. He had gotten his first hard lesson in what has come to be known as "dual-use" technology. "Dual-use" simply means a given technology could have a military application as well as a commercial one. The phrase provided both buyer and seller great latitude to dissemble, and—on the subject of encryption—dissemble they often did and worse.

"This was pretty scary to me," says Hill. She had good cause to be scared. Encryption is ominous stuff, the stuff of spy novels and real-life thrillers. The Soviets, for instance, compelled convicted spy Aldrich Ames to encrypt the computer file information he passed to them. American spy John Walker had surely enhanced the Soviets' knowledge of encryption by selling them top-secret encryption codes for some twenty years.

Jonathan Pollard delivered his purloined encryption codes to the Israelis. Arrested in 1985, Pollard, an American citizen, still sits in a North Carolina prison for handing over these codes to an *ally*. For their part, the Israelis have been accused of refusing to give them back. This may explain why Clinton denied Prime Minister Netanyahu's request to spring Pollard, even when offered as a condition of the Wye River accords—a deal Clinton desperately needed to close on the eve of the 1998 congressional elections.[4]

Encryption is the kind of technology for which nations are willing to sacrifice. One particular reason stands out: encrypted radio communications transmitted via satellite can assure secure worldwide communications for military and commercial use. To the degree that a nation controls this technology, it controls the world.

Brown found himself involved in encryption technology from the moment he opened his door for business at Commerce. The Clinton administration had inherited a high priority project that went under the name of the "CLIPPER Chip." There is perhaps no subject that can stir the soul of the conspiracy-minded like this one. And not without reason.

Developed by the National Security Agency (NSA), the CLIPPER had two essential functions. One was to enable users to secure seemingly private communications. The other was to allow certain government agencies, under prescribed conditions, all but total access to those communications. Before industry rebelled, the Clinton administration hoped to impose the technology on the private sector either through "mandatory" legislation or a "voluntary" system of taxpayer backed payments.[5] The CLIPPER chip had Orwellian potential and was a subject of great international interest.

Even the least suspicious have to be intrigued by the Clinton officials assigned to oversee this project. They included Associate Attorney General Webster Hubbell, White House counselors Vince Foster and Bernie

Nussbaum, and Ron Brown. Within three years of their involvement, all four would be gone from the White House, none of them voluntarily. Two would die under mysterious circumstances, and one would find himself in prison. In the case of both Foster and Hubbell, the NSA would intervene to suppress evidence.[6]

Hubbell, however, could take some comfort in the $100,000 grant he received from two men who also had a keen interest in encryption technology: James and Mochtar Riady of Indonesia. Indeed, the Riady's man in America, John Huang, would be briefed thirty-seven times by the CIA on the subject of encryption technology, and still no one can explain why.

Several other Commerce Department employees schooled themselves in encryption technology as well. Much of the controversy swirls around a Commerce attorney named Ira Sockowitz. A former administrative law judge from New York, Sockowitz attracted the attention of the Clinton team by organizing early support for the 1992 Clinton/Gore campaign. Contrary to rumor, he was not a fund-raiser.[7]

Shortly after Brown's death, Sockowitz left the Department of Commerce with 2,800 pages of intelligence documents, much of which dealt with sensitive and highly secret satellite and encryption technologies. Sockowitz stashed the documents in the safe of his new office at the Small Business Administration (SBA). And there they might have remained were it not for a series of Freedom of Information Act requests filed by Larry Klayman and Judicial Watch.

Although the documents include a classified NSA study of the international market for computer software with encryption and other studies like one on uranium transactions in Russia, Sockowitz argues convincingly that he moved them in all innocence and quit the SBA in October 1996 only "to end any controversy" before the election.

Others disagree. "He knew what he was doing," said one congressional investigator. "He had to. He held one of the highest levels of clearance—top secret with code word."[8]

Innocent or otherwise, Sockowitz drew so much heat because these documents could have been tremendously helpful to a company like Motorola or its offshoot Iridium, which was created by Motorola to help construct a worldwide telecommunications network.

With a sharp eye for talent, Iridium hired four Commerce Department employees with high-level security clearance soon after Brown's death. The most notable of these was the inescapable Lauri Fitz-Pegado, she of "Baby Doc" and incubator baby fraud fame. Although admittedly Fitz-Pegado had no experience in the business, she started her Iridium career as the vice president of its Global Gateway Management division. Larry Klayman, who deposed Fitz-Pegado, believes they hired her for one reason above all: "access to Clinton."[9]

In 1994, Motorola began to pressure Brown and others in the administration on the subject of encryption. As point man, the company used a former Clinton National Security Council member. The pressure Motorola applied through him was relentless and well-targeted. The goal: to allow Motorola to sell encrypted radios and cellular phones to the Chinese People's Armed Police.

Not surprisingly, the State Department objected. The People's Armed Police, after all, ran the *lao gai*, China's notorious prison camps. They were also entrusted with executing dissidents and selling their organs for cash. Just five years after the Tiananmen Square massacre, there was not a lot of enthusiasm at State to empower the Chinese police any further.

In February 1995, frustrated by State's hand-wringing over human rights, Motorola's Tooker directly appealed to Ron Brown. There was no "Dear Ron" on this letter. With "$100 million worth of two-way radio business tied up by the lack of a waiver," Tooker let his anger show.

"Export controls administered by the State Department at the behest of the National Security Agency (NSA)," he wrote Brown, "should NOT be referred for endless delay to the human rights bureau and myriad others in State." Finally, in July 1995, after much scurrying around by Brown and others, Clinton dismissed the objections of State and approved the export with his signature.[10] Thus, the "Dear Ron" letter.

In the run up to the 1996 election, encryption was just one of many high tech, dual-use technologies being shopped abroad. The Clinton administration would also facilitate the export of high performance computers, satellite technology, advance machine tools, communications systems, and much more.

To be fair, there are those who view Clinton's efforts to "liberalize" export controls as a kind of necessary reform. They include much, if not most, of the high-tech corporate leadership and at least a few academics. One of the latter is Richard Cupitt, author of *Reluctant Champions*, an authoritative and appropriately dust-dry work on strategic export controls.

The Clinton one meets in this book continually takes the ingenuous Cupitt by surprise. As Cupitt acknowledges, Clinton did not seem a likely reformer. He campaigned stridently against Bush's "too lenient controls on exports to China,"[11] and picked a running mate in Al Gore, who had a record of supporting the tough export controls Clinton promised.[12]

And then, lo and behold, Clinton changed. On September 15, 1993, the president sent a rather remarkable letter to Silicon Graphics president Edward McCracken. "By some estimates unnecessary export controls cost U.S. companies $9 billion a year," wrote Clinton. "One reason I ran for president was to tailor export controls to the realities of a post–Cold War world."[13]

As they say, there is no zealot like a convert. The House Select Committee, better known as the Cox Committee, would reveal in painful detail that the major beneficiary of the president's newfound faith in exports was—no surprise here—China. Within a year or so of the letter to McCracken, his administration removed controls on encryption technology including advanced fiber-optic communications, radiation-hardened encrypted satellite control systems, encrypted radios and cellular phones, and encrypted navigation systems. It also liberalized controls on stealth technologies, exempted U.S. satellites from Pakistan-related sanctions, approved the sale of advanced machine tools from a B-1 bomber plant, and, as discussed earlier, dispatched Ron Brown on a floating high-tech swap and shop to Hong Kong and the People's Republic.[14]

These exports could not have taken place without the personal signature of Clinton and the intervention of Brown. In the first two years of his tenure at Commerce, Brown lobbied incessantly against the Reagan-era controls aimed at preventing the leakage of technology to Russia and China. He and the president and their industry allies struggled to wrest the controls of these dual-use exports away from the departments of State and Defense where serious people still cared about the security of America.

The more authority Brown secured, the deeper he enmeshed himself in the various financial transactions that greased the wheels of politics and commerce. Says Hill, "Ron felt like the more dirty work he did the more indispensable he was."

What Brown sometimes forgot was that he was a mere cog in these wheels. His position was more important than he was. By doing the dirty work, he made himself more vulnerable than indispensable. The White House could always use that dirt against him. If he ever chose to respond in kind, he would put any number of highly unscrupulous people at risk. Hill saw the precariousness of his position long before Brown did. Only toward the end did Brown begin to see that more than his job was at stake.

The president's zeal for export reform shone through in October 1995 when the administration adopted what Cupitt calls "the most sweeping liberalization of export licensing requirements in the history of export controls."[15] Cupitt, however, never quite comes to grip with why Clinton adapted so readily.

Unfortunately for the future of the nation, neither did congressional Republicans. By pursuing one inquiry into Clinton's fund-raising and another into his otherwise inexplicable high tech give-away, they failed to make the connection between the two in the public mind. The result is that even academics like Cupitt could credibly look for the rationale behind Clinton's change of heart everywhere except to the obvious: Clinton's obligation to the Riadys and his increasingly desperate need for money.[16]

As it happened, a month before the October 1995 reforms, at a key meeting in the White House treaty room, Dick Morris made an impassioned plea to the president. "We will decide the outcome of the election right here and now," Morris declared. What was needed was a massive new infusion of money to ramp up the TV ad campaign against the Republicans. There was only one problem from Morris's perspective: "The DNC had no cash on hand for such spending and eventually had to borrow much of the money."[17]

Morris had chosen not to know where that money was coming from. The Clintons had no such luxury. On Sunday night, September 10, 1995, Bill and Hillary met with Al Gore, Chief of Staff Leon Panetta, aide Harold Ickes, and DNC chair Don Fowler to determine whether or not to go forward with Morris's plan for a massively expensive ad campaign. Says Dick Morris, "The entire fate of Clinton's presidency hinged on this decision."[18]

For all the talk of Ron Brown's role in the 1992 campaign, he was never invited to these sessions or involved in these decisions. No minorities ever were—no minorities, that is, except for the Riadys. Three days after the September 10 meeting, Clinton met in the Oval Office with James Riady and the ubiquitous John Huang. At this meeting, the improbable decision was made to ship Huang to the DNC. There, he would have the title vice financial chairman, an honorific created uniquely for him.

The DNC was not enthused by this turn of events. Fowler and Finance chair Marvin Rosen knew too much about Huang's reckless fund-raising history, and they resisted. Finally on November 8, the president took Rosen aside at a DNC fund-raiser at the Historic Car Barn in Washington and laid down the law: John Huang was to be hired.[19] Between the September meetings and the November ultimatum, Huang made sixteen visits to the White House, visiting not only with the president and vice president but also with Mrs. Clinton.[20]

Others of Chinese descent were not as fortunate as Huang. Some time after the Motorola deal was consummated, heroic dissident Harry Wu attempted to enter China through a remote border in his relentless attempt to expose the *lao gai*. He was not successful. The People's Armed Police intercepted him. They had been communicating, Wu noticed, on their brand-new Motorola encrypted radios.[21]

22   HEAT

I t was some time early in 1996. Nolanda Hill does not remember the exact date. An extremely anxious Ron Brown removed from his ostrich skin portfolio a packet of documents about an inch thick and showed them to Hill.

As Hill would later testify under oath, she looked at the top five or six. They were letters on Commerce Department stationery signed by Melissa Moss, the director of the Commerce Department's Office of Business Liaison. Brown never really trusted the former DNC staffer. He always imagined Moss to be a White House mole.

It was not Melissa Moss's signature that troubled Hill. It was the contents of the letters. Each was addressed to a trade mission participant, and each, according to Hill's testimony, "specifically referenced a substantial financial contribution to the Democratic National Committee."[1]

After a year of shocking revelations, Hill realized in a flash she still wasn't shock proof. Here in front of her was the trade mission investigation's proverbial "smoking gun," the elusive documents Judicial Watch had been seeking for more than a year under court order.

Hill had had enough. She and Brown had ample problem with the Office of the Independent Counsel. The last thing either of them needed was another scandal. This was no time for polite indirection. She told Brown straight out that if he wanted to save his career he had better turn the documents over and fire Moss pronto. Brown could not play dumb much longer. He was going to have to do something.

For Brown, it was just one more wrench of the gut. The last year of his life had easily been the most desperate, and it was getting more so. Larry Klayman's public interest group, Judicial Watch, had added its own considerable heat to a simmering fire stoked by Congress and the Justice Department.

Dismissed by the media as a right-wing gadfly—at least until Judicial Watch sued Vice President Dick Cheney—Klayman and his associates were doing nothing more incendiary than forcing the administration to honor the law, and nowhere was the law more dishonored than at Commerce.

Judicial Watch had started in on Brown in late 1994 when its attorneys got wind that the Commerce Department might just be selling seats on its trade missions. Judicial Watch sent the Commerce Department a series of Freedom of Information Act (FOIA) requests asking for relevant documents. These requests, Judicial Watch notes, "were thwarted at every turn."[2]

In October 1994, Melissa Moss telephoned Klayman, hoping to persuade him to limit the scope of the FOIA request. When Klayman refused, Moss angrily slammed the phone down. The next day, however, Moss sent Klayman a fax, presumably to build a paper trail. The fax claimed Judicial Watch had voluntarily agreed to limit the scope of its FOIA request to a list of trade mission participants. This was a lie, and Moss knew it.

Commerce continued to stonewall. In January 1995, Judicial Watch filed suit in federal district court to force Commerce staff to hand over the information requested in the FOIAs. The Commerce Department agreed to comply but only if Judicial Watch would pay some $13,000 in search and duplication costs. This bit of dilatory mischief did not amuse the court. The judge ordered Commerce to produce the appropriate documents and waive the fee.

Still playing games, Commerce responded by turning over 28,000 pages of random documents. Not found among them, however, were any notes or letters from Brown or any kind of anything from the White House or the DNC on the subject of trade missions.[3]

These documents did exist. Hill was not the only one to have seen them. Under oath, several Commerce Department staff members would later testify both to their existence and to the knowing failure of Commerce to turn them over. They were understandably anxious about testifying. Commerce executive Sonya Stewart, for instance, presented her affidavit "with great trepidation and grave concern about retribution and retaliation which may be directed at me, both professionally and personally."

Despite her fears, Stewart admitted her staff's efforts to honor the

FOIA process "were thwarted and obstructed by Commerce Department officials." As the architect of this obstruction, Stewart cited Melissa Moss. According to Stewart, Moss "refused to cooperate in producing documents responsive to Judicial Watch's FOIA requests." Stewart shared one incriminating detail after another about how the White House conspired with Commerce to lose or withhold just about all relevant documents, including a diskette flagrantly labeled "contributions/trade missions."[4]

Although Moss may have been coordinating the resistance, Brown was surely aware of it. As both Hill and the Department's FOIA secretary would testify, Brown made the "highly unusual" decision to move the Judicial Watch requests from the FOIA office to his own. The White House was pressuring him to control both the flow of information and the timing of its release.[5]

According to Hill, two of the president's top deputies, White House Chief of Staff Leon Panetta and Deputy Chief of Staff John Podesta, had ordered Brown to do just that. By having Brown defy court orders, the pair hoped to push the resolution of the suit back until after the 1996 elections. Hill made no bones about this when questioned before Federal District Judge Royce Lamberth in March 1998:

> *Q*: Now, do you remember Ron saying to you that Panetta and Podesta wanted him to, quote, "slow pedal" the case until after the [1996] elections? Those were the words that were used, was it not?
> *A*: Yes.
> *Q*: And that Ron mimicked Leon Panetta and laughed when he used the words "slow pedal"?
> *A*: Well, he did a pretty good Leon Panetta.

Panetta and Podesta obviously did not come up with this scheme on their own. About this, Hill was forthcoming as well:

> *Q*: And did [Brown] not say to you that—and I am kind of paraphrasing—Hillary believes that every thing is politics and politics is driven by money; correct?
> *A*: He did say those—close to those words, recall [*sic*].
> *Q*: And he told you that, in fact, it was Hillary's idea to use the trade mission to raise money; correct?

A: He initially believed that she was very instrumental, and he gave her a lot of credit.[6]

Although her information was admittedly secondhand, Sonya Stewart also implicated Hillary Clinton in the trade mission scheme. If Hillary Clinton were involved, however, she was not acting without the advice and counsel of the president. Hill made this clear in her testimony:

A: Ultimately, [Brown] believed that the president of the United States was, at least tangentially.
Q: Involved?
A: Yes sir. It was his reelection that was at stake.
Q: Ron believed that the president of the United States knew the trade missions were being sold and their purpose being perverted?
A: Yes, sir.[7]

Still, for all of the heat coming from Judicial Watch through early 1996—and it was considerable—Klayman had no independent authority. The Office of the Independent Counsel, by contrast, had almost no restraint. Nolanda Hill found this out the hard way.

In October 1995, Hill and her seventy-nine-year-old mom were driving a Ryder truck full of documents from Dallas to her attorney's office in Kentucky. As they were passing through Memphis, a crew of agents from the DEA—as in Drug Enforcement Agency—stopped them. They ordered Hill and her mother from the truck and spread-eagled Hill against it.

DEA agents detained the pair for five rainy hours in a parking lot while they brusquely searched Hill and the truck. During this grim, humiliating shakedown, the proverbial lightbulb flashed over Hill's head. She thought, "I know what this is all about." The First International case could not have generated this kind of heat. The independent counsel had to be on to something bigger, something hotter, and that something had to be Oklahoma.

Hill was right. The always entertaining Gene and Nora Lum, in their heedless pursuit of wealth and power, had covered their tracks no better than O.J. Simpson. FBI agents followed their paper trail from Washington back to Hawaii and on to California.

The agents were particularly curious as to what happened to that APAC money raised in their Torrance, California, warehouse for the 1992 presidential campaign. Alas, the Lums had no records. As they told the authorities, a car just happened to crash into the corner of their house where they kept their paperwork, destroying it all.[8]

From California, the FBI tracked the Lums to Oklahoma. The Lums eased the FBI's work through their sheer recklessness. Truth be told, they knew little about a business other than how to loot it. In an April 1995 suit, a Dynamic Energy shareholder, Linda Price, accused the Lums of doing just that—to the tune of $3 million. As the reader recalls, Ron Brown helped the Lums launch Dynamic Energy and become instant millionaires in the process.[9]

The independent counsel had no trouble discovering the quid pro quo. And here, for Ron Brown, was the tragic rub: the quid passed through his son, Michael. One of the Lums' first major acts as majority shareholders in Dynamic Energy was to hire Michael, then just twenty-eight. Michael, of course, had no more experience in this business than the Lums or his father, but his father had put the deal together. This was surely payback time.

As described in Linda Price's lawsuit, Nora Lum had given Michael a 5 percent share in the company worth about $500,000 and a consulting fee of $7,500 per month. On top of that, she awarded Michael a $60,000 corporate membership in an exclusive Robert Trent Jones golf club, just about a thousand miles due east of Tulsa in suburban Virginia. Before his first year on the job was out, Michael would be named the company's acting president.[10] When confronted by PBS *Frontline* producers, Nora Lum explained she had so favored Michael because she and Gene thought of him as the son they never had.[11]

In a further bit of what the Center for Public Integrity would call "unseemly incestuousness," the Lum's daughter Trisha secured a high-level job at Commerce and then, after a couple of swell trips to Asia with Brown, left Commerce to work for Dynamic Energy. So did Gilbert Colon. Tellingly, Colon had served as the former chief of Commerce's Minority Business Development Agency.[12] It had been Ron's dream, Hill remembers, to get his hands on an energy company that could serve "as a pass-through for preference contracts." Colon could help.

The Linda Price suit made at least one other painful revelation beyond the rewards offered to Michael Brown, namely that he "provided no services or value to the corporation in exchange for said transfers."[13] When deposed in this same lawsuit, Linda's husband, Stuart Price, explained why Michael was hired:

> He absolutely is there for them to gain influence with the Department of Commerce, and that's it, and [the Lums] think he's a buffoon, and their discussions with me is that because they want influence, and that's why he is getting paid, and that's why they gave him five percent of the stock for free.[14]

Linda Price added detail. She claimed Ron Brown's attorneys had met with Nora Lum and Michael Brown in March 1995 "to discuss personal, legal, and public relations issues regarding his father."[15] It did not take FBI agents long to realize here in the gas and oil fields of the Sooner state, they had struck black gold. Ron Brown had surely "accepted things of value." Their wildcatting days were over.

In an October 1995 article in the *Legal Times*, Brown attorney Reid Weingarten dismissed the allegations. Said Weingarten, "The suggestion that Secretary Brown was involved in the business affairs of a small energy company called Dynamic Energy Resources Inc. . . . while at Commerce is completely false."[16]

Weingarten, who openly scorned Hill, had been trying to direct the attention of the investigators and the media away from Oklahoma and on to Hill. During the ordeal in the rain, however, Hill came to understand that the only way the independent counsel could get Brown was through the Oklahoma affair. It could never have made a successful case on either her or Brown through First International. From that moment on, she resolved to say not a word about anything to anyone "without a full walk on the table."[17] She'd had enough, and she was not about to compromise her future for the sake of the Lums or Michael Brown.

When the DEA ended their fruitless search in Memphis, Hill continued on to Kentucky, then drove her mother back to Dallas, and then turned right back around and drove to Washington. As soon as she arrived she called Ron Brown from a pay phone.

"There are some major league problems," she told him. "You and the boy are in trouble."

Hill had learned about the Oklahoma deal only after the fact, and it pained her to be "hung out to dry" because of it. "Ron was not innocent on that deal," remembers Hill, and as to Michael, "There was no question he was guilty as a goose."

Hill remembered the day it all went down. Brown was at her office reviewing his finances.

"What's my tax hickey?" he had asked.

"Knowing what I know," she answered, "here's about what I think you're going to need." The amount Hill estimated was $60,000, the same amount as the fee for the Virginia golf club or the first eight months of Michael's salary.

Brown went to the phone. For security purposes, Hill made him use the phone on her fax machine. He called Michael and explained how much money Michael had to funnel him. At the time, Hill did not know Michael was in Oklahoma.

"You're sure that's going to do it?" Brown asked Hill.

"What's this all about?" she asked.

"It's just a deal Michael's in," Brown answered weakly.

When Hill persisted with her questioning, Brown accused her of trying to scotch any action she could not control, and he dropped it at that. "Of all they had done on the independent counsel thing," remembers Hill, "this was the only thing they had. *They had it!*"

As both Hill and Brown sensed, the one part of the Oklahoma deal the independent counsel had yet to discover was the Mack McLarty connection. Indeed, had Pearson and his agents known where the trail was leading, they might not have pursued it.

Brown had gotten involved in Oklahoma only at the White House's urging. Hillary Clinton had even thanked him for handling this affair for Bill's old friend and chief of staff. Although the president had gently dumped McLarty in June 1994—and he did have some justification other than Oklahoma—the White House had to be worried this tinderbox could still blow open. To make matters worse, the impetuous Nora Lum reinforced the White House connection by visiting eighteen times in Clinton's first term alone.[18]

In November 1995, Hill saw Brown three or four times and each time she saw him she implored him, "You better tell me what you know," but Brown was still in denial. In late November, discreetly and without any public notice, Janet Reno sent the request to court for the independent counsel to add Michael Brown to the case. In late December and early January, after Michael had been officially but quietly targeted, Ron Brown turned serious.

Hill had been privy to much confidential information throughout Brown's tenure. After Michael was formally brought into the investigation, she insisted on full disclosure from Brown. She and Brown agreed Hill would review all potential areas of Brown's liability as it related to the independent counsel. Brown also understood if he failed to inform Hill about any action that could adversely affect her case, she "would plead out in a nano-second."

"I looked at pieces of paper you wouldn't believe," says Hill. These included the trade mission documents. One weekend she and Brown spent up to fifteen hours each day going through the files in his home. To complicate matters, Ron's wife Alma had to pick Hill up and take her back to her hotel. Although Hill thinks highly of Alma Brown, that weekend, she admits, "Alma was awful to me." And at this point, Alma did not yet know about Michael.

If a weak case could be made that Ron Brown deserved the fruits of minority capitalism, no such case could ever be made for Michael. Tall, athletic, good-looking, Michael had grown up with every advantage afforded an American child. Indeed, he had been even more indulged than the young Bill Clinton. And unlike Clinton, Michael had a natural father in the home, one who loved him deeply and spoiled him consummately.

As he entered young manhood, Michael stood poised to build on his father's legacy in all of its dubious glory. "Michael tried very, very hard to emulate his father," says Hill, "but he didn't have the same brains." Despite attending the best of private schools as a boy, Michael had a difficult time getting through college and especially law school at the University of Delaware.

"I know for a fact that Ron arranged to have his grades changed," says Hill. "Ron got somebody to fix it." The Middlebury spirit lived on. Michael had an even harder time passing the bar exam.

On the quiet, Brown had arranged for a law firm to handle Michael's scarily serious problem with the independent counsel. But he could not keep this news under wraps forever. When Alma found about Michael's fix, she fell apart. She was understandably livid with Brown for dragging Michael in.

In January 1996, Hill drove into Washington about 7:00 AM on the morning the Justice Department was to issue a press release on Michael's involvement. She had a terrible headache after weathering a West Virginia snowstorm. For discretion's sake, Hill checked into a small Holiday Inn not too far from the Commerce Department office, and Brown met her in her room. He knew the press statement was coming. "I had never seen him like that," says Hill. "He was shaking."

"Ron, it's over," Hill told him. "I'll tell you what I have been offered." Brown had to steady himself. For the first time, he realized the independent counsel's office had put a deal on the table for Hill. As Hill explained, the only reason she had not told what she knew about Oklahoma was the independent counsel was not yet ready to let her walk.

As heartsick as Brown was, he could not address the issue at the moment. He was off on still another trade mission with all that a trade mission implied. Hill was angry, and she let him know it. He had to stop doing the Clintons' dirty work, she told him, and get the pressure off her and Michael. The independent counsel's office wasn't after them. It was after him.

For the first time, Hill implored Brown to seek a private meeting with the president to get him to call this all off. Hill had a more realistic case than it might seem, and Brown had a stronger hand. They held at least two trump cards. The first was the shared knowledge that the path through Oklahoma led straight to the White House.

The second, the truly scary one, was China.

23 | MILO MINDERBINDER

At a meeting in November 1995, after proving to the president's satisfaction that General Colin Powell could not get the Republican nomination, Dick Morris looked across the table at Clinton and said with a dramatic flourish, "The election is now over. Congratulations, you won."[1]

By February 1996, with Morris's ads still running full tilt, Clinton was polling 53 percent in a conceptual one-on-one against Bob Dole. A year earlier, before Morris's multi-million dollar ad campaign, Clinton was polling 33 percent in the same imagined race.[2] During that year, Clinton had done almost nothing presidential to merit the boost. His comeback was a tribute to the powers of unethical advertising, illicit fund-raising, and a quiescent media. Observed Robert Reich acidly, "The only process we have is Dick Morris."[3]

To understand who financed the "process" and why, one does well to reread Joseph Heller's classic World War II novel, *Catch-22*. If, at the time of its publication in 1955, the novel seemed a wee bit hyperbolic, by 1995 it rang eerily true, particularly the character Milo Minderbinder, a dead-on fictional incarnation of the Loral honcho Bernard "Bernie" Schwartz.

Here Minderbinder explains to the novel's protagonist, the morally "simplistic" Yossarian, why he is selling the German army a "medium bomber and crew":

> Sure, we're at war with them. But the Germans are also members in
> good standing of the syndicate, and it's my job to protect their rights
> as shareholders. Maybe they did start the war, and maybe they are

killing millions of people, but they are paying their bills a lot more promptly than some allies of ours I could name. Don't you understand that I have to respect the sanctity of my contract with Germany? Can't you see it from my point of view?[4]

One can hear Schwartz making an almost identical pitch to Ron Brown and Bill Clinton. He had purchased the rights to do so. His money spoke with such clarity that in early February 1996 the White House dispatched Brown to collect a major chunk of it in person. No doubt, Schwartz could have mailed it in. But by sending a cabinet member, the White House signaled both its respect for Schwartz and its recognition of his intent, namely to secure waiver approval for Loral's satellite launches.

Brown also afforded the Clintons a degree of insulation should the media ever catch on to the exchange. "Oh, you know Ron Brown," one can almost hear the anonymous Clinton aides whispering to their pals in the media. With a subtle intra-tribal nod, they would not need to even mention Brown's race. That would be understood.

In return for staying "on board" Brown's sinking ship, Nolanda Hill insisted on being apprised of any action that might threaten her freedom and his. Increasingly uneasy about his situation, Brown welcomed a second opinion. On his February trip to New York to see Schwartz, he needed one.

The meeting was brief and to the point. Although Hill did not attend, she was in New York and met with Brown immediately afterwards. Still reeling, Brown showed her the two checks Schwartz had given him. Hill could not believe what she was seeing. Combined, they totaled $1.2 million. Hill does not "think" the total was $1.2 million. She "knows" it was and told the Justice Department as much in a pre-sentencing interview.

The checks must have unnerved even the DNC, as they were never logged in. Still, Schwartz got his point across, and before this election cycle was over he would officially donate more than $630,000 in soft money to the DNC, fifty times what he had given in the last presidential election. No Democrat gave more.[5]

In February 1996, Schwartz's money mattered. The Clintons were just beginning to smell victory. To secure it, they had to continue feeding the TV beast. They had fully ignored all FEC restrictions and were using soft money as though it were hard. Better still, the media had chosen not to see. Yes, Schwartz deserved his own bagman.

Schwartz did not make his gesture in an informational vacuum. According to the *New York Times*, February 1996 represented a moment of keen impasse between warring forces within the Clinton administration. With his generous support, Schwartz surely was hoping to breach the enemy's defenses.

The enemy in this case was his own Pentagon and intelligence community. Much to Schwartz's frustration, they were standing firm on the question of commercial satellites. Given the vital technology contained therein, much of it secret, they had convinced Secretary of State Warren Christopher in October 1995 to keep the satellites on the so-called "munitions list," an inventory of the nation's most sensitive military and intelligence-gathering equipment.

Almost immediately, Deputy National Security Advisor Sandy Berger had begun plotting to undermine Christopher. In November, Berger sent a memo to Christopher's deputy and long time Clinton buddy, Strobe Talbott. Berger claimed that Ron Brown, who "was far more sympathetic to the satellite makers,"[6] would appeal Christopher's ruling to Clinton. Clearly, Berger was setting up a paper trail that led directly to the hapless Brown. He then added, as if Talbott needed to be told, "I, too, have real questions about the wisdom" of Christopher's decision.[7]

Berger, a trade lawyer by profession, had no real foreign policy experience before becoming the number two man at the NSA. Like Talbott at State and Hubbell at Justice, Berger functioned more or less as the "political officer" within his department. According to the *Times*, critics described Berger as "the point man for the White House's China policy."[8]

Still, despite Berger's machinations, and the president's obvious support, the serious professionals within the NSA, State, and Defense were resisting the wholesale transfer of licensing authority for these satellites to the Commerce Department. Once moved to Commerce, the military feared it would lose veto power over exports.

The president also faced strong resistance from the genuine liberals within the administration. In the margin of a December 1995 document, for example, senior advisor George Stephanopoulos scrawled a vulgar note strongly criticizing the president's China policy.[9] Although not particularly liberal, Nolanda Hill was likewise appalled. For all the compromises of her Washington life, she retained her red-blooded Texan vigor. She loved her country, warts and all, and damned if she didn't know where those warts were. What Brown and Schwartz were doing was treasonous, she thought, and said so in no uncertain terms.

The case for treason would only grow stronger. Soon after he returned from New York, Brown learned he would be meeting—by order of the White House—with a character by the name of Wang Jun. The sheer bravado of Wang Jun's petition and the brazenness of the Clintons in welcoming him leave one awestruck.

Wang Jun chaired Poly Technologies, a company controlled by the People's Liberation Army. According to a Rand Corporation report forced from the U.S. Department of Commerce by a federal lawsuit, one of Poly Technologies' profit centers was the "importation and distribution of semi-automatic rifles for the U.S. domestic market." Between 1987 and 1993, the company and its affiliates sold more than $200 million worth of these guns in the United States. When Clinton piously signed into law the banning of certain semi-automatic weapons in 1994, Poly Technologies only profited. They exploited export loopholes to circumvent the ban and ultimately resorted to old-fashioned smuggling.[10]

In the mid-1990s, these weapons were flooding the inner cities of California. The always-feisty Los Angeles congresswoman Maxine Waters made Brown aware of the impact of these weapons on the young people in her district. Although Brown could barely stomach Waters, her message resonated. In his moral shipwreck of a life, Brown had always found a refuge in children, his own and others. He had a genuine fondness for them, especially adolescents. On a discreet, unscheduled trip to China in late January or early February 1996—ostensibly to warn the Chinese off Taiwan—he confronted the Chinese with their illicit gun dealing. It was one of his nobler moments.[11]

On the day of the Wang Jun meeting, February 6, 1996, Hill was staying at the Watergate Hotel. At the time, neither Hill nor Brown knew about Wang Jun's arms trade. Brown only knew the meeting was to be about satellite export controls. This makes sense as Wang Jun also owned a huge stake in a Hong Kong satellite company. Brown showed Hill the briefing book on the meeting. His task was to assure the Chinese that America intended to be a most friendly trading partner and if Wang Jun ever had any problems dealing with the United States, he could call Brown directly at anytime. Hill was beside herself.

"You're putting us at risk with all this Chinese money and Loral crap," she told him. She and Brown were under so much scrutiny already they could scarcely afford drawing any more heat. If Brown were naïve about Wang Jun's likely PLA connections, Hill was not. "The Red Army owns everything in that country," she told him. Hill implored him to pass on the meeting, but the White House had ordered him to go.

"Ron did not have any choice in the matter," says Hill.

Later that afternoon, the White House also insisted Brown join Wang Jun at an intimate "coffee" with President Clinton. It was an only-in-America kind of moment. Wang Jun, who had cut arms deals with Chinese allies in places like Libya, Iran, Serbia, Iraq, and Afghanistan, now found himself at a cordial private coffee with—of all people—the president of the United States.

Clinton pal Charlie Trie had greased the Wang Jun meeting with a $50,000 payment. Evidence suggests Trie laundered the money through a Wall Street player named Ernest Green. Under oath, Green would later attribute the multi-thousand dollar traveler's checks he received from Charlie Trie to "a gentlemen's bet on a basketball game."[12]

Green too deserves a sidebar. For no career arc, even Brown's, more clearly tracks with the sad decline of the civil rights movement. Green had parlayed his childhood role as one of the "Little Rock Nine" into a position in Jimmy Carter's Labor Department. From there he moved to Lehman Brothers on Wall Street and from there to a key role in the DNC fund-raising machine. In fact, he showed up in Hong Kong on Brown's 1994 junket and impressed even Brown with his Asian connections. Completing the descent, he eventually pled guilty to scandal-related tax charges.[13]

To the president's humble credit, as the Thompson Committee would later report, he did admit that the meeting with the PLA arms dealer, Wang Jun, was "clearly inappropriate." The president did not apologize, however, for signing waivers for four more satellite launches by Chinese rockets on that same February day. The president approved these waivers despite reports the month before that China continued to export nuclear technology to Pakistan and missiles to Iran, the latter deal Wang Jun was suspected of brokering.[14]

Just a week or so after Wang Jun's excellent Washington adventure, a Chinese Long March 3B rocket carrying the Loral-built Intelsat 708 satellite crashed just after liftoff and killed or injured at least sixty people in a nearby village. This was the third Long March failure in the last three years involving U.S.-built satellite payloads.[15]

The Pentagon welcomed the news. With the collapse of the Soviets, the People's Republic had emerged as America's most serious potential enemy, and its leaders weren't afraid to say so. Just a few months earlier, in fact, a Chinese military officer had warned American ambassador Chas Freeman, "If you hit us now, we can hit back. So you will not make those threats [about Taiwan]." The officer then proffered the following not so cryptic caveat: "In the end you care more about Los Angeles than you do about Taipei."[16]

American technical advice was making Chinese missile-rattling more than an empty threat. And yet in their relentless drive to raise money, the Clintons were fully prepared to broker that advice. In March 1996, Berger pressed on and managed to finesse a compromise that sent satellite control to Brown at Commerce and cost the Pentagon its veto power.[17]

According to the *Times*, which reviewed thousands of pages of unclassified documents, the deal was closed in a series of telephone calls involving Berger, Talbott, Brown, and John White, the deputy defense secretary. Tellingly, the *Times'* review "found no indication that Mr. Christopher was personally involved in the president's decision." On March 12, 1996, the president signed off on a "decision memorandum" that reversed Christopher's decision and awarded authority over satellite-export licensing to Commerce. Said an attached memo, "Industry should like the fact that they will deal with the more 'user friendly' Commerce system."[18]

In a likely show of contempt for both the president and of democracy in general, the People's Republic of China celebrated the decision by lobbing a few ballistic missiles into Taiwanese waters during Taiwan's March democratic elections.[19]

Indifferent to the fate of Taiwan and feeling confident about his relationship with the president, Schwartz up and dispatched a Loral-led review team to China to assess the February 1996 failure of the Long March 3B rocket and suggest refinements. The Cox Committee would later describe Schwartz's actions as "an unlicensed defense service for the PRC that resulted in the improvement of the reliability of the PRC's military rockets and ballistic missiles."[20]

So serious was the offense that in 1998 the Criminal Division of the Justice Department launched an investigation. Incredibly, while the investigation was in process, Berger, now national security adviser, sent a memo to the president urging him to "waive the legislative restriction on the export to China of the communications satellites and related equipment for the Space Systems/Loral (SS/L) Chinasat 8 project."[21]

This waiver would present a huge problem for the prosecution. Berger admitted as much: "Justice believes that a jury would not convict once it learned that the president had found SS/L's Chinasat 8 project to be in the national interest." But Berger was not about to let that stop him: "We will take the firm position that this waiver does not exonerate or in any way prejudge SS/L with respect to its prior unauthorized transfers to China." Berger was blowing smoke, and he knew it. A waiver would make prosecution all but impossible.

The president could only issue a waiver, however, if it served America's "national interest." Berger made an almost comically specious case that it did, arguing satellite technology would give remote Chinese villagers access "to people and ideas in democratic societies." During these misbegotten years, one trembles at what the villagers might have learned about American democracy.

For its part, Loral had no greater cause than its own bottom line. "If a decision is not forthcoming in the next day or so, we stand to lose the contract," Loral lobbyist Thomas Ross wrote Berger. "In fact, even if the decision is favorable, we will lose substantial amounts of money with each passing day."[22]

So much for the national interest. Ross then added the kicker, sure to win the president's heart: "Bernard Schwartz had intended to raise this issue with you at the Blair dinner, but missed you in the crowd." Schwartz knew he had a friend in the White House. The president approved the waiver, and the prosecution came to naught.[23]

This story merits its own book, but what deserves immediate comment is the willingness of the Clintons to risk everything to keep the cash pipeline open. Schwartz kept it open and full. Before he was through, Schwartz and Loral would donate roughly $2 million to the Clinton cause.[24] Whether Schwartz gave additional money or favors off the books is a question that deserves asking.

Wang Jun ran into problems of his own when on May 23, 1996, CNN breathlessly reported "the largest seizure of smuggled automatic weapons in U.S. history." The San Francisco Bureau of Alcohol, Tobacco, and Firearms had infiltrated a smuggling ring and confiscated two thousand fully automatic AK-47 rifles imported from China. The weapons were found on board a COSCO ship, the enterprise that had been trying to secure the Long Beach Naval Station. CNN traced the rifles to Wang Jun's Poly Technologies.[25]

Wang Jun, however, had not wasted his investment. Someone in the know did the arms merchant a large favor by leaking the news of the BATF gun smuggling investigation well before it was wrapped up. The Bay-area bust was premature. The BATF was not able to nail the operation's ringleaders.

Ron Brown knew Bernie Schwartz. He knew Wang Jun. He knew the Riadys and the Lums and John Huang. He knew about the Chinese navy's attempt to secure a bridgehead in Long Beach. He even knew about Mack McLarty and the Oklahoma deal. Did he ever. He knew what money was involved and where it went, and he transported a whole lot of it, much of which was never recorded. Ron Brown, in fact, knew way too much at a time when the media knew almost nothing. If there was any one man in America whose knowledge could undo the "process" and sink Bill Clinton, it was Brown.

Later that same month as the Schwartz and Wang Jun meetings, February 1996, in a private session in the White House family quarters, the president finally came to understand this.

24 | END GAME

In December 1995, after a lifetime of indifference, Ron Brown began going to church. For anyone looking closely, this sudden turn to the spiritual rightly suggested a soul in turmoil. As daughter Tracey acknowledges, "He was not a particularly religious man."[1]

Prayer came hard for Brown. He had worshipped too long and too devoutly at the altar of Mammon. But when the independent counsel targeted his son, Brown lost much of his faith in the here and now. He needed the kind of help that could not be purchased by the hour, and he knew it. For Brown, this was the beginning of wisdom. The shame was it had to come so late.

To help Brown find peace of mind, Nolanda Hill turned to a Christian mystic friend of hers who offered a Native American talisman. She in turn gave it to Brown, and he would carry this kit with him, wherever he went, right to the end. In an ironic twist, the kit would prove its value after his death. It was, however, not magic enough to save his life.

Brown needed immediate, temporal help as well. This, only the president could provide. And so Brown sought a private meeting with Clinton, one-on-one. They had a lot to talk about. Highest on Brown's list of priorities was the fate of Michael Brown, now just thirty and the father of twins. Brown loved the boy dearly. He could not bear the thought of his son going to jail. He knew it would all but kill Alma. And he knew finally that he was the one responsible. After all, it was he who had involved Michael in Oklahoma. How to explain that even to himself?[2]

Nolanda Hill did not share Brown's affection for the often-obtuse

Michael, but she cared deeply about Ron. For all her tough talk, she loved Brown unapologetically. Michael was his son. Her destiny and Michael's were joined whether she liked it or not.

It was Hill who pushed Brown to seek the meeting with Clinton. After Michael was publicly named, the pushing got easier. "I was absolutely convinced that Michael was looking at jail time," says Hill. She was convinced too that the independent counsel would charge Brown with unreported income and illegal use of his office, and that the charges would stick.

For Brown, however, seeking a meeting was no longer the same as securing one. "The number one stumbling block," says Hill, "was that he had to get the appointment." Brown could not just pick up the phone and call the president. They did not have that kind of a relationship.

The road to an appointment led through the acutely political Leon Panetta, Clinton's chief of staff. To arrange a private meeting—in the White House family quarters, where such meetings were held—Brown needed a rationale, a "ploy" as Hill calls it. She suggested fund-raising and the pressures thereof. Brown nixed that. He needed more. He needed an explanation the president would buy. Fund-raising wouldn't do it.

Hill ventured perhaps Brown might go through his longtime friend, Alexis Herman. She was hosting many of the White House "coffees" and had direct access to the president. Brown rejected this option too. He was convinced that Herman, his closest confidante in the White House, "had cast her lot with the president." This thought distressed him even more.

Brown never did tell Hill how he arranged the meeting or through whom, but he arranged it nonetheless. He told her about it only after the fact. She was staying at the Watergate where Brown came to debrief her. She traces the date to mid-February.

"I'll never forget it *as long as I live*," says Hill. The possibility exists Brown made up the details, but this seems unlikely. As Hill says, "He so knew I was so on his side that lying to me was like lying to himself."

It is possible too Hill conjured up the meeting or distorted its content, but a woman facing a very real independent counsel had no cause to fictionalize a meeting about the same. Besides, of all the parties involved in this drama, Hill's record for telling the truth is the strongest. The men who have sought her testimony under oath, Larry Klayman and Stephen Dresch, both vouch for her general reliability. If she protects herself just a little, implies Dresch, who wouldn't? As to the meeting itself, the only person in a position to refute her account will not do so short of his deathbed. And if he did, based on his history and hers, the disinterested observer would still have to believe Hill.

As Hill tells it, the meeting at the White House family quarters did not go well. The fastidious Brown had to read contempt into Clinton's odd choice to greet him in his stocking feet. Still Brown persisted. He told the president to call off the dogs, to shut down the independent counsel, to do whatever had to be done because he was not about to let Michael do jail time.

The president kept his peace and let Brown talk, much as he had with Lani Guinier. After Brown had finished, the president told Brown he doubted that he could do anything for him. The die had been cast. The case was out of his hands.

Brown dissented. Without the IRS and the FBI, the independent counsel could not function, he reminded the president. If Reno wanted to starve the investigation, she could do just that and say no more. Sure, she might have a public relations problem, but Reno loved her job so much she would do just about anything to keep it. This was her weakness, and both Clinton and Brown knew it.

In February 1996, more than a year into his mad scramble to retain the presidency, the president couldn't have cared less about Reno or her reputation. The only reputation he worried about was his own. He likely calculated the political risk to his reelection chances and ruled against intervention on the spot. He was not cold about it. He did not want to estrange Brown irrevocably, but he held out little hope.

When Brown did not get the response he wanted from Clinton, he resorted to his ultimate bargaining chip. If he had to, he told Clinton, he was prepared to reveal the president's treasonous dealings with China, almost none of which had yet to make the news. It was on this subject—the president's ultimate Achilles' heel—that Hill had been focusing Brown.

Before Clinton had a chance to assess the threat, Brown unthinkingly upped the ante. He told the president he had "lost control" of Hill. Clinton said nothing directly, but he surely must have read this remark for the implicit warning that it was.

So ended what may well have been the most critical and uncomfortable meeting of the Clinton presidency. The details of this meeting the president would not have shared with Leon Panetta or Vernon Jordan or even Dick Morris. The one person he would have told was his wife. He and Hillary could not have failed to recognize that if Brown went public on

......a, Clinton would certainly lose the election, probably the nomination, and quite possibly his freedom. The potential for disaster was that real and that imminent.

Hill did not see much of Brown after the meeting. The White House had him on the road almost constantly, leaving the burden of dealing with the case almost entirely on her shoulders. Still, Brown and Hill talked often. Brown worried openly about Hill's safety. Above all, he feared the Chinese. After their attempted seizure of the Long Beach Naval Station, says Hill, "He never stopped being afraid."

Now, the stakes were higher still. There was so much money involved, so many deals on the table. Brown had impulsively advertised Hill as the one other person willing to blow it all open even if he backed down. A government that had eliminated a few thousand of its own at and after Tiananmen Square was not likely to get squeamish about one or two more. Brown went so far as to call Hill's sister, with whom she stayed from time to time, and insist Hill not be allowed to go out jogging alone.

In March, Brown flew to South and Central America on still another trade mission. In Nicaragua, he made the acquaintance of Violeta Chamorro, the charismatic president whose 1990 election shocked the Sandinistas and the world.

Unmoored, looking for a safe harbor, Brown found it in Chamorro. In one five-hour stretch he called Hill three times, indiscreetly pleading with her to come to Nicaragua and share in Chamorro's wisdom. The line was unsecured. "He should not have been saying what he was saying on the phone," says Hill. "A lot of it was explosive. It was dangerous for us and our family."

Throughout early 1996 Judicial Watch intensified the pressure on Brown. On March 14, under court order, Brown submitted a sworn statement Judicial Watch would later claim to be "patently false and misleading."[3]

In his finely parsed words, Brown swore he had played no role "in determining the scope of the Department of Commerce's search for and/or preparation of response to the Freedom of Information Act requests made the basis this suit." Brown was perjuring himself. While he was writing the statement, he had some of the requested documents in the same room with him.

Even the judge was moved to comment on Brown's "obviously careful wording." Brown might have said there simply were no such documents, but this was too flagrantly false. Needing more information, Judicial Watch went ahead and scheduled Brown for a deposition in early April, but that was not to be.

On March 19, the independent counsel's office ratcheted up the pressure as well. Daniel Pearson obtained subpoenas for more than twenty individuals and organizations. He wanted to see the records of the DNC, the Lum's infamous Asian Pacific Advisory Council and their even more potentially explosive Oklahoma entity, Dynamic Energy Resources.[4] If they were unaware before, the Clintons had to know now just where Pearson was heading, and they could not have been pleased.

Soon after the subpoenas were issued, Brown informed Hill of another trip, this time to the Balkans. Brown likely knew about the trip earlier. Ira Sockowitz claims credibly that he started preparing for the trip about six weeks out, which would have been mid to late February.[5] This would have been just after Brown's private meeting with Clinton. The dating of each is too imprecise to confirm that the meeting precipitated the trip, but it may very well have. In any case, six weeks suggests haste. Preparations for the 1994 China trip began at least six months out. As soon as Hill learned of the trip, she was worried. "I felt a real foreboding," she remembers. "I tried to talk him out of going."

Everything about this "drop-in" junket seemed wrong. At first, Brown was told the State Department had asked for the trip, but this made no sense as State typically wanted as little to do with Commerce as possible. The military could not have sought it either. Less than six months after the signing of the Dayton accords, the Balkan countryside remained unsettled and dangerous. Security would not come cheaply or easily.

Nor could Hill see the commercial logic of the trip. "Why would anyone want to invest over there?" she asked Brown. "We aren't even through blowing stuff up." The American business community did not appear to see the point of it either. Brown had to make calls and twist arms to assure there were enough people on the plane. And even then he could not attract the high level CEOs for whom these trade missions were designed.

"This trip makes no sense," Hill told him more than once. Brown did not disagree. The trip did not even make sense from a fund-raising perspective.

Hill continued to lean on Brown to cancel the Balkan trip. Beyond her premonitions, she desperately wanted to arrange a meeting for the two of them and their lawyers. With Hill's lawyer in Kentucky, that would not be easy. Hill knew she was being hard on Brown, but there was too much at stake not to be.

"Hillary and Chelsea have just gone," she said of the Clinton family trip which would touch down in Bosnia ten days before Brown's. "Isn't that enough?" Brown, however, could not call the trip off on his own. The White House was organizing it.

Brown had one last White House meeting scheduled before he departed. Under pressure from Hill, he found a minute alone with the president and asked him to send someone else to the Balkans. The president refused. Brown called Hill immediately afterwards from his car and told her. "He was just low," says Hill.

At home, Brown's anxiety was beginning to bleed through. Although Alma was bedridden with the flu, Brown insisted she accompany him to the bank to refinance the mortgage at a lower rate. The day before he was to leave, he ignored Alma's objections and all but lifted her out of bed to get the mortgage signed. As Tracey Brown observes of her mother, "She couldn't understand his intensity."[6]

The night before he departed for the Balkans, Brown visited his mother, then hospitalized for schizophrenia, in New York City. Afterwards, he returned to her apartment. He had not been there in years. Sitting alone in the dark, Brown called Hill and for three tearful hours walked her through the ruins of his life. "I was his old comfort," says Hill. "I was home to him."

The day Brown left for Europe, he spent with "Sonny Junior," as Brown called his beloved son. They played golf together, ironically enough at the Robert Trent Jones Golf Club, the club whose membership the Lums had purchased. Brown appeared to be in good spirits. After golf, his chauffeur arrived at the Brown residence to take him to the airport. Brown kissed the still ailing Alma good bye, and he was off.[7]

Brown called Hill, then in Dallas, from the car. The conversation went badly. She asked that he "step up to the plate" and shoulder his share of the burden imposed by the independent counsel. He accused her of putting "negative thoughts" in his head. Despite the increasing unease attached to them, he had lately found a measure of escape in these journeys—in Europe, they could care less about the independent counsel—and he was vainly trying to find it now.

On March 31, Brown arrived in France and headed up to Lille, two hours north of Paris, for a G-7 conference on employment. There, as fate would have it, he met up with Labor Secretary Robert Reich, gracious and sincere as always.

Standing together at the top of a grand stairway for their entrance, the two gloried in their shared Americanness. It mattered little that Reich was Jewish or that Brown was a foot or so taller. They had found common ground. Brown regretted he had ever disparaged the man. As for Reich, he would cite Brown's death as the reason he would soon quit the cabinet.[8]

After the two-day conference, Brown returned to Paris where he stayed with Pamela Harriman, the *grande dame* of the Democratic party and then ambassador to France. That afternoon, he and Harriman went for a long walk through the *arrondissements* of Paris.

The account Hill and Tracey Brown give of the walk and, in Tracey's words, the "most unusual" event that followed is essentially the same. Brown had found a small chapel named for Saint Catherine Labouré. After the outing with Harriman, he had a staff person drive him back to the chapel. He stayed so long in prayer that he came late to the reception Harriman was holding in his honor. Brown had never done anything like this before.[9]

Afterwards, Brown called both Alma and Nolanda and told them about the experience. Alma, still ailing, paid it little mind. Nolanda took it seriously. He apologized for his outburst in the car. As he often did, he shared his boyish wonder at the elegance around him. He then promised Hill that when he returned he would cease these endless trips and devote his attention to their case before the independent counsel.

Brown also shared his misgivings about the Balkan leg of the trip, how disorganized and improvised it all seemed. He was not even sure who was coming. "Ron," said Hill, "there is something wrong with this." Brown did not disagree, but it was Hill's safety about which he worried, more so than his own.

As they talked, Brown began a slow, emotional descent through the hell of his own psyche, one level at a time. "I heard something in his voice," says Hill, something she had first heard a few nights earlier at his mother's, a keen sense of isolation and regret. "I have never been so lonely in all my life," he confessed.

After the reception on April 2, Brown boarded a military plane at the Villacoublay airport in France and headed to the Croatian capital of Zagreb. There he landed around midnight. Croatian ambassador Peter Galbraith and Brown aide, Morris Reid, met him at the airport, as did Croatian prime minister Zlatko Matesa.

Brown was originally scheduled to meet Croatian strongman and president Franco Tudjman the next day in Zagreb. But Matesa informed him the meeting site had been changed to Dubrovnik, allegedly to help promote the walled city's potential as a tourist site. This added leg could not have pleased Brown. He would have to take a change of clothes with him when he left the hotel the next morning at 5:30 AM for a trip to Tuzla in Bosnia.[10]

According to daughter Tracey, Brown ordered his aide Morris Reid to stay behind in Zagreb "to take care of a problem that had arisen with Enron." Writing in those innocent days when Democrats took such interventions in stride, Tracey blithely describes Enron as "a Texas-based natural gas company that was negotiating an agreement with the government of Croatia." The Enron executives would take their own plane to Dubrovnik the next day.[11]

In Tuzla, Brown was to meet with American troops stationed there. Prior to leaving France, he had persuaded a McDonald's manager in Zagreb to give him two hundred Big Macs to carry to the troops. Needless to say, the soldiers were delighted by the gesture.[12] He met with one group for breakfast and another for lunch, and in between he schmoozed with local officials.

At about 1:30 PM Croatia time, shortly before his departure from Tuzla, Brown called Hill from a satellite phone. The troops had greatly boosted the spirits of this former Army captain. He felt like he had brought something to their lives. Maybe, he told Hill, "That was God's purpose." The words disarmed Hill. She had never heard him speak in those terms before. Previously, it had always been, "What's in it for me?"

Brown overrode her objections about flying and reassured her the weather had improved. He would call as soon as he found a phone that worked in Dubrovnik. "I want you not to worry," he said. "I'm fine." It was about 5:30 AM in Dallas. Hill promised him she would stay up until he phoned.

"You'd have been so proud of me, sweet angel," said Brown of his visit with the troops. "I'll call you. I love you." Those were the last words from Ron Brown that Hill would ever hear.

25 | ST. JOHN'S PEAK

A s the world knows, Ron Brown's plane never did reach its destination. Why it did not is another question. What follows is a straightforward, multi-sourced account of that last flight.[1]

At 2:10 PM Croatia time on April 3, 1996, Captain Amir Sehic landed a twin-engine corporate jet at Cilipi Airport about ten nautical miles south of Dubrovnik on the Adriatic coast. For the record, a nautical mile equals 1.15 statute miles. All future references will be to nautical miles.

Sehic's jet carried Croatian Prime Minister Zlatko Matesa and American ambassador Peter Galbraith. After Galbraith disembarked, he heard another plane descending and thought it might be Brown's. It wasn't. It was a Swiss Air charter carrying the Enron executives, one of five planes to land routinely on the airport's sole runway in the hour before Brown's plane was scheduled.

About fifteen minutes earlier, at 1:55 PM, Ron Brown's CT-43A, the military version of a Boeing 737, call sign IFO-21, left Tuzla in Bosnia, 130 miles to the northeast. At this stage, the plane was five minutes ahead of schedule. When Brown boarded the plane he was wearing a polo shirt Nolanda Hill had given him and an all-weather jacket. He turned right after entering, towards a compartment in the back, and there changed into a suit and tie.[2]

A few minutes after take-off, IFO-21 contacted Air Force weather service and asked for Dubrovnik weather at the planned arrival time. The weather report was 500 feet broken, 2,000 feet overcast, five miles visibility

Ron Brown's Fatal Flight

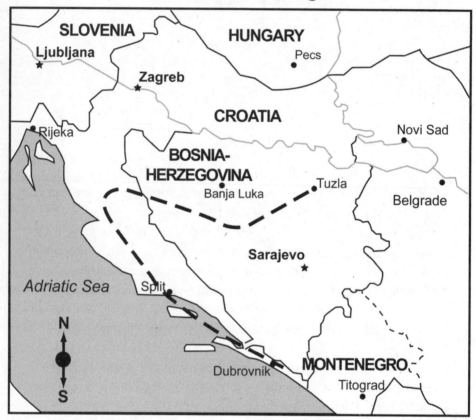

SLOVENIA
Ljubljana

HUNGARY
Pecs

Zagreb

CROATIA

Novi Sad

Rijeka

BOSNIA-
HERZEGOVINA
Banja Luka

Tuzla

Belgrade

Sarajevo

Adriatic Sea

Split

N

S

Dubrovnik

MONTENEGRO

Titograd

and rain. Technically, this was below the legal minimum for landing, but the pilots proceeded apace. The weather had been highly variable all day. It would likely change again.

Sixteen minutes out of Tuzla, the pilots started a turn to the south before being reminded by NATO controllers that this projected route was not in one of the authorized corridors. The controllers redirected them to a northern corridor. This maneuver put the plane about ten minutes behind schedule.

At 2:34 PM the plane, now at 21,000 feet, crossed over the sophisticated VOR transmitter at Spit and banked southeast out over the Adriatic towards Dubrovnik's Cilipi Airport one hundred miles away. The Zagreb Center, which was controlling the plane, cleared it to descend first to 14,000 feet and then 10,000. At that latter point, Zagreb transferred control to the Dubrovnik tower at Cilipi.

Captain Sehic sat in the cockpit of his Challenger facing north to keep an eye out for Brown's plane. He watched as the rain ceased and the sky brightened. At 2:48 PM, he called the incoming plane from his cockpit and told the pilots several other planes had successfully landed and the weather was, in his words, "on the minima," meaning above the minimum standards needed to land. If they needed to execute a missed approach, however, he recommended a route over the Adriatic to the right. "It is easy approach [sic]," he would tell USAF investigators. "I was not concerned."[3] Now at about 5,000 feet and some sixteen miles away, U.S. Air Force Captains Ashley J. Davis, thirty-five, and Tim Shafer, thirty-three, thanked Sehic for his words of welcome.

At 2:53 PM, the control tower told another flight the weather was "500 broken and 2,000 overcast." This was below minimum. Davis and Shafer likely heard this, but they themselves did not ask for the current weather from the tower. If they had, it would have been on tape and they could have been reprimanded for starting an illegal approach. The only way they could get in trouble is if they crashed and they certainly did not expect to do that. They were well aware there was a mountain just 1.8 miles to the left of runway 12 and that mountain was shrouded in clouds. Whatever they did, they were not going to fly left of the final approach course. "If you're going to err," Captain Paul Frydenlund would casually acknowledge after testing the course post-crash, "you want to err to the right side."[4]

Because of the weather, the crew was required to fly an instrument approach into Cilipi. The only ground instrument the pilots could follow into this relatively primitive airport was a non-directional radio beacon

(NDB) on Kolocep Island. This was not of great concern to Davis. As an evaluator pilot—that is, one who is skilled enough to evaluate other pilots— he did not lack confidence. He himself had recently tested "proficient" on this kind of approach. As the USAF report acknowledged, "The mishap pilot and copilot were described as the two best pilots in the flight."

The pilots, however, were in the midst of a long and busy day. With a dignitary on board, there is no doubt they wanted to stay on schedule. If, once they reached their minimums of 2150 feet mean sea level—about 1600 feet above the runway—they could not see the runway environment, they could always execute a "missed approach procedure" and climb out safely and easily to the Adriatic on their right and head back to Spit or try again.

At 2:54 the plane passed over the radio beacon, seemingly on course, if a little too fast. The crew called the tower—"We're inside the locator, inbound"—and was then cleared for a landing. The published approach charts required the pilot to fly a 119-degree course from this beacon on Kolocep Island, the "final approach fix."

To the pilots, all seemed in order. This was a routine landing. They descended through the clouds at an appropriate approach speed to an altitude of 2200 feet smoothly and consistently, guiding themselves by the one beacon behind them. The tower took the pilots at their word. It had nothing else on which to rely. It had no radar.

Lenadra Gluhan, an off-duty air traffic controller, knew something was wrong the moment she heard the plane pass *behind* her house. She lived just north of the airport. She could hear clearly because the light rain had ceased altogether, and she had just thrown open her rear windows. As Gluhan knew, the plane should have been in front.[6]

Only in the final seconds of their young lives did Pilots Davis and Shafer realize they were off course. But they could not have begun to comprehend how far and how fatally. Before the plane's Ground Proximity Warning Systems could activate, just three minutes after last contact with the control tower, St. John's Peak rose up right in front of them.

Davis would have instinctively yanked back on the control wheel and firewalled the throttles, but it was too late for either.[7] At 2:57 PM the plane's inertia carried the hundred thousand pound craft at 150 knots into the jagged hillside, clipping its right wing and engine and cracking off the tail before any of the passengers even had a chance to pray for deliverance. The fuselage then skidded violently across the rocky slope, breaking up as it slid, disgorging its passengers randomly, and finally crunching to a fiery halt with the crew, likely dead or unconscious, trapped inside.

Those at Cilipi, a little less than two miles from the crash, knew nothing. At 3:01 PM the tower tried to contact the pilots but without success. At 3:10 PM the tower announced to Morris Reid, Galbraith, and the others that it had lost contact with Brown's plane. No one was particularly worried. They presumed the pilots had chosen to divert to another airport.

Ten minutes later, Prime Minister Matesa lamented that all contact with the plane had been lost. Galbraith returned to Matesa's plane and called the State Department in Washington. He reached Undersecretary Peter Tarnoff and expressed his concerns. Galbraith then turned his attention to organizing a multinational rescue operation. It would not be until 4:30 PM Croatia time that word reached the president in the Oval Office. It was 9:30 AM in Washington, a seven hour differential due to Europe's early move to Daylight Savings Time.

Nolanda Hill was concerned long before the president. The plane should have arrived about 7:00 AM Dallas time. Hill was still up, sitting by the wall phone in the kitchen of her suburban Dallas home, refusing to use a portable for fear the call would be intercepted. As the hours passed, Hill grew more and more anxious.

Finally, the phone rang. Hill answered and felt that sudden wrench of the heart that comes with the dashing of an anxious hope. It was not Brown. It was her brother-in-law, Louis Blaylock. His tone frightened her.

"Sue, do you have the television on?" he asked. "No," she answered, now alarmed.

"Don't turn it on until someone gets there."

"What's wrong?"

"Ron's plane went down. Your mother and Mary Lou are on the way."

Hill dropped the phone, stood up, and then slumped to the floor as her legs gave way underneath her. Her young cousin Jennifer, who had been staying with Hill, heard the fall and came running down the stairs. For a moment, Hill could not find the words to say anything.

"Ron's plane crashed," she whispered finally, simply. When Hill regained at least some hint of composure, she called her longtime friend from Patton Boggs, Joe Reeder, then undersecretary of the Army. Reeder told her, "I've got men in the water, and they think they have found it."

Back in Washington, Alma Brown also waited for a call that never came.

When the phone finally did ring, the voice on the other end said, "Alma, Alma is that you? This is Bill Clinton."[8]

In Croatia, Morris Reid, Galbraith, and others huddled numbly in the airport police station while search and rescue operations proceeded apace. Lacking helicopters in the Dubrovnik area, Croatian authorities called on NATO for help. Two French helicopters took off from nearby Ploce at about 4:50 PM—nearly two hours after the crash—and began searching.

The first coordinates given to the French placed the crash site in the water between Kolocep Island and Dubrovnik. For the next hour, the French pilots continued to fly over and around the old city of Dubrovnik. "We didn't know anything about the location of the crash," conceded Lt. Col. Jean Francois Dupleix.[9]

At 6:45 PM, two American helicopters arrived. They had crossed the Adriatic looking for a T-34, a single engine, training plane. They were not only looking for the wrong plane, but they were also looking in the wrong places. They had not been informed about the direction of approach for Brown's plane. After only a few minutes on site near Dubrovnik, however, they "pretty much knew it was on land."[10] They saw no indication of the plane in the water, and the plane's crash position indicator was emitting a telltale signal. The weather, however, prevented an inland search, and so they landed at Cilipi airport, there to sit for the next frustrating few hours.

At 6:45 PM Croatian time, almost four hours after the disappearance of the plane, a local villager named Ivo Djurkovic called the police to tell them that earlier in the afternoon he had heard a plane fly low overhead, followed by a loud "grating sound" and then an explosion.[11] Given the time and place, he assumed it was a grenade. But then the fog finally lifted off a nearby mountain called Sveti Ivan, or in English, St. John's Peak, one of the highest mountains in the area at 2400 feet. And there, to his horror, he saw the shattered wreckage of Ron Brown's plane.

With no phone in the village of Velji Do, he drove his small Fiat five miles down a narrow winding road to a friend's house and called the police. At that moment Cavtat police chief Vitomir Bajac was driving towards the hills for the simple reason that this "was the area that wasn't searched so far."[12] When the message was relayed to him, he headed towards St. John's Peak. At 7:20 PM he called in the first official visual confirmation of the wreckage, and he reached the site on foot about fifteen minutes later.

About fifteen minutes after that, police instructor Damir Raguz arrived with a group of about thirty other police. By this time, the rains were torrential and visibility non-existent. Some mystery surrounds how many survivors the rescue workers found or at exactly what time they found them. According to Commerce Department documents, kept secret for three years before being unearthed by court order, Commerce attorney Ira Sockowitz called Washington at 8:58 PM Croatia time to report that two passengers "have been recovered alive from the crash."[13] Sockowitz was in Sarajevo doing advance work for the trip. He denies making such a call, and his denial rings true.[14]

According to his own testimony, it was not until 8:30 PM that Raguz spotted two women lying under debris in the tail of the plane. The tail had broken off but remained largely intact after the crash. He had presumed them both dead until at 9:30 PM, he heard one of them, Tech Sergeant Shelly Kelly, thirty-six of Zanesville, Ohio, make an "ah" sound. He and the others pulled the debris off Kelly. She was bleeding from her mouth and nose and from her leg. Raguz bandaged her leg and laid her on her side so she wouldn't choke. At 9:35 PM, he first alerted the outside world that there was at least one seriously injured survivor.[15]

At 10:36 PM a U.S. MH-53 helicopter took off from Cilipi for the peak in an attempt to airlift the survivor out but was repeatedly beaten back by the weather. By 11:15 PM, Croatian police realized they would have to transport the survivor. They put her on a stretcher found inside the plane and carried her down the hill. At the bottom of the mountain, they transferred Kelly to a waiting ambulance. An accompanying Croatian physician pronounced her dead on the way to the hospital. She likely died on the way down.

Rumors would spread that Kelly was seen climbing onto a rescue helicopter under her own power, only to succumb later of a slashed femoral artery. The New York Times may have fed the rumors by claiming Djurkovic and two policemen had found her alive two hours earlier than they actually had and that "she tried to stand up, and lost consciousness."[16] But the Times was wrong, and rumors of her murder were just that.

An entirely credible autopsy would confirm she died of an "ill-defined cervical fracture"[17]—a broken neck—likely aggravated by her forced extrication from the plane and a rough trip down the slope by well-meaning rescuers. She also had a broken leg and severe internal injuries. She would not have been able to walk onto anything, even if there had been a helicopter. The tales of a second survivor may well have focused on Kelly's seatmate, fellow flight attendant and tech sergeant, Cheryl Turnage, thirty-seven, of Lakehurst, New Jersey, whose body was intact but who did not survive the crash.

More might have been known about what transpired at the scene were it not for an odd exchange of information at 9:40 PM Croatia time. Again, according to Commerce Department documents, Deputy Secretary of State Strobe Talbott was reported to have made a "strong request" that "HRT TV team in Dubrovnik not film at the crash site."[18] HRT is the acronym for Hrvatska Radiotelevizija, or Croatian Radio Television. Croatian officials readily complied.

While the Croatians scoured the hillside for survivors, President and Hillary Clinton left the Brown residence and headed over to the Commerce Department to deliver a "eulogy" for Ron Brown and the other victims, at least one of whom was still very much alive. One labors to find a rationale for the Clintons' haste other than beating the deadline for the evening news. At this point, they could not have known who was living and who was not. As shall be seen, "haste" will shape much of the ensuing investigation.

Back in Dallas, reality settled in and shock and sorrow yielded to thoughts of survival. Nolanda Hill called Brown's people at the Commerce Department. At Commerce, Brown kept a locked drawer filled with sensitive documents he had never turned over.

"Don't let anyone get in that drawer," Hill told them. She then called Michael Brown on his cell phone and expressed her concerns. Still in shock at the loss of his father, Michael had the presence of mind to tell her, "Any kind of documents that need to be shredded are being shredded as we speak." He was already one step ahead of her.

That same afternoon, Hill received an unexpected call that notched up her anxiety level even higher. One of Tommy Boggs' partners called to ask whether she knew anything about a possible assassination attempt on Boggs, then in Capetown. The partner had gotten a heads up from a friend in the media. With her son Andrew in Mali on a business deal, Hill was nearly apoplectic, fearing some sort of wider conspiracy. The story about Boggs never broke through to the major media, but it circulated just below the surface for years.

Hill later confronted Boggs and asked him straight out if anyone did ever try to kill him in South Africa. Boggs just laughed and changed the subject. Hill was not amused. "One of the things you and I have in common is Ron Brown," she told him, "and he's dead." Boggs would say no more.

In Croatia, later that first night, Galbraith, Reid, and others drove the narrow, difficult road to the base of St. John's Peak. There they saw a crowd of Croatian military and police. Galbraith and some of the others tried to climb the peak in the rain and fog, but the going was slow, and rescue workers discouraged them from continuing. They all returned to the hotel save for Brown's loyal factotum, Morris Reid. He watched the rescue workers retrieve Kelly and nine crash victims and affirmed none of them was Brown.

The first three American rescuers from the Special Tactical Squad would not reach the peak until 2:30 AM Croatia time. At 4:00 AM American military personnel set up a communications post at the base of the mountain. Towards morning, Reid prevailed upon them to allow him to climb the two uphill miles to the crash site. The hike took more than an hour. Amidst the debris and carnage, he saw Ron Brown's body, the remains of a tie still around the neck. Reid climbed back down and called the Brown family. It was 9:00 AM in Croatia, 2:00 AM in Washington. Michael Brown took the call.[19]

Seven hours later, at 9:00 AM Washington time, President Clinton called Alma Brown. He told her Brigadier General Michael Canavan, special operations commander on site, had identified her husband.[20]

On April 4, without any hard information, the political people hastened to dispel any notion of terrorism or sabotage. In the run up to the 1996 election, in the face of an unpopular and ill-explained Balkan policy, a terrorist attack on a plane carrying a popular black leader could have some unpleasant ramifications.

"The weather yesterday, as the plane flew in, was terrible," said Peter Galbraith. He then shifted from overstatement to outright misinformation. "In fact, people in Dubrovnik say that this is the worst storm in a decade."[21] As ambassador to Croatia, he was in a position to know better. His remark was picked up widely by the media and, without any substantiation, transformed into fact. "Brown's entourage boarded an Air Force T-43 for the coastal town of Dubrovnik," asserted *Time* magazine a week or so later, "where one of the worst storms in a decade was raging."[22]

Defense Secretary William Perry had flown on the same plane only days earlier. So had Hillary and Chelsea a week or so before that. In an oddly indiscreet moment, Perry told reporters on his way back to Washington from Egypt, "It was a classic sort of an accident that good instrumentation should be able to prevent."[23] He was in no position to know that or say it.

At the Pentagon, Lt. Gen. Howell Estes of the Joint Chiefs of Staff seemed yet unaware of political efforts to spin the story. "It's a safe approach," said Estes. "Many aircraft have landed at the airport there at Dubrovnik with no difficulties, and, in fact, as you know, some landed that morning and early afternoon prior to Secretary Brown's aircraft's scheduled arrival."[24] He was saying the obvious, but in time the obvious would not be explanation enough.

Although the Commerce Department logs casually note "the flight data recorder has been recovered," Estes' impolitic response here gives greater credibility to his claim, as improbable as it sounds, that the plane did not seem to have a cockpit voice recorder or a flight data recorder, the so-called black boxes.[25] The reason he cited is the Air Force procured the plane for training purposes, and it was not so equipped when it came from the factory.

As to the president, he had made the serendipitous connection between this sad day—April 4, a day after the crash—and a comparably sad one twenty-eight years earlier when Martin Luther King was slain in Memphis. Like King, claimed the president, Brown died "answering a very important challenge of his time."[26] Clinton did not elaborate that this "important challenge" was getting him reelected by whatever means necessary. Jesse Jackson laid it on even thicker:

> On this day twenty-eight years ago, I learned a painful lesson about the strength of faith on a hotel balcony in Memphis. Dr. Martin Luther King, Jr. spent his last day finding ways to improve the lives of the poor, and expanding opportunities for workers. In their way, Ron Brown and his delegation were doing the same thing.[27]

Were he alive, Brown would never have dared to profane King's achievements by comparing them to his own. But he was not alive, and so throughout the day and beyond, Clinton, Jackson, and others would exploit the King-Brown connection for all it was worth.

The media would reliably pick up the theme. After all, as *Time* reported, Brown's resume also "contained a gold-plated series of civil rights achievements." As to the charges against Brown, none of which were "ever proved," these were largely the product of "G.O.P. budget cutters who were targeting the Commerce Department for elimination."[28]

If the president had not seen it already, Ron Brown's death offered a whole lot more silver lining than cloud.

26 | DEPARTED SOUL

Chief Petty Officer Kathleen Janoski glanced from time to time at the classroom's muted TV screen, and all she saw was Ron Brown. "That's odd," she thought.

At the end of class—an FBI course in photography at Quantico—someone turned up the volume, and it all became clear. Ron Brown's plane had disappeared. Janoski knew without being told that she had her work cut out for her.[1]

That work was forensic photography. For the past year, Janoski had served as a forensic photographer in the Office of the Armed Forces Medical Examiner (OAFME) at the Armed Forces Institute of Pathology (AFIP), an inter-service institute managed by the Army.

After twenty years in the Navy, Janoski accepted the reality that this was still a man's world and always would be. When she started in forensics, she could easily anticipate the gamut she would have to run. A good-looking blonde, with an as yet un-barnacled freshness about her, she was sure her new colleagues would think of her "as a lightweight bimbo." To survive, she would have to quickly disabuse them of that notion. She had done it before.

Medical forensics presented a higher level of challenge than her previous postings. Janoski knew she would have to confront death on a daily basis. She did not know, however, the first death she would have to confront would be her own mother's. Her mom died back in Pittsburgh just as Janoski was starting her new job.

When Janoski returned from leave, still emotionally wrought, she had to fly immediately to the site of a helicopter crash in Oklahoma. This first assignment could not have come at a more unsettled time. Still, despite her personal anguish, the one-hundred-degree heat of an Oklahoma summer, and the horrific sights and smells of catastrophic death, Janoski "didn't puke or pass out," and that alone she considered a moral victory.

Janoski had toughened up over the years. One has to in the Navy. A steelworker's daughter, she had come to the task with more than her share of survival skills, joining, over her parents' objections, just a few years out of high school. In 1976, girls did not do such things. The Navy made this one girl happy, though, when it actually sent her where she had asked to be sent—photo school. Better yet, her first posting was in Pensacola, Florida.

In 1988, the year Ron Brown first surfaced on the national horizon, Janoski started her grittiest gig yet, this time on the "hot, noisy, dirty" repair ship, the *L.Y. Spear*, hull number AS-36. For the next three years, as Brown ran the DNC, Janoski ran the *Spear's* improbable photo lab. It was on board this ship that she learned just how vulnerable she was to the sway of the sea, a real liability for a sailor.

"There were times," says Janoski, "that I wished I would have died." Seasick or not, she persisted. "You have no choice," she adds. "In the Navy, you just suck it up and do it."

As happens in the Navy, her fate soon reversed course. By 1992, she had snagged her best job yet, working as a personal photographer to a two star admiral and getting, as always, impeccable evaluations. Better still, she was living in Washington, a city she loved, with her husband, a helicopter pilot assigned to the Pentagon.

Given her background, especially her family's union sympathies, Janoski had always considered herself a liberal and a Democrat. In 1992, like Nolanda Hill, she voted for Bill Clinton. Soon after the election a Job-like series of events severely tested her will. Her father died. Her husband asked for a divorce. And the wife of her only sibling was diagnosed with cancer. To help fill the void, she volunteered to answer the mail for the White House, the reward for which was the occasional private tour of the famed West Wing and a photo of herself with Hillary Clinton.

On Good Friday, 1996, two days after the crash, Janoski finished her photo course and drove up to the medical examiner's office in Washington. There, while gathering up her gear, she ran into team leader, Navy Cmdr. Edward Kilbane, looking smart in his dress blues. When she teased him about his attire, he told her cryptically, "I had to go to the West Wing of the White House." At the time, Janoski had no idea what Kilbane's comment meant or that she would soon be causing that same West Wing a world of trouble.

The next morning, Holy Saturday, Janoski drove alone through the cool gloom to the Dover Air Force Base in Delaware where the thirty-three American bodies from the Balkan crash would soon be arriving. With little to do that first day but set up, she looked forward to the arrival of the president. That afternoon, he and Hillary, the Brown family, and a few of Brown's close friends flew in on Air Force One. Although not particularly close to Ron Brown at the end, Tommy Boggs had been assigned a seat on board. "His job," suggests Nolanda Hill, "was to contain the toxicity."

The Clintons visited individually with each of the other thirty-two families. Afterwards, the president spoke to about a thousand friends and family sitting on makeshift bleachers in the gray sepulchral chill of the late afternoon. Again, as at the Commerce Department, he talked almost exclusively about "the noble secretary of Commerce," Ron Brown.[2] Brown's rehabilitation was continuing apace. Janoski watched in her own dress blues with a colleague, Naval Criminal Intelligence Service (NCIS) agent, Jeanmarie Sentell, and was appropriately moved.

The next morning, Easter Sunday, Janoski and her colleagues went to work at the base's huge mortuary, a building about the size of an airplane hangar and with roughly the same ambiance. After the bodies were unloaded from the trucks, they passed in assembly line fashion from one station to the next: triaging and personal effects, fingerprints, dental X-rays, full body X-rays, and then into the morgue for inspections, DNA, and body charting by the AFIP's pathologists. Set up for a large-scale disaster, the morgue area was large enough to accommodate six or more examination tables.

Janoski was the chief of the photography team. Fully aware of the controversy around White House counselor Vince Foster's ill-handled death, she took the responsibility for photographing Ron Brown's body. The purpose was to document the extent of the injuries or the absence of the same, and this she was prepared to do with extra care.

Janoski can still picture Brown on the table in front of her. She recalls the ragged pants, the tie, and particularly his black dress socks, now pointless in their formality. For all the savagery of the crash, the body was fully intact. Janoski could see the chemical burns to Brown's torso and face and the lacerations on the front and sides of his head as well as on the top, but none of these injuries, she believed, would have been lethal. Brown also suffered a broken pelvis, but that injury would not have killed him either.

Janoski proceeded to test the exposure system on her Nikon F4. By some providential stroke, she did so by shooting Brown's X-rays, which were posted on the light box. When ready, she mounted a stepladder and began to photograph the body starting at the head. She had scarcely begun when she saw something that took her breath away.

"Look at the hole in Brown's head," she exclaimed. "It looks like a bullet hole."

Col. William Gormley, the pathologist examining Brown, instinctively shushed her, but a buzz quickly ran through the room. U.S. Army Lt. Col. David Hause, an experienced deputy medical examiner, left his examining table to take a look. "Sure enough," he remembers saying. "It looks like a gunshot wound to me, too." He would later add that the wound "looked like a punched-out .45-caliber entrance hole."[3]

Gormley consulted with the other pathologists present, including Cmdr. Kilbane, and they all agreed it looked like "an entrance gunshot wound." Gormley would admit this on Black Entertainment Television.[4] Yet despite this consensus, Col. Gormley, the highest-ranking AFIP officer then at Dover, did not do the obvious. He did not call in the FBI. He did not ask the Brown family to permit an autopsy. Nor did he take the opportunity to look for an exit wound or test for gunshot residue.

These oversights perplexed Janoski at the time, but she was hardly in a position to challenge Gormley. Meanwhile she continued to take photos, more than two hundred in all, ignoring the pressure to hurry up and "get the bodies out." That pressure, as contract investigator Bob Veasey told her, came directly from the White House.

From the examination station, Brown's body passed through the next phases: embalming, wrapping/dressing, and casketing. By the end of the process, there could be no more examinations of Brown without undoing a lot that had been done. Indeed, a day later, Brown's body lay in state in the rotunda of the Commerce Department. Inexplicably, his casket was closed. Janoski cannot understand why. His head wounds were not that severe. It would have been easy work to make him presentable.

That same day, April 8, Lt. Col. Steve Cogswell, a doctor and deputy medical examiner, arrived at St. John's Peak in Croatia. As was standard, the AFIP had sent one of its pathologists to the scene—in this case, one of its best—to help his colleagues back at Dover establish the cause and manner of each victim's death. A self-described "short, fat, bald guy," the modest Cogswell would prove to be a much more formidable figure than he looked.[5]

Cogswell had no sooner descended on the scene than Col. Gormley called with a request. He wanted Cogswell to look for an object that might have punched a ".45 [inch] inwardly beveling, perfectly circular hole in the top of [Brown's] head." These were Gormley's words as Cogswell noted them at the time.[6] The previous day's exam had apparently alarmed Gormley.

For Cogswell, the search for a part was a second step. The first one was obvious. "Open him up," he told Gormley. "This man needs an autopsy. This whole thing stinks."[7] As they both knew, what Gormley described sounded like a wound from a .45 caliber weapon. Even more suspicious, Brown was the only person on the plane with a hole in his head.

There was much about this crash that seemed suspicious to Cogswell. For starters, the Air Force chose to skip the "Safety Board" phase of the investigation. With twelve years of experience at crash scenes, Cogswell could not understand why. This was the first time in his experience that there was no Safety Board.[8]

On the scene in Croatia, Cogswell dutifully searched for a rod or bolt that might have caused the hole. Those that were appropriately round he measured and had photographed. None matched the hole. He also wondered how any object could have entered and exited Brown's skull like a drill punch and left a perfectly circular hole, especially with everyone and everything in violent motion.[9] He found no answers. There are reports as well, albeit unsubstantiated, that a comparable search was undertaken on a clone plane at the Ramstein Air Force base in Germany.

Back at Dover, the AFIP crew continued their work, lightened as always by a salty dose of graveyard humor. Janoski had a knack for this coping skill and could more than hang in there with the boys. She and her colleagues got a juicy morsel to chew on that same Monday, April 8. The Associated Press was reporting that the man responsible for the Cilipi Airport's navigation system, maintenance chief Niko Jerkuic, had shot himself in the chest an hour after the bodies of Brown and the other Americans had been flown out of the airport on Saturday.[10]

Jerkuic had not been working on Wednesday, the day the plane crashed. The Croatian interior minister was quick to deny that his suicide had "any connections with the tragic crash of the U.S. aircraft," although it would have made perfect sense if it had.[11] The *New York Times* was reporting that a "failed romance" had left the forty-six-year-old bachelor despondent.[12] For Janoski and her colleagues, Jerkuic's death was just more grist for the mortuary's dark humor mill. Among them, they had seen enough suicides to know that the chest was an unlikely place for an individual to deposit a fatal bullet.

In Washington, grieving for Brown continued, much of it painfully sincere, some of it less so. After a memorial service for Brown at St. John's Chapel near the White House, a TV cameraman captured the quintessential Clinton moment. As Clinton and the Reverend Tony Campolo were walking back to the White House, they were discussing, as Campolo recalls, the typically joyous black funerals they had attended in the past, and the conversation turned mirthful.[13]

As Clinton leaned back to laugh, he suddenly locked on to the camera and reflexively downshifted to a funereal gear, dropping his head in seeming sadness and wiping an imagined tear from his eye. Campolo attributes the mood switch to a switch in conversation, claiming he confronted the president with the issue of the partial birth abortion bill recently passed by Congress. But the fact is that Campolo, unaware of the camera, kept on talking and laughing. Fairly or unfairly, the media would have hung that transitional moment around the neck of a less favored president.[14]

If Clinton's sentiments were suspect, the Brown family's were not. They deeply loved their husband and father, as did a few other people, among them Nolanda Hill. At a delicate moment for everyone, Alma Brown overruled her family and placed Hill on the "friends and family" list for the funeral service scheduled for Wednesday morning, April 10, at the Washington National Cathedral.[15]

Says Hill, "Alma is a very classy person." She was also an astute one. Adds Hill, "She knew I knew a lot."

Hill met with about seventy-five other Brown friends at a site near the Brown home, and from there they were bused to the cathedral. On the bus, no one would sit next to her. At the cathedral, her reception was cool at best. The looks she got from Commerce Department insiders like Lauri Fitz-Pegado and Melissa Moss, the signatory on the Commerce fund-raising letters, were "real ugly." Hill believes their motive was to send her a signal, to wit, "Go away. Keep your mouth shut. We are not going to be supportive."

Alma Brown, however, took the high road. When she saw Hill later that day she embraced her and said merely, "We lost our Ronnie." Moved by Alma's gesture, Hill could only respond, "I know."

The service was relatively short and decorous. Johnny Cochran attended. So did Stevie Wonder and many other black luminaries. Hill marveled that several of the speakers, like Robert Johnson, chairman of Black Entertainment Television, were not all that close to Brown. But then again neither were Bill and Hillary Clinton. And there they sat front and center, Bill, as usual, appropriately mournful.

After the service, the funeral cortege made its way to Arlington National Cemetery. This was an oddly fitting place for Brown to come to rest. It was only in the Army that he ever honored his potential. It was only at the Army bases in Bosnia that he had experienced any real joy in the last weeks, maybe months, of his life. He was coming home.

Nolanda Hill was among the small group invited. Robert Reich was also there. So were the president and Mrs. Clinton. It was cool and misty and even snowed briefly. TV newswoman Cokie Roberts, Tommy Boggs's sister, and her husband Steve Roberts stood by Hill at the graveside, and Hill was enormously appreciative. Others were treating her "like [she] had AIDS." A cameraman in a tree captured an image of Hill and beamed the shot all over the world.

She was crying. She was devastated by the loss and overwhelmed by fear. Her faith was not strong enough to block it. She had felt as long as Brown was alive he would expose the truth, and the truth would protect her. Now that he was gone, she was alone. And the manner of his death did nothing to reassure her.

The day of the funeral, a friend in a position to know had told Hill "for [her] own safety" that Brown had been found forty yards from the plane. "It looked," he said, "like he was trying to get away." Neither he nor Hill could have known about the hole in Ron Brown's head.

Immediately after the burial, the president retreated to the White House. There, in the media shadow of Brown's funeral, in a move that was cynical even by his own standards, he vetoed the partial birth abortion bill that had been sitting on his desk for the past two weeks. The Senate would sustain the veto, and the grisly practice would continue.

The day after the funeral, April 11, as she was wrapping up her gear to head back to Washington, Kathleen Janoski was given one more photo assignment, one that would ultimately make her aware of Hill and lead to a hellish last year in the U.S. Navy.

Brown's personal effects had finally arrived at Dover. These included several oval-shaped gold medallions Brown had bought for his family in Paris. Each featured a raised image of the Virgin Mary and the inscription: *O Marie, concue sans peché, priez pour nous qui avons recours a vous.*

"Oh Mary," the words translated, "conceived without sin, pray for us who have recourse to you." Taped inside the briefing book of this man of little apparent faith was an extraordinary prayer to Mary's husband, St. Joseph. The prayer concludes, "When [Jesus] reposes in your heart, press him in my name, kiss his fine head and ask him to return the kiss when I draw my dying breath. St. Joseph, patron of my departed soul, pray for me."[16]

"Why did Dad have religious medals and a prayer?" Tracey Brown asks, "Did he have a premonition? Could that be why he had been so insistent on refinancing the mortgage before he left?"[17] No, not a premonition exactly. His fears had been much more grounded than that.

Jeanmarie Sentell, the NCIS agent, had placed one item of particular interest on a gurney and asked Janoski to shoot it. "We have something sensitive for you," Sentell told her when she handed it over. The item in question was the Native American medicine kit Hill had given Brown and that he carried everywhere in his diplomatic pouch. Janoski and the others joked that it looked like drug paraphernalia. The authorities might have thought so too.

Contrary to all policy, they put it aside to be destroyed. Before they were through, the authorities would destroy evidence much more critical than this.

27 | THE TERROR SUMMER

An unrivaled master of feigned sincerity, Bill Clinton had used the funeral service at the National Cathedral to his advantage. Here, he was speaking not just to the Brown family and their friends but also to all of black America. And he had their number.

"On a personal note," said Clinton in his inimitably convincing way, "I just want to say to my friend one last time: Thank you. If it weren't for you, I wouldn't be here."[1] His words moved the congregation. Said BET's usually savvy Robert Johnson, "The things he said at Ron Brown's funeral. That was just off the charts."[2]

Immediately after the funeral service, the Clintons and the rest of the cortege drove through the historic Shaw neighborhood around Fourteenth and U streets where Brown had been born. They could see hundreds of people lining the streets, many of them holding signs inscribed with sentiments like "WE LOVE YOU, RON BROWN" and "GOODBYE OLD FRIEND."[3] One can understand if the Clintons felt more relieved than sad. Had Brown lived and talked and turned the emotional power of the African American community against them, there would have been no second term.

That particular April, emotions were running high. "An epidemic of terror"—in the words of the assistant attorney general for civil rights, Deval Patrick—had seized black America.[4] Since the beginning of the year, the media had been stoking the nation's anxiety with sporadic tales of arson attacks against black churches in the South.

In March 1996, shortly before Brown's death, the Atlanta-based Center for Democratic Renewal had held a highly publicized press conference to shed light on "the well-organized white-supremacist movement" behind the church burnings.[5] The major media took it from there. A database search turned up more than 2,200 articles on the subject by July—including three huge layouts in *USA Today* on consecutive days.[6] *Time* magazine captured the spirit of the coverage, describing the phenomenon as a "national epidemic of violence against black churches."[7]

Ron Brown's plane crash on April 3 only intensified fears of a wide-ranging conspiracy against African Americans. The Clintons were aware of the fears. According to Nolanda Hill, they went to work immediately on Alma Brown, "separating her from her world," making her an ally. The fact that Independent Counsel Daniel Pearson immediately ceased his investigation of Brown did not hurt the cause. The hail of hosannas for Brown from the White House and the media further dimmed any rumbles of conspiracy.

For Hill, the terror was much more personal. Soon after the funeral, she went to see her attorney in Kentucky to make some sense out of her legal situation. Although the inquiry into Brown had been closed, her case and Michael's remained open. Getting answers would not prove easy.

For all her real anxiety about her legal status, Hill had a deeper concern, and that was her safety. Says Hill unabashedly of Brown's death, "I was then and am now convinced he was murdered." Alone in the world and unprotected, Hill fled to a friend's weary, time-worn lodge on a small island off the coast of Massachusetts called Cutty Hunk. Only a ferry connected the island to the mainland. She kept her eye on it.

Hill's long, lonely summer on Cutty Hunk stretched into fall. She wandered ceaselessly around the island, replaying her past and praying on the future. With Brown gone, she had only the Psalms to soothe her and remind her she was not alone. Each day Hill read them from beginning to end. It seemed almost as if they were written for her.

> I am the scorn of all my adversaries, a horror to my neighbors, an object of dread to my acquaintances; those who see me in the street flee from me.
>
> I have passed out of mind like one who is dead; I have become like a broken vessel. For I hear the whispering of many—terror all around!—as they scheme together against me, as they plot to take my life.

> But I trust in you, O LORD; I say, "You are my God." My times are
> in your hand; deliver me from the hand of my enemies and persecutors.[8]

For Kathleen Janoski, that spring and summer of 1996 passed without such burden. The hole in Ron Brown's head had already devolved into something of a darkly ironic joke among her colleagues at the AFIP. Janoski, in fact, would tease Colonel William Gormley with his failure to do anything about it.

One day, in the fall of 1996, Janoski was standing in the hallway of the AFIP annex, talking to Naval criminal investigator Jeanmarie Sentell, when Gormley happened by. As was her habit, Janoski started ribbing Gormley about the hole, and he, flustered, stuttered out some vague response, threw up his hands in mock helplessness and kept on walking. After Gormley passed, Sentell volunteered an extraordinary bit of information.[9]

"Did you know the first set of Brown's head X-rays were destroyed?" she said conspiratorially. When Janoski asked why, Sentell confided they showed a "lead snowstorm."

Janoski had to ask what a "lead snowstorm" was. Sentell explained that it referred to a pattern of metal fragments one might see after a gunshot wound. Sentell then offered another stunning tidbit: "They took a second set of X-rays and made them deliberately less dense."

Janoski did not have a whole lot of respect for Sentell to begin with. She describes her as a "scrawny bimbo" who "couldn't investigate her way out of a paper bag." Nor apparently was the Naval Criminal Intelligence Service highly regarded by the folks at the AFIP. They joked that NCIS stood for "No Crime Is Solved."

Still, Sentell was on the scene when Brown's body was examined. Given her position as an investigator, she may well have known more than her colleagues. Janoski took her at her word. When confronted later by a reporter, Sentell would not deny Janoski's charges.[10]

Janoski found the conversation with Sentell unnerving, "Twilight Zone-ish." Immediately afterwards, she went back to her office to see if she could find the 35 mm color slides of Brown's X-rays she had casually taken at Dover to help calibrate her camera. This was no easy task in that she had just moved up to the Rockville facility, and her boxes were not yet unpacked. But Janoski was in full Nancy Drew mode by this time, and there was no stopping her.

Eureka!

Janoski found them, the head X-rays included. She got hold of the one person she most trusted at the AFIP, Lt. Col. Steve Cogswell. He put the images in his projector and flashed them up on the wall. There it was. Even in a photo of the X-ray, they could see the "lead snowstorm." Always careful, Cogswell did not claim—and never would—that these whitish specks in the front of Brown's skull were bullet fragments. But they certainly deserved more attention than they had gotten.

Later, but before the AFIP brass became aware of her suspicions, Janoski went to the AFIP library and asked to pull two sets of X-rays. One set was Ron Brown's. The other set she pulled just for cover. When Janoski laid Brown's out on the light box, she came to still another unnerving realization: the head X-rays were missing. The X-rays were numbered sequentially from one to fifteen, without gaps, which meant the head X-rays had never been included, even the "less dense" ones Sentell had discussed. That is when Janoski realized her slides were the only proof.

"I was scared," admits Janoski, before adding with a bit of Navy bravado, "That was the only time."

No word of the hole in Ron Brown's head had yet reached the media. Janoski did not feel that she was in a position to say anything, and the culture of the military did not at all encourage whistle-blowing. She did, however, start paying more attention to the Ron Brown story.

For his part, Cogswell took a more active role. In charge of training for the AFIP, he had added the Ron Brown case to a slide show he presented at professional conferences and to FBI agents in homicide courses. He called the presentation, "Mistakes and Failures in Forensic Pathology."

Brown's was one among many cases Cogswell featured. Indeed, he had been involved with more than one hundred civilian and military crash investigations since joining the Air Force. But Brown's was the most provocative, the one that would eventually catch the attention of reporter Christopher Ruddy and cost Cogswell and Janoski their careers. That would come later.

For sixteen United States Air Force officers, terror came in the form of a stunningly ruthless purge following the investigation into the crash of Brown's plane. In the way of background, major Air Force commands like the 86th Airlift had long enjoyed the discretion to use various airports in Eastern Europe as the need dictated. That began to change in 1994 when the Air Force directed these commands to review approaches not under the control of the Department of Defense before authorizing flights into them.

The 86th Airlift Wing, working as it did in Eastern Europe, understood the impact this new directive would have on its operations and requested a waiver. In January 1996, U.S. Air Forces in Europe headquarters turned down the waiver request. Three months after that, Ron Brown's plane flew into an airport that had not been reviewed or approved.

Heads rolled. On August 6, 1996, the Air Force announced the final tally of who and how many. Brig. Gen. William E. Stevens, commander, 86th Airlift Wing, and Col. John E. Mazurowski, commander, 86th Operations Group, were relieved of command for dereliction of duty. Col. Roger W. Hansen, vice commander, 86th Airlift Wing, was relieved of duty the same day. Maj. Gen. Jeffrey G. Cliver, former director of operations, headquarters, USAFE, received a letter of reprimand. Four colonels and two lieutenant colonels received letters of admonishment. Two lieutenant colonels and two majors got letters of counseling. Two lieutenant colonels received verbal counseling. And had the pilots survived, they too would have been disciplined. The USAF report had found them negligent in any number of ways.[11]

The irony, from a civil rights perspective, was that Brown's death had resulted in the cashiering of the highest-ranking black officer in the Air Force, Brigadier General Stevens. Needless to say, there was no mention of his race on the way out.

If Nolanda Hill needed any more reason to feel anxious about the forces of government arrayed against her, General Fogleman provided it. During a June 1996 press conference, he responded to the question of whether Brown had overruled staff members who had worried the weather was too treacherous to fly to Croatia, a claim Hill had allegedly made to a *New York Times* reporter.

Hill's charge was fairly innocuous. Brown hadn't overruled the crew, merely the timid among his own staff. But Fogleman overreacted. He charged not only that Brown had said no such thing but also that Brown had never called Hill at all, let alone right before the flight. As proof, he cited Brown's escort, a brigadier general, "who never saw Secretary Brown use a telephone." Fogleman strongly implied, despite a sworn affidavit from Hill, that Hill was lying.[12] She wasn't, and she was able to prove it. Made aware of its mistake, the Air Force later sent Hill a letter of apology. The media did not cover the apology, of course, and the public impression that Hill was a liar remained unchallenged.

In the spring and summer of 1996, Bill Clinton nursed his own sense of terror and had even given it a name: "Greg Norman." On April 14, 1996—four days after Ron Brown's funeral—Clinton had watched in shock as Norman, his one buddy in the Republican-friendly world of professional golf, blew a six-stroke lead in the final round of the Masters, the greatest choke in the tournament's history.

"Yes," Clinton would tell press aide, Mike McCurry, "that's going to be the new *theme* for the campaign, that we're not going to allow ourselves to be Greg Normanized."[13] Bill Clinton was horrified in a way few around him could understand. "We could have a major crisis go bad on us," he fretted constantly.[14] Clinton knew something his staff did not: Ron Brown's death had spared him just such a crisis. "Greg Norman," he would repeat to his staff. "Greg Norman."[15]

Dick Morris, who likely did not know about the close call with Brown, reinforced Clinton's anxiety. He did not shy from telling him that despite his lead, Clinton had "a soft underbelly," namely that the majority of the voters did not particularly trust or respect him.[16]

Morris worried that a terrorist act could expose that underbelly in the months leading up to the November election. In what he now routinely refers to as "the terror summer of 1996," Morris has identified "three attacks" in a six week stretch had put the whole White House on edge.[17] The first was the June truck bombing of Khobar Towers in Saudia Arabia that left nineteen American servicemen dead. The second was the still unexplained destruction of TWA Flight 800 off the coast of Long Island on July 17. The third was the Centennial Park bombing at the Atlanta Olympics on July 28 that killed two and injured more than one hundred.

As Robert Reich has bitterly observed, Morris's mantra in the run-up to the 1996 election was, "Things are wonderful."[18] To preserve the illusion, Clinton would "utter no word that challenges America." As Morris well knew, however, a terrorist act against America could dispel the illusion of "wonderful" in a literal flash. It had "Greg Norman" written all over it. With a twenty-point lead over Bob Dole in the mid-summer polls, the last thing Clinton or anyone in the White House wanted was a test of the president's tenuous grip on his role as commander-in-chief.

Much better to stall for time. For Khobar and TWA 800, overly deliberate investigations would put off any real response for years. For Centennial Park, there was always Richard Jewell, the hapless security guard who had found the bomb in the first place. The Clinton administration would serve up the transparently innocent Jewell as fodder to the media all the way through October.

Domestic terror was another issue altogether. Clinton had revived his presidency at Oklahoma City by exploiting the bombing of the Murrah building. He and his supporters had ruthlessly linked Timothy McVeigh to Newt Gingrich, Rush Limbaugh, and other "purveyors of hate and division" on the Right.[20] The nicely-timed church burnings presented an opportunity to repeat the coup. Responding to the presumed "epidemic," Clinton told a national radio audience that "racial hostility is the driving force" behind the church burnings. "I want to ask every citizen in America to say," continued the president, "we are not slipping back to those dark days."[21]

If the president was discreet about who was responsible for the presumed arsons, his allies on the Left were not. In an article written for the September/October issue of the *Columbia Journalism Review*, all the more damning for its attempts not to be, Joe Holley cites instance after instance of activists and journalists pinning the blame on the "the resentful, fear-driven rhetoric" of the political Right.[22] In its June 3 issue, for instance, *Newsweek* quoted Jesse Jackson instinctively finessing the guilt from white supremacy to a "'cultural conspiracy'—a seeming intolerance fed by white politicians' attacks on affirmative action and immigration."[23]

Holley may have pulled his punches, but science writer Michael Fumento did not. Writing in the July 8 issue of the *Wall Street Journal,* Fumento cut right to the chase. "OK, Mr. President, I'll say it. I'll say it because this supposed 'epidemic of hatred' is a myth, probably a deliberate hoax. There is no good evidence of any increase in black church burnings."[24] Fumento had the numbers to prove it. The only surge in church burning had come after the media hype as a result of copycat crimes, targeted at no particular race, and perpetrated not by Christian right-wingers but by self-described "satanists" more than any other identifiable group.

Sheepishly, in time, the major media would come to accept the verdict of Fumento, Holley, and others, but the damage had been done. Black Americans had understandably grown more alienated and more fearful. Who better to protect them this election year than that great friend and patron of Ron Brown, Bill Clinton, the first black president?

It was a good thing all around that the president's African American loyalists did not focus much attention on the one fatal church burning during his first term, the one that claimed the lives of twenty-eight of their brethren, the one at the Mount Carmel Community on the dusty plains outside of Waco, the one set ablaze—directly or otherwise—by their patron's own forces.

28 | NATURAL CAUSES

The Friday morning after Thanksgiving, 1996, the Associated Press broke a minor news story. It scarcely registered in the consciousness of most Americans, but in the hearts of at least a few, the story must have struck something close to terror.

> WASHINGTON (AP)—Police were investigating the death of a woman whose body was found today in an office at the Commerce Department.
>
> Anne Luzzatto, press secretary for Commerce secretary Mickey Kantor, said the woman's body was found this morning by a Commerce Department employee, who notified security personnel in the building. "It is my understanding that someone found the body in an office on the fourth floor," Luzzatto said.
>
> She said that District of Columbia police were conducting an investigation but that she had no details on a cause of death. The woman's name was being withheld pending notification of relatives.[1]

The Clintons heard the news that morning at Camp David. They were unique among elected first families in that they had no home—no Crawford ranch, no Kennebunkport, no Santa Barbara, no Plains, no San Clemente, no LBJ ranch, no Hyannisport. But at least they would have Camp David—and the White House—for four more years.

Dick Morris had seen to that. By following his Faustian plan, the

Clintons had done the seemingly undoable and retained the presidency. If Robert Reich thought Clinton had sold his soul to win, the media were typically much more forgiving.

"Redemption and renewal are peculiarly American graces," gushed Newsweek's Evan Thomas in his book on the campaign, "and in 1996 Bill Clinton embodied them."[2]

True, it got a little dicey at the end. "A flap over Democratic campaign money," lamented Thomas, had managed to "spoil a perfect campaign."[3] But the Clintons prevailed in any case—even if late exposure of their illicit fund-raising suppressed Clinton's popular vote and kept the final tally under 50 percent.

That Thanksgiving the Clintons were a little less enthused about themselves than Thomas was. The Republicans had held Congress, both houses. In a week, Senate leadership would announce the beginning of a major investigation into that untidy little "flap over Democratic campaign money," the historic Thompson Committee. Meanwhile the House and Judicial Watch were still demanding Commerce hand over documents related to Ron Brown's activities, a demand Commerce was resisting. And now, this morning, there was a dead woman in the Commerce Department itself.

The Clintons had to have learned of the death immediately. No doubt, Mickey Kantor, the new Commerce secretary, called them soon after the body was discovered. His spokeswoman would not have talked to the Associated Press without Kantor's approval, and Kantor would not have given it without the president's. Unlike Brown, Kantor was trusted by the Clintons. As U.S. trade representative, he had pulled insider rank on Brown often enough that Brown grew to despise him. It would have galled him to know Kantor now had his job.[4]

The dead woman's name was Barbara Wise. A co-worker had found her bruised and half-naked body on the fourth floor in Commerce's International Trade Administration office at 7:45 AM. Wise had worked in this office for fourteen years. This was the same office in which John Huang, soon to become a household name, had also worked.

Wise was reportedly "very close to Ron Brown," according to Insight magazine editor Paul Roderiquez, who tracked this case closely. Apparently she had been "under enormous pressures," emanating in part "from within the Department of Commerce not to cooperate with ongoing investigations on Capital Hill."⁵ Nolanda Hill confirms Wise used to regularly brief Brown.

About two hours after the body was found, in what would have seemed a coincidence in any other administration, the president, Hillary, Chelsea Clinton, and producer Harry Thomason boarded Marine One for Washington. According to the AP, the group "*unexpectedly* left Camp David in the Catoctin Mountains of western Maryland, where [Clinton] and his extended family had enjoyed Thanksgiving, to return to the White House."⁶

On this otherwise slow news day, ABC News chose to report on the president's unexpected trip. White House reporter Jerry King asked press secretary Mike McCurry the motivation behind it. Said McCurry, "Mr. Clinton did not have some of the books he wanted to research for example to find poetry to be read at the [inaugural]. So, he flew in the official helicopter, Marine One, back to the White House to pick up the books."

The inaugural was nearly two months away. McCurry's less than credible answer startled King into skepticism. He asked, "Could the research not have been delivered cheaper?"

"Well, sure," McCurry answered.⁷ And that was that.

McCurry offered an equally dubious explanation as to what Clinton had done after arriving. "He spent an hour in the Oval Office with television producer Harry Thomason," said McCurry, "discussing the themes and program of his second inaugural."⁸ He offered no explanation, however, as to why the two had to come to Washington to do the planning.

If Thomason had a reason for traveling with Clinton other than to provide cover, it was not obvious. Besides, Thomason had a penchant for skullduggery. It was he, after all, who had led the Clintons into the morass known as Travelgate.

About two hours after arriving at the White House, as reported by the venerable Helen Thomas of the UPI, Clinton "carried a briefcase as he strolled to the waiting helicopter for a return flight to Camp David." Thomas added one more intriguing detail: Clinton "was followed by an aide carrying a huge box of inaugural papers."⁹

One can forgive Ms. Thomas for not inquiring more deeply. At the moment, the Clintons' motives were far from obvious. It is likely they knew little more about Wise's death than anyone else did. Their hasty, improvised return to Washington suggests as much.

The Clintons did, however, have a history of removing files from offices under suspicion before the forces of justice could do the same. Undoubtedly, it was Hillary Clinton who had orchestrated the purge of Vince Foster's office after his death. Among the first into that office to do the hands-on work was the always-reliable Patsy Thomasson.

The Clintons knew Patsy from Arkansas. There she had served as number two person at Laster & Co. She even ran the company while her boss and Clinton confidante, "Bond Daddy" Dan Lasater, served hard time for distributing cocaine, one of the many illicit adventures in his infamous career. Despite her involvement with Lasater—she had made at least one Central American run with him that the FBI investigated—the Clintons appointed Thomasson special assistant to the president and director of the Office of Administration for the White House.[10]

Foster's office was not Thomasson's only file-purging job. As *Time* magazine reported just three weeks before Wise's death, FBI agents had recently scoured Thomasson's home looking for Travelgate documents. "It was Thomasson's files that contained a memo portraying Mrs. Clinton as a central figure in the firings," said *Time*, "a role the first lady has denied."[11]

In short, it would not have been out of character for the Clintons to dispatch their staff to Huang's old office and, if need be, clear it out. One is hard-pressed to recall the president's carrying his own briefcase on other occasions, and if he were truly retrieving "inaugural papers," he would not have needed a "huge box."

One other curiosity. Although it was in large part Hillary Clinton's "extended family" that remained behind at Camp David, she stayed on in Washington, allegedly to oversee the decoration of the White House for Christmas.[12] In her book *Living History*, however, Hillary misleads the reader into thinking she spent the whole long weekend at Camp David, and she does so deliberately.

"At dinner we voted on which movie to watch that night in the camp's theater," she writes, "and in the event of a tie, or strong dissent, we sometimes ran a double feature."[13] Sometimes? Who would guess she was gone by Friday morning?

At 5:21 PM that same Friday after Thanksgiving, the AP put on the wire a story quietly at war with itself. "The name of the forty-eight-year-old woman was being withheld pending notification of relatives," the article relates before adding, "District of Columbia police spokesman J.C. Stamps said that an autopsy was being performed."[14]

In short, less than ten hours after a professional woman's body has been discovered, and before her relatives had been contacted, the DC medical examiners had it opened up on the table. This happens rarely if at all in the real world. It certainly did not happen to Ron Brown. One senses pressure from above.

There was one good reason for the pressure. A finding of "natural causes" could put a quick lid on an extremely explosive story, to wit, a semi-naked woman, reportedly close to Ron Brown, found dead in John Huang's old office in the midst of a swelling fund-raising scandal and this just months after Brown's unlikely death.

At 5:36 PM the AP posted another article that was testament to the power of spin. "Scaring a pondful of ducks," reads the story's lead, "President Clinton enjoyed an afternoon of golf with family members on Friday after returning briefly to the White House to work on the program of his second inaugural."[15]

Clinton's media people clearly spoon-fed the reporter this non-story. It not only reinforced the rationale for the Washington trip, but it also suggested how blithely oblivious Clinton was to any unpleasantness in Washington, like, say, what the DOA found in John Huang's old office. The cynic might even suggest the president could afford to relax only because the first lady was on the job, back in Washington, tending to eventualities.

At 1:30 AM Saturday morning, AP identified the dead woman as Barbara Alice Wise, forty-eight, of Gambrills, Maryland. The DC police claimed, "She died of natural causes." They also acknowledged, however, the autopsy was "unable to determine the cause of death."[16]

In its final edition that same Saturday, November 30, the *Washington Post* picked up the story. The *Post* was the only major media outlet to do so. It added some useful details. Bruises had been found on Wise's body although there was no external sign of death. A neighbor confided that Wise had been hospitalized often over the last six months. An unnamed official volunteered that Wise's office was responsible for helping U.S. companies export their products around the world. Another suggested the death had unnerved those at work on Friday, especially those in nearby offices.[17]

The *Post*, however, made no connection to John Huang or Ron Brown or the brewing Commerce Department scandal, at the heart of which was the issue of export controls. Reporters did not check with the House Republicans or Judicial Watch. They made no allusion to the Clintons or their unexpected return. To them, the death might just as well have occurred at the Smithsonian or at a local Starbucks. And the *Post* was the *most* inquisitive of the major media.

In an article just 116 words long, the AP wrapped up its reporting a week after it began on December 6. At this time, DC police were saying Wise "probably died from natural causes," but they could not be certain until the medical examiner's office completed a toxicology test. Otherwise, despite the bruises, there was "no evidence of foul play."[18]

Although the police showed unusual discretion by refusing to release copies of the final report, *Insight's* Paul Roderiquez had a reliable source within the department. The source convinced him the woman had been despondent and a heavy drinker and on the night in question, Thanksgiving eve, she had suffocated on her own vomit while in the depths of an alcoholic haze. The police theorized she had taken off her blouse at one point to clean up the vomit.[19] Roderiquez was not inclined to protect the Clintons. *Insight* is the magazine of the conservative *Washington Times*.

Wise probably did die as Roderiquez describes. Had it been planned, there would have been no need for all the last minute scurrying about. And yet, there may have been a force afoot in the land over which the Clintons had lost control. The toxicology test suggests a link, admittedly tenuous, to a death at the other end of the *Guanxi* pipeline, Oklahoma. If Wise's death was likely natural, this one likely was not. Kudos to the *Oklahoma Constitution* whose excellent reporting makes much of this next story possible.

The story centers on one of the good guys in the simmering Oklahoma scandal, Ron Miller, co-owner of a natural gas company called Creek Systems. It was Miller whose lawsuit threatened to expose bribery and other crimes committed not only by Oklahoma Natural Gas but also by Arkla and its executives, former Clinton chief of staff Mack McLarty likely among them.

In a deal closed in November 1993, Miller had sold his enterprise to the Hawaiian hucksters, Gene and Nora Lum. After making a down payment, the Lums had promised to pay the rest in installments. A couple of years down the road, the Lums reneged. Their failure to pay drove Miller to near bankruptcy. When Miller made his case to Don Sweatman, the Lum associate who had brokered the deal, Sweatman told him not to worry, "Hillary said that you'll get your money." Sweatman had worked with the Lums on their APAC fund raising scam in California. There, he reportedly presented himself as "Bill Clinton's personal representative."[20]

Miller had more than his memory to rely on. He had made at least 165 tape recordings of his conversations with the Lums and their associates. During this time, he worked closely with FBI agent John Hippard, a relationship based on mutual trust and respect.

In January 1997, a little more than a month after Barbara Wise's death, Miller made another appeal to Sweatman for the money due him and was told to back off: "You haven't been shot at yet." Miller promptly filed a police report. Stated the report, "The subjects he is dealing with have made a number of references to certain people wanting Mr. Miller dead."[21]

Gene Lum may have been one of those people. Reportedly, former Lum partner Stuart Price had heard Lum say that if someone is giving too much trouble, "just have him killed." When the *Constitution* staff contacted Price about this incident, he told the reporters he was getting ready to eat dinner and promised he would call back. He never did.[22]

Throughout 1997, Miller endured a steady siege of intimidation. He received any number of threatening phone calls. Prowlers tried to tamper with his car. A helicopter menacingly buzzed his office on State Highway 9 in Norman, an event attested by several neutral eyewitnesses.

In early August 1997, under subpoena, Miller turned over the tapes to the FBI's Hippard. Staff from the House committee chaired by Representative Dan Burton interviewed Miller a few days later. The committee also subpoenaed documents from Miller on the subject of Brown, the Lums, and their company, Dynamic Energy Resources.

On September 5, 1997, the Burton Committee deposed Mack McLarty. The committee asked him about Arkla lobbyist Bill "Tater" Anderson, but McLarty's lawyers succeeded in having him avoid questions about Oklahoma corruption. McLarty did admit knowing about Dynamic Energy, and he had talked to Brown about Michael's placement on its board, but he denied knowing Gene and Nora Lum. As mentioned earlier, however, he had attended a breakfast with them at the APEC conference in Seattle six days after the Dynamic deal was closed.[23]

The Burton Committee was scheduled to begin its formal proceedings on October 8, and Ron Miller was to testify. Rashly perhaps, Miller had told a colleague that after his testimony, "Al Gore will never become president."[24]

Miller never did get a chance to testify. On Wednesday, October 2, he took ill with what he thought was the flu and cancelled a scheduled meeting with Sweatman. His condition worsened the next two days, and on Saturday the fourth he was admitted to Norman Regional Hospital. There the doctors treated his pneumonia-like symptoms, and by Tuesday, he was stable.[25]

On Wednesday, however, Miller lapsed into respiratory distress with his temperature spiking at 105 degrees. Doctors transferred him to the more sophisticated Integris Baptist Hospital where his condition only worsened. He died on October 12.

After the autopsy, which FBI agents attended, the Oklahoma Chief Medical Examiner's office classified Miller's death as a "possible threat to public health" and "under suspicious circumstances." As to cause of death, the examiner originally inscribed "pending investigation." In time, this was changed to "natural."

Even before the anthrax scare of late 2001, the *Constitution* staff investigated the possibility of inhalation anthrax in Miller's death. Reporters had contacted Dr. John Cooper, the pathologist who performed the autopsy, and he admitted anthrax was a "possible" cause of death. The recorded cause of death, as he remembered, was "an unknown, an undetermined."

In fact, many of Miller's recorded symptoms were consistent with inhalation anthrax. Evidence suggests that Baptist medical staff considered this possibility when Miller was transferred there a week into his illness. On one form Baptist nurses recorded, "No specific exposure or activity that would suggest animal-related illness." Anthrax typically involves animal contact. Records also show an unidentified "co-worker" had come by the hospital and was quoted as saying, "Mr. Miller was in Iowa and Nebraska three to four months ago looking at horse ranches."[26]

By 1999, forensic economist Stephen Dresch had gotten involved on the Oklahoma end. He had gathered enough evidence to persuade Oklahoma's chief medical examiner that the cause of Miller's death should be officially reconsidered. Upon further review, the medical examiner did just that, changing the listed cause from "natural" to "unknown."[27]

Dresch, who still expects to solve Miller's death, has slowly come to a chilling conclusion. Although not certain about anthrax, he says, "I can almost guarantee you it wasn't natural causes."[28] When asked by the *Oklahoma Constitution* staff whether Miller's fate was in any way tied to the Clinton administration, Cleveland County District Attorney Tim Kuykendall said, "There are just too many connections to be coincidental."[29]

29 | GOING PUBLIC

It was a hard November, that November of 1996. Still in "full-blown hide," Nolanda Hill had taken refuge with her sister and family on an isolated spread in Sherman, Texas. Here, deep in the Texas countryside, Hill could spot a stranger coming for miles.

It was in Sherman that Hill watched the 1996 election returns. As the evening wore on, her dread turned to despair. The Clintons had secured four more years, and Republicans had secured at least two. For her, it was the worst possible combination.

Had Clinton lost, the Republicans in Congress would have let her case die. Had the Democrats won the House, they too would have let it die. As things turned out, it would still be open season on Hill. Brown would have been hard to ignore, but with him dead, the White House had all the more incentive to smear and isolate Hill. She could do scant damage if no one believed her.

Those who wanted to bring Hill down had one problem. There was not much with which to bring her down. "A pile of mishmash" is how Hill describes the charges against her. One prosecutor after another walked away from the case. Hill believes they did so because it so lacked in substance. For months at a time, there would be no U.S. Attorney assigned at all. "They just twisted me, twisted me, twisted me," says Hill.

To stay close to her attorney in this oft-mutating case, Hill moved to Kentucky. The attorney's wife found her a room nearby. Each evening after leaving her attorney, she would drive to an isolated monastery, checking her rearview mirror all the way. She would park and walk beyond its quaint church, through the parking lot in back, up the hill for a hundred yards or more and across the footbridge to an ungainly doublewide used primarily for storage. Once inside, she finessed her way through a large front room filled with bunk beds, down a narrow hallway, and into a "little bitty" room at the end. There was no other soul within shouting distance. No one would find her here.

Hill slept in a dismantled bunk bed in that chilled, cramped room. Had she known that the next time she would be compelled to sleep in a bunk bed she would be incarcerated and her ladder-less bunk would be on top, she might have been more appreciative. But those caught in a downward spiral take little solace knowing they have yet to hit bottom.

To keep her sanity during this period, she found a piano on the monastery grounds and played it passionately. She walked a good deal and ran and reviewed the path of her imperfect life and looked hard to the guidance of the Bible. "Do not remember the sins of my youth or my transgressions. According to your steadfast love remember me, for your goodness' sake, O LORD."

When Bill Clinton carried his Bible into church, he made sure to carry it on the camera side of his body. That's the kind of Christianity Washington understood. In that city of brittle surfaces, one distrusted his fellow citizens to the degree they took anything to heart. That Hill was then besieged and alone and locked in a spiritual struggle more intense than they would ever know counted for nothing.

In early 1997, after several years of lawyer-induced silence, Hill ignored her attorney's advice and went public. Telling the truth would add an unwelcome footnote to the ongoing hagiography of Brown, but there could be no salvation for her without it. She hoped the truth would set her free— in this case, literally.

For the first time, she allowed reporters into her life. Peter Boyer, writing a lengthy piece for the *New Yorker*, went deep and personal. Not everything revealed in his June 1997 article flattered Hill. Boyer talked in painful detail about Hill's relationship with Brown, her split with Billy Hill because of it, and her resulting estrangement from her adolescent son.

After interviewing countless friends and foes, however, Boyer came to a then novel conclusion: "Most of her story was confirmed by others who knew her and Brown well." Boyer even confronted Jesse Jackson with Hill's provocative charge that Brown had delivered millions of dollars to him for the campaign. Although he put a "you need an infrastructure" spin on the transaction, Jackson did not deny the charge.[1]

True to form, in its review of the startling Boyer article, the *Washington Post* treated Hill's story no more seriously than it would an episode of *Dallas*.

"Hill is not the most reliable of sources, but she sure can dish," wrote media reporter Peter Carlson. "My favorite revelation is that Brown carried a medicine pouch made by Hill's Native American spiritual guru, a dude named Dude Perry. It contained an arrowhead, a feather, and a half-smoked cigarette." Having stuck the knife in Hill's back, Carlson then twisted it, "Obviously [the medicine kit] did not protect Brown from old friends with big mouths."[2]

If nothing else, Carlson nicely captured the frivolous worldview of late century Washington. In an article that revealed the finally lethal connection between Michael Brown and the Lums—Boyer had also produced the excellent PBS *Frontline* piece "The Fixers"—Carlson could find nothing more interesting than the medicine kit. He also reveals how casual was the distaste for anyone who dared to reveal the secrets of this particular White House.

As fate would have it, at least one *Washington Post* reader found the medicine kit as interesting as Carlson did. That just happened to be Chief Petty Officer Kathleen Janoski, the woman who had photographed the kit at Dover.

After reading the *Post*, and then the *New Yorker*, Janoski learned for the first time the desperate mess that was Ron Brown's life. She also learned the kit had been a gift. Brown obviously treasured the gift as he carried it in his diplomatic pouch. Orders to destroy it had to come from high up. "I was confused," says Janoski. "I knew that something was wrong."[3]

She asked her colleagues, "How could the family ask for it back if Nolanda Hill is the one who gave it to him?" Later, Janoski learned from NCIS investigator Jeanmarie Sentell that the kit had been purposefully destroyed. When she heard this, Janoski was perplexed. "We don't destroy anything."

For Janoski, the removal of the kit from a secure diplomatic pouch and its subsequent destruction showed "mindset," especially since the Medical Examiner's office placed so much emphasis on the integrity of personal effects. "It was mind-boggling to think we deviated from standards so dramatically," says Janoski. "It was almost an outrage."

Janoski had to wonder, "What else did they destroy?" Now that she knew about Brown's troubles, she had to wonder if authorities hadn't purged everything in the diplomatic pouch that might have proved embarrassing, possibly even telltale documents about the trade missions.

Janoski shared her concerns with Lt. Col. Steve Cogswell, who was then lecturing about the Brown case among others. It would still be months before reporter Christopher Ruddy found his way to the Armed Forces Institute of Pathology, but thanks to the *Post's* unwitting revelation, he would meet with a receptive audience when he got there.

Nolanda Hill meanwhile continued to shock those who were listening with her unvarnished candor. On June 18, 1997, she appeared in a segment on ABC's *Prime Time Live* and came out swinging:

> *Nolanda Hill*: [Brown] came up in the era of drugs are OK. I mean, you know, he was a 60s child.
> *Brian Ross*: (on camera) As secretary of Commerce, did he use drugs?
> *Hill*: Um, yes.
> *Ross*: Were you there?
> *Hill*: Yes.
> *Ross*: (voice over) It happened, she said, frequently at her Washington apartment, where Brown would come to relax after work.
> *Hill*: He smoked pot, and he once did a line of cocaine.

Brown's drug use may very well explain why the medicine kit was destroyed. Someone likely thought it drug paraphernalia, especially given the "half-smoked cigarette" found with it. Brown was not a smoker. When Ross checked with Brown lawyer Reid Weingarten about Hill's drug allegation, Weingarten sounded flustered and evasive.

> *Weingarten:* Preposterous. I mean, I guess anything's possible. There may be a tyrannosaurus rex outside when we leave this building. It sounds preposterous to me.

The contrast between Hill and Weingarten, here and throughout, favored Hill. Like Boyer, Brian Ross had come to believe her. This became clear on two critical subjects, Vietnam and Oklahoma. After Hill explained the details of the Vietnam bribe effort, including the fact there had been a foreign bank account set up to receive the money, ABC showed an old clip of Brown denying everything.

> *Ross*: (on camera) Is that truthful?
> *Hill*: No.
> *Ross*: He lied?
> *Hill*: Yes.
> *Ross*: (voice over) But Hill says no money ever changed hands, and the bank account was not used because Brown got a tip the FBI was on to him, something FBI agents on the case have told ABC News they always suspected.

Ross's last comment reveals the FBI had felt its mission had been betrayed—presumably by someone in the Justice Department—and its agents had obviously shared the same with ABC. Again, Weingarten would hear none of it.

> *Weingarten*: The Justice Department completely exonerated Ron Brown.
> *Ross*: For lack of evidence?
> *Weingarten*: Lack of evidence. There was no evidence. There was no evidence to support the allegation whatsoever.
> *Ross*: Nolanda Hill did not testify.
> *Weingarten*: She had no connection with the investigation. She had no direct information except this bald lie about what Ron Brown may or may not have said.

It was on the issue of Oklahoma, though, that Hill's statements had the most relevance. This case was ongoing and up for grabs.

> *Ross*: (off camera) In 1993, the Lums took over an Oklahoma gas company called Dynamic Energy Resources that sought special government contracts as minority-owned business. Then, the Lums hired Brown's twenty-eight-year-old son, Michael, and made him a well-paid officer of the company—a convenient way, Hill says, to move money to the father.
> *Hill*: I know that Ron received money that had been paid to Michael.

Ross: (on camera) From the Lums at Dynamic Energy?

Hill: Yes.

Ross: Why would the son give the father money?

Hill: Well, the official version from Reid Weingarten is to pay back some of his law school fees, which I fought with Ron about and told him that was the dumbest thing I ever heard. And I even told Reid that that was stupid to say that.

Ross: What did Ron tell you was going on?

Hill: Ron needed money to pay his taxes.

Ross and ABC had set a well-deserved trap for Weingarten, and he walked right into it.

Weingarten: Let's start with the facts. It's always a good place to start. The Lums never paid off Ron Brown. And Ron Brown never did anything for the Lums.

Ross: (voice over) When pressed, Weingarten said just what Nolanda Hill predicted he would.

Weingarten: Ron was an incredibly generous dad. When Michael came of age—when Michael started kicking in professionally— Michael would be in a position to repay some of the responsibilities that Ron assumed.

Ross: (voice over) Hill says she tried to get Brown to use a different story.

Hill: I talked to Ron about this, and I said, you know, "Why don't you say, 'There's nothing I can do for the Lums as secretary of commerce'?" And he said, "But that's not true. I don't want to say that, because that's not true." And I said, "Well, it's not true that this all of a sudden is to pay you back for college either." He said, "Well, nobody can prove that."

Michael Brown, then with Patton Boggs, "declined to talk" with *Prime Time Live* about the allegations. Just as well. Weingarten had stumbled badly enough, and he was allegedly skilled at this sort of thing. The perceptive viewer had to know who was telling the truth and who was not. With Hill's credibility established, Ross encouraged her to go even deeper, and she did.

Ross: (voice over) One question many want answered is how the man now at the center of the FBI's investigation of illegal fund-raising—John Huang—how did he get a top-level job at Ron Brown's Commerce Department? Nolanda Hill says she knows.

Hill: Ron told me that the White House put him there, and it was Ron's opinion the White House meant Hillary in this instance.

Ross: (on camera) That she put him there.

Hill: He believed that she was the person that had made the call.

Ross acknowledged that Hill's "going public" was risky for her as a grand jury was still reviewing her case. Weingarten drove that point home with more than a hint of menace: "I think there's perhaps a likelihood that she's going to be indicted," he warned, "and charged with serious felonies."

"We may be seeing a lot more of Nolanda Hill this summer," ABC's Sam Donaldson added, but that was not to be. The White House had its way of taking her out of the news.[4]

On August 28, two months after Hill's appearance on ABC, Michael Brown pled guilty to one misdemeanor charge of illegally giving $4,000 to Ted Kennedy's 1994 Senate campaign. Specifically, Brown had given $2,000 to his secretary and $1,000 apiece to two co-workers, which they in turn gave to Kennedy's people.[5]

Amazing as it might have seemed to anyone paying attention, when Brown pled guilty to this one misdemeanor, his slate was wiped clean. The Justice Department agreed it would "not prosecute the defendant for any other conduct by the defendant of which the Public Integrity Section . . . [is] presently aware."[6]

Michael Brown did not leave the courthouse kicking his heels, but one could excuse him if he had. Raymond Hulser, the same prosecutor who had passionately sought to imprison the innocent Billy Dale in the Travelgate disgrace, had let Michael Brown slide with the gentlest of rebukes. Despite a ton of evidence, there would be no charges at all brought against him for passing illegal gratuities on to his father.

"I knew I was in serious trouble when Michael got off," says Hill. "He was the only one in the whole deal who should have gotten hard time."

To allay any suspicions of an inside deal, the Justice Department let it be known that, as condition for the wrist slap, Michael Brown had agreed to testify against Hill. This proved to be untrue, but it gave the Justice Department cover for the brief spin cycle in which Michael Brown was news.

Any stigma attached to the plea faded quickly. A month and a day after he pled guilty, the press found Michael teeing up with a jaunty President Clinton for the second annual Ronald H. Brown Memorial Golf Tournament. Young Brown needed a break from his work as international trade and public policy specialist at Patton Boggs and president and CEO of the Ronald H. Brown Memorial Foundation.[7] Within a few months, Washington insiders would be bruiting his name about as a likely candidate for mayor of the District of Columbia.[8] Ron Brown had died in vain. Michael was following in his footsteps. The father's death had taught the son nothing.

At the time, his father's Commerce Department was still very much in the news. On October 27, 1997, the *Los Angeles Times* shared one story out of many that illuminated the dark corners of Ron Brown's bailiwick. The story concerns an Indonesian by the name of Arief Wiriadinata and the inescapable John Huang.[9]

While still a Commerce employee, Huang had illegally solicited donations to the DNC from Wiriadinata and his wife. Between November 1995 and July 1996, the couple would donate $450,000. In fact, this money was not theirs to give. A Riady business partner had laundered it through them.

Wiriadinata shared his story with the media for a reason lost on most westerners: the early news accounts caused him to lose face, not because they revealed how he had broken the law, but because they referred to him as "a gardener." At the time, in fact, he was manager of the Lippo-owned Sea World in Jakarta.

Wiriadinata would add a new and memorable phrase to the nether-Bartlett's of the Clinton years. Under pressure, the White House released a videotape of him shaking hands with the president and confiding: "James Riady sent me." In the Washington of Bill and Hillary Clinton, those four words could get a soul just about anywhere.

On November 21, 1997, Michael Brown learned what the penalty would be for his misdemeanor—three years' probation and a $5,000 fine. He also had to perform 150 hours of community service and pay an additional $7,818 for the costs of his probation.[10]

Michael Brown and golf buddy, Bill Clinton, likely thought they had put the whole affair to bed that day. Just three days later, however, they would learn how very wrong they were. As it turned out, Nolanda Hill was not the only one to go public in 1997. Lt. Col. Steve Cogswell decided to do so as well.

To Kathleen Janoski
with best wishes,

Hillary Rodham Clinton

30 | CONSPIRACY COMMERCE

"Oh s—," Kathleen Janoski remembers thinking, "Cogswell is right. We're in trouble."

On December 3, 1997, Janoski was home on leave in Pittsburgh. She got the sense something was up when a tech sergeant called from the AFIP office wanting the combination to her safe. That was just the first of many phone calls that morning, including one from Lt. Col. Steve Cogswell.

At Cogswell's urging, Janoski went out and grabbed the paper. "Experts Differ on Ron Brown Head Wound" screamed the page one headline.[1] Although the series on Brown had opened on November 24, this was the first article to refer to the hole in Brown's head or mention Cogswell by name. Janoski bought ten papers. Although she had yet to go public herself, it was clear back at AFIP that she was part of Team Cogswell. Or maybe more than "part."

"Since it was a Pittsburgh paper," says Janoski, "they thought I was the ring leader."

The Clintons were well aware of the *Pittsburgh Tribune-Review*. The White House had documented the vexatious *Tribune-Review* and the "media food chain" that nurtured it in a 332-page report that bore the *Austin Powers*-like title, *Communication Stream of Conspiracy Commerce*. In its unapologetic paranoia, the effort recalled nothing so much as the final days of the Nixon administration.

"What is striking about the document," observed the *Washington Post* earlier in 1997, "is that it lays down this suspicion-laden theory about how the media works in cold print, under the imprimatur of the White House."[2] According to the document, here is how "the stream" worked:

> First, well-funded right-wing think tanks and individuals underwrite conservative newsletters and newspapers such as the *Western Journalism Center*, the *American Spectator*, and the *Pittsburgh Tribune Review*. Next, the stories are reprinted on the Internet where they are bounced all over the world.

From the Internet, according to the report, the stories go through the right-wing British media, back through the respectable right-wing American press, into Congress, "finally to be covered by the remainder of the American mainstream press as a 'real' story."[3]

The mechanics the *Communication Stream* describes are not entirely fanciful. What it fails to address, though, is whether or not these stories were accurately reported. If its account of Ron Brown's death is indicative, the *Tribune-Review* hews to a journalistic standard at least as high as its respectable rivals and probably higher.

The Brown article in question was straightforward, specific, and comprehensive. It covered many of the more damning details of the case, including the famous "lead snowstorm" and what Cogswell matter-of-factly called "an apparent gunshot wound."[4]

There was nothing matter-of-fact about the AFIP response. The next day, the institute came out firing. "This is a closed case," insisted the public affairs officer. Officials had conducted a "full discussion" of Brown's injuries, including the head wound, and had dismissed any possibility of foul play.[5]

On December 5, the AFIP imposed what was essentially a gag order on Cogswell. He was forced to refer all press inquiries on the Brown case to AFIP's public affairs office and told he could leave his office only with permission. More intimidating still, military police escorted him to his house and seized all of his case materials on the Brown crash. When Janoski returned from Pittsburgh, under suspicion for her friendship with Cogswell, she and others were restricted to their floor and could not even go to lunch without permission.

The AFIP would soon clarify that neither Cogswell nor anyone else was under "house arrest." The institute was merely conducting an internal investigation to make sure no "internal policies or procedures were violated—

unrelated to the forensic findings—and it is important that Dr. Cogswell be available during this review."

This was a stunning admission. The AFIP was prepared to investigate Cogswell's media relations but not Gormley's forensics. And lest anyone be uncertain of the outcome, the AFIP publicly chastised Cogswell for bringing "unnecessary grief to the families of those who died in this tragic accident."[6] This, by the way, was the exact strategy used to discredit critics of the ongoing TWA 800 investigation.

On that same December 5, F. Whitten Peters, acting secretary of the Air Force, sent an angry, apologetic letter to the families of the crash victims. "The alleged 'bullet fragments' mentioned in the [*Tribune-Review*] reports were actually caused by a defect in the reusable x-ray film cassettes," Peters wrote. "Medical examiners took multiple x-rays using multiple cassettes and confirmed this finding." He went on to claim that Brown had died of "multiple blunt-force injuries" suffered in the crash. Despite the hole in Brown's head and the apparent "bullet fragments" that necessitated multiple X-rays to explain, Peters saw no reason for the medical examiners to pursue an autopsy. "Had there been suspicion regarding the nature of Mr. Brown's death," they certainly would have.[7]

On December 6, Howard Kurtz of the *Washington Post* did his best to help the AFIP undermine Cogswell and his claims. Kurtz gleefully cited the article's presumably tainted source and its movement up the now famous "media food chain." An experienced media critic, Kurtz was able to deconstruct the story with a phone call or two.

"Cogswell never actually examined the body," Kurtz revealed as though this were news. He then added with unwarranted certainty, "There definitely was no bullet because there was no exit wound."

Here, Kurtz cited Gormley as his authority. If Gormley were not authority enough, Kurtz fell back on an "army spokesman," who had assured him the case was "closed." With this assurance, the case was closed for Kurtz and the once-inquisitive *Washington Post* as well.[8]

If Kurtz or the AFIP thought the outbreak had been contained, they were in for a surprise. In a refreshingly noble gesture, Lt. Col. David Hause ignored the heat and went public on December 9 in support of Cogswell.

Unlike Cogswell, Hause had been present for the examination. The authorities and their media friends could no longer write off Cogswell as some lone eccentric. Hause, who had won a purple heart in Vietnam as a combat infantryman, had been involved in autopsy procedures for twenty-five years. He was not one to be taken lightly.

Hause added one other bit of useful evidence. When the *Tribune-Review* had interviewed Gormley, he insisted that whatever caused the hole could not have been a bullet because it did not perforate the skull. No brain was allegedly visible.

Hause begged to differ. "What was immediately below the surface of the hole was just brain," he asserted. To Gormley's claim that there was no exit wound, Hause and Cogswell both agreed a bullet could have traveled down the neck and lodged elsewhere in the body.[9] Although Janoski had not yet said so publicly, she knew one other fact of critical importance: Gormley had never even looked for an exit wound.

The AFIP fired back that same day with a press release rich in the kind of detail that would make a good defense lawyer cringe. "Due to the initial appearance of Brown's injuries," Gormley was quoted as saying, "we carefully considered the possibility of a gunshot wound. However, scientific data, including X-rays, ruled out that possibility." Gormley repeated publicly Peters' claim that the alleged "bullet fragments" were "actually caused by a defect in the reusable X-ray film cassette." For Gormley, there was not "the slightest suspicion" regarding the nature of Brown's death.[10]

What the release did not say, but what the AFIP finally had to admit, was those multiple new X-rays were all now missing, as were the original ones. "Wecht's law," famed coroner Cyril Wecht called the phenomenon. The more controversial a case, the more likely evidence is to turn up missing. He cited the Brown case as a classic example of the same. In real life Wecht described as "very, very rare" the times key X-rays actually disappeared.[11]

Not about to back off, the *Pittsburgh Tribune-Review* had brought Wecht in to review the case. A prominent local Democrat, the Pittsburgh coroner could not be easily dismissed as a trafficker in Republican conspiracy commerce. He noted the "perfectly circular" nature of the wound, its "inwardly beveling path," the "tiny pieces of dull silver-colored" material around the edge of the wound, the "lead snowstorm" shown in the photo of the X-ray, and came to an unequivocal conclusion:

> There was more than enough evidence of a possible homicide to call
> in the FBI so that [the autopsy could have been conducted] and a gun-
> shot could have been ruled out. The military had a duty to notify the

family, and if the family didn't allow an autopsy, go to another authority and have it conducted.[12]

As Tracey Brown would later concede, she learned about the hole only from the media and then more than a year and a half after the crash. "Had my family known about the suspicious wound at the time," says Tracey, "we would have requested an autopsy."[13]

Wecht was not the only problem for the White House. Although the mainstream media were still largely avoiding the subject, the story, like some rogue salmon, made an unusual jump from the conservative media stream to the black-oriented one.

On December 11, the *Chicago Independent Bulletin* ran a story headlined "Pastor Demands Investigation into Late Ron Brown's Death."[14] Two days later, the influential *Baltimore Afro-American* ran a lengthy front-page story, "Brown Head Injury Suspected Bullet Wound."[15] If the White House could ignore the conservative media, it could not ignore the black media. Nor could the Brown family. In December, the family asked for and got an audience with the AFIP. After looking at a photo of her father's lifeless face, Tracey Brown came to a startling conclusion.

"I stopped caring how my father died," writes Tracey. "It may seem strange, but whether his death was an accident or an assassination, he's not coming back."[16] In any case, the Browns did nothing publicly to pacify the black community.

To head off the unrest, Col. Gormley appeared on *BET Tonight*, a national cable show hosted by Tavis Smiley.[17] By this time, Gormley knew the *Tribune-Review* had run actual photos of Brown's wound, and the brain was clearly visible. He conceded he had been wrong on that point and wrote off his mistake to faulty memory. Still, he insisted the X-rays showed no metal fragments, and there was no exit wound.

It had to have been an excruciating time to be Col. Gormley. He was by no means a White House operative. It's as likely his botched examination resulted from a generalized pressure to move quickly as it did from any direct order. And yet, as Gormley unwittingly admitted to Smiley, he had chosen not to pursue an autopsy based "on discussions at the highest level from in Commerce (sic), at the Joint [Chiefs of Staff], and the [Department of Defense], the White House."[18]

In other words, Gormley was sufficiently concerned about the wound to consult with his superiors at the time of the examination. This inquiry reached the White House. According to the relevant law that covers executive assassination, 18 U.S.C. § 351, the president should have referred the case to the FBI.[19] At the very least, he should have informed the Brown family. That he did neither suggests he had good reason not to.

Now Gormley was being hung out to dry. The pressure on him was specific and surely exerted by a high authority. That authority was compelling Gormley to invent answers, even on national TV, and his inventions were increasingly transparent. A quick summary:

- The lead snowstorm seen in the Janoski photos of the Brown head X-rays was a result of a defective X-ray cartridge.
- A second set of X-rays had been taken, and they showed no fragments.
- Unfortunately, all the head X-rays were now missing from Brown's files.
- Despite what Gormley had said earlier, Brown's brain was visible. Gormley had forgotten.
- Although there was not the "slightest suspicion" of foul play, examiners took multiple X-rays to explain away the apparent lead snowstorm, commissioned a search for some part that could explain away the hole, and referred the case to the White House.

Janoski could see right through Gormley's uneasy dither. She had followed Brown's body all the way until embalming, which came right after the examination. She had wondered, even at the time, why Gormley did not look for an exit wound or test for gunshot residue.

Janoski could not imagine when a second set of X-rays could have been taken. Besides, at the morgue she had heard no talk at all about a problem with the original X-rays. More to the point, naval investigator Jeanmarie Sentell had long ago confided in her that the original X-rays had been deliberately destroyed precisely because they showed a lead snowstorm.

At the time, Janoski was making no friends among the brass. She and several others refused to talk to investigators. A smooth, southern colonel had been assigned to ease the story out of her, but Janoski had been around the Navy block too many times to fall for his sweet talk.

Janoski felt that her colleagues had no choice but to go public. They could not appeal to a chain of command that had ignored the presidential assassination statute, denied Brown an autopsy, concealed the wound from his family, lied about his examination, and possibly destroyed evidence, including critical X-rays.

"This was not textbook 'how to be a good petty officer' stuff," says Janoski. "We were naive. We had no idea we could get in so much trouble for telling the truth."

Meanwhile, the pressure from the black community was growing more insistent. On December 18, the AP was reporting that the head of the NAACP, Kweisi Mfume, was now taking the Brown case to the White House and demanding answers.[20]

That pressure turned nightmarish on Christmas Eve. Possibly for the first time in its history, protestors showed up at the AFIP headquarters at Walter Reed Army Medical Center in Washington. Leading the charge was veteran activist and former comedian Dick Gregory. He staged a protest and prayer vigil that culminated in the TV-friendly gesture of wrapping yellow crime scene tape around the area.

DC police obliged Gregory by arresting him. He vowed he would not pay any bail and would spend Christmas in jail until he could make his case before a judge. "We are not going to allow this to pass," he vowed. "There is very strong evidence the AFIP found a gunshot wound on Brown's head and decided to cover-up this evidence."[21]

The mainstream media largely ignored Gregory, just as they had Mfume. But there was one black leader neither the media nor the White House could ignore. That was Jesse Jackson, and he came forward on January 5. In 1998 Jackson still had the perceived moral force to shake up Washington, and now he was exerting that force to call for an investigation.[22]

With Jackson on board, reporters finally raised the Brown question at a press conference on that same day. They obviously struck a nerve.

"The Pentagon, I think, has very thoroughly and in very gruesome detail, and no doubt in ways painful to the Brown family, addressed this issue. And it's time to knock this stuff off," snapped press secretary Mike McCurry. "I'm not going to talk about this further or take any further questions on the subject."[23]

For all of McCurry's bluster, the White House could not just blow Jackson off. It had to respond. On January 8, the administration's designated buffer, Janet Reno, held a press conference to announce that the Justice Department had, in fact, consulted with the Defense Department in the past month but saw no reason to investigate further.

"The department is not looking into the matter," Reno said, before adding the meaningless sop, "If there is credible information developed that a crime has been committed, then we will pursue it immediately."[24]

The next day, January 9, the *Washington Post* clarified what had gone on behind the scenes to justify Reno's decision. As reported by Michael Fletcher, the AFIP had convened an internal panel of pathologists to review the Brown case, and the panel, including the presumed dissident Hause, "unanimously backed" Gormley's findings.[25]

In the January 11 issue of the *Tribune-Review* Hause roared back in dissent. "Fuming," he denied he had ever said any such thing. Like the others, he had been asked in private whether he thought Brown's wound was from a gunshot.

Hause had answered that he thought it more likely to have come from an "exotic weapon," like a captive-bolt gun. Designed to kill livestock, the gun had been used by drug traffickers to kill an American DEA agent in Mexico in 1985. In any case, Hause had told his AFIP interviewer that "Secretary Brown's body should be exhumed and an autopsy performed by someone not associated with AFIP."[26]

In that same issue of the *Tribune-Review*, a third pathologist, Air Force Maj. Thomas Parsons, also came forward. Although not present at the examination, he agreed the hole was "suspicious and unusual" and worthy of an autopsy. Like Hause, he firmly denied he had ever signed off on a report backing Gormley's findings and just as firmly argued for an autopsy.[27]

Appalled by the treatment of Cogswell and Hause, Chief Petty Officer Janoski decided to talk on record, and her account appeared two days later.[28] Although lacking the clout of a pathologist, Janoski strengthened the group's hand considerably. She had discovered the hole. She had been with Brown's body longer even than Gormley. She had heard firsthand about the purposeful destruction of property and X-rays, and on top of that she was a woman and a Democrat. She fit no one's profile of a right-wing kook. And when she talked to the *Tribune-Review*, she told them everything.

With momentum still building in the black community, the *Washington Afro-American* ran a lengthy front-page story on January 17 focusing on Janoski's claims.[29] At this moment in time, the story had enough substance and enough bi-racial support to breach the walls of the mainstream media and shake Washington to its foundation, but this was not to be.

In one of the great ironies of modern media, a separate stream of conspiracy commerce had been simultaneously gathering force. This second stream followed much the course the White House report had described. One could trace its genesis to a January 1994 article in the Richard Mellon Scaife-funded *American Spectator.* The *Spectator's* "Troopergate" story exposed the sexual escapades of then Governor Clinton and his involvement with one woman whose first name accidentally sneaked into the text—"Paula," as in Paula Jones.[30]

With the help of civil-liberties legal firm Rutherford Institute, Paula Jones sued the president for sexual harassment. Had the *Washington Post* allowed into print even a portion of Michael Isikoff's exquisitely researched piece on Jones, Clinton might have gotten a necessary wake-up call. But the *Post* spiked the story and forced it underground, and Clinton continued misbehaving.[31]

On the same day and in the same city that Kathleen Janoski was talking to Christopher Ruddy, Linda Tripp was talking to Ken Starr. She presented Starr with tapes on which Monica Lewinsky recounted how the president and Vernon Jordan had encouraged her to lie under oath in the Jones suit.

Six days after Janoski went public, so did Matt Drudge. An Internet maverick and veritable poster child for the conspiracy stream, Drudge broke a new Isikoff story that *Newsweek* was suppressing. So powerful was this stream—and so rich was it in those tawdry details that the public loves—the major media had no choice but to open the floodgates. By January 21, the Monica tale had inundated the land and left every other news story gasping for breath.

Jesse Jackson had a choice to make. He could either pick away at the administration on a story that had just lost its legs, or he could ride the rising tide of resentment in the black community and come to the besieged president's aid.

As Elmer Smith told DeWayne Wickham, "Once those right-wingers went after [Clinton] he became a martyr in the black community."[32] These were the same right-wingers, after all, who only recently were burning down black churches. The media had un-told the arson story only in whispers, and now they were about to paint Starr as the kind of zealot who could easily have been passing out the torches.

Nothing if not clever, Jesse Jackson chose to embrace the president once more. In an unintentionally comic saga, Jackson emerged as the president's spiritual advisor and, with the aid of his comely assistant Karin Stanford, comforted the repentant president in the midst of his moral crisis.

In August, after the president's grudging TV apology, Chelsea Clinton reportedly asked that Jackson come to the White House to counsel her and her mom. Hillary, breathless, had presumably just found out the truth. The three were said to have prayed together for two hours. Jackson then praised Hillary for her strength and her love of her husband, and Hillary's poll numbers shot up.[33] In the black community at least, so did Bill Clinton's. In August 1998, they clocked in at an astounding 93 percent, higher even than Jackson's.[34]

Jackson wasn't through. In December of that same year, he led an anti-impeachment rally at the Capitol. The day before the rally, he presided over an online chat through the *Washington Post*. One participant asked him about the president's impending impeachment-eve war on Iraq and whether Jackson was willing to "condemn Bill Clinton for being willing to slaughter brown people as a political survival tactic." Jackson hemmed and hawed and did admit that yes, the timing was indeed "awkward," but that did not dim his support.

"What [Clinton] did," said Jackson "does not fit the definition of high crimes; it was a little crime. High crime would be treason, crimes against the state, threat to national security."[35] To be sure, Jackson's "high crimes" definition did not fit the Monica affair nearly as well as it did the China business in which the president and Brown were involved.

Speaking of awkward, just months before this vigil, Jackson's comely assistant, the one photographed with him in the Oval Office when she was four months pregnant, had given birth to Jackson's now famous "love child." A $40,000 moving fee courtesy of Rainbow/PUSH and a $10,000 a month retainer would help keep the young Jackson child out of the news for more than a year.[36]

As expected, Jackson's support for the president did not come without a price. A *Business Week Online* article unconsciously suggests the nature of the likely payoff:

> As House impeachment managers began laying out their case in the Senate for the conviction of Bill Clinton, the president sought solace in a favorite, if unusual, haven: Wall Street. . . . [Clinton] is scheduled to speak on Jan. 15 to a Wall Street conference organized by Jesse L.

Jackson. Jackson's meeting was designed to prod the financial industry both to hire more minority employees and to invest more money in economically distressed areas. Clinton plans to outline a series of steps to leverage billions of dollars in investment in inner cities and poor rural communities, sources tell *Business Week Online*.[37]

In the face of all those fresh minority capitalism dollars and all that easy access to power, Jesse Jackson and the DC civil rights enterprise forgot about Ron Brown just about as quickly as they had forgotten about Lani Guinier.

To his credit, Dick Gregory is still protesting.

31 | RETRIBUTION

When she signed her affidavit for Judicial Watch on January 17, 1998, Nolanda Hill was not at all in the flow of the conspiracy streams then swirling through Washington.

She did not know who Kathleen Janoski was. Nor was she aware Janoski had gone public about Ron Brown's death just four days earlier. She had never heard of Linda Tripp or Monica Lewinsky. Nor did she know on that very day Bill Clinton was about to swear under oath that he didn't know much about Monica Lewinsky either.

All Hill knew is she did not want to be doing what she was doing. The problem was she had run out of options. In the nearly three years since Janet Reno had aligned the sundry forces of government against her, Hill had spent hundreds of thousands of her own dollars on legal fees, and she had no more dollars to spend.

And then there was always Larry Klayman. For some time now, he had a subpoena with Hill's name on it, and all he had to do was find her. Only she had the knowledge that could move his trade mission investigation to the next level. Hill had not made it easy for him. It wasn't that she feared Klayman. Rather, she feared the Clintons and the retribution that would surely follow if she cooperated.

By January 1998, however, Hill could run no more. She literally could not afford it. Emotionally and financially exhausted, she finally agreed to submit an affidavit to Klayman if he could keep it under seal. He believed that he could.

The resulting affidavit was short and to the point, less than a thousand words long. Under oath, Hill first established the intensity and intimacy of her relationship with Brown and then cut straight to the heart of the matter.

After the election debacle of 1994, she attested, "The trade missions were being used as a fund-raising tool for the upcoming Clinton-Gore presidential campaign and the Democratic Party." Brown had told her that companies "were being solicited to donate large sums of money in exchange for their selection." He also shared his displeasure that these missions "were being perverted at the direction of the White House."[1]

According to the affidavit, Hill and the Commerce counselor, Jim Hackney, had encouraged Brown to pay heed to Judicial Watch's FOIA requests. That was not to be: "The White House, through Leon Panetta and John Podesta, had instructed him to delay the case by withholding the production of documents prior to the 1996 elections." This was damning stuff, and there was more.

Again, according to the affidavit, when Brown showed Hill the solicitation letters signed by Melissa Moss, she encouraged Brown to fire Moss. At Hill's urging Brown did call her and promise to set up a meeting, but that meeting never came to pass. Brown died in the interim. Hill had since seen Moss's deposition video, and she affirmed that Moss "has not told the truth."

"Because of a fear for my personal and my family's well-being and safety," Hill said in conclusion, "I ask that this affidavit be kept under seal and that a mechanism be set up by the court for me to come forward to tell all I know." Klayman submitted the affidavit to the court on January 28. This was the day after Hillary Clinton had revealed to the world the presence of a "vast rightwing conspiracy." If there were such a conspiracy, no one had told Hill about it. With Ron Brown dead, and his son Michael—her other alleged co-conspirator—out golfing with the president, Hill felt like the loneliest person in the world.

When he read the affidavit, Judge Royce Lamberth understood its import. However brief, this was the wedge needed to force open the whole unholy 1996 election mess. It was too powerful to remain under seal, and this meant, as Hill relates, "hauling my butt up there for open court."

Although Lamberth instructed the attorneys from the civil side of the Justice Department not to communicate with those from the criminal side, Hill feared the worst. Consequently, she had her lawyer, Stephan Charles, talk to Deputy Attorney General Eric Holder, a friend of Brown's and a Clinton insider. Holder, however, was not sympathetic. He told Charles that Hill's statements "were getting her into trouble." Later, under pressure from Judge Lamberth, Holder would deny he ever communicated with Hill's attorney, let alone threatened Hill.

For Hill, the hammer came down on March 13, ten days before her scheduled evidentiary hearing before Judge Lamberth. The Clinton Justice Department indicted Hill, as well as her business partner, Ken White, on fraud and tax evasion charges. The improbably naïve lead of the *New York Times* called the indictment "a vivid example of how an investigation can outlive its target," as if some unconscious legal force blindly pushed the case along.[2]

Larry Klayman knew better. In a motion to the court, he would write, "The timing of these events is neither accidental nor coincidental. Ms. Hill's indictment was likely an effort to retaliate against her and deter her from giving any further damaging testimony at the March 23, 1998 hearing."[3]

Specifically, the indictment charged Hill with conspiring to defraud the Internal Revenue Service between 1990 and 1995 and the Federal Deposit Insurance Corporation between 1989 and 1993, as well as aiding and assisting in the preparation of false federal income tax returns.

Regardless of the charges, Hill knew well what her real "crimes" were. The independent counsel had targeted her only to get at Brown, reduced her to the status of "unnamed person." The Justice Department had indicted her only to shut her up. If Hill's claims of being hounded strike the reader as paranoid, the Justice Department press release proved otherwise. Boasted Justice, "This case was investigated by the IRS, the FDIC, and the FBI; and by the U.S. Department of Justice, Fraud Section, and the Tax Division."

A few days after the indictment, Hill turned herself in at the District of Columbia jail. Some eight agents in trench coats met her there, more than enough to intimidate. Unfortunately, none of them knew quite exactly what to do, and so together, they stumbled through the already humiliating process of getting Hill booked.

The officer in charge at the jail, an African American, took an interest in Hill's plight. Upon learning who she was, he asked a question much on the minds of black America, "Do you think Ron Brown was murdered?" When Hill answered in the affirmative, he replied, "That's what we think too." He then asked why there was no investigation. To that question, despite her circumstances, Hill could only laugh.

Fearing self-incrimination, as the White House knew she would, Hill attempted to back out of the evidentiary hearing. The court, however, insisted she testify, and Hill nervously complied. On March 23, 1998, she reported to Washington's Federal District Court for the hearing, *Judicial Watch v. Department of Commerce*. Just in from Kentucky, the normally stylish Hill wore jeans, a shirt she had just picked up at Wal-Mart, and her son's oversized blazer. So anxious was she about testifying in public that when Judge Lamberth called her to the bench she had to rush to his own restroom to throw up. Hill had spotted certain White House operatives in the packed courtroom, and she knew there would be hell to pay for telling the truth.

Lamberth demanded no less than the truth. He sat Hill so she would face him, stared right through her to gauge her honesty, and watched intently as Klayman grilled her. The proceedings lasted seven hours. Hill answered truthfully and consistently under oath, refusing at every turn to be led. At the end of the day, she knew that Lamberth too believed her.

Hill did not know about the Ron Brown investigation on the other side of the Washington metro, a "Command Investigation." The AFIP was not investigating Brown's death, mind you, but rather the embarrassing disclosures of its own incompetence and/or complicity in the woefully inadequate examination of Ron Brown's body.[4]

Although told this was an informal inquiry, a way to improve internal communications and the like, Kathleen Janoski and her colleagues knew better. One clue was investigators were warning them to get lawyers. In desperation, Janoski turned to one attorney who knew and cared more about Ron Brown than anyone else.

"Larry Klayman is my hero," says Janoski. "If it wasn't for Judicial Watch I would have been toast."

The AFIP had been pressuring the four dissenters to sign a statement. Klayman called an attorney from the Army's celebrated Judge Advocate General's corps to get some clarification. "What's going to happen to Janoski if she doesn't talk?" he asked. The officer said a court martial was a possibility.

"And if she doesn't talk then?" The JAG officer listed the theoretical outcomes, including "the death penalty." He had to have regretted that bit of Roy Beanish bravado the moment he said it, and Klayman was not about to let him forget it.[5]

In researching the Uniform Code of Military Justice, Klayman came quickly to a surprise finding. Janoski and the others did not have to talk. Not talking, however, only aggravated the situation at the AFIP. Janoksi heard rumbles that the four photographers under her would be taken away. After she was seen using the fax machine, her superiors had it locked up. Many of her colleagues avoided her altogether. "It was really such a tough time," says Janoski. "I had an outstanding career and now I was made out to be some kind of dirtbag."

One day in early April 1998, while Janoski was on the phone, Cogswell walked by and left a note on her desk. It simply read, "You are going to be reassigned." The orders came soon after. Janoski was so angry at the crudeness of it all that she could scarcely drive downtown. When she confronted the assigning officer about the reason for the transfer, the officer refused to give one.

The brass had snatched Janoski away from that nest of conspirators in Rockville and dispatched her to the Washington headquarters where they could keep an eye on her. Only in retrospect did she realize her last day at Rockville just so happened to mark the second anniversary of Brown's last day on earth, April 3.

Janoski started at her new assignment immediately. On day one, her new boss pointed to a desk and said simply, "You are going to be sitting here." Intentionally or otherwise, he had assigned her a chair that was too low at a desk that was too high in a corner where the erratic fluorescents flickered torturously overhead. Janoski lacked only a dunce cap to complete her public humiliation.

"We might have you work on a project," said the boss, a civilian. Gone were the staff, the responsibilities, the $250,000 inventory, all the real challenges of useful adult work. In despair by day's end, Janoski left her new office only to find that her '84 Mazda pickup had been ticketed. "I almost lost it," says Janoski.

For the first few months on this presumed job, no one dared talk to Janoski. From time to time, her boss found her some meaningless make-work, but mostly she just sat. "It is so hard to do nothing all day," she remembers. Disgusted, this twenty-three-year veteran retired from the Navy less than a year later. She credits Klayman with saving her backside and her benefits.

If anything, Cogswell was treated worse. Just the year before, he had been cited as the number one forensic pathology consultant in the Department of Defense and was called, ironically enough, "AFIP's expert on gunshot wounds." No more. In late January 1998, after ten years of the best possible reviews, Cogswell received a negative evaluation. Cogswell knew this was a career killer. He did not have to wait long to find out just how dead his career was. Despite his exceptional skills as a forensic pathologist, he was banished to dental pathology. There he would spend his days reviewing slides of mouth tumors, a task at which he had no special gifts.[6]

The AFIP soon barred Lt. Col. David Hause and Maj. Thomas Parsons from doing autopsies and told them they really needed to find someplace else to work. Soon Hause was transferred to Fort Leonard Wood in Missouri and Parsons to Andrews Air Force Base, both in hospital pathology, the specific field of neither. In one of those rare moments of nobility in the face of bureaucracy, none of the group yielded to the pressure to back down or turn on his or her colleagues.[7]

"The four of us stuck together," says Janoski, "and that was very important."

Hill, however, was feeling very much alone. After the indictment and the FOIA hearing, Hill returned to Dallas to comfort her aging mother, who was devastated by the prosecution. Hill also had to borrow money against her house to afford a defense. She was not there long when she learned she would have to return to Washington. The Justice Department was going to re-indict her, allegedly because of typographical errors in the first indictment. Klayman suspected another motive. "Most likely," he argued to the court, "this re-indictment and re-arraignment was another warning by the Clinton administration to this material witness."[8]

Hill had had enough Washington. She sought refuge once again in the Kentucky monastery, "as far underground as you can get." She was no longer worried about subpoena servers. She was worried about assassins. For the next year, she had little work to do other than to save herself from prison.

In assessing her chances at trial, Hill and her attorney could not overlook one very real but sensitive issue: the likely makeup of a DC jury. To be the white "mistress" of a married black man before a jury composed largely of black women did not augur well for Hill. Worse, the Clintons and their cronies would do their best to poison the jury pool. They controlled the media spin, not Hill.

Hill had an additional problem. Alexis Herman, now secretary of labor, had a particular grudge against her. Just a week before the Monica scandal broke, Herman realized she had a scandal of her own to contain. A businessman from Cameroon, Laurent Yene, had publicly accused Herman of selling access to the White House during Clinton's first term. In an interview with ABC News's Brian Ross in January 1998, Yene described how he delivered cash to Herman to help a client secure, of all things, an FCC license:

> *Laurent Yene*: I went to her house and gave her this envelope.
> *Brian Ross*: You gave her an envelope of cash?
> *Yene*: Personally.
> *Ross*: To Alexis Herman?
> *Yene*: Absolutely.

Yene provided Justice lawyers and ABC News with bank statements and other documents. He also passed a lie detector test.[9] Janet Reno called for an independent counsel, and predictably the White House spin machine proceeded to slander Yene unmercifully, much as it had Ly Thanh Binh years before.

Yene was just one of the "liars" making life miserable for the Clintons in 1998. He joined the ranks of Hill, Janoski, Cogswell, Wecht, Lewinsky, Tripp, Paula Jones, Juanita Broaddrick, and Kathleen Willey among others. The fact the accusers were mostly women or people of color and virtually all Democrats seemed to escape those who invested paranoid faith in Hillary's vast rightwing conspiracy.

In due course, the independent counsel declined to press charges against Herman.[10] As Hill knew and the independent counsel had to, Herman had a powerful reach in the District's black community. This too worried Hill. Although not involved romantically, she and Yene were good friends. He had escorted her in fact to one of Brown's memorial services. Hill saw what the White House had done to Yene. Its minions would go harder still on her.

Anxious, alone, and broke, facing as many as seventy years in prison if convicted, Hill chose to negotiate a deal. The judge, however, refused to accept the plea that had been negotiated. Apparently, the law she was alleged to have broken applied only to lawyers and accountants. The prosecutor and her own attorney finally prevailed upon the judge to relent.

Three years and a few days after Ron Brown's funeral, Hill accepted her sentence. On June 15, a day before her fifty-fifth birthday, she reported to a halfway house in Seagoville, Texas, some thirty miles south of Dallas, just in time for a typically torrid Texas summer with on and off again air-conditioning.

From day one, Hill missed the dismantled bunk beds of Kentucky. She now bunked on top in a space so tight she could not sit up. To reach her bed, she had to use a chair. There was no ladder. Inexplicably, she was not allowed a pillow or blanket. Hill was easily the oldest of the twelve women in a facility that also housed ninety men.

For all the discomforts and petty humiliations, "It wasn't an all bad thing at all," says Hill. To many of her housemates, she became the mother they never really had. For Hill, after three years of fruitless isolation, it was a role she was more than willing to play. She helped them, male and female, with their paperwork, their career plans, and their spiritual life. "Sometimes," says Hill, "it was a matter of letting them express how afraid they were."

Several reciprocated by sending Hill notes and cards, the most touching she had ever received. One woman, in for prostitution and drug addiction, wrote her life story at Hill's urging. Upon leaving, she presented Hill with the three spirals notebooks of autobiography. "This is the only gift I can give you," the woman wrote Hill, "because you gave me my life."

Four months after checking in, Hill got her own life back or at least a part of it. She had to wear an ankle bracelet for another four months and spend a year on probation. Try as hard as she could, Hill just could not completely wipe away the bitterness.

The thought that Michael Brown and Huang and Herman and Holder and Wang Jun and the Riadys and Schwartz and Sockowitz and Panetta and Podesta and Fitz-Pegado and McCarty and Moss and Madsen and the ninety-two listed members of the Burton Committee's "pled or fled" club and, most of all, Bill and Hillary Clinton would skate through their own high crimes and/or misdemeanors without ever wearing so much as an ankle bracelet had to rankle, and it did.

Hill could take some small comfort knowing in September 1997 Gene and Nora Lum had been sentenced to ten months in custody, half in a community confinement center, the other half in home detention, but not much. The pair had pled guilty only to arranging about $50,000 in illegal contributions and those just in 1994 and 1995 for congressional campaigns, the mere tip of their illicit iceberg.

Curiously, the Justice Department prosecutor alluded to the "abortive

FBI investigation of public corruption" in Hawaii as well as "the support from Ronald H. Brown" in setting up the Lums' California operation, but there was no further pursuit of either. Nor, of course, were there any charges related to their Oklahoma gas company and their relationship with the Browns.[11] Almost unbelievably, Michael Brown would emerge from the muck as the DNC's national finance vice chair, a position he holds at the time of this writing.

Hill spent the year after her release looking over her shoulder and did not really begin to relax until January 20, 2001. She did not, however, vote in the 2000 election. Felons are not allowed to.

For all her travails, Hill has not grown jaded. "I mean to tell you I have lost millions," says Hill. "I have been harassed, harangued. I have been incarcerated unjustly, but I'm as blessed an individual as ever walked this earth."

As fate would have it, Kathleen Janoski feels much the same way. "I had a very interesting career," says Janoski. "I have no regrets." The quickest way to irritate the Navy vet is to suggest she was a "victim." For her, the harrowing last year at AFIP was merely "my big test in life." She takes great consolation in knowing she and her three amigos all passed.

"We're Inside The Locator, Inbound."

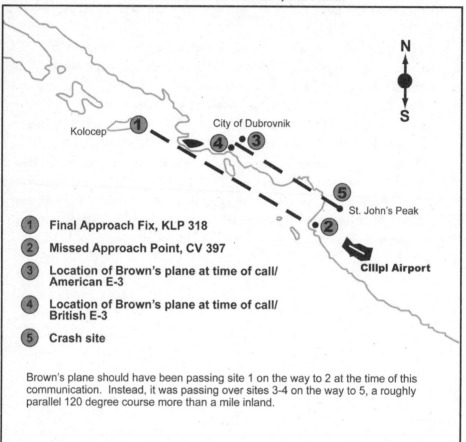

N
S

Kolocep ①

City of Dubrovnik

④ ●: ③

⑤
St. John's Peak

②

Clllpl Airport

① Final Approach Fix, KLP 318

② Missed Approach Point, CV 397

③ Location of Brown's plane at time of call/
American E-3

④ Location of Brown's plane at time of call/
British E-3

⑤ Crash site

Brown's plane should have been passing site 1 on the way to 2 at the time of this
communication. Instead, it was passing over sites 3-4 on the way to 5, a roughly
parallel 120 degree course more than a mile inland.

32 | OCCAM'S RAZOR

When I first heard of the Ron Brown plane crash in 1996—please forbear the switch in voice from third person to first; its necessity will become obvious—I presumed it was just that, a crash, an accident. It was not until the revelation of the hole in Brown's head in late 1997 that I began to question the simplicity of the earlier explanation.

Still, even when I proposed this book, I cautioned the publisher not to expect a clear verdict at book's end. I believed the most likely explanation would prove to be either an accident or possibly a terrorist incident covered up for the sake of political expediency. For that reason, I chose to focus on why the plane went up rather than why it came down. I expected to conclude that in its illicit pursuit of campaign cash, the White House frequently and needlessly put its principal bagman, the secretary of commerce, in harm's way.

In exploring Ron Brown's life, however, I came to see just how desperate were its circumstances, especially at the end. I also came to see how deeply—and willfully—flawed was the investigation into his death.

To restore logic and order to that investigation, I turn to the fourteenth century philosopher, William of Occam.[1] He proposed a theory that makes as much sense today as it did then. We know it as Occam's Razor, and it is often stated thusly, "The simplest explanation is usually the best." The original Latin adds a wrinkle. Said William, "*Pluralitas non est ponenda sine neccesitate.*" This translates roughly, "Multiple variables are not to be posited without necessity."

Take, for instance, the unfortunate crash of JFK Jr.'s plane. The simplest theory—an inexperienced pilot flying on a foggy night—is fully sufficient to explain the tragedy. That does not mean the theory is correct, but it needs to be challenged, even discredited, before one proposes a more complex theory.

What has retarded the investigation of his father's assassination is that so many of the theories violate Occam's principles. In the movie *JFK*, for instance, Oliver Stone posits an extraordinary number of interdependent variables that simply ignore the realities of human nature and American character. Forgive my naïveté, but I refuse to believe the American military would conspire to murder an American president—or a secretary of commerce for that matter.

Still, Occam warned only of *unnecessary* variables. The simplest theory about Brown's death has to accommodate four variables, the first three of which are absolutely necessary, the fourth of which is nearly so.

- The justified state of fear in which Brown lived
- The plane crash
- The apparent bullet hole in Brown's head
- The presumed suicide of Cilipi supervisor, Niko Jerkuic

STATE OF FEAR

Imagine, for instance, identical circumstances had surrounded the death not of Ron Brown but of Labor Secretary Robert Reich. As with Brown, "G.O.P. budget cutters" targeted his department for extinction, making him likely fodder for a vast right-wing conspiracy. Reich, however, gave the imagined conspirators no ammunition. He managed his personal and political affairs prudently and honestly.

Had Reich been found on St. John's Peak with a hole in his head, the simplest explanation would still have been accident or possibly terrorism. Only the delusional would have contemplated a conventional murder. Upon discovering the hole, pathologists likely would have recommended an autopsy to rule out terrorism. Their superiors would have approved, not fearing the results. Case closed.

Ron Brown's case, however, remains wide open. A quick synopsis of his life suggests why. Indulged as a child and treated preferentially thereafter, Brown lost his balance. He came to feel "entitled" and grew reckless as a result. He was able to justify to himself one progressively more corrupt deal after another. For its own purposes, the White House enabled Brown's corruption and exploited it.

The Clintons differed in one major way from any of their predecessors in the White House. They had lost almost all sense of American exceptionalism. This loss diminished their patriotism and enabled them to deal with nations like Indonesia or the People's Republic of China as though they were worthy trading partners. In a political season as desperate as 1995-1996, there was little the Clintons were not willing to trade. They approved any number of deals that would endanger their reelection if exposed. Brown was the "bagman" on many of them.

For all of his flaws, Brown never lost his core humanity. He was still capable of love, especially towards his children. When justice finally caught up with Brown and, more critically, his son, Brown reacted as a father would. He threatened the Clintons and their associates with exposure as leverage for his son's freedom.

The Clintons' Indonesian, Chinese, and American corporate allies had invested much in the Clintons and could have cared less about Ron or Michael Brown or the affection between them. Any number of them would—and did—benefit greatly from his death. Whether accidental or not, Brown's death preserved their investments and likely saved the Clinton presidency.

PLANE CRASH

At the June 1996 press conference summarizing the crash investigation, chief of staff of the Air Force, Ronald R. Fogleman, made a rather remarkable response to an unremarkable question. Asked whether a cockpit voice recorder would have clarified the cause of the crash, Fogleman replied, "It would help explain these apparently inexplicable actions such as flying the wrong course."[2]

"Inexplicable"? Yes, finally, inexplicable. For no firm reason that any official has been able to proffer, the CT-43A veered nine degrees off course in the last four minutes of the flight and crashed into a mountainside nearly two miles northeast of the airport. This was a unique event. Indeed, the Air Force's seventeen specially fitted Boeing CT-43A military aircraft had logged more than 300,000 hours of flying without a previous crash.[3]

"The Fatal Mistake Remains a Mystery," reads the subhead of a comprehensive *New York Times* article more than three weeks after the crash.[4] The possible explanations for the crash ranged far afield, among them bad instruments, bad weather, even an imagined "electrical storm" that Croatian authorities suggested "could have thrown off the compass."[5]

Although refreshingly honest in some respects, the Air Force's accident report offers no better explanations than do the Croatians. On the positive side, the Air Force avoids easy excuses. Says the report, for instance, "All aircraft systems were operating properly at the time of accident."[6]

The ground-based navigation aids were operating properly as well. The Air Force had an FAA Hawker-Siddeley Aircraft come and test them five days after the crash. "The frequencies of the navigation aids were sufficient to shoot the approach," said General Ronald Fogleman, "and it passed an FAA certified check in terms of the ground based navigation aids."[7]

As to the weather, despite the overheated claims of Ambassador Peter Galbraith, it "remained good enough to allow the aircraft to land at Dubrovnik using an instrument approach" and was not "a substantially contributing factor or a cause of this mishap." And although the pilots crossed the site of the first beacon too fast, the plane "descended to 2,200 feet which is consistent with the published minimum descent altitude of 2,150 feet and they slowed to a normal final approach airspeed."

The Air Force bluntly defined the causes of the accident as three: "the failure of command, aircrew error, and an improperly designed instrument approach procedure." The command failure would cause heads to roll, but it essentially meant that, despite an order to the contrary, planes were allowed to fly into unapproved airports.

The airport's approach procedure was old and outmoded, but it was undeniably functional. "It's a safe approach," Lt. Gen. Howell Estes candidly admitted soon after the crash. "Many aircraft have landed at the airport there at Dubrovnik with no difficulties, and, in fact, as you know, some landed that morning and early afternoon prior to Secretary Brown's aircraft's scheduled arrival."[8]

Trouble comes, as it often does, with the elusive notion of pilot error. In fact, the Air Force blames the sober, highly skilled, and reasonably well-rested crew for "a series of errors" while planning and executing the "mishap flight." At its press conference, the Air Force cited four primary errors.

For one, the pilots crossed the final approach fix too fast and without properly configuring the aircraft. For another, they began their final approach without specific clearance from the tower. These two errors, however, were minor and correctible. It was the third and fourth errors in this series that proved fatal:

> [The pilots] selected a heading which placed the aircraft on an incorrect course, nine [degrees] left of the published course. Most significantly, the pilots failed to identify the missed approach point and consequently failed to execute the missed approach procedure.

On the surface at least, this seems true enough. But one reads the report in vain trying to discover how two experienced pilots in a sturdy plane on a day with a light wind and tolerable conditions could miss an airport by nearly two miles when they were on course only twelve miles out.

The Croatians were likewise perplexed. In her fourteen years of service as an air traffic controller at this very airport, Nives Baraba could recall "no incident of a pilot flying left of course" when approaching from the north.[9] "We cannot believe it really," said airport manager Tonci Peovic, "because this never happens [sic] here before."[10]

In a chapter of his admirable book, *Silent Knights*, aviation safety authority Al Diehl makes a credible case for pilot error greatly aggravated by poor training and inadequate equipment, but he does not fully answer this question either.

"To make matters worse," writes Diehl, "[Capt. Ashley Davis] is on the wrong course. He is nine critical degrees left of the proper track and heading towards the towering mountains just north of his intended flight path."[11] Yes, much worse.

"It's easy to screw up these approaches," Diehl argued convincingly in a follow-up interview.[12] Beyond the problems of weather and obsolete approach procedures, the aircraft apparently had only one automatic direction finder, or ADF. The ADF, which is displayed on the pilot's instrument panel, converts the radio signal coming from a beacon into a readable instrument.

As the pilots on Brown's plane approached the airport they would tune in to the signal from that first beacon—known as the "final approach fix" (FAF). The pilots' charts sited the beacon about twelve miles out and identified it as 318 KLP. The "318" refers to the radio frequency. The KLP refers to Kolocep, the island on which the beacon is located. The pilots could confirm the beacon's identity, as it would continuously repeat K-L-P in Morse code.

The sole runway at Cilipi Airport bore the number 12. This told pilots the runway ran roughly 120 degrees to the southeast. Their charts would tell them the exact heading was 119 degrees.

Pilots sometimes call the single ADF needle the "bird dog" because it points straight on at the beacon emitting the signal. As the pilots set the course at 119 degrees on their radio magnetic indicator, they aimed to fly right at the beacon and align the "bird dog" with the 119 setting. As the plane passed over the beacon the needle would swing around 180 degrees ideally to a 299 reading and the pilots would calculate their direction towards the airport from the tail of the needle.

If there were two automatic direction finders, the pilots would have been able to navigate from the first beacon while they monitored the second beacon, 397 CV, located only two miles from the airport, the so-called "missed approach point." With only one automatic direction finder, however, the pilots would and did ride that first signal all the way in.

When Brown's plane crossed Kolocep Island, twelve miles out, it appears to have been on course. Diehl cites "the very high mental workload" that surely burdened the pilots as they attempted to land. The pilots would have been configuring the plane for landing, correcting for the wind, and "hoping and praying that they get a visual"—in other words, seeing the runway.

But neither Diehl nor the Air Force has a definitive answer as to how the pilots could have flown so far off course. As the Air Force admits, Davis was an evaluator pilot "fully qualified for the flying activities he was performing at the time of the [crash]."

Still, if there were no other necessary variables to consider, "pilot error" would be the fall back hypothesis. "No one with a lot of credibility has suggested it was anything but an accident," says Diehl.

To be fair, Diehl and the Air Force were reporting in something of a vacuum. They did not know enough about the other critical variables to make them suspicious. Diehl, for instance, was aware of the hole in Brown's head, but given the scant coverage in the mainstream media, he did not know how seriously to take it.

THE APPARENT BULLET HOLE

In fact, this wound needs to be taken very seriously. The reasons to be suspicious are many and compelling:

- The circular hole struck the forensic photographer and attending pathologist as having the size and shape of a gunshot wound.
- Out of thirty-five passengers, only Brown received such a wound.
- Other pathologists on site at the Dover mortuary agreed the hole looked like a gunshot wound.
- When alerted to the hole, the pathologist, Col. William Gormley, did not check for an exit wound or test for gunshot residue.
- Gormley did not order an autopsy or even request one.
- Members of the Brown family were not informed of the hole at the time. If they had been, they would have ordered an autopsy.
- Gormley was, however, sufficiently concerned that he told Lt. Col. Steve Cogswell, then in Croatia, to look for a part that might have caused the hole.
- When Cogswell strongly recommended an autopsy, Gormley ignored him.
- Despite strenuous efforts, Cogswell could not find any part of the appropriate size.
- Nor could Cogswell envision a scenario in which a hole could have been so perfectly drill-punched into Brown's head.
- A comparable search for a circular part was reportedly undertaken on a clone plane in Germany.
- Apparent "metal fragments" on the original X-ray allegedly led the AFIP to run multiple tests of its X-ray cassettes.
- Despite these efforts, Gormley claimed he did not have "the slightest suspicion" regarding the nature of Brown's death.
- Despite the absence of suspicion, decision-making on an autopsy reached the White House.
- Gormley publicly stated a bullet could not have made the hole in question because no area of brain was visible.
- When another pathologist corrected him about the brain's visibility, Gormley claimed he had forgotten.

261

- CPO Kathleen Janoski learned at Dover that U.S. Navy investigators were prepared to violate regulations and destroy property removed from Brown's diplomatic pouch, namely the Indian medicine kit.
- For Janoski, this established a "mindset" and made her wonder what other possibly incriminating material of Brown's might have been destroyed.
- A U.S. Navy criminal investigator informed Janoski the first set of X-rays had been destroyed because they showed a "lead snowstorm."
- The investigator said a second set had been taken at a less dense setting.
- When Janoski checked Brown's official file, there were no head X-rays at all.
- The AFIP would later admit all head X-rays were missing.
- The 35 mm slides Janoski took of the head X-rays did show a likely lead snowstorm.
- Upon examining the evidence, famed pathologist Cyril Wecht insisted there should have been an autopsy.
- A panel of AFIP pathologists convened under pressure were said to agree "unanimously" that the hole was irrelevant and Brown died of accident-related injuries.
- Two of the pathologists went public claiming they had said no such thing.
- Three military pathologists and a forensic photographer had their careers ruined for telling the truth.

There is one more curious piece of evidence, this one found deep in the twenty-two volumes of the official Air Force report. Filed in Zagreb on April 17, eleven days after the crash, the "Report of the Death of an American Citizen Abroad" for Ronald Harmon Brown lists the cause as "blunt force injuries to head." He is unique in this regard. Every other passenger died from "multiple blunt force injuries." Remember, too, that both Gormley and the acting secretary of the Air Force, F. Whitten Peters, had earlier sworn that Brown had died from "multiple blunt force injuries."

The photos of Brown after death suggest no other potentially fatal head wound save for the circular hole on top, the one AFIP officials had done their best to minimize or ignore. Among those officials was Cdr. Edward Kilbane, whose name is on Brown's death report. When I called Kilbane to inquire not only about this report but also about his visit to the White House immediately after the crash, he laughed nervously and said he would get back to me. He has not.

In his biography of Brown, *New York Times* reporter Steven Holmes does his best to explain away the head wound, but he only succeeds in reinforcing the case for foul play. In Holmes' account, Col. Gormley is anxious enough about the wound to order a second full set of X-rays to be taken, as well as a third set "taken later."[13] The reader is not told when exactly that "later" was. Holmes must not realize that Brown's body immediately went to embalming after Gormley's cursory examination and soon after that to Washington to lie in state.

"The mystery deepens even more," adds Holmes, "when the air force [*sic*] admitted it had lost the original X-rays taken of Brown during postmortem examination." As to the alleged "lead snowstorm," Holmes tells us this was "probably caused by dust on the X-ray film."[14] As the reader recalls, both Gormley and acting Secretary Peters had earlier blamed not dust, but "a defect in the reusable X-ray film cassette."[15] The story was mutating over time.

Holmes, alas, offers still more evidence of journalistic complacency during the Clinton years. He is investigating what appears to be a bullet hole in the head of a troubled public figure. He learns that the first set of X-rays did show a lead snowstorm but that those X-rays were somehow lost. Incredibly, he is not the least bit suspicious.

Holmes implicitly asks us to accept his authority because he writes for the *New York Times*, and Christopher Ruddy does not. "First of all," sniffs Holmes in dismissing any talk of conspiracy, "there was the newspaper that broke the story."[16] In fairness, much of the reporting the *Times* did was quite good. The newspaper had a stake in the story. One of its own reporters, Nathaniel Nash, died in the crash.

Towards the end of my research, I had a long talk with forensic economist Steven Dresch. He asked a question I had asked myself, "Presuming a gunshot, why shoot Brown in the top of the head? Would that not be too obvious?"[17]

It would be far less obvious, I responded, than shooting him in the face or mouth, especially since the presumptive shot entered through an existing laceration. The scalp had been ripped up and off at that spot. Given its nearly perfect circularity, the hole was almost assuredly punched out after the laceration. Were Janoski not so vigilant it is quite likely the hole would have been missed altogether.

Without an autopsy, all talk of a bullet hole remains speculative, and the parties involved acknowledge as much. The forensic and behavioral evidence is so strong, however, that any serious discussion of Brown's death has to take that hole into account.

THE NIKO JERKUIC SUICIDE

If the suicide of a White House counselor in a public park still defies easy explanation, the suicide of anyone in war-ravaged Croatia is exponentially harder to prove or disprove—let alone the maintenance chief responsible for the Cilipi Airport's navigation system. Some considerations:

- Jerkuic had reportedly not been at work on Wednesday, the day the plane crashed.[18]
- His duties, according to the AP, "included keeping the navigation system working properly."
- Jerkuic reportedly shot himself in the chest an hour after the bodies of Brown and the other Americans had been flown out of the airport on the Saturday following the crash.
- He died, again according to the AP, "before the U.S. team got a chance to question him" about the navigation aids.
- Those aids were later found to be in perfect working order.
- The Air Force report revealed a Non-Directional Radio beacon had been "stolen" during the 1992-1995 conflict. Although it was replaced, the original was never recovered.
- The Croatian interior minister was quick to deny Jerkuic's suicide had "any connections with the tragic crash of the U.S. aircraft," although it would have made perfect sense if it had.[19]
- The *New York Times* reported a "failed romance" had left the forty-six-year-old bachelor despondent.[20]
- Heading up the investigation into Jerkuic's death was Miroslav Tudjman, Croatian intelligence chief and son of Croatia's neo-fascist strongman president, Franjo Tudjman.[21]

Even Dresch, who had Russian associates working for him on the ground in Croatia, made no real headway in this instance. As it happens, however, the Jerkuic investigation shared one critical understanding with the inquiries into the plane crash and into the hole in Brown's head: from beginning to end, all three were conducted as if foul play were not even a possibility.

As mentioned, the Air Force bypassed the Safety Investigation Board phase and moved directly to an Accident Investigation Board. This was only the second time the Air Force had ever done so and the first time on friendly soil.[22] Even more troubling, the decision was made on April 4, just hours after American investigators had arrived on site and long before anyone could have ruled out hostile fire or sabotage with any certainty.

In fairness, the Safety Board invites its own kind of corruption, especially since its contents are "privileged." Nevertheless, confidentiality tends to produce better results. The Accident Board, by contrast, is open to public review. "Its ostensive purpose is to establish legal responsibility," writes Al Diehl, "but its real objective is public relations." According to Diehl, the reports generated by the Accident Board "at best . . . simply describe what may have happened and whom the investigators think should be punished."[23] The Accident Board also begins, of course, with the presumption that the cause of the crash was an accident.

In *Living History*, Hillary Clinton writes breathlessly about her own flight into Tuzla in Bosnia just nine days before Ron Brown's. In this case, her excitement was understandable. She and Chelsea had to wear flak jackets and sit in a reinforced cockpit in case of snipers or ground-to-air missiles. The pilot also undertook a variety of evasive maneuvers to minimize risk. Contrary to rumor, these pilots were not Davis and Shafer. Davis had, however, flown the Clinton women on a different leg of the same trip.[24]

Less than six months after the Dayton Accords, in the wildly unstable Balkan countryside, pilots feared accidents far less than they did intentional shoot-downs. Without prompting, several search and rescue personnel expressed their anxieties to the Air Force investigators.

Helicopter pilot Steve Kelly, for instance, told of a warning by the NATO command center not to venture too far south of the Cilipi airport lest he run afoul of an active SA-6 surface-to-air missile site.[25] Cilipi, after all, is just a few miles from the Bosnian border. Air Force investigators, however, were not about to pursue this line of inquiry. Although they started interviews within days of the crash, long before they could have known its cause, they asked no questions about missile batteries or other belligerent activity in the area.

An accident is all that was ever considered for the hole in Brown's head.

The AFIP went to some lengths to find an accidental explanation for the hole both at the site of the crash in Croatia and reportedly on a veritable clone plane at the Ramstein Air Force base in Germany. The AFIP brass, however, did not take the simplest steps at Dover that might have proved otherwise. There was no search for an exit wound, no forensic test for residue, and no interest at all in an autopsy.

In Croatia, authorities immediately ruled Jerkuic's death a suicide. If they looked any deeper, they certainly have not shared the results with the world. The Air Force expressed a conspicuous lack of interest as well. In none of the interviews with his airport co-workers did investigators ask a single question about Jerkuic, his life or his death.

Seven centuries back, philosophers like Occam employed a logical concept known as "inference to the best explanation." To explain a phenomenon, they would choose from a pool of likely options the one option that best fit the observed data. In the case of the plane crash, the bullet hole, and Jerkuic's death, investigators consciously removed "murder" or "terror" from the pool *a priori*. The fact that Brown had reason to fear for his life should have strengthened the murder option but, if anything, it had the opposite effect.

One errs greatly to think the Air Force and the AFIP personnel were active participants in a grand conspiracy to coverup the murder of Ron Brown. Conspiracies do not work like that. If I could venture my own "razor" it would be this:

> Most seeming participants in a cover-up are either largely ignorant of any criminal intent or willfully blind to that intent. If they are covering up anything, it is their own failure to stop or solve the activity in question.

Participants, however, do respond to what Janoski calls a "mindset." They instinctively sense whether the controlling authority wants the truth or something less. If the Clintons had really wanted the truth, they could have established as much with a phone call. They did not.

What follows are four possible explanations for what did happen on the afternoon of April 3, 1996, in the skies above Dubrovnik.

NO. 1: THE ACCIDENT SCENARIO

There is not sufficient evidence to rule out an accident. As to the plane crash itself, credible people have proposed scenarios in which pilot error and faulty instrumentation might have caused it.

Less credible are the pathologists who ignored the hole in Brown's head and ruled that he died of blunt force injuries. Nevertheless, their dissembling does not necessarily make their analysis wrong. A still unknown object could have punctured Brown's head and no one else's and left a nearly perfectly circular bullet-sized hole. And even if a bullet did create the hole, the shooting could have been the work of an early scavenger on the scene.

Maintenance supervisor Niko Jerkuic might well have shot himself in the chest because of a failed romance just three days after the most calamitous accident in the history of Croatia took place at the airport he supervised. With the Tudjmans controlling the investigation, one cannot even begin to prove otherwise. There has been no discussion in any official American report or media outlet of the relevant forensic evidence.

And finally, the desperate anxiety in which Brown passed the last few weeks of his life might have had no bearing at all on his untimely death. If so, one could fault the White House for exploiting Brown's corrupt dependency, for exposing him to people who were capable of killing, for dispatching him all too frequently on hasty and dangerous missions, and even for capitalizing on his death, but not for conspiring to kill him.

NO. 2: THE HIJACK SCENARIO

Brown's fatal flight departed from Bosnia, a Muslim country still simmering from a brutal civil war. The media tended to portray Bosnia as weak and peace-loving, but they, like the Clinton administration, chose not to look as thousands of Islamic *mujahideen*—holy warriors—streamed into Bosnia from throughout the Islamic world in the early 1990s.[26]

CIA Director George Tenet would admit as much to the Senate Armed Services Committee. "U.S. and other international forces are most at risk in Bosnia," said Tenet, "where Islamic extremists from outside the region played an important role in the ethnic conflicts of the 1990s."[27]

The Islamic world was sending more than men. Starting in 1993, Croat and Bosnian Muslims began to receive planeloads of Chinese-made artillery and anti-tank rockets. They did so in violation of a NATO embargo enforced by the Europeans and Russia. The arms arrived in Bosnia on Iranian C-130 cargo planes. At the time, the White House knew of the shipments and did nothing to stop them. In 1997 this embarrassing revelation would prevent Clinton national security advisor, Tony Lake, from being confirmed by the Senate as director of Central Intelligence.[28]

Iran contributed to the cause in still more valuable ways. In 1996, for instance, NATO forces discovered in Bosnia a base for Vavak, the Iranian Ministry of Intelligence and Security. Ali Fallahan, the head of Vavak, had been there as well. At the time, Fallahan presided over the planning committee that approved Iranian sponsored terrorist attacks abroad.

The information retrieved at the Vavak base revealed a good deal about Fallahan's activities. Apparently, he had earlier traveled to Germany and set up the assassination of Kurd rebel leaders exiled in Berlin. He also organized a huge purchase of advanced encryption and communications equipment that he shipped to Iran in 1994 and 1995. NATO forces recovered some of this equipment in the Bosnian Vavak raid. In April 1996, Fallahan was still at large. A year later he would be found guilty in the assassination of the Kurdish leaders, but only in absentia.[29]

This is not to suggest Vavak was involved in the death of Ron Brown but rather that there were people on the ground quite capable of executing the fully speculative scenario that follows.

⌇

Shortly before the plane is to depart, an unknown man approaches Ron Brown and asks to come along. To assure his passage, he says the magic four words that can open the door of even the Oval Office: "James Riady sent me."

Brown would not turn him down. Nolanda Hill acknowledges he often took passengers with him on these trips who were not on the manifest. This may have been one such trip. The Department of Defense briefing lent credence to this possibility:

> Another issue the board examined was passenger-manifesting procedures. Aircrews are directed to prepare a passenger manifest prior to each take-off to account for passengers onboard. These manifests are then maintained by the European Operations Center. No passenger manifest was found after this accident. A passenger list had to be reconstructed by the U.S. Embassy in Zagreb.[30]

For the first fifty-five minutes of the flight, the man sits quietly and perhaps talks to Brown. A *mujahideen*, still nursing a deep grudge against the Great Satan, he is prepared to sacrifice his own life to accomplish his mission. Fallahan is prepared to sacrifice the man as well, partly to embarrass America but largely to ingratiate himself to the Chinese arms dealers.

A moment after the pilots make their last communication to the control tower, the man calmly stands up, shoots a dozing Brown in the top of the head, and walks swiftly past the astonished passengers to the cockpit where he wrestles the plane away from the pilots and steers it into the mountainside.

⁓

"Something had to have happened in that cockpit," a veteran flight instructor told me. "With a day's training even a novice pilot would know enough not to fly into a mountain."[31] As it happens, unholstered weapons were recovered amidst the crash debris.[32]

From Occam's perspective, the hijack scenario addresses the first three of the necessary conditions and falls short only on the fourth one, the Jerkuic suicide. The suicide, however, could be explained by Jerkuic's despondency over the plane crash at his airport. This scenario also absolves the Croatians of any involvement. It might have involved no wider conspiracy than a China-friendly Indonesian financier, aware of Brown's willingness to blow the whistle, and an opportunistic Iranian intelligence chief.

The scenario, however, does add at least one new variable that needs to be addressed, the absence of a thirty-sixth body. True, there were two Croatians on board, but Dresch had them checked out, and neither seemed a likely assassin. One, in fact, was a woman. It would not have been hard to "lose" a body at the scene, but that would have involved the active participation of the Croatian authorities or the American military.

Finally, what undermines this scenario is the absence of any sense of anxiety or desperation on the part of the pilots right up until the end. In fact, the last seven miles of the flight were smooth, straight, and consistent. The pilots might have been flying under duress, but here we are adding variables and confounding Occam.

NO. 3: THE MISSILE SCENARIO

In her flight to Bosnia a week or so earlier, Hillary Clinton worried openly about ground to air missiles and with good reason. During their war against the Soviets in the 1980s, the *muhajideen* who streamed into Afghanistan became quite adept with U.S.-supplied Stinger missiles. They used them to destroy Soviet jets and attack helicopters and in so doing turned the tide of war. More recently, Islamic terrorists have used shoulder-fired missiles in attempting to bring down U.S. military aircraft in Saudi Arabia and an Israeli airliner in Kenya.

Commercial aircraft are most vulnerable when landing and taking off. The shooter simply aims at a plane's heat sources, namely its engines, "locks on" the target for about six seconds, and fires. A pilot would rarely have the chance to see a missile coming and could generally react only after the missile hit an engine or exploded nearby.

In Croatia in 1996, any group seeking to upset the delicate Dayton Accords would have advanced its cause greatly by shooting down Ron Brown's plane. Remember, World War I began with an assassination in Bosnia.

The White House would have all the reason in the world to cover up the real cause. A terrorist shoot-down of Ron Brown's plane had Greg Norman potential. It would have shattered any illusion of diplomatic success in that area and demanded some kind of military response. Three months later, after the destruction of TWA 800 off the coast of Long Island, the White House would again move to eliminate all talk of missiles even when missiles seemed the likeliest explanation.[33]

As rational as the missile scenario sounds, however, it accommodates none of the four necessary variables—the pilot's smoothly deviant course, the hole in Brown's head, Jerkuic's suicide, or Brown's pre-existing fears.

NO. 4: THE ROGUE BEACON SCENARIO

Safety authority Al Diehl firmly believes Ron Brown's plane crashed due largely to pilot error, the result of faulty training and inadequate equipment. "To me it has all the earmarks of a classic accident," Diehl told me, "but . . ."

"But what?" I asked.

"But if I were looking for another explanation," he said, there is always the possibility of *meaconing*. Although the word has passed from common usage, meaconing has an interesting history. Apparently, during the early days of World War II, German bombers flying over England pioneered the use of radio signals to guide their bombing runs even in bad weather.

The British were quick to respond. They came up with two options. One was to jam the beams, so enemy aircraft could not receive the signals. The second was to mask the enemy's transmitting beacons by picking up and repeating German signals. The enemy aircraft would not be able to distinguish between the signal from its home beacon and the one from the interfering station in the U.K. and would drop their bombs in some harmless place of British choosing. The British gave this practice the unlovely name of "meaconing" from "masking beacon."[34]

According to Diehl, the Soviets used this trick often. In my subsequent conversations with pilots who flew in Vietnam, I learned that our enemies there did as well. Even today, various pilot guides warn of the practice.

Early in my research on Brown's life and death, I came across suggestions that this is the trick that deceived the pilots. The sources, however, were always a bit unsteady and their data unreliable. It was not until I began to speak to veteran airline pilots and flight instructors who followed the case and who too believed that meaconing might have caused the crash that I began to take the possibility seriously. Consider the following scenario, again speculative:

છ

Niko Jerkuic does not report in for work on the morning of April 3, but he has a busy day ahead of him. He is not looking forward to it. Just two days earlier, April 1, two large gentlemen from the Croatian intelligence services gave him an assignment he did not feel free to turn down. For reasons of national security, the agents needed to down a certain plane, and they required his assistance. Electronics experts themselves, they would help as needed. To ease his resistance, they also offered Jerkuic a substantial sum of money if he were successful.

The project is not technically difficult. Jerkuic has seen a lot in his forty-six years. He knows all about meaconing or "spoofing" as it is sometimes generically known. Since the 1940s, portable Non-Directional Radio beacon (NDB) stations have been available to military and civilian operators and have proved especially useful in war torn areas like this one.

· The agents with whom he is working have brought along a gasoline driven generator, a tunable transmitter, and a temporary antenna, all loaded into the back of a pickup truck. Together, they drive to an isolated spot just outside of Dubrovnik and only about three or four miles east-southeast of Kolocep Island, the site of the first beacon, the final approach fix.

Jerkuic has all the time he needs on April 3 to set it up. As much as he dreads the assignment, he has to admire the new Motorola radiophone the agents have given him to coordinate communications. Jerkuic sets the frequency of his portable beacon at 318 kilohertz to match that of the Kolocep beacon, the final approach fix, and encodes the KLP Morse code identifier. He cannot power it up, however, until all the earlier scheduled flights have landed.

Meanwhile, the doomed flight is cleared "direct to the KLP NDB." The pilots are told they are "number one for beacon approach" and assume they will get an approach clearance prior to KLP and will not have to enter "holding."

When the word comes from the Dubrovnik tower that Brown's plane has checked in at 2:46 PM local time and the other planes have landed, Jerkuic shuts down the normal NDB and activates the "rogue" NDB. The automatic direction finder in the plane now points to Jerkuic's beacon near Dubrovnik.

At this distance, the needle shift is negligible. Davis and Shafer scarcely notice. "Hmm," Davis thinks to himself when he sees it, "the NDB's a little further east than I thought." But given its 318-kilohertz frequency, Davis naturally assumes the radio signal to be coming from Kolocep and flies towards it. Remember, the Dubrovnik tower has no radar. At this stage, the radio signal is the pilots' only real guide to the world below the clouds.

As the signal strengthens, Davis gradually aligns the "bird dog" needle with the posted 119-degree setting. At 2:54 PM, he watches as his automatic direction finder swings back around to the bottom, now at a 299-degree reading. He has passed over the beacon and will navigate from the tail of the ADF needle.

"We're inside the locator, inbound," he radios the tower, and the tower clears his approach and landing. At that moment, the charts tell the pilots the airport is twelve miles straight ahead on a 119-degree course. They will be able to see the runway in about three minutes. In fact, however, the plane is now heading right towards St. John's Peak about eight miles away.

Word of the crash comes over Jerkuic's radio. He shuts down the temporary transmitter and reactivates the Kolocep beacon. Still, the whole process sickens him. He has no stomach for this. The agents assigned to him sense his unease, but they have work to do, like finding the plane and making sure the person they were assigned to kill is dead. They make their way to St. John's Peak and up the mountain, their passage concealed by the low hanging clouds. They smile when they see the plane. Damned if they didn't pull this job off. Better still, the bodies are scattered, and there are only a few black men among them. They pull out the photo of Brown and start checking.

Brown is not hard to find. But what stuns the men is that he is farther from the plane than is anyone else. He appears to have crawled there.

"Oh, Christ," says the leader. He kneels down next to Brown and turns him over on his back. He is still not sure whether Brown is dead or not. He pulls out his pistol and fires skillfully into the wound on the top of his head. In this part of the world, no one even blinks at the sound of gunfire.

The men look around quickly for other survivors and seeing none hustle back down the hill. Their colleague back at the airport is going to try to misdirect the search as long as he can. But the men on the hill do not want to hang around any longer than necessary. They exit the area with their beacon, drive to a bluff overlooking the Adriatic, and deep six it.

Three days after the crash, Lauri Fitz-Pegado, Morris Reid, and Ira Sockowitz among others attend a memorial service at Cilipi for those who died in the crash. They then board the plane with the thirty-three American dead and take the long grim flight back to Dover.

Just hours later, Niko Jerkuic answers the knock on his door and greets the two men who recruited him. He is still anxious, and they can see it. The Air Force investigators have arrived and will start interviewing airport personnel in two days. The Croatian agents cannot afford to let the Air Force talk to Jerkuic.

"We hate to do this," says the one agent as he casually shoots Jerkuic in the chest. They don't even try too hard to arrange a suicide scenario. They know who will be investigating.

⤳

This preceding scenario is the only of the four that satisfies all four of the necessary conditions, and it does so with chilling neatness. What is more, the tracking data provided by the Air Force would seem to support the scenario.

Air Force personnel reconstructed this data after the fact from Zagreb radar and the radar from two NATO E-3 Airborne Early Warning (AEW) aircraft, one American and one British. Only the two E-3's, which monitor the skies primarily for defense purposes, tracked the final approach. The Air Force freely acknowledges a certain imprecision. The reconstruction appears, however, to be an honest one.

One airline pilot with whom I consulted, retired TWA international captain Raymond Gentile, accepted my challenge to review the data, but he offered to go public with his findings only on the condition that he have access to the full twenty-two-volume Air Force report. This I secured through the Freedom of Information Act, and he and I both reviewed it in depth, as did at least one other airline pilot, who has chosen to remain anonymous but who confirmed Gentile's findings.

As the Air Force report notes, coordinates for the real Kolocep Island beacon are 42.40.2 north and 18.01.6 east. At 2.53.58, the crew reported, "We're inside the locator, inbound." The swing in the ADF needle as they passed over the beacon would have told them this. At that moment, the data generated by the Air Force's E-3 AEW aircraft show Brown's plane to be at 42.39 North and 18.08 East, a mile south of the real beacon on Kolocep Island, but some seven miles east, inland.

The Air Force report also contains a readout from the British E-3. This analysis shows that at 2:53:56, just two seconds before the pilots called in their crossing of the beacon, Brown's plane was at 42.38.24 north latitude and 18.06.46 east longitude, roughly five miles east and a mile and a half south of Kolocep. In other words, the data from both E-3s show Brown's plane to be dramatically east of the normal KLP beacon at the time its pilots reported crossing that beacon. These coordinates can only be found in the body of the report, not in the ninety-four-page summary, but they cry out for explanation. The unlikely possibility that the pilots delayed their call in to the tower does not explain the startling eastward skew of these coordinates.

The final data derive from those few seconds before the crash when the two E-3s last registered the transponder code of Brown's plane. Based on the actual crash site coordinates, the British E-3 tracking information was highly accurate, certainly at the end, and the Air Force's was somewhat less so. Extrapolating backwards from the crash site and correcting for discrepancies, Gentile was able to fix the site of the reported beacon crossing of both E-3s within one mile of each other.

"If the flight reported passing KLP shortly after actual passage," says Gentile, "the only conclusion a reasonable person can make is that they reported passing a rogue NDB which was in fact transmitting in an area east of the normal NDB."[35] It astonished Gentile that the Air Force report narrative made no note of this discrepancy.

This much said, as Gentile points out, there were still real problems with the approach. When the pilots crossed the KLP beacon, they had not been cleared for the approach. This clearance should have been received when the plane was outside the beacon. If approach clearance were not received, the crew should have entered a holding pattern at the beacon.

Once inside the beacon, the pilots had to descend to minimums of 2,150 feet from 4,000, reconfigure the airplane for landing and decrease their speed from more than 200 knots to 130 knots. Assuming the rogue beacon hypothesis, the only way this could have been done, while descending, was with idle power, full flaps, and gear extended. Given the difficulty of this assignment, the pilots should probably have called it quits and executed a "missed approach" to the right over the Adriatic. But they had a VIP on board, presumably on important affairs of state, and they likely felt pressured to complete their mission.

In spite of the imperfect approach leading up to KLP, once they crossed the beacon, the pilots did what Gentile calls "an admirable job of decreasing altitude and airspeed," the proof of which is they were at minimums and on speed at the time of impact.

Maintaining the inbound course would have been greatly simplified because of the wind direction. As the flight was cleared to land, the tower reported wind on the ground at 120 degrees at 17 knots. Fifty-five seconds later, the tower gave another aircraft the ground wind as 120 degrees at 12 knots. In both cases, the wind direction was right down the runway.

Chief Croatian pilot Amir Sehic confirmed a 14-knot headwind.[36] Pilot Mario Sarinic, who also arrived at Cilipi in the hour before Brown's plane, told the Air Force the drift angle was "almost nothing" because the wind was "pretty much in line with the runway." According to Sarinic, the wind did not change in the hour following his landing.[37]

The report does state that the wind at the aircraft's approach altitude was 160 degrees at 25 knots, but the Air Force determined this wind value after the fact and with data pulled from upper air soundings at Brindisi,

Italy, 117 miles away. "If valid," notes Gentile, "these winds would have affected the flight during the early segment of the approach, but their effect would become negligible in the latter stages of the approach."

One more critical bit of evidence needs to be considered. As the USAF report observes, "Ground and aerial compass readings indicated that the airplane's initial ground impact marks were oriented along a magnetic heading of approximately 120 degrees." One hundred and twenty degrees is roughly the course the plane was supposed to be flying from the fixed KLP beacon on Kolocep Island, the one that would have sent the plane right down runway 12.

The Air Force report ignores these findings. According to the report, the pilots "selected a heading which placed the aircraft on an incorrect course, nine [degrees] left of the published course." As a result, the aircraft "tracked outbound on approximately a 110-degree bearing from KLP to the impact location." But there is no evidence at all that the pilots "selected" the wrong heading and flew straight from Kolocep Island to St. John's Peak on a 110-degree course as the report implies. Given the clarity of the pilots' charts, the high level of their experience, and the admittedly good working order of all instruments and navigation aids, such a scenario would seem well nigh impossible.

The data from the two E-3 AEW aircraft, when combined with the ground impact marks, argue for another scenario altogether. They show Brown's plane tracking not from Kolocep Island but from a site near Dubrovnik, roughly three to five miles southeast of Kolocep Island and a mile or so off the charted course. From there, the pilots flew a nicely con-trolled flight roughly parallel to the 119-degree course dictated by their flight plans, but, tragically, more than a mile or two inland from that course. For Gentile, these combined observations "unequivocally" indicate "the aircraft was in fact tracking 120 degrees from the rogue NDB."

The final alleged pilot error, and the least well explained, was the failure to identify the missed approach point. At the press conference announcing the Air Force's findings, the head of the Accident Board, Maj. Gen. Charles Coolidge, observed, "Had the missed approach procedure been executed in a timely manner, the accident would not have occurred."[38] The reporters alertly zeroed in on what seemed like a gratuitous assignment of blame. One asked, "What would [the pilots] have seen to alert them that they've missed the approach point?"

Coolidge admitted the aircraft did not have "a buzzer or a light" to alert the pilots. He also observed that with just the one automatic direction finder, the Air Force dictates the pilots "not detune a station that is providing the course guidance on final approach." In other words, the pilots have to stay tuned to the first beacon they crossed, the final approach fix, the one presumed to be on Kolocep Island.

The General then added that the pilots' automatic direction finder was, in fact, "found tuned to the final approach fix." The reporter then asked, "So, they followed the procedure?" Coolidge hemmed and hawed out a "yes" and then succeeded in losing his audience in a sea of double talk.

What the generals did not say was this: with only one automatic direction finder, the pilots had no way at all of tuning into a second radio beacon that served as the missed approach point. Besides, if they were following a rogue beacon, they would have thought that they were perfectly on course and still short of the airport and thus not even worrying about a missed approach.

The Air Force report would fault the pilots for having "failed to determine the approach could not be flown with only one ADF receiver." This is simply not true. The approach can be flown with one ADF receiver, not legally perhaps, but usually without much difficulty. The second receiver adds an element of insurance. In this case, however, that insurance would have been critical.

"The fact that IF0 21 was not equipped with a second ADF is the primary cause of the accident," says Gentile. "If they had the second ADF, the fact that they were navigating on a rogue KLP would be immediately evident to the pilots." As Gentile observes, "The criminals who set the stage had to have extensive knowledge of aviation and aircraft navigation. They had to know the aircraft had only one ADF."

Beyond the issue of pilot error, the portable beacon theory also makes sense of several other loose ends:

- The change of flight plans to Dubrovnik
- The timing of that change
- The misdirected search
- The "non-functioning" crash position indicator
- The "disappearance" of IFD 98
- The foreign locale

THE CHANGE OF FLIGHT PLANS

Tracey Brown offers the most detailed account as to why Brown went to Dubrovnik. In her retelling, Croatia Prime Minister Zlatko Matesa changed "the meeting between Dad and President Tudjman" from Zagreb to Dubrovnik primarily "to publicize the city's ability to attract tourists."[39]

The real problem in this account is not the reason for the switch, dubious as it sounds, but the presence—or absence—of Tudjman. Where was he? In no reporting of the hours before and after the crash is there any mention of him. He certainly was not at the airport to greet Brown. Nor is he mentioned at all in the Air Force report. One can argue that at seventy-four and ailing Tudjman would not have involved himself in the search and rescue. But at seventy-four and ailing would he really have volunteered to fly to Dubrovnik just to help it "attract tourists"?

The best evidence that he never left Zagreb is a press release from the Croatian government dated April 3. "Croatian President Franjo Tudjman on Wednesday evening formed a government commission to investigate the circumstances of a U.S. Air Force plane near Dubrovnik," reads the release. A notation found on the Commerce Department logs from the morning of April 4 strongly suggests that Tudjman was in Zagreb when he formed that commission:

> Chief of Protocol Misetic called. President Tudjman will chair a GOC commemoration ceremony this evening at 2030. He would like Ambassador Galbraith to join. Expects Prime Minister Matesa to fly back this afternoon. Ambassador could accompany.[40]

THE TIMING OF THE CHANGE

According to the Air Force report, "The pilot of the flight was known for very thorough mission planning and briefing." And yet when the crew planned the mission on April 1, that plan did not list a stop in Dubrovnik.

The Dubrovnik stop was not added until 7:45 PM on the night of April 1. Commerce Department officials Claudia Rayford-Williams and Thomas DeSeve would separately tell Air Force investigators the Croatian government "insisted" a Dubrovnik stop be added.[41]

Given the security planning involved, a change of this nature was by no means normal. CT-43A pilot, Capt. Deanna Ketterer, who had flown Hillary and Chelsea on their visit, made this clear. According to Ketterer, these flight plans are "never, never changed. I never saw a change given once we left Ramstein [Germany]."[42]

The portable beacon scenario would only work, however, if the skies were overcast and if the conspirators could be confident of the same. DeSeve, a special agent working security for Commerce, observed that the weather turned sour on March 31, continued growing cloudier and rainier, and "was not expected to improve."[43] It surely did not. The weather in the twenty-four hours after the crash was worse still. The Dubrovnik detour was added in full knowledge that the gloomy skies would hold through April 3 and, if anything, undermine the city's tourist potential.

THE MISDIRECTED SEARCH

Virtually all searching by helicopter, French and American, was done over the sea or over the Dubrovnik area. Air Force investigators tried to pin down the source of this misdirection but without success. Their final report traces the problem to the Zagreb NATO air traffic control center but holds no one accountable.

British major, Rocky Swearengin, who was chief of the NATO cell at Zagreb, was less diplomatic. According to Swearengin, the Croatians provided him the wrong coordinates for the crash site and were "adamant" that NATO helicopters had verified the same. When he tried to call the Dubrovnik tower, Croatian officials would not talk to him. "The night of the accident," said Swearengin, "when we really needed [Croatian] assistance, they were very uncooperative; nothing could get done."[44]

This, of course, could all be written off to bureaucratic confusion. But when Air Force investigators talked to Swearengin in Croatia ten days after the crash, he took them aside and implied something "was not quite the way it should be." He claimed the Croats were serving up "ringers" to the investigators, "people who weren't directly involved."[45] None of Swearengin's concerns—and he was not alone in these charges—surface in the official Air Force summary.

THE CRASH POSITION INDICATOR

On a related issue, Croatian authorities were telling the *New York Times* in the weeks after the crash that the plane's crash position indicator (CPI, also known as an emergency locator transmitter), a device that emits a signal from a downed plane, "did not work." The *Times* reporter contended that if it were working, "The crash site should have been located immediately."[46] Although the *Times* overstates the ease of finding the site, the Croatians misled the *Times* about the indicator. As the Air Force report makes clear, it was indeed working when recovered.

On this question, some of the higher-ranking Croatian authorities proved elusive at best. In the hours after the crash, Jure Kapetanovic, the assistant minister for Civil Aviation, told airport manager Tanci Peovic the CPI was emitting its signal from somewhere "between Kolocep Island and the old part of Dubrovnik,"[47] the area to which the helicopter pilots had been directed. When questioned, Kapetanovic attributed this bad information to the U.S. and NATO. "I think they lost a couple hours, at least two hours," he chided.[48]

What turned this lost time from inconvenience to tragedy was the death of Shelly Kelly. A coincidence of names compounded the regrets of American helicopter pilot Steve Kelly. From the moment his helicopter arrived, he was getting "good hits" on the CPI, but it kept telling him "to go inland."[49] By this late in the day, however, the weather had grown worse still and thwarted his best efforts.

THE DISAPPEARANCE OF IFD 98

At 2:52 PM the pilots of flight IFD 98 checked in with Dubrovnik Tower and were advised that they were number two for the approach behind Brown's plane. At 2:54, the pilots asked for the latest weather report. The flight was further cleared to 5,000 ft, and at 2:58 the pilots were told to "expect a holding pattern overhead KLP."

At this point the plane disappears from the official record. There is no further mention of it in the USAF report. The reader does not even know whether the plane landed or was diverted elsewhere. At the very least, the pilots of this plane would have been in an excellent position to comment on the weather. More significantly, the NATO E-3 AEW aircraft that tracked

Brown's plane would have tracked this plane as well. The E-3s could have provided radar data on IFD 98's track over the ground as it flew directly to the same radio beacon at the same time that beacon was guiding Brown's plane. The IFD 98 then entered a holding pattern, one whose center point was that same beacon. The interested observer is left to speculate on the location of that beacon at that moment and the fate of IFD 98.

THE FOREIGN LOCALE

Occam might ask, if the goal were to kill Brown, would it not have been much simpler to have Brown commit suicide back in Washington the way Jerkuic allegedly did in Dubrovnik? No, it wouldn't. As fate would have it, the heat generated by Vince Foster's suicide in Fort Marcy Park three years earlier made a Ron Brown suicide unthinkable. This is just as true if Foster really did commit suicide as if he did not.

In sum, from Occam's perspective, the portable beacon scenario works much better than any other, including the accident scenario. It accounts for all essential variables and several important, if non-essential, ones.

There is only one major complication. The portable beacon scenario demands agency. Accidents may not require motive, but murder most surely does.

33 | BANQUO'S GHOST

Avaunt! and quit my sight! let the earth hide thee!
Thy bones are marrowless, thy blood is cold;
Thou hast no speculation in those eyes
Which thou dost glare with!
—William Shakespeare, *Macbeth*

When I first met with Tom Fitton and Larry Klayman at Judicial Watch's offices in Washington, Klayman asked me straight out who I thought had murdered Ron Brown.

The question took me aback. As I was just beginning my inquiry, I answered honestly, "I don't know that Brown was murdered." Klayman just smiled. He did not press the point.

Only later, once I had inquired more deeply into Brown's life, did I understand the challenge implicit in Klayman's question: If I were willing to investigate Brown's death, I must inevitably prepare myself to ask, "Who did it?" It was not enough to shout "conspiracy."

Nolanda Hill has asked herself this question many times. One night, towards the end of my research, she called me to talk about it. The call startled me. This was the first time that she had initiated the contact.[1]

Hill was crying. She had just spent the evening moving materials out of storage and came across any number of reminders of her relationship with Brown. She wanted to talk. And after about thirty hours of previous conversation, few could talk about her relationship to Brown more knowingly than I.

To this point, however, we had not spoken at all about the mechanics of how Brown might have died. When I told her that I had just talked to Stephen Dresch and he had suggested Pakistani involvement, Hill shot back, "Dresch is wrong." Her firmness took me by surprise.

"If not the Pakistanis," said I, "then who?"

"The Chinese," she answered. "I am absolutely convinced."

I began to understand why Hill was so upset. This was the first time that she had confronted her own overwhelming sense of responsibility, "guilt out the wazoo" as she expressed it in her colorfully profane way even in the midst of tears.

"Don't you see," she said, "Ron looked to me when he did not know what was happening, and I absolutely focused him on treason. He went in and told Clinton he was going to blow the whistle on Asia and treason, and I put him up to it—just to get the independent counsel shut down."

As Hill admitted, she had tried to save Brown and herself, and now she had to accept some measure of blame for his death. She should not have been the only one, or even the primary one, to do so. There were others far more culpable. This thought, however, offered no consolation.

In fact, Hill had come a long way since her self-seeking days as a would-be media impresario. There is no understanding that journey without understanding her maturing faith. It preserved her and strengthened her and brought her to the point, finally, where she could face the truth about her life with Brown, a truth that she was willing to share as the cautionary tale it was.

When Hill asked what I thought had happened to Brown, I walked her through Occam's logic. "There are only two credible explanations," I said, "accident or rogue beacon." When I explained the latter, she said unhesitatingly, "That's it."

As we both realized, however, it is one thing to say "Chinese" and "rogue beacon," and another thing altogether to create a credible scenario around those two elements that explains the death of Ron Brown. Hard questions have to be asked. Someone would have had to commission Brown's assassination. Someone else would likely have had to broker it. And a third party would have had to execute it. For so egregious and risky a venture, all parties would have had to have both the means and the motive.

To explore this issue is indeed uncomfortable, especially for Hill. But to stop here, or to pull one's punches lest one be labeled a conspiracy theorist, does the reader an injustice. The evidence that follows is circumstantial and may even be coincidental, but any serious analysis demands its consideration.

THE EXECUTION

The execution end of the presumed crime is the most obvious. If Brown were murdered, the Croatians almost surely did the dirty work. I speak here of a small group of well-wired insiders, not the rank and file who proved so helpful in the search operation. The motives here are not hard to calculate. Croatia had spent the last five years in a bloody civil war that brutalized just about everyone involved. The threat of war crimes trials hovered over the heads of many of its leaders, including President Franjo Tudjman.

Tudjman could not have expected much sympathy in the court of public opinion. Indeed, his trial would have had the whiff of Nuremberg about it. A former communist turned nationalist, if not neo-fascist, Tudjman was also something of an historian. In 1989, the year before he was elected president, he had written a harrowing book that included passages like the following: "A Jew is still a Jew. Even in the camps they retained their bad characteristics: selfishness, perfidy, meanness, slyness and treachery."[2]

Tudjman was as responsible as anyone in the Balkans for the civil wars that broke out in 1991. Having evaded the United Nations arms embargo then in place, he drove the ethnic Serbian populations out of Croatia and attempted to establish a Croatian state within Bosnia. Although he disliked Muslims as much as Jews, he eventually acquiesced to a fragile federation between Croatia and the Bosnian Muslims. They were better armed than he had anticipated.

In 1996, there were three things that Tudjman would have wanted out of any deal. The most obvious was arms. They were more valuable than money, as money could not always buy them. At this point, no one really expected the Dayton Accords to hold.

His freedom concerned him even more. At his age, Tudjman did not want to be dragged up to The Hague and tried as a war criminal. And this is where the Enron Corporation re-enters the picture. If Ron Brown had any pressing economic incentive to visit the Balkans, it was to advance a deal that would have given Enron rights to build a power station in Croatia. One major reason Tudjman entertained the Enron offer was to finesse his way out of a war crimes trial.

According to the *Financial Times* of London, audio tapes made public after Tudjman's death in 1999 revealed that he linked a possible Enron deal to a variety of political demands, chief among them "avoiding his arrest and that of other senior figures by the Hague-based International Criminal Tribunal."[3]

As the understanding played out, Enron would run the power station for twenty years and sell electricity to HEP, the state electricity company, at above-market rates.[4] The terms of this deal would prove scandalous when revealed, but by then Brown was long since dead.

Revelations since Brown's death confirm a disturbing fact: Even if the plane crash were accidental, Brown and thirty-four others died for no higher purpose than to secure a sweetheart deal between a fascist dictator and a notoriously corrupt American company. This was the "very important challenge of his time" that inspired President Clinton to compare Brown to Martin Luther King.

For all of his concern about arms and a potential trial, Tudjman had a third and still more immediate worry in 1996. And that was his health. He had cancer. Somewhere along the way, however, he found a guardian angel. In November 1996, just months after Brown's death and one week after President Clinton's reelection, Tudjman traveled not to The Hague but to Walter Reed Hospital in Washington for cancer treatment.[5]

One has to wonder if the White House pushed the treatment back until November to avoid political fall-out. In any case, this brutal anti-Semite would live three more years in Clinton's good graces and never would be tried. Although it is hard to track arms shipments with any precision, Tudjman's forces had ample arms in 1997 to drive ethnic Serbs out of their remaining enclaves within Croatia. As to the power plant, it was never built. Tudjman may have found other means to secure his personal agenda.

One other historical fact is worth noting. Shortly after World War II, Tudjman's parents were found shot dead in their house. The police said the two had committed suicide. Four decades later, Tudjman was still contending that his parents had been killed by the Communist secret police.[6] In other words, Niko Jerkuic's suicide may have had a precedent in Tudjman's own life.

THE BROKERING

It seems inconceivable that an American in power would have negotiated directly with the Croatians. There had to have been a go-between. Although there is any number of likely suspects, many of whom had visited the White House, identifying the most likely among them remains elusive.

As mentioned earlier, Stephen Dresch implicated Pakistan.[7] He cited, in particular, Asif Ali Zardari, the notoriously corrupt husband of Pakistan Prime Minister Benazir Bhutto. According to Dresch, Zardari and Brown had conspired on a complicated deal involving the purchase of American F-16s, the exposure of which would have doomed the shaky Bhutto presidency.[8] Had the White House alerted Zardari to Brown's threat, he would have had ample reason to silence Brown. Dresch suggested that the Pakistanis were deeply involved in Bosnia and had Chinese arms to offer the Croatians as an inducement.

Of note, Benazir Bhutto would not have ascended to power had it not been for a plane crash that killed her predecessor, Gen. Mohammed Zia ul-Haq. Newspaper accounts describe the crash as "mysterious" and little more.[12] When I asked my Pakistani sources what actually happened to the plane, they could provide no answers. At the time, Pakistani media offered none. Although all the surrounding details of his story checked out, I have no other source on Brown's involvement in the deal other than Dresch.

As to potential Chinese involvement—and remember, the Riadys are ethnic Chinese—Hill and I reviewed the list of likely suspects. When I volunteered the name Wang Jun, the Chinese arms dealer whose visit to the White House even President Clinton deemed "inappropriate," she assented immediately.

About two weeks after Wang Jun's meetings with Brown and the President in February 1996, the White House commissioned Brown's trip. The timing is too uncertain to know whether the trip was arranged to set Brown up, but given its haste and pointlessness, the possibility has to be considered.

Hill also believes that Wang Jun or someone like him could have contracted with the Croatians on his own authority. He would not have needed an American commission. Having consulted extensively abroad, Hill believes that authorities in many of the world's rougher quarters respect wealth more than political power. They would have the highest respect for wealth that could be converted to arms. Here she alluded not just to Asian wealth like Wang Jun's or the Riadys', but to American wealth as well, like that of Bernard Schwartz.

One other name surfaced late in my research, that of Zdenka Gast, a Croatian-born American citizen. U.S. Ambassador to Croatia Peter Galbraith entered her name into the official record. When questioned by the Air Force, Galbraith observed that Gast had arrived at the Cilipi airport on a Swiss Air Charter with the executives from Enron minutes after he did. At the time she was serving as liaison between Enron and the Croatian government.

Intriguingly, Gast had been scheduled to fly with Brown but thought better of it. Said Galbraith, "There were problems in—in—in this—in concluding this deal where they wanted to sign a letter of intent, and so, rather than—than go on the Brown trip, she stayed with the Inron [*sic*] people to do the final negotiations."[9]

"We've been looking for her," volunteered Air Force Capt. John Cairney. The Air Force obviously did not look too hard. Investigators conducted 148 witness interviews, but Gast was not among them. I found her in five minutes of searching. When I reached her contact person, I was told, "Don't be surprised if she gets back to you in just a few minutes." I am still waiting.

Inquiring into Gast's background, I came across a Croatian language magazine named *Gloria*. Although I could not read the text, the photo that graces this article leapt off the page at me. In the center of three smiling women, all linked arm in arm, is Zdenka Gast, an attractive, full-figured redhead. On her left is the then secretary of labor, Alexis Herman. On her right is none other than Hillary Clinton. This was one article that I had to get translated. I did, and here is what I learned.

The story details a wedding reception for Alexis Herman at the White House, hosted by the Clintons.[10] The reception took place a few weeks after Herman's wedding in mid-February 2000. Only forty people were in attendance. Those named included Bill and Hillary Clinton, Al and Tipper Gore, John Podesta, as well as "several governors and senators." One suspects that the Brown family was there as well. Alma Brown had earlier hosted a private wedding reception dinner for Herman.

Among the handful of relatively unknown people is Gast. "I was a visitor to the White House before," Gast tells the reporter, "but this was truly something special."

Nolanda Hill had not heard of Gast but has known Alexis Herman well for twenty-five years. "Unless Gast was doing something big for her," says Hill, "or had done something big, Alexis would not have included her in the White House reception."

Gast claims that she had grown close to Herman after the unfortunate death of "*Ronu Brownu, amerièkom ministru trgovine*," the man who had allegedly introduced her to Herman in the first place. The article notes that Gast had been "in the media spotlight because of her involvement in the controversial contract between HEP and Enron." This exposure obviously did not deter the Clintons from inviting her. If nominally a Republican, Gast boasted that she was an active supporter of Hillary in her Senate run and that "Hillary paid special attention to me."

Although Gast seems too insubstantial to have brokered a deal between the White House and the Croatians, the Air Force investigators would have done well to interview her about Brown's death. At the very least, she might have known why Brown had been dispatched to the Balkans, something Brown himself did not know. Gast might have even known more, enough perhaps to keep her off Brown's plane on its Dubrovnik leg.

Gast continued to work for Enron at least through the summer of 2000. When the deal between a new Croatian government and Enron began to sour in June of that year, Gast used her influence to mobilize the Clinton White House in Enron's behalf. The Croatian journal, *Nacional*, claimed, in fact, that "the political relations between the United States and Croatia, as well as the upcoming visit by President Mesic and Premier Racan to the White House [were] connected to the successful signing of the Enron deal with Croatian Electric (HEP)."[11]

It is unlikely that this deal was a high priority for the Clintons, but its general squalor should help dispel any lingering Democratic pieties about Republican relations with Enron.

THE COMMISSIONING

Hill's comments on Wang Jun recall the fate of the devout English priest Thomas à Becket. As is well known, some eight hundred years ago, he refused the demand of King Henry II to yield the church's power to the crown. When Henry learned of his defiance, he imprudently burst out, "Who will rid me of this turbulent priest?" Four knights in attendance took him at his word and made quick work of Becket.[12]

If not a priest, Ron Brown was surely turbulent. In early 1996, he posed a more immediate threat to the Clintons' precarious kingdom than Becket did to Henry's. Possibly, President Clinton expressed similar exasperation at Brown's defiance and likely desertion, and a Wang Jun or a John Huang or a James Riady or an Asif Ali Zardari or a Bernard Schwartz or some other trusted advisor like a Bruce Lindsey took him much more literally than he ever intended.

If indeed Brown were murdered, I would like to think that something along this line happened, that the commissioning of this crime was somehow inadvertent. The alternatives are much more disturbing. I could not, however, convince myself of this possibility for one reason: No sane

Croatian conspirator, however war-hardened he might be, would execute so potentially disastrous a plan without specific American guarantees. That guarantee had to be a necessary condition.

To infer to the best explanation, if Ron Brown was murdered, some American of power must have commissioned that murder. That power would almost surely have derived from the higher reaches of the White House. The person wielding that power would have to have been calculating, cold-blooded, and authoritative. And the list of potential suspects is short. It inevitably, if uneasily, includes the Clintons.

If Brown were murdered, there had to have been a moral calculus involved. No White House conspirator would have sacrificed Brown merely for the sake of reelection. No, he or she would have done so only to achieve a larger, nobler goal like, say, the continued "human reconstruction" of the American people, a project that did, admittedly, hinge on reelection.

If the death of Ron Brown could be so justified, the death of thirty-five innocent people could not. I do not know of an American in power who would have commissioned the destruction of that Air Force plane. Hillary Clinton's visit to the cockpit of a CT-43A in Bosnia ten days before the crash was surely coincidental. I cannot imagine her inquiring into its capacity to decode radio signals.

Her trip to Bosnia, however, raises questions. This side-trip was shoehorned in as part of a longer sojourn to Greece and Turkey. Daughter Chelsea accompanied her. At the time, Hillary's own stated motive was "to visit our troops and to say 'Thank you.'"[13] The White House even made a point of noting that "no first lady since Eleanor Roosevelt has made a trip into such a hostile military environment."

In *Living History*, however, Hillary offers a more nuanced reason for her visit: "The administration wanted to send a strong signal that the peace accords were to be honored and would be enforced."[14] She raises the question of why she and her husband willingly exposed Chelsea to such danger and answers it by saying that the experience would help her mature. As the father of adolescent daughters, I have a problem with that answer.

If Ron Brown were murdered, Hillary's trip to the Balkans makes sense as the kind of "strong signal" the Croatians would need before executing so harrowing a plan. There would be no need for conversation. That would be done through the broker, but a Croatian conspirator would want some powerful reassurance that the planned hit on Brown was authorized by the

White House. It is possible, in fact, that Hillary was used to this end without her knowledge.

One other variable argues for White House involvement: the rumored assassination attempt on Tommy Boggs that same April 3 in South Africa. This may have been no more than rumor. Boggs refused Hill's request for clarification and did not respond to mine. But what is certain is that the story did indeed surface. The question lingers as to who would craft so detailed a story so quickly after Brown's death and why.

There is one good answer. Not knowing the details of Brown's impending death, the American conspirators contrived a cover story. If there had been an attempted hit on Tommy Boggs, or more likely the appearance of one, the combined action would have seemed like blowback on a Patton Boggs job gone bad. One can envision the headlines: "Assassins Kill Commerce Secretary Brown in Croatia: Ex-Partner Boggs Nearly Killed in Capetown." Quite possibly, the cover story was leaked before the conspirators realized it was unnecessary.

If the Boggs story increases the possibility that the commissioners of the presumed crime did not know the means of execution, what cannot be denied—and has to be faced—is that they did not want to know.

THE VERDICT

It is time now to end the speculative part of this essay and focus on the verifiable.

As in the case of Barbara Wise, the Commerce employee found dead in her office, or Vincent Foster for that matter, no one in power was eager to learn the truth about Ron Brown's death. There would be no safety board investigation, no speculation about a missile attack, no ruminations about a rogue beacon, no questions about Niko Jerkuic, no interview with the crew of IFD 98, no interview with Gast, no autopsy, no valid X-rays, no alerting the Brown family, no inquiry into the Boggs story, and no exploration of any possibility at all other than "accident."

Without question, the U.S. Air Force and the Armed Forces Institute of Pathology consciously narrowed their investigations to avoid exposing inconvenient facts. At the AFIP, the "narrowing" took an arguably criminal turn. In neither case, however, was it the idea of the military to limit the inquiry. Orders almost undoubtedly came from the White House.

Without more information, however, the prudent reader will accuse Bill or Hillary Clinton of nothing more sinister than dreading the unknown. For fear of what they might have found—in this, the most desperate political season of their lives—the Clintons chose not to look.

The Air Force was—and is—more willing to confront the facts. When I initially balked at the price of securing the full Air Force report, in excess of $1,000, the Air Force waived the fee and sent it anyhow. As I said in my thank-you note, "This is the nicest thing my government has ever done for me." The Air Force has, after all, an abiding interest in the truth. An "inexplicable" plane crash needlessly ruined sixteen Air Force careers and ended six worthy Air Force lives.

Joining those six in death were twenty-nine civilians, the most celebrated among them the uniquely vital Ron Brown. For all his imperfections, no one can deny the life force that Brown was and continues to be. Irrepressible even in death, he "dost glare" from his grave as unredeemed as Banquo's Ghost, and until his story is told and the truth revealed, there can be no redemption.

NOTES

Introduction
1. Enron "Press Room," 3 April 1996.
2. Byron York, "Why Ron Brown Won't Go Down," *American Spectator*, April 1996.
3. CNN Interactive, "Ten Bodies Pulled from U.S. Plane Crash," 4 April 1996.
4. White House Press Release, "Remarks By The President About Secretary Of Commerce Ron Brown," The White House Office of the Press Secretary, 3 April 1996. Says Clinton, "[Herman} told me that his favorite Scripture verse was that wonderful verse from Isaiah." Brown's daughter Tracey attributes the suggestion to her mother. Tracey's mistake is likely an honest one. All other comments made by Clinton to Commerce employees come from this source.
5. Tracey Brown, *The Life and Times of Ron Brown: A Memoir by His Daughter* (New York: William Morrow and Company, 1998), p. xv.
6. Reflections on Brown's state of mind, especially in the last weeks and months of his life, unless otherwise noted, derive from a series of interviews undertaken by the author with Brown's closest confidante, Nolanda Hill, who was also co-targeted with Brown by independent counsel, Daniel Pearson. The first of these interviews, an extended one, took place in Fort Worth on 12 March 2003, much of it in the presence of her son, Andrew Hill. The rest were conducted by phone through 9 September 2003 for a total of about thirty hours.
7. Nolanda Hill, 27 January 1998, from testimony at Washington's Federal District Court for a Freedom of Information Act (FOIA). Hill's oral testimony confirmed written testimony she had given to Judicial Watch in an affidavit on 17 January 1998.
8. This quote was first reported by Christopher Ruddy, "Fourth Expert Claims X-ray Evidence Destroyed," *Pittsburgh Tribune-Review*, 13 January 1998. It was confirmed by the author in an extended in-person interview, 21-22 August 2003.

Chapter 1: The Handshake
1. The photo appears in Tracey Brown's book and is dated 1955.
2. The early biographical information comes from four principal sources: Tracey Brown's *The Life and Times of Ron Brown*; Steven A. Holmes, *Ron Brown: An Uncommon Life* (New York: John Wiley & Sons, 2000); Harry Jaffe, "Mr. In-Between," *Washingtonian*, November 1992 (an 8500 word article written with

Brown's cooperation); and the author's interviews with Nolanda Hill. The sources track with some consistency. Inconsistencies and direct quotes will be noted.

3. W.E.B. DuBois, "The Talented Tenth," *The Future of the Race*, reprint eds., Henry Louis Gates Jr. and Cornel West (New York: Vintage Books, 1997), p. 145.

4. DuBois, p. 175.

5. DuBois, p. 164.

6. Brown, p. 55.

7. Author's interview with Nolanda Hill.

8. Author's interview with Nolanda Hill.

9. Shelby Steele, *A Dream Deferred: The Second Betrayal of Freedom in Black America* (New York: Harper Collins, 1998), p. 44 and following.

10. Steele, p. 44.

11. Holmes, p. 47.

12. Holmes, p. 53.

Chapter 2: Ron Beige

1. DuBois, p. 100.

2. Brown, p. 188.

3. Jaffe, *Washingtonian*, November 1992.

4. Hillary D. Rodham, Wellesley College, student commencement speech, May 31, 1969, www.wellesley.edu/PublicAffairs/Commencement/ 1969/053169hillary.html.

5. Rustin's comments can be found at www.britannica.com.

6. Malcolm X, "The Chickens Come Home To Roost," from *The Black Revolution from the End of White World Supremacy: Four Speeches by Malcolm X*, ed. Imam Benjamin Karin, www.bcpl.net/~dbroida/chicken.html.

7. Malcolm X, *The Black Revolution from the End of White World Supremacy: Four Speeches by Malcolm X*.

8. Rodham's speech is cited above.

9. Text of "Bill Clinton's Letter to Eugene Holmes," www.assumption.edu/WebVAX/other/Clinton3Dec69.html.

10. Brown, p. 107.

11. Holmes, p. 56.

12. Holmes, p. 56.

13. Holmes, p. 60.

Chapter 3: Coming Home

1. Steele, *A Dream Deferred*, p. 47.

2. Brown, p. 84.

3. Nolanda Hill, interview with the author.

4. Brown, p. 134.

5. Holmes, p. 87.

Chapter 4: Cashing In

1. Holmes, p. 91.

2. In 1980, the married Jordan was shot in the back in the parking lot of a Fort Wayne motel at 2:00 A.M. in the presence of a blond divorcee.

3. David Corn, "Secret Agenda Man," *Salon.Com*, March 3, 1998.

4. Nolanda Hill, interview with the author.

5. John D. Skrentny, *The Minority Rights Revolution* (Cambridge, Mass: The Belknap Press, 2002), p. 149.

6. Steele, *A Dream Deferred*, p. 62.

7. Skrentny, p. 143.

8. Malcolm X, "God's Judgment of White America," New York City, December 4, 1963, ed. Benjamin Karim, BlackCommentator.com/42/42.

9. Kent Hoover, "SBA Minority-Contracting Effort Favors the Few," *Sacramento Business Journal*, 8 October 2001.

10. Steele, p. 81.

11. Steele, p. 35.

12. John B. Judis, "Sleazy Genius," *New Republic*, 15 May 1995. The firm would soon drop "Blow" from its name as does the text.

13. Nolanda Hill, interview with the author.

14. Jaffe, *Washingtonian*, November 1992.

15. Jaffe, *Washingtonian*, November 1992.

16. Holmes, p. 124.

17. Holmes, p. 126.

18. Brown, p. 158.

Chapter 5: Nolanda

1. Unless otherwise noted, information about Nolanda Hill derives from a series of interviews undertaken by the author beginning on 12 March 2003 through 9 September 2003 for a total of about thirty hours.

2. John B. Judis, "Sleazy Genius," *New Republic*, 15 May 1995.

3. Brown, p. 269.

4. Holmes, p. 130.

5. Holmes, p. 131.

6. Keith Bradsher, "Commerce Inquiry Focuses on a Brash Motivator," *New York Times*, 5 March 1995.

7. Ann E. Weiss, *Tune In, Tune Out: Broadcasting Regulation in the United States* (Boston: Houghton Mifflin Company, 1981), p. 29 and following.

8. The best single source on this subject is an academic essay, Chris Paterson, "The Making of a One Station Town: Television Broadcasting Comes to Austin, Texas," 1993, www.usfca.edu/fac-staff/paterson/mi-ktbc.html.

9. Robert Caro, *Master of the Senate* (New York: Alfred A. Knopf, 2002), p. 226.

10. Holmes, p. 129

Chapter 6: Haiti

1. Nolanda Hill, author interview. Unless specified otherwise, Hill provides the insight into Brown's thinking.

2. "Human Rights" section of the "1992 Democratic Party Platform: A New Covenant with the American People."

3. DeWayne Wickham, *Bill Clinton and Black America* (New York: Ballantine Books, 2002), p. 103.
4. Wickham, p. 103.
5. Robert E. White, "Haiti: Policy Lost, Policy Regained," *Cosmos Journal*, 1996.
6. "United States Dual-Use Exports to Iraq and Their Impact on the Health of the Persian Gulf War Veterans," 25 May 1994, U.S. Senate Committee on Banking, Housing, and Urban Affairs, Washington DC. Faircloth's remarks provide the most reliable source of verified information on Fitz-Pegado.
7. Bruce McColm, "A Communist Beachhead in Baby Doc's Haiti?" *Business Week*, 18 April 1983.
8. Brown, p. 159-160.
9. Brown, p. 160.
10. Holmes, p. 132.
11. Brown, p. 159. Brown specifically refers to this junket as a "trade mission."
12. The information on Brown's inglorious role comes from Nolanda Hill.
13. Holmes, p. 135.
14. Holmes, p. 136.
15. Holmes, p. 136.
16. Brown, p. 78.
17. Peter Boyer, "Ron Brown's Secrets," *New Yorker*, 9 June 1997.
18. Holmes, p. 136.
19. Wickham, p. 104.
20. Wickham, p. 134.

Chapter 7: Jesse
1. Brown, pp. 167-168.
2. Jaffe, *Washingtonian*, November 2002.
3. Holmes, p. 148.
4. Holmes, p. 148.
5. Jaffe, *Wahingtonian*, November 2002.
6. Holmes, p. 149.
7. Jaffe, *Wahingtonian*, November 2002.
8. Jaffe, *Washingtonian*, November 2002.
9. Larry J. Sabato, "Jesse Jackson's 'Hymietown' Remark—1984," "The Washington Post Special Report: Clinton Accused," *Washingtonpost.com*, 1998. Sabato provides a good overview of the whole incident.
10. Sabato, *Washingtonpost.com*, 1998.
11. Robert Shogan, "New Democratic Chief," *Los Angeles Times*, 9 February 1989.
12. Holmes, p. 170.
13. Holmes, p. 165.
14. Shogan, *Los Angeles Times*.
15. Shogan, *Los Angeles Times*.
16. Howard Fineman, "The Go-Between," *Newsweek*, 25 October 1993.
17. Brown, p. 181.
18. Brown, p. 184.

19. Brown, p. 182.
20. The story that follows first appeared in Peter Boyer's *New Yorker* article of 9 June 1997. Hill confirmed it to the author.
21. Boyer, *New Yorker*, 9 June 1997.
22. Holmes, p. 200.
23. Holmes, p. 201.

Chapter 8: Entitled

1. The Engler story was told to the author by Stephen Dresch, a former college administrator turned high level forensic economist, who testifies frequently in court.
2. The information on the evolution of preferences in the FCC comes from the "History of the License Application Process," prepared for the Federal Communications Commission by KPMG LLP Economic Consulting Services, November, 2000, pp. 9 and following.
3. Jerry Knight, "NBC to Forgive Loan to Firm Owned by Brown, Others," *Washington Post*, 25 February 1995.
4. Byron York, "Ron Brown's Booty," *American Spectator*, June 1995.
5. Stephen Labaton, "Commerce Nominee's Lobbying Prompts Scrutiny, *New York Times*, 20 December 1992.
6. Jaffe, *Washingtonian*, November 1992.
7. Nolanda Hill, interview with the author.
8. Kevin Flynn, "City Stink Forces Sludge Firm Out," *Newsday*, 8 November 1991.
9. Kevin Flynn, "High-Rent District: City Pays Double for Its Sludge Site," *Newsday*, 31 March 1992.
10. Flynn, *Newsday*, 8 November 1991.
11. Jaffe, *Washingtonian*, November 1992.
12. Holmes, p. 137.
13. York, *American Spectator*, June 1995.
14. Holmes, p. 137.
15. Knight, *Washington Post*, 25 February 1995.
16. Nolanda Hill, interview with author.
17. Catherine S. Manigold, "Ron Brown Re-emerges in Halls of Power, and Thrives," *New York Times*, 12 April 1994.
18. York, *American Spectator*, June 1995.
19. Shelby Steele, *The Content of Our Character* (New York: Harper Perennial, 1991), p. 103.

Chapter 9: Guanxi

1. Michael Kirk and Peter J. Boyer, "The Fixers," *Frontline*, #1511, Public Broadcasting Service, 14 April 1997.
2. Kirk and Boyer, "The Fixers."
3. Kirk and Boyer, "The Fixers."
4. Cause no. PUD 980000188, Before the Corporation Commission of the State of Oklahoma, prepared by Stephen P. Dresch. Confirmed in an 8 September 2003 interview with the author.

5. Kirk and Boyer, "The Fixers."

6. Maely Tom, "Remembering Ron Brown: Honoring a Consummate Advocate for Asian Pacific Americans," *Asia Week*, 12 April 1996. Among other jobs, Tom served as James Riady's liaison to the DNC.

7. Evelyn Iritani, "Wooing Asian Voters: Growing Ethnic Group Seen As a Key Element in Presidential Race," *Seattle Post-Intelligencer*, 20 April 1992.

8. Iritani, *Seattle Post-Intelligencer*, 20 April 1992.

9. Edward Timperlake and William C. Triplett II, *Year of the Rat* (Washington: Regnery Publishing, 1998), p. 9.

10. For all the interest in doing business with China, the first book-length study of Guanxi was only recently published: Yadong Luo, *Guanxi and Business* (Singapore: World Scientific Publishing Company, 2000).

11. Timperlake and Triplett, p. 10.

12. DNC Document Production E 0000140 (Exhibit 3); House Government Reform and Oversight Committee, also known as the Burton Committee.

13. Chapter 13, Investigation of Illegal Activities in Connection with 1996 Federal Election Campaigns, Final Report, U.S. Senate Committee on Governmental Affairs, Senate Report 105-167, 10 March 1998, also known as the Thompson Committee.

14. Thompson Committee report, Chapter 13.

15. DNC Document Production E 0000627-629 (Exhibit 5). Burton Committee.

16. Alan C. Miller, "DNC Seen as Exploring Foreign Funding in 1991," *Los Angeles Times*, 30 August 1997.

17. DNC Document Production F 0010739 (Exhibit 4), Burton Committee.

18. Kirk and Boyer, "The Fixers."

19. Tom, *Asia Week*, 12 April 1996.

20. Bill Clinton and Al Gore, *Putting People First: How We Can All Change America* (New York: Times Books, 1992), pp. 157-58.

21. Cited on "The China Trade Debate," *Online Newshour*, 18 May 2000.

22. Timperlake and Triplett, p. 10.

23. Richard Cooper, "How DNC Got Caught in a Donor Dilemma," *Los Angeles Times*, 23 December 1996.

24. Evelyn Iritani, *Seattle Post-Intelligencer*, 20 April 1992.

25. Kirk and Boyer, "The Fixers."

26. "Easy Reader," *Hermosawave.net*, 16 November 2000.

27. Kirk and Boyer, "The Fixers."

Chapter 10: Mirror Image

1. Brown, p. 211

2. Bill Clinton, 22 September 1991, posted on the Claremont Institute Web site, www.claremont.org/writings/020708higgins.html.

3. Nolanda Hill, interview with author, as are all Hill references in this chapter.

4. Brown, p. 145.

5. Brown, p. 249.

6. Brown, p. 250.

7. Brown, p. 226.
8. Holmes, p. 183.
9. Holmes, p. 240.
10. Joe Klein, "Joe Klein on Bus Trips and Conventions," *Newsweek*, 14 September 1992.
11. Joel Achenbach, "Clinton and Gore: New Heart-throbs of the Heartland," *Washington Post*, 22 July 1992.
12. Eleanor Clift, quoted from the 25 July 1992 *McLaughlin Group* in "Clinton's Magical Mystery Bus," *Newsweek*, 3 August 1992.
13. Joe Klein, *Newsweek*, 14 September 1992.
14. Howard Kurtz, "When the Media Are on a Role, the Candidate Rides a Wave," *Washington Post*, 25 July 1992. For a good overview of the collective media swoon, please read Tim Graham, *Pattern of Deception* (Alexandria, Virginia: Media Research Center, 1996).
15. Jaffe, *Washingtonian*, November 1992.
16. Brown, p. 236.

Chapter 11: New World Order
1. Edward Timperlake and William C. Triplett II, *Year of the Rat* (Washington: Regnery Publishing, 1998), p. 13.
2. Brown, p. 234.
3. Holmes, p. 242.
4. Holmes, p. 244.
5. Brown, p. 238.
6. Holmes, p. 242.
7. Brown, p. 236.
8. Kevin Phillips, *Wealth and Democracy* (New York: Broadway Books, 2002), p. 52.
9. Herbert Hoover Presidential Library & Museum, Digital Archives, www.ecomm-code.com/hoover.
10. Phillips, p. 311.
11. Phillips, p. 311.
12. Phillips, p. 312.
13. Harry Truman, "Address at Mechanics Hall in Boston," 27 October 1948, accessible through www.trumanlibrary.org.
14. "1992 Democratic Party Platform: A New Covenant with the American People."
15. "1992 Democratic Party Platform: A New Covenant with the American People."
16. Phillips, p. 353.
17. Phillips, p. 383.
18. Phillips, p. 353.
19. Phillips, p. 353.
20. Roper Center poll for the Freedom Forum of 139 Washington bureau chiefs and congressional correspondents, released April 1996.
21. Holmes, p. 250.
22. Holmes, p. 267.
23. Holmes, p. 249.
24. Holmes, p. 249.

NOTES

Chapter 12: Oklahoma
1. Michael Kirk and Peter J. Boyer, "The Fixers," *Frontline*, #1511, Public Broadcasting Service, 14 April 1997.
2. Skrentny, p. 151.
3. There are four principal sources for the story that follows: "The Fixers" as referenced above; Steve Byas, et al., "Natural Gas Price Hearings, Oklahoma Natural Gas Overcharges Tied to Clinton White House," *Oklahoma Constitution*, Spring 2001: Benjamin Wittes, "The Browns' Oklahoma Connection," *Legal Times*, 16 October 1995; Cause no. PUD 980000188, Before the Corporation Commission of the State of Oklahoma, prepared by Stephen P. Dresch. The four sources track consistently and cover much of the same material. Direct quotes and exceptions will be noted.
4. Kirk and Boyer, "The Fixers."
5. Kirk and Boyer, "The Fixers."
6. Kirk and Boyer, "The Fixers."
7. Kirk and Boyer, "The Fixers."
8. Kirk and Boyer, "The Fixers."
9. Kirk and Boyer, "The Fixers."
10. Byas, et al., *Oklahoma Constitution*, Spring 2001.
11. Kirk and Boyer, "The Fixers."
12. Kirk and Boyer, "The Fixers."
13. Byas, et al., *Oklahoma Constitution*, Spring 2001
14. Thomas F. (Mack) McLarty, counselor to the president of the United States, revised July 1994, clinton1.nara.gov/White_House.
15. Nolanda Hill, interview with author. Hill also testified at the hearing before the Oklahoma Commission prepared by Stephen Dresch.
16. Kirk and Boyer, "The Fixers."
17. Kirk and Boyer, "The Fixers."
18. Kirk and Boyer, "The Fixers."
19. Kirk and Boyer, "The Fixers."
20. Testimony of Stephen Dresch, Volume I of II.
21. Testimony of Stephen Dresch, Volume II of II.
22. Nolanda Hill, interview with author.
23. Byas, et al., *Oklahoma Constitution*, Spring 2001.
24. Byas, et al., *Oklahoma Constitution*, Spring 2001.
25. Reported by Byas, et al., in the *Oklahoma Constitution* and confirmed by author. In an interview with Byas on 10 October 2003, he stated that a banker had verified the source of the loan but that he used the word "allegedly" in his article under legal advisement. He also used the phrase "big buddies" to describe the relationship between Alice Walton and Hillary Clinton.
26. Testimony of Stephen Dresch, Volume II of II.

Chapter 13: Vietnam
1. The details of this story were widely and consistently reported. Noted will be all quotes and specific and/or controversial details.

2. Jerry Seper, "Haitian Woman Key in Probe of Brown; She Lives in Posh House He Bought," *Washington Times*, 21 October 1993.

3. Jason DeParle, "Businessman Details Case Involving Commerce Chief," *New York Times*, 4 October 1993.

4. Nolanda Hill, interview with the author.

5. DeParle, *New York Times*, 4 October 1993.

6. Seper, *Washington Times*, 21 October 1993.

7. Marcy Gordon, "Vietnam Veterans Group Demands U.S. Commerce Secretary Resign," *Associated Press*, 1 October 1993.

8. DeParle, *New York Times*, 4 October 1993.

9. The affidavit was reprinted in William P. Hoar, "Ron Brown's Hanoi Kickback," *New American*, 15 November 1993.

10. Brown, p. 246.

11. Gordon, *Associated Press*, 1 October 1993.

12. Holmes, p. 251.

13. Michael Kranish, "US Probe of Brown Near End; Secretary Denies Influence Peddling," *Boston Globe*, 24 October 1993.

14. DeParle, *New York Times*, 4 October 1993.

15. "Commerce Secretary Ron Brown Dodges Media Questions," CNN, *Insider Politics*, 29 September 1993, Transcript #429.

16. CNN, 13 August 1993, as reported in *The Hotline*, 16 August 1993.

17. CNN, 13 August 1993, as reported in *The Hotline*, 16 August 1993.

18. Jerry Seper, "FBI Questions Commerce Secretary in Vietnam Probe," *Washington Times*, 15 October 1993.

19. DeParle, *New York Times*, 4 October 1993.

20. Holmes, p. 251.

21. DeParle, *New York Times*, 4 October 1993.

22. DeParle, *New York Times*, 4 October 1993.

23. Margaret Carlson, "The Company He Keeps," *Time Magazine*, 11 October 1993.

24. Gordon, *Associated Press*, 1 October 1993.

Chapter 14: The Black President

1. Toni Morrison, "Talk of the Town," *New Yorker*, 5 October 1998.

2. DeWayne Wickham, *Bill Clinton and Black America* (New York: Ballantine Books, 2002), p. 49.

3. Wickham, p. 1.

4. Wickham, p. 1.

5. Wickham, p. 40.

6. Wickham, p. 62.

7. Wickham, p. 27.

8. Wickham, p. 71.

9. Wickham, p. 130.

10. Bill Clinton, "On the Fortieth Anniversary of the Desegregation of Central High School," 25 September 1997, as reprinted in Wickham, p. 268.

11. Bill Clinton, "On Affirmative Action," 19 July 1995, as reprinted in Wickham, p. 245.

12. Bill Clinton, "Presidential Radio Address to the Nation," 8 June 1996, www.clinton6.nara.gov.
13. Virginia Kelley, *Leading with My Heart* (New York: Simon & Schuster, 1994), p. 24.
14. Kelley, p. 28.
15. As reprinted in Carl Limbacher, "GOP Warming to 'Racist' Label? Lott Attacked, Byrd Ignored," *NewsMax.com*, 9 December 2002 and elsewhere.
16. Larry Patterson, *More Than Sex: The Secrets of Bill and Hillary Clinton Revealed by Arkansas State Trooper* (Washington: NewsMax.com, 1999).
17. Reprinted in *Italian Info*, www.italianinfo.net/finalmente-page1.html.
18. "Bill Clinton, 1992: Road To The White House," *All Politics*, CNN TIME, 1997. This article refers to the tape as "purported" but does not qualify the apology.
19. Kelley, caption on photo after p. 128.
20. Kelley, p. 110.
21. Kelley, p. 172.
22. David Maraniss, *First In His Class: The Biography of Bill Clinton* (New York: Touchstone, 1996), p. 37.
23. Maraniss, p. 49.
24. Jim Johnson, a retired state Supreme Court justice, in a letter sent to Mr. Clinton on 9 June 1996. *Washington Times*, 10 June 1996, page A10.
25. Jodie T. Allen, "This Is (Not Quite) Your Life," *Slate*, 20 November 1997.
26. Maraniss, p. 55.
27. Maraniss, p. 63.
28. Maraniss, p. 75.
29. Maraniss, p. 81.
30. Bob Woodward, *The Agenda: Inside the Clinton White House* (New York: Simon & Schuster, 1994), pp. 40-41.
31. Wickham, p. 47.
32. Wickham, p. 25.
33. Steele, *A Dream Deferred*, p. 163.
34. Wickham, p. 253.
35. Wickham, p. 163.
36. Wickham, p. 36.
37. Wickham, p. 108.
38. Roger Morris, *Partners in Power: The Clintons and Their America* (New York: Henry Holt and Company), 1996.
39. Wickham, p. 58.
40. Woodward, p. 38.
41. Nolanda Hill, interview with the author.
42. Woodward, pp. 15-16.
43. Jerry Oppenheimer, *State of a Union: Inside the Complex Marriage of Bill and Hillary Clinton* (New York: Harper Collins, 2000), p. 153.
44. Carl Limbacher, "Bodyguard Details Hillary's Jew Bashing into the 1990s," NewsMax.com, 15 July 2000.
45. Carl Limbacher, *Hillary's Scheme: Inside the Next Clinton's Ruthless Agenda to Take the White House* (New York: Crown Forum, 2003), pp. 93-96.

46. Nolanda Hill, interview with the author.

47. On 17 October 1998, H.R. 3616, the Fiscal Year 1999 Defense Authorization Act was signed by the President and became law. Among the measures contained in the law was a provision denying the President the authority to issue a waiver allowing COSCO to lease a terminal at the former Long Beach Naval Station.

Chapter 15: Betrayal

1. Lani Guinier, *Lift Every Voice: Turning a Civil Rights Setback into a New Vision of Social Justice* (New York: Simon & Schuster, 1998), p. 24.

2. Guinier, p. 25.

3. Guinier, p. 31.

4. David Thibodeau and Leon Whiteson, *A Place Called Waco* (New York: Public Affairs (Perseus Books Group), 1999). At the end of this well-reviewed book, survivor Thibodeau lists the names and ethnicity of all eighty victims. He makes no issue of it. He may have presumed that everyone knew.

5. Guinier, pp. 51-52.

6. Guinier, p. 43.

7. Guinier, p. 50.

8. Hillary Clinton, *Living History* (New York: Simon & Schuster, 2003).

9. Guinier, p. 50.

10. Guinier, p. 113.

11. Guinier, p. 120.

12. Guinier, p. 122.

13. Guinier, p. 125.

14. Guinier, p. 126.

15. Guinier, p. 127.

16. Guinier, pp. 136-38.

17. Wickham, p. 148.

18. Susan Garland, "A Dilemma Called Ron Brown," *Business Week*, 11 October 1993.

19. "Commerce Secretary Ron Brown Dodges Media Questions," CNN, *Insider Politics*, 29 September 1993, Transcript # 429.

20. Jerry Knight, "Justice Dept. Set to Clear Ron Brown; Jury Finds Vietnam Allegations Unproven," *Washington Post*, 2 February 1994.

21. Nolanda Hill, interview with author.

22. "Mystery Woman," *Prime Time Live*, ABC News, 18 June 1997.

23. Knight, *Washington Post*, 2 February 1994.

24. Catherine S. Manegold, "Ron Brown Re-emerges in Halls of Power, and Thrives," *New York Times*, 11 April 1994.

25. William McGowan, *Coloring the News: How Crusading for Diversity Has Corrupted American Journalism* (San Francisco: Encounter Books, 2001), p. 41.

26. Guinier, pp. 133-45.

27. Guinier, p. 143.

28. Guinier, p. 135.

29. Guinier, p. 146.

Chapter 16: Most Favored Nation
1. Catherine S. Manegold, "Ron Brown Re-emerges in Halls of Power, and Thrives," *New York Times*, 11 April 1994.
2. Cited on "The China Trade Debate," *Online Newshour*, 18 May 2000.
3. "Judicial Watch's Historic Record of Holding Bill and Hillary Clinton Accountable at Law for Their Crimes," an executive summary produced by Judicial Watch, 2003, p. 2.
4. Timperlake and Triplett, p. 39.
5. Nolanda Hill, interview with author.
6. Timperlake and Triplett, p. 26.
7. Timperlake and Triplett, p. 28.
8. Timperlake and Triplett, p. 13.
9. Bill Clinton and Al Gore, *Putting People First: How We Can All Change America* (New York: Times Books 1992), p. 157.
10. Chapter 13, U.S. Senate Committee on Governmental Affairs, Senate Report 105-167, 10 March 1998, also known as the Thompson Committee.
11. Thompson Committee report, Chapter 13.
12. "Clinton Renews MFN for China," *Voice of America* editorial, 14 June 1993.
13. "President Clinton's Visit to China in Context," *Human Rights Watch*, www.hrw.org/campaigns/china-98.
14. "Clinton Renews MFN for China," *Voice of America* editorial, 14 June 1993.
15. "CSR Issue Brief," Carnegie Endowment for International Peace, 6 December 1996.
16. Patrick Tyler, *A Great Wall, Six Presidents and China: An Investigative History* (New York, A Century Foundation Book, 1999), p. 399.
17. "President Clinton's Visit to China in Context," *Human Rights Watch*, last updated 8 December 1998.
18. Christopher Hitchens, "Done Deal," *London Review of Books*, 5 April 2001.
19. Tyler, p. 407.
20. Tyler, p. 409.
21. Tyler, p. 406.
22. Steven Greenhouse, "Christopher Feels Capitol Hill Heat on China," *New York Times*, 25 May 1994.
23. "President Clinton's Visit to China in Context," *Human Rights Watch*, last updated 8 December 1998.
24. "The US and China: An Uneasy Relationship," *BBC News*, 24 May 1999.
25. Tyler, p. 387.
26. Timperlake and Triplett, pp. 36-37.
27. Thompson Committee report, Chapter 13.
28. Thompson Committee report, Chapter 13.
29. "Mystery Woman," *Prime Time Live, ABC News*, 18 June 1997.
30. Thompson Committee report, Chapter 14.

Chapter 17: Flying High
1. Holmes, p. 258

2. Holmes, p. 258

3. Holmes, p. 238.

4. Holmes, p. 239.

5. "Tamraz: Contributions Bought White House Access," *All Politics, CNN Time,* 18 September 1997.

6. "Tamraz Testifies," *ONLINE NewsHour,* PBS, 18 September 1997.

7. Charles Smith, "Clinton export policy helped India hide the bomb," *WorldNetDaily,* 4 August 1998. The actual documents dated 10 February 1994 and obtained through the Freedom of Information Act can be viewed at www.us.net/softwar/tamraz.html.

8. Robert B. Reich, *The Next American Frontier: A Provocative Program for Economic Renewal* (New York: Penguin Books, 1984), p. 248.

9. Robert B. Reich, *Locked in the Cabinet* (New York: Alfred A. Knopf, 1997), p. 247.

10. Reich, inside flap.

11. Reich, p. 24.

12. Reich, *Locked in the Cabinet,* p. 151.

13. Paul Klebnikov, "What He Wants, Bernie Gets," *Forbes,* 7 October 1996.

14. Juliet Eilperin, "GOP Says U.S. Gave China Nuclear Edge," *Washington Post,* 6 May 1998.

15. Jeff Gerth and John Broder, "The White House Dismissed Warnings on China Satellite Deal," *New York Times,* 1 June 1998.

16. Ken Timmerman, *Selling Out America* (Washington: Xlibris Corporation, 2000), pp. 191-92.

17. George Stephanopoulos, *All Too Human: A Political Education,* (Boston: Little, Brown and Company, 1999), p. 337.

18. Woodward, *The Agenda,* p. 142.

19. Reich, *Locked in the Cabinet,* p. 180.

20. Reich, *Locked in the Cabinet,* p. 171.

21. Available through Charles Smith, Softwar, www.softwar.net/rscotxt.html.

22. Available through "Foreign Trade Missions," Center for Public Integrity.

23. "So You Want to Buy a President," *Frontline,* PBS, available through www.pbs.org/wgbh.

24. Charles Smith, "Toy Story: Bejing Style: Failed U.S. Company Linked to Clinton Administration, Chinese Military," *WorldNetDaily,* 24 May 2000.

25. "Rocky Mountain High-Flier," *The Public,* newsletter of The Center for Public Integrity, June 1995.

26. John Ellis, *Boston Globe,* 30 May 1999.

27. Available through Charles Smith, Softwar, www.softwar.net/rscotxt.html.

Chapter 18: Calamity

1. Nolanda Hill, interview with author.

2. In researching an article on casino gambling in Missouri the author came across the 1995 first person testimony of Nat Helms, a former and reformed spokesperson for "Vote Yes Amendment 6 Committee." His account of how one buys the inner city vote is priceless. It is available through www.casinowatch.org.

3. Stephanopoulos, p. 321.

4. Stephanopoulos, p. 321.

5. Reich, *Locked in the Cabinet*, p. 199.

6. Reich, *Locked in the Cabinet*, p. 200.

7. Robert Woodward, *The Choice: How Clinton Won* (New York: A Touchstone Book, 1997), p. 18.

8. Woodward, *The Choice*, p. 20.

9. Reich, *Locked in the Cabinet*, p. 200.

10. Dick Morris, *Behind the Oval Office: Winning the Presidency in the Nineties* (New York: Random House, 1997), p. 33.

11. Reich, *Locked in the Cabinet*, p. 201.

12. Evan Thomas, et al., *Back from the Dead: How Clinton Survived the Republican Revolution* (New York: Atlantic Monthly Press, 1997), p. 8.

13. Stephanopoulos, p. 436.

14. Bruce Nelan, "Business First, Freedom Second," *Time Magazine*, 21 November 1996.

15. Stephanopoulos, p. 322.

16. Nolanda Hill, interview with the author.

17. Bill Clinton, "Remarks to the International Business Community in Jakarta, Indonesia," 16 November 1994.

18. Nelan, *Time*, 21 November 1996.

19. Charles Smith, "Indonesian Power Deal Blows Financial Fuse," *NewsMax*, 27 January 2001.

20. Charles Smith, "CIA Refuses to Release Documents on Corrupt Deals," *NewsMax*, 17 October 2002. Documents available at www.softwar.net/kkn2001.html#CIA.

21. Charles Smith, "CIA Agents Named in John Huang Files," *WorldNetDaily*, 13 February 2000.

22. Charles Smith, "Indonesian Power and Corruption" *WorldNetDaily*, 15 June 1999.

23. Wolf Blitzer, "Clinton Declares Utah Canyons a National Monument," *CNN.com*, 18 September 1996.

24. Government Reform and Oversight Committee, public archives, FBI Interview summaries for John Huang, Volume II.

25. Charles Smith, "CIA Refuses to Release Documents on Corrupt Deals," *NewsMax*, 17 October 2002.

Chapter 19: Dark Buddha

1. Woodward, *The Choice*, p. 68.

2. Chapter 4, U.S. Senate Committee on Governmental Affairs, Senate Report 105-167, 10 March 1998, also known as the Thompson Committee.

3. *Cato Handbook for Congress*, Cato Institute, 106th Congress, p. 134. From the perspective of the next Congress, Cato had an even harsher view of Commerce.

4. *Cato Handbook*, p. 135.

5. Clinton, *Living History*, p. 252.

6. Dick Morris, "Setting the Record Straight: An Open Letter to Hillary Clinton," *National Review Online*, 12 January 2003.

7. Morris, *Behind The Oval Office*, p. 110.
8. Morris, p. 25.
9. Morris, p. 115.
10. Morris, p. 110.
11. "Additional Views of Chairman Fred Thompson," Thompson Committee report.
12. Morris, p. 139.
13. Morris, pp. 138-39.
14. Morris, p. 147.
15. Thompson Committee report, Chapter 4.
16. Morris, p. 150.
17. Morris, p. 139.
18. Woodward, *The Choice*, p. 239.
19. Thompson Committee report, Chapter 4.
20. Woodward, *The Choice*, p. 435.
21. Woodward, *The Choice*, p. 436.
22. Thomas, *Back from the Dead*, p. 177.
23. Thompson Committee report, Chapter 4.
24. Joe Klein, "Foreword," *Back from the Dead*, p. xii.
25. Holmes, p. 261.
26. Morris, p. 149.
27. Stephanopoulos, p. 328.
28. Stephanopoulos, p. 336.
29. Reich, *Locked in the Cabinet*, p. 325.
30. Reich, p. 273.
31. Nolanda Hill, interview with author.
32. Deposition of Terence Richard McAuliffe, by Judicial Watch, Civil Action 95-0133, Washington, D.C., 30 April 1999.
33. Larry Klayman, interview with author, Washington DC, 20 February 2003.
34. Morris, p. 151.

Chapter 20: Co-Targeted
1. For an accessible summary of the act, please read "The Independent Counsel Act," *All Politics, CNN Time*, 27 March 1997.
2. John Harris, "Special Counsel to Probe Brown; Clinton Stands by Commerce Chief," *Washington Post*, 18 May 1995.
3. Keith Bradsher, "Commerce Secretary Is Accused Of Failing to Disclose Income," *New York Times*, 27 January 1995.
4. Sara Fritz and Robert L. Jackson, "Entrepreneur Plays Key Role in Brown's Financial Dealings," *Los Angeles Times*, 22 February 1995.
5. See for instance Byron York's "Ron Brown's Body" in *American Spectator*, February 1998.
6. Sara Fritz and Rich Connell, "Secretary of Commerce linked to Slum Housing," *Los Angeles Times*, 9 April 1995.
7. Fritz and Jackson, *Los Angeles Times*, 22 February 1995.
8. Keith Bradsher, "Inquiry on Commerce Chief Focuses on Campaign Video,"

New York Times, 17 February 1995.

9. Keith Bradsher, 17 February 1995.

10. Boyer, *New Yorker*, 9 June 1997.

11. Sharon Walsh, "Dramatic Flair, Deal-Making Put Nolanda Hill in Spotlight; Ambition Drives Ron Brown's Former Partner," *Washington Post*, 27 March 1995.

12. Holmes, p. 271.

13. Holmes, p. 269.

14. Lou Dobbs, "Reno Announces Investigation of Secretary Ron Brown," *CNN.com*, 17 May 1995.

15. Harris, *Washington Post*, 18 May 1995.

16. Harris, *Washington Post*, 18 May 1995.

17. Holmes, p. 271.

18. Harris, *Washington Post*, 18 May 1995.

19. Brown, p. 268.

20. Holmes, p. 270.

Chapter 21: Dear Ron

1. "Letter from Motorola to Ron Brown," *NewsMax*, 16 May 2001, as referenced in Charles Smith, "Clinton's Exports Abet Chinese Suppression," *NewsMax*, 17 May 2001.

2. Part III, CommerceGate/ChinaGate, "Judicial Watch Interim Report on Crimes and Other Offenses Committed by President Bill Clinton Warranting His Impeachment and Removal from Elected Office."

3. Chapter 10, U.S. Senate Committee on Governmental Affairs, Senate Report 105-167, 10 March 1998, also known as the Thompson Committee.

4. Batsheva Tsur, "Clinton To Review Pollard Case Today," *Jerusalem Post*, 19 January 1999.

5. Charles Smith, "MYK-78 Clipper Chip Encryption/Decryption on a Chip," available on Smith's Web site, *Softwar.net*.

6. Charles Smith, "The Secrets of the Clipper Chip," *WorldNetDaily*, 12 January 1999.

7. Ira Sockowitz, interview with the author, 18 September 2003.

8. Tim Maier, "Nation: Ira Sockowitz," *Insight Magazine*, 1 September 1997.

9. Maier, *Insight Magazine*, 1 September 1997.

10. Letters available through Charles Smith's Web site under "Dear Ron—Forget Human Rights—We want to SELL!" *Softwar.net*.

11. Richard T. Cupitt, *Reluctant Champions: U.S. Presidential Policy and Strategic Export Controls* (New York: Routledge, 2000), p. 160.

12. Timmerman, *Selling Out America*, p. 286.

13. Timmerman, *Selling Out America*, p. 286.

14. Timmerman, p. 29.

15. Cupitt, p. 191.

16. Timmerman, p. 287.

17. Morris, *Behind the Oval Office*, p. 149.

18. Timperlake and Triplett, *Year of the Rat*, p. 64.

19. Thompson Committee report, Chapter 15.

20. Timperlake and Triplett, p. 66.
21. Charles Smith, "Motorola, Clinton, and the Red Gestapo," *WorldNetDaily*, 8 December 1998.

Chapter 22: Heat
1. Affidavit of Nolanda Butler Hill, C.A. No. 95-0133 (RCL), *Judicial Watch, Inc., Plaintiff, v. United States Department of Commerce*, Defendant, in the United States District Court for the District of Columbia.
2. Part III, CommerceGate/ChinaGate, "Judicial Watch Interim Report on Crimes and Other Offenses Committed by President Bill Clinton Warranting His Impeachment and Removal from Elected Office."
3. "Judicial Watch Interim Report."
4. Declaration of Sonya Stewart, C.A. No. 95-0133 (RCL), *Judicial Watch, Inc., Plaintiff, v. United States Department of Commerce*, Defendant, in the United States District Court for the District of Columbia.
5. The name of the Commerce Department FOIA officer is Brenda Dolan as noted in Part III, CommerceGate/ChinaGate, "Judicial Watch Interim Report."
6. "Judicial Watch Interim Report."
7. "Judicial Watch Interim Report."
8. Kirk and Boyer, "The Fixers."
9. Benjamin Wittes, "The Browns' Oklahoma Connection," *Legal Times*, 16 October 1995.
10. Wittes, *Legal Times*, 16 October 1995.
11. Kirk and Boyer, "The Fixers."
12. Wittes, *Legal Times*, 16 October 1995.
13. Wittes, *Legal Times*, 16 October 1995.
14. Byron York, "Michael Brown Goes Free," *American Spectator*, November 1997.
15. Wittes, *Legal Times*, 16 October 1995.
16. Wittes, *Legal Times*, 16 October 1995.
17. Nolanda Hill, interview with the author.
18. Steve Byas, et al., "Anthrax Death in Oklahoma?" *Oklahoma Constitution*, Summer 2001.

Chapter 23: Milo Minderbinder
1. Morris, *Behind the Oval Office*, p. 157.
2. Morris, p. 277.
3. Reich, *Locked in the Cabinet*, p. 41.
4. Joseph Heller, *Catch-22* (New York: Dell, 1955), pp. 262-63.
5. The figure comes from the Center for Responsive Politics and was widely reported. It was based on soft-money contributions to the Democratic National Committee and its affiliated committees for the years 1995-96. Based on data from the Federal Election Commission and Common Cause.
6. Eric Schmitt and Jeff Gerth, "White House Memos to President Reveal Strategy to Shift Purview Over Satellite Sales," *New York Times*, 18 July 1998. The description of Brown is that of the reporters.

7. Schmitt and Gerth, *New York Times*, 18 July 1998.
8. Schmitt and Gerth, *New York Times*, 18 July 1998.
9. Schmitt and Gerth, *New York Times*, 18 July 1998.
10. Charles Smith, "Smoking Gun: Made in China," *WorldNetDaily*, 9 February 2000.
11. Nolanda Hill, interview with the author.
12. Byron York, "The End of the Scandal: The Final Gasps of the Campaign Finance Investigation," *National Review Online*, 8 January 2002.
13. York, *National Review Online*, 8 January 2002.
14. Unsigned editorial, *Washington Times*, 22 May 1998.
15. Volume II, Chapter 6, U.S. House of Representatives, Select Committee on U.S. National Security and Military/Commercial Concerns with the People's Republic of China. House Report 105–851, 3 January 1999. Also known as the Cox Committee.
16. Review & Outlook, "Why China Hates NMD," *Wall Street Journal Interactive Edition*, 11 July 2000.
17. Schmitt and Gerth, *New York Times*, 18 July 1998.
18. Schmitt and Gerth, *New York Times*, 18 July 1998.
19. Editorial, *Washington Times*, 22 May 1998.
20. Volume II, Chapter 6, Cox Committee report, 3 January 1999.
21. "Text of Correspondence on Waiver to Permit Satellite Export," *New York Times*, 23 May 1998.
22. "Text of Correspondence on Waiver to Permit Satellite Export."
23. "Text of Correspondence on Waiver to Permit Satellite Export."
24. Loral Space & Communications Ltd., New York/Bernard Schwartz. $1,949,500—Compiled by the Center for Responsive Politics based on soft-money contributions to the Democratic National Committee and its affiliated committees from January 1991 through June 1999. Based on data from the Federal Election Commission and Common Cause.
25. "Sting Nabs Alleged Chinese Arms Smugglers: Seizure Billed as Largest in U.S. History," *CNN.com*, 23 May 1996.

Chapter 24: End Game
1. Brown, p. 10.
2. Nolanda Hill, interview with author. Unless specified otherwise Brown's reflections are filtered through Hill as she remembers them.
3. Part III, CommerceGate/ChinaGate, "Judicial Watch Interim Report on Crimes and Other Offenses Committed by President Bill Clinton Warranting His Impeachment and Removal from Elected Office."
4. Christopher Ruddy, "Questions Linger about Ron Brown Plane Crash," *Pittsburgh Tribune-Review*, 24 November 1997.
5. Ira Sockowitz, interview with the author, 18 September 2003.
6. Brown, p. 6.
7. Brown, p. 7.
8. Reich, *Locked in the Cabinet*, p. 334.
9. Brown, p. 10.

10. Brown, pp. 11-12.
11. Brown, p. 13.
12. Kevin Fedarko, "The Joyful Power Broker: Washington Mourns the Secretary of Commerce Who Conquered Barriers and the World," *Time Magazine,* 15 April 1996.

Chapter 25: St. John's Peak
1. The primary source for this chapter is "The Summary of Facts" from the *Accident Investigation Board Report,* United States Air Force CT-43 A, 3 April 1996, Dubrovnik, Croatia. These notes will only cite additions and exceptions, including quotes.
2. Nolanda Hill, interview with author, as are all other reflections by Hill.
3. *Accident Investigation Board Report,* pp. V 393-98.
4. *Accident Investigation Board Report,* p. V 2581.
5. Dr. Shiela Widnal, Secretary of the Air Force, et al., Department of Defense Briefing, 7 June 1996. (This document and extensive Q & A that followed will be referred to as "DOD Briefing.")
6. *Accident Investigation Board Report,* p. V 193.
7. Alan Diehl, *Silent Knights: Blowing the Whistle on Military Accidents and Their Cover-Ups* (Washington: Brassey's, 2002), p. 220.
8. Brown, p. 17.
9. *Accident Investigation Board Report,* p. V 1157.
10. *Accident Investigation Board Report,* p. V 1447.
11. *Accident Investigation Board Report,* p. V 761.
12. *Accident Investigation Board Report,* p. V 215.
13. "A Chronology of Events as Logged by Personnel at Embassy Zagreb in Connection with Secretary Brown's Plane Crash," as summarized in Carl Limbacher, "Documents Reveal Two May Have Survived Initial Impact of Ron Brown Plane Crash," *NewsMax,* 24 September 1999.
14. Ira Sockowitz, interview with author 18 September 2003. Sockowitz was in Sarajevo and was not in a position to know.
15. *Accident Investigation Board Report,* pp. V 158-162.
16. Tim Weiner, "A Special Report: In Crash That Killed Brown, Signs of Safety Shortcomings," *New York Times,* 28 April 1996.
17. Lt. Col. Steve Cogswell and the other whistleblowers in the saga to follow confirm that Kelly died of a broken neck.
18. Limbacher, *NewsMax,* 24 September 1999.
19. Brown, pp. 24-25.
20. Brown, p. 25.
21. Kwame Holman, "Unfinished Mission," transcript, *PBS,* 4 April 1996.
22. Fedarko, *Time Magazine,* 15 April 1996.
23. Tony Smith, "Officials Still Stumped by Cause of Brown Crash," *Associated Press,* 4 April 1996.
24. Holman, "Unfinished Mission," *PBS,* 4 April 1996.
25. Limbacher, *NewsMax,* 24 September 1999.

26. White House Press Release, "Remarks By The President About Secretary Of Commerce Ron Brown," The White House Office of the Press Secretary, 3 April 1996.

27. Jesse Jackson, "Ron Brown: A Man Who 'Made History,'" press release, 4 April 1996.

28. Fedarko, *Time Magazine*, 15 April 1996.

Chapter 26: Departed Soul

1. Kathleen Janoski, interview with the author, in person on 22-23 August and several phone and e-mail exchanges thereafter. Janoski provides the details of the scene at Dover.

2. Brown, p. 280.

3. Christopher Ruddy, "Second Officer: Wound Appeared To Be from Gunshot." *Pittsburgh Tribune-Review*, 9 December 1997.

4. *BET Tonight*, Black Entertainment Television, 11 December 1997. Transcript was included as attachment with Judicial Watch's petition to order continuation of the independent counsel's investigation into matters related to former Secretray of Commerce, Ronald H. Brown (In re Ronald H. Brown, Division No. 95-2).

5. Janoski, interview with the author.

6. Christopher Ruddy, "Experts Differ on Ron Brown's Head Wound," *Pittsburgh Tribune-Review*, 3 December 1997.

7. Ruddy, *Pittsburgh Tribune-Review*, 3 December 1997.

8. Ruddy, *Pittsburgh Tribune-Review*, 3 December 1997.

9. Ruddy, *Pittsburgh Tribune-Review*, 3 December 1997.

10. Tony Smith, "Airport's Navigations System Maintenance Chief Kills Himself," *Associated Press*, 8 April 1996. The AP calls him "Jerkic." Other accounts say "Junic." The most frequently cited is "Jerkuic." Note how uncritically the AP accepts suicide as the cause of death.

11. Smith, *Associated Press*, 8 April 1996.

12. Weiner, "A Special Report," *New York Times*, 28 April 1996.

13. Tony Campolo, interview with author, 5 September 2003.

14. The video clip is still widely available on the Internet.

15. Nolanda Hill, interview with the author.

16. Brown, p. 10.

17. Brown, p. 10.

Chapter 27: The Terror Summer

1. Brown, p. 286.

2. Wickham, p. 115.

3. Brown, p. 287.

4. Joe Holley, "Who Was Burning Black Churches," *Columbia Journalism Review*, September/October 1996.

5. Joe Holley, *Columbia Journalism Review*, September/October 1996.

6. Michael Fumento, "A Church Arson Epidemic? It's Smoke and Mirrors," *Wall Street Journal*, 8 July 1996.

7. Holley, *Columbia Journalism Review*, September/October 1996.

8. Psalms 31: 11-15.

9. Kathleen Janoski, interview with author. Following information comes from same source.

10. Christopher Ruddy, "4th Expert Claims X-ray Evidence Destroyed," *Pittsburgh Tribune-Review*, 13 January 1998.

11. Linda D. Kozaryn, "16 Air Force Officers Punished Over Brown Crash," *Armed Forces Information Service*, 6 August 1996.

12. Q & A that followed Department of Defense Briefing, 7 June 1996.

13. Woodward, *The Choice*, p. 421.

14. Woodward, *The Choice*, p. 367.

15. Thomas, et al., *Back from the Dead*: p. 79.

16. Morris, *Behind the Oval Office*, p. 277.

17. Dick Morris, *Off With Their Heads: Traitors, Crooks & Obstructionists in American Politics, Media & Business* (New York: Regan Books, 2003), p. 105.

18. Reich, *Locked in the Cabinet*, p. 276.

19. Reich, p. 273.

20. For a good accounting of this phenomenon see Graham, *Pattern of Deception*, p. 217.

21. Fumento, *Wall Street Journal*, 8 July 1996.

22. Holley, *Columbia Journalism Review*, September/October 1996.

23. Holley, *Columbia Journalism Review*, September/October 1996.

24. Fumento, *Wall Street Journal*, 8 July 1996.

Chapter 28: Natural Causes

1. "Police Investigating Death at Commerce Department," 29 November 1996. (Credit here to Missy Kelly for assembling the timeline.)

2. Thomas, et al., *Back from the Dead*, p. 201.

3. Thomas, et al., p. 196.

4. Nolanda Hill, interview with author.

5. Paul Roderiquez, on the *Mary Matalin Radio Show*, 21 August 1997.

6. "Clinton Enjoys a Round of Golf," *Associated Press*, 29 November 1996. Emphasis added.

7. Jerry King, *ABC News*, 29 November 1996.

8. "Clinton Enjoys a Round of Golf," *Associated Press*, 29 November 1996.

9. Helen Thomas, "Clinton Reviewing Inaugural Plans," *United Press International*, 29 November 1996.

10. Roger Morris, *Partners in Power* (New York: Henry Holt and Company, 1996), p. 422.

11. Jeffrey Birnbaum, "Kenneth Starr Works His Way Towards the Clintons," *Time Magazine*, 4 November 1996.

12. Helen Thomas, *UPI*, 29 November 1996.

13. Hillary Clinton, *Living History*, p. 390.

14. "Commerce Department Employee Found Dead in Office," *Associated Press*, 29 November 1996.

15. "Clinton Enjoys a Round of Golf," *Associated Press*, 29 November 1996.
16. "Female Commerce Worker Found Dead," 30 November 1996.
17. Robert E. Pierre and Martin Weil, "Commerce Department Employee Found Dead in Office," *Washington Post*, 30 November 1996.
18. "Natural Causes Probable Explanation for Commerce Department Death," *Associated Press*, 6 December 1996.
19. Paul Roderiquez, on the *Mary Matalin Radio Show*, 21 August 1997.
20. Steve Byas, et al., "Natural Gas Price Hearings: Oklahoma Natural Gas Overcharges Tied to Clinton White House," *Oklahoma Constitution*, Spring 2001.
21. Steve Byas, et al., "Natural Gas Price Hearings."
22. Steve Byas, et al., "Anthrax Death in Oklahoma," *Oklahoma Constitution*, Fall 1999.
23. Cause no. PUD 980000188, Before the Corporation Commission of the State of Oklahoma, prepared by Stephen P. Dresch, Volume II of II.
24. Steve Byas, et al., "The Strange Death of Ron Miller," *Oklahoma Constitution*, Spring 1998.
25. Steve Byas, et al., "Anthrax Death in Oklahoma."
26. Steve Byas, et al., "Anthrax Death in Oklahoma."
27. Steve Byas, et al., "Anthrax Death in Oklahoma."
28. Stephen Dresch, interview with author, 8 September 2003.
29. Steve Byas, et al., "Natural Gas Price Hearings."

Chapter 29: Going Public
1. Peter Boyer, "Ron Brown's Secrets," *New Yorker*, 9 June 1997.
2. Peter Carlson, "Salinger, Elusive As Ever; Esquire's Story Is a Classic Bait-and-Switch," *Washington Post*, 3 June 1997.
3. Kathleen Janoski, interview with the author.
4. Brian Ross, "Mystery Woman," *Prime Time Live, ABC News*, 18 June 1997.
5. "Ron Brown's Son Gets Probation," *CNN.com*, 21 November 1997.
6. Byron York, "Michael Brown Goes Free," *American Spectator*, November 1997.
7. York, *American Spectator*, November 1997.
8. Loose Lips, "The Search for Candidate X," *Washington City Paper*, 23-29 January 1998.
9. Allan Miller and Glenn Bunting, "Indonesian Couple Break Silence on DNC Donations," *Los Angeles Times*, 27 October 1997.
10. "Ron Brown's Son Gets Probation," *CNN.com*, 21 November 1997.

Chapter 30: Conspiracy Commerce
1. Christopher Ruddy, "Experts Differ on Ron Brown Head Wound," *Pittsburgh Tribune-Review*," 3 December 1997.
2. John Harris and Peter Baker, "White House Memo Asserts a Scandal Theory," *Washington Post*, 10 January 1997.
3. Associate White House counsel Mark Fabiani commissioned the *Communication Stream of Conspiracy Commerce*, excerpted here. A young aide named Christopher Lehane wrote it.
4. Ruddy, *Pittsburgh Tribune-Review*, 3 December 1997.

5. "M.E.: Brown Should Have Had Autopsy," *Associated Press*, 4 December 1997.
6. "Statement from the Armed Forces Institute of Pathology Regarding the Ron Brown Case," press release, 9 December 1997.
7. Letters to Families of Victims, reprinted in *Newsmax.com*, 27 December 1997.
8. Howard Kurtz, "Demise of a Buddy System," *Media Notes, Washington Post*, 8 December 1997.
9. Christopher Ruddy, "Second Officer: Wound Appeared To Be from Gunshot," *Pittsburgh Tribune-Review*, 9 December 1997.
10. "Statement from the Armed Forces Institute of Pathology Regarding the Ron Brown Case," 9 December 1997.
11. Christopher Ruddy, "Wecht: Autopsy Needed in Brown Case," *Pittsburgh Tribune-Review*, 17 December 1997.
12. Christopher Ruddy, *Pittsburgh Tribune-Review*, 17 December 1997.
13. Brown, p. 299.
14. Hurley Green III, "Pastor Demands Investigation into Late Ron Brown's Death," *Chicago Independent Bulletin*, 11 December 1997.
15. James Wright, "Brown Head Injury Suspected Bullet Wound: At Second Glance," *Baltimore Afro-American*, 13 December 1997.
16. Brown, p. 299.
17. *BET Tonight*, Black Entertainment Television, 11 December 1997.
18. *BET Tonight*, Black Entertainment Television, 11 December 1997.
19. The law is sometimes unofficially referred to as the "presidential assassination statute."
20. "NAACP Leader Asks Administration about New Questions over Brown's Death," *Associated Press*, 18 December 1997.
21. "Death Cover-up Press Release" from Dick Gregory, 24 December 1997.
22. Paul Shephard, "Jesse Jackson Calls for Investigation of Ron Brown's Death," *Associated Press*, 5 January 1998.
23. "Officials Back Up Brown Crash Findings," *Air Force News Service*, 5 January 1998.
24. "Justice Concludes No Evidence of Crime in Ron Brown Death," *AllPolitics, CNN Time*, 8 January 1998.
25. Michael Fletcher, "Justice Dept. Declines to Probe Death of Brown," *Washington Post*, 9 January 1997.
26. Christopher Ruddy, "Pathologists Dispute Claim in Brown Probe," *Pittsburgh Tribune-Review*, 11 December 1998.
27. Christopher Ruddy, *Pittsburgh Tribune-Review*, 11 December 1998.
28. Christopher Ruddy, "Forensic Expert Claims Military Bungled Probe of Brown's Death," *Pittsburgh Tribune-Review*, 13 January 1998.
29. James Wright, "Brown's Death Botched, Fourth Expert Says," *Washington Afro-American*, 17 January 1998.
30. David Brock wrote a series of articles for *American Spectator* beginning in January 1994 under the general rubric, "Troopergate." Although he has apologized for doing so, he has never denied their truthfulness. The *Los Angeles Times* ran with the same story in late December 1993 and has stuck by its guns.

NOTES

31. Morris, *Partners in Power*, p. 443.
32. Wickham, *Bill Clinton and Black America*, p. 87.
33. Mary Leonard, "Mrs. Clinton Admiration Grows 'in a Jerry Springer' World," *Boston Globe*, 19 August 1998.
34. Wickham, p. 1.
35. "Direct Access: Jesse Jackson," *Washington Post.com,* 16 December 1998.
36. Jon Dougherty, "'The Other Jesse' Blasts Jackson Says News of Civil Rights Leader's Affair 'No Surprise'," *WorldNetDaily*, 24 January 2001.
37. Richard Dunham, "Clinton Retreats to Safer Ground in New York," *Business Week Online*, 14 January 1999.

Chapter 31: Retribution
1. Affidavit, in the United States District Court for the District of Columbia, 17 January 1997.
2. Judicial Watch, In re Ronald H. Brown, Division No. 95-2, Petition to Order Continuation of the Independent Counsel's Investigation into Matters Related to Secretary of Commerce, Ronald H. Brown.
3. Judicial Watch petition, In re Ronald H. Brown, Division No. 95-2.
4. Kathleen Janoski, interview with author.
5. Kathleen Janoski, interview with author.
6. David Stout, "Investigation of Ron Brown Leads to Other Indictments," *New York Times*, 14 March 1998.
7. Judicial Watch, "Plaintiff's Motion for In Camera Review by the Court of Federal Grand Jury Proceedings Regarding Nolanda Hill," Civil Action No. 95-133 (RCL) (JF).
8. Judicial Watch, Civil Action No. 95-133 (RCL) (JF).
9. "Justice Investigates Herman: Businessman Alleges Cash-for-Access Swap," *ABCNews.com*, 14 January 1998.
10. "Independent Counsel: No Indictment of Labor Secretary Alexis Herman," *CNN.com*, 5 April 2000.
11. George Lardner Jr., "Judge Sets 10-Month Term in Political Donations Case," *Washington Post*, 10 September 1997.

Chapter 32: Occam's Razor
1. William of Occam, the Franciscan nominalist and *"doctor invincibilis,"* was born at Occam in 1280 and died in Munich on 10 April 1349.
2. Dr. Shiela Widnal, Secretary of the Air Force, et al., Department of Defense Briefing, 7 June 1996. (This 6500 word document and extensive Q & A that followed will be referred to as "DOD Briefing.")
3. Rowan Scarborough, "VIP Jet's Safety Record Flawless," *Washington Times*, 4 April 1996.
4. Weiner, "A Special Report," *New York Times,* 28 April 1996.
5. Tim Weiner, *New York Times,* 28 April 1996.
6. The primary source for flight data is "The Summary of Facts" from the *Accident Investigation Board Report,* United States Air Force CT-43 A, 3 April 1996,

Dubrovnik, Croatia. Subsequent notes will only cite additions and exceptions, including quotes.

7. DOD Briefing, 7 June 1996.

8. Kwame Holman, "Unfinished Mission," transcript, *PBS*, 4 April 1996.

9. *Accident Investigation Board Report*, p. V 140.

10. *Accident Investigation Board Report*, p. V 945.

11. Alan Diehl, *Silent Knights: Blowing the Whistle on Military Accidents and Their Cover-Ups* (Washington: Brassey's, 2002). P. 221.

12. Alan Diehl, interview with author, 13 September 2003. Subsequent quotes from same source unless otherwise specified.

13. Holmes, p. 283.

14. Holmes, p. 283.

15. "Statement from the Armed Forces Institute of Pathology Regarding the Ron Brown Case," 9 December 1997.

16. Holmes, p. 282.

17. Stephen Dresch, interview with the author, 8 September 2003.

18. Tony Smith, "Airport's Navigations System Maintenance Chief Kills Himself," *Associated Press*, 8 April 1996. Following AP citations come from same source.

19. Tony Smith, *Associated Press*, 8 April 1996.

20. Tim Weiner, *New York Times*, 28 April 1996.

21. Stephen Dresch, interview with the author, 8 September 2003.

22. The first was the friendly-fire shoot-down of a Blackhawk helicopter over Iraq on 14 April 1994.

23. Diehl, p. 9.

24. Clinton, *Living History*, p. 342.

25. *Accident Investigation Board Report*, p. V 1420.

26. Gregory Piatt, "West Feeling the Fallout of Efforts To Aid Bosnian Muslims a Decade Ago," *Stars and Stripes*, 14 April 2002.

27. George J. Tenet, "Worldwide Threat—Converging Dangers in a Post 9/11 World," Testimony Before The Senate Select Committee on Intelligence, 6 February 2002.

28. "Anthony Lake Withdraws," *Online NewsHour, PBS*, 12 March 1997.

29. Charles Smith, "How Clinton Created Serb War," *WorldNetDaily*, 6 April 1999.

30. DOD Briefing, 7 June 1996.

31. Interview, 29 September 2003. This person runs a major flight school, has read the Air Force summary, and has asked to remain anonymous.

32. Carl Limbacher, "Documents Reveal Two May Have Survived Initial Impact of Ron Brown Plane Crash," *NewsMax.com*, 24 September 1999.

33. See Jack Cashill and James Sanders, *First Strike: TWA Flight 800 and the Attack on America* (Nashville: WND Books, 2003).

34. "Mow Cop's War Effort," Congleton Chronicle Series.

35. Gentile has prepared a detailed 5,000-word analysis of the USAF report, which is available upon request.

36. *Accident Investigation Board Report*, p. V 187.

37. *Accident Investigation Board Report*, pp. V 170-79.

38. DOD Briefing, 7 June 1996.
39. Brown, p. 11.
40. Limbacher, *NewsMax.com*, 24 September 1999.
41. *Accident Investigation Board Report*, pp. V 1801, 1978.
42. *Accident Investigation Board Report*, p. V 1264.
43. *Accident Investigation Board Report*, p. V 1980.
44. *Accident Investigation Board Report*, pp. V 469-93.
45. *Accident Investigation Board Report*, p. V 498.
46. Tim Weiner, *New York Times*, 28 April 1996.
47. *Accident Investigation Board Report*, p. V 946.
48. *Accident Investigation Board Report*, p. V 1320.
49. *Accident Investigation Board Report*, p. V 1421.

Chapter 33: Banquo's Ghost
1. Nolanda Hill, interview with the author, 9 September 2003.
2. The book is called *Impasses*. It was cited in his *New York Times* obituary, 11 December 1999.
3. Robert Wright, "Enron's Curious Croatian Client," *Financial Times*, 31 January 2002.
4. Robert Wright, *Times*, 31 January 2002.
5. *New York Times* obituary, 11 December 1999.
6. *New York Times* obituary, 11 December 1999.
7. Stephen Dresch, interview with the author, 8 September 2003.
8. John Burns, "House of Graft: Tracing the Bhutto Millions," *New York Times*, 9 January 1998.
9. *Accident Investigation Board Report*, p. V 362.
10. "Svadba u Bijeloj kuæi," *Gloria.com*, 2000 (otherwise undated).
11. "The First Diplomatic Miss by Racan's Government," *Nacional*, Croatia, Issue 243.
12. In some versions, Henry II uses "meddlesome" or "low born" instead of "turbulent."
13. Bill Nichols, "First Lady to U.S. Troops: 'Thank You'," *USA Today*, 26 March 1996.
14. Hillary Clinton, *Living History*, p. 431.

ACKNOWLEDGMENTS

On the evening of my first meeting with Nolanda Butler Hill, while we warily assessed each other's motives in the lounge area of the venerable Fort Worth Club, a news announcer interrupted the regular programming on the lounge TV. Elizabeth Smart had been found alive, a triumph of faith over probability, and a sign to both of us, I suspect, that it was time to tell Nolanda's story. For hers too is the triumph of faith and courage, not so much over probability as conscious persecution. Without her help, this would have been a ghost of a book. Thanks too to Nolanda's son, Andrew Hill, who aided his mother in the vetting process that first day in Fort Worth.

When Kathleen Janoski volunteered her assistance, the story gained more heart still. Kathleen is one of the great, unsung heroines of the Clinton era. She and her colleagues at the AFIP—pathologists Hause, Parsons, and especially Cogswell—deserve a medal for courage under bureaucratic fire.

At the outset of this project, when the scope of it seemed overwhelming, a good friend, retired engineer Don Covington, volunteered his technical and research assistance and helped me shepherd the project throughout. Thanks Don.

Thanks as well to retired TWA Captain Raymond Gentile. Ray volunteered to help me sort through and make sense of the twenty-two volumes of the Air Force report and proved willing to put his name on his findings. A tip of the hat to whoever it was in the Air Force (or above) that waived the otherwise daunting fees and expedited the FOIA request.

Stephen Dresch introduced me to Nolanda Hill and graciously shared his excellent and original research with me throughout. A retired New Jersey homicide detective, John Stankard, introduced me to Dresch. John also made a key introduction for *First Strike*. Thanks also to my Croatian analyst/interpreter, Dominik.

That *Time Magazine* has yet to name Larry Klayman "man of the year" is a failure of *Time's*, not Klayman's. The work he and Judicial Watch did on the Brown case is stunning. Thanks as well to Tom Fitton of Judicial Watch for his encouragement.

Some seriously good and bold primary research made the telling of key parts of this story possible. Kudos here to Christopher Ruddy and the *Pittsburgh Tribune-Review*, Steve Byas and the staff of the *Oklahoma Constitution*, Edward Timperlake and William C. Triplett II, authors of *Year of the Rat*, Peter Boyer and PBS's *Frontline*, Ken Timmerman and Byron York for *The American Spectator*, independent researcher Missy Kelly, and Charles Smith of *Softwar*.

Useful too were the previous biographies of Ron Brown by Steven Holmes and Tracey Brown. This whole ordeal has to have been hell for the Brown family, and I apologize in advance for extending it. That Brown could raise a daughter who loved him dearly enough to write the book she did is a tribute to his better angels.

My own daughters and my wife, Joan, deserve credit too for gracefully enduring one more plunge into the abyss, not to mention Joan's help with the footnotes.

And finally again thanks again to the people in the WND Books family who made this all possible: Janis Reed, Joe Farah, Wes Driver, and editor Joel Miller, among others.

INDEX